Sherman's
Forgotten General

Shades of Blue and Gray Series
Edited by Herman Hattaway and Jon L. Wakelyn

The Shades of Blue and Gray Series offers Civil War studies for the modern reader—Civil War buff and scholar alike. Military history today addresses the relationship between society and warfare. Thus biographies and thematic studies that deal with civilians, soldiers, and political leaders are increasingly important to a larger public. This series includes books that will appeal to Civil War Roundtable groups, individuals, libraries, and academics with a special interest in this era of American history.

Sherman's
Forgotten General

HENRY W. SLOCUM

Brian C. Melton

University of Missouri Press
Columbia and London

Library of Congress Cataloging-in-Publication Data

Melton, Brian C., 1976–
    Sherman's forgotten general : Henry W. Slocum / Brian C.
Melton.
        p.   cm.
Summary: "Biography of Union major general Henry W. Slocum.
Author explores Slocum's attitudes and tactics while serving
under various Civil War generals such as George McClellan,
Joseph "Fighting Joe" Hooker, and William Tecumseh
Sherman"—Provided by publisher.
    Includes bibliographical references and index.
    ISBN 978-0-8262-1739-4 (alk. paper)
1. Slocum, Henry Warner, 1826–1894.   2. Slocum, Henry
Warner, 1826–1894—Military leadership.   3. Generals—United
States—Biography.   4. United States. Army—Biography.
5. United States—History—Civil War, 1861–1865—Campaigns.
6. Command of troops—Case studies. I. Title.
    E467.1.S63M45 2007
    973.7'3092—dc22
    [B]   2007002244

This paper meets the requirements of the
American National Standard for Permanence of Paper
for Printed Library Materials, Z39.48, 1984.

Designer: Jennifer Cropp
Typesetter: BookComp, Inc.
Printer and binder: Thomson-Shore, Inc.
Typefaces: Palatino, Caxton

*The University of Missouri Press offers its grateful acknowledgment to
an anonymous donor whose generous grant in support of the publication of outstanding dissertations has assisted us with this volume.*

To my parents, Dale and Margaret,
and to my patient wife, Kami

Soli Deo Gloria

Contents

Acknowledgments

I would like to acknowledge the efforts of everyone who contributed to the assembly of this manuscript. Special thanks are due Dr. Steven Woodworth, Dr. D. Clayton Brown, Dr. Mark Gilderhus, and Dr. Todd Kerstetter for the invaluable time they committed to serving on my dissertation committee. Rebekah Ambrose of the Onondaga Historical Association was a great help and consistently went far above the call of duty in aiding my research. Elizabeth Redkey of SUNY Albany helped me a great deal and was a pleasure to work with. Pompeytown historian Sylvia Shoebridge provided a good deal of useful information and several leads. Quotations from the Joseph Howland manuscript and "War of 1861–1865 Letters" are courtesy of the New–York Historical Society. I would like to thank Mr. John A. Slocum for sharing his family memories with me. Thanks are also due Peter Bedrossian, Michael Peets, James Shockley, and David Jay Webber for the help they rendered with their research regarding the 150th New York and the bushwhacking incident in Tennessee in 1863. I greatly appreciate the comments and improvements made by the copy editor, Pippa Letsky, and I thank her for doing such a thorough job. April Wold did an excellent job helping to secure photographs for this volume.

Portions of Chapter 6 were previously published as the article "Wading in 'Deep Water' with a 'Driveling Cur': The Slocum-Hooker Feud and the Chattanooga Campaign," in the Spring 2006 issue of the *Tennessee Historical Quarterly*.

Excerpts from Stephen W. Sears's *Chancellorsville*, *Landscape Turned Red*, and *To the Gates of Richmond* are reprinted by permission of the Houghton Mifflin Company.

Excerpt from *Gettysburg: Culp's Hill and Cemetery Hill* is reprinted by permission of the University of North Carolina Press.

Abbreviations

GNMP   Gettysburg National Military Park Archives

Lincoln Papers   Abraham Lincoln Papers, Library of Congress

NA   National Archives

NYHS   New-York Historical Society.

OHA   Onondaga Historical Association, Syracuse, New York.

OR   U.S. War Department. *The War of the Rebellion: A Compilation of the Official Records of the Union and Confederate Armies.* 128 vols. Washington, D.C.: GPO, 1881–1901.

Sherman's
Forgotten General

Introduction

Sherman's Forgotten General

Henry Warner Slocum could be remembered in history for so much: he was a successful politician, a flourishing business man, railroad tycoon, colonel, brigadier, major general, corps commander, and even army commander. Some individuals spend their entire lives pursuing just one of these titles. Slocum played an important role fighting in the Civil War eastern theater from Bull Run to Gettysburg, was post commander at Vicksburg, and then served in nearly every battle in the western theater from the capture of Atlanta to Johnston's surrender. Yet traditionally Slocum has been either ignored altogether or interpreted almost exclusively through his lackluster performance at the Battle of Gettysburg.

There are reasons why this happens. Primary sources from Slocum, or that even deal with him on a personal level, are virtually nonexistent. Slocum has no assembled papers, and only a scant few letters lie scattered in repositories across the country. Locations that would seem logical places to find materials on Slocum—such as the Brooklyn Historical Society (Slocum resided in Brooklyn from 1865 until his death), the New-York Historical Society (NYHS), or the New York State Library—have few original autographs. A call to Brooklyn, for example, reveals only a single battle report, already available in the *Official Records*. In the National Archives (NA), only a few references scattered here and there turn up even a single letter (most of them professional, not personal correspondence). The notes of William MacGregor Downs seem promising, until they are obtained. These notes of a postwar speech by Slocum, really more of a vague rebuttal written while Slocum happened to be speaking, are of little use. The Slocum family papers ought to be a gem, but they contain only one lonely letter from Slocum petitioning Lincoln to appoint one of his nephews to West Point. The John O. Slocum papers at the Onondaga Historical Association (OHA) hardly

1

mention his more famous brother. Document trails uncovered during research have an annoying habit of coming up dry. For instance Slocum carried on a sporadic correspondence with Sherman after the war; copies of the letters and references to them are found in both of Slocum's biographies and in newspaper articles. But the single reference to Slocum in the finding aids of the Sherman collection at Notre Dame regards a copy of William Fox's *In Memoriam: Henry Warner Slocum,* and only one copy of a letter from Slocum to Sherman has been found. The list of repositories where I have not found Slocum materials could form a book in itself. The Slocum family does not retain any related papers that have not already been donated to the National Archives.[1]

The situation improves only a little when looking at contemporary secondary evidence, such as newspapers. After Johnston's final surrender, Slocum made a decision that resulted in his being publicly buried under an avalanche of poor press: Slocum, the lifelong Republican, became a Democrat and dared to run for office. Republicans, especially in his home state of New York, treated him like a traitor and excoriated him in editorial after editorial. The Democrats seemed less than enthusiastic about such a recent convert and, though quite happy to make use of his military record, did not accept him with open arms. Defeated for election, Slocum sank back into relative obscurity while other soldiers rocketed to new heights of postwar fame. This meant that in historical arguments over position and importance Slocum rarely made his side of the story heard.

The scarcity of evidence has led to one of two approaches in dealing with Slocum. One approach involves ignoring him or treating him as a nonentity. In the more than seventy thousand books written on the Civil War since its end, there are only two full biographies of Slocum and both predate the First World War. Many historians who have written about Slocum since

---

1. William T. Sherman Papers, University of Notre Dame, online at http://www.archives.nd.edu/findaids/ead/index/SHR001.htm. Regarding the Slocum Family Papers, I spoke to the one identifiable member of Henry Slocum's branch of the family, Mr. John A. Slocum of Lynchburg, Virginia. He had kept the majority of the family's various documents until donating them to the National Archives, and even those documents contained little about Henry Slocum. I wrote to every Henry Slocum now living in America on the offhand chance one might have inherited papers somehow forgotten, but none replied. It is possible that when William F. Fox began compiling his memorial for Slocum, he obtained the originals of both Sherman's and Slocum's letters. This would explain their absence from Sherman's papers and Slocum's family. What Fox may have done with them, if anything at all, is unknown. It could also be that Slocum's immediate family found things inside them so embarrassing that they destroyed them outright. This is all pure speculation.

then have not advanced our understanding much. A. Wilson Greene referred to the "relatively anonymous" hierarchy of Slocum's Twelfth Corps, while Lee Kennett's *Marching through Georgia* does not even have an index listing for Slocum though some of his subordinates appear. In *Battle of Despair*, Robert Paul Broadwater mistakenly assigns Slocum to brigade command at First Bull Run. Even the excellent Albert Castel repeatedly refers to Slocum as "Henry B." in his authoritative book on the Atlanta Campaign, *Decision in the West.* Many of these authors simply assume that Slocum was a competent commander, though they rarely take the time to explain why they think so. This is not out of sorts, given that Slocum is not their topic, but it does not translate into a well-developed body of reasoned scholarly opinion of the man.[2]

Yet there is one place in history where Slocum seems to be known, where he can hardly be avoided, and this place has produced a second school of Slocum historiography: the Gettysburg Slocum. For decades, almost as soon as Lee retreated from that bloody field, what might be termed the Gettysburg Paradigm became the lens through which much of the war has been viewed. According to this mythology, everything prior to two o'clock in the afternoon of July 3, 1863, was nothing more nor less than a lead up to the Confederacy's crescendo at Pickett's Charge, and everything past it was little more than an afterthought. Carol Reardon's *Pickett's Charge in History and Memory* dealt with this phenomenon explicitly. If adopted, the paradigm often means that a person's actions, personality, and abilities are seen solely from the perspective of how that person performed at Gettysburg.[3]

Given the paucity of other evidence on Slocum's life, the Gettysburg Paradigm tends to affect him more thoroughly than it might other generals. No historian has encountered a full, researched, objective depiction of the whole of Slocum's life, for the simple reason that one has yet to be produced. The memory of Slocum exists only in topical snippets scattered through the entirety of Civil War literature. The only place one can consistently encounter Slocum to any depth is the campaign studies of Gettysburg in general and of Culp's Hill in particular.[4] Since Slocum's performance there was

2. A. Wilson Greene, "A Step All-Important and Essential to Victory," 89; Lee Kennett, *Marching through Georgia: The Story of Soldiers and Civilians during Sherman's Campaign;* Robert Paul Broadwater, *Battle of Despair,* 19; Albert Castel, *Decision in the West: The Atlanta Campaign of 1864.*

3. Carol Reardon, *Pickett's Charge in History and Memory.*

4. There are several examples: Stephen W. Sears, *Gettysburg;* Harry W. Pfanz, *Gettysburg: Culp's Hill and Cemetery Hill;* Edwin B. Coddington, *The Gettysburg Campaign: A Study in Command;* Samuel P. Bates, *History of the Battle of Gettysburg.*

peculiarly lacking, historians have often interpreted the rest of his career in this light.

His defenders, on the other hand, are usually found on the other extreme of the Paradigm. One of the earliest accounts of Slocum's life appeared on April 29, 1894, just after his death, when Oliver O. Howard delivered a eulogy to Slocum's memory at the Plymouth Church in Brooklyn, New York. Every biography of Slocum, including this present one, makes use of this document. Having met together with others there to sing the praises of his friend, Howard portrayed Slocum's wartime career in a dazzling light, making him shine as brightly as either Grant or Sherman. It is difficult to read this eulogy and not think that Howard's grasp on history and Slocum's place in it are somewhat tenuous.

Rather than cast such aspersions on Howard's personality, it is necessary only to point out what he was attempting that day. He did not address an assembly of historians or a gathering of Civil War enthusiasts. He wrote and delivered a eulogy, not serious history. Howard wanted to have his audience focus exclusively on the good aspects of Slocum's role in the war. It would be a rare and unpopular eulogy indeed that included a significantly critical look at the worst decisions the deceased had made. So Howard understandably offered no criticism of Slocum's performance on the first day at Gettysburg, though he speaks of it elsewhere. Instead he stated, "But for Slocum the waters of Rebellion would have passed around the heights and the 'high-water mark' would not have been found on that Cemetery crest."[5] Given Howard's purpose, lauding Slocum was not out of place. But the reader must remember why Howard wrote his speech and not expect to see an especially objective view of Slocum's career.

Since the Civil War, only two authors aside from the present have succeeded in writing an extended researched account of the life of Henry Slocum. The first, William F. Fox, did so as part of the dedication of Slocum's statue at Gettysburg in 1902. Of all the authors thus far attempting to undertake this project, Fox had the best access to the man himself. He had known Slocum, had access to his papers, and also knew many of his fellow officers. However, his work would not meet the standards of modern history for the simple reason that, like Howard, Fox was not aiming to meet those standards. *In Memoriam: Henry Warner Slocum* is just that: a memorial. Fox was not interested in supplying his readers with

---

5. Oliver O. Howard, "To the Memory of Henry Slocum: A Eulogy by Oliver O. Howard."

a critical look at the general's life. Indeed he is just as likely as Howard to ignore the man's foibles. The memorial is also relatively short. Fox's narrative of Slocum's life takes up only 54 pages of a 325-page book, though there is much pertinent information on Slocum throughout. For the sake of space he often skims over important events. Again, such an approach was perfectly understandable for his purposes, but the fact remains that it does not translate into good professional history. Still, even with these difficulties, Fox's memorial is a great source of information. He seems to have been an honest author and generally felt no need to exaggerate Slocum's role in the war. He also reproduced primary source documents that are no longer available elsewhere. For instance he reprints letters to and from Sherman that reveal some of Slocum's personality and motivations for important decisions.

Slocum's more recent biography demonstrates hagiography at its best, or worst, as the case may be. In 1913 Charles Elihu Slocum of Toledo, Ohio, published *The Life and Services of Major-General Henry Warner Slocum.* He did not content himself to simply focus on highlights; in some cases he almost manufactured them. Taking nearly four hundred pages to complete it, he stuffed the book full of verbatim reports from the *Official Records,* letters taken from the pages of Fox's memorial, and the like, all available elsewhere. Not only accenting every favorable word ever written about the general, Charles Slocum sweetened his narrative to the point that some readers might find it noxious. He made a few unique claims and provided a few new leads, but his book exhibits such poor documentation that it is next to impossible to follow up on any of those leads. He gave fewer than 130 references in the entire book, the vast majority of which prove to be simple quotations from the *Official Records.* Yet, unfortunately, Charles Elihu's book is the best-known of Slocum's biographies.[6]

Many professional historians who have written on Slocum have carried their depictions to the other extreme, thanks to Gettysburg. The first virulently negative accounts of Slocum appeared during his own lifetime. Samuel P. Bates wrote one of the first thoroughly critical accounts of Slocum's performance, around 1875. Bates's work originated many of the criticisms of Slocum that still echo today. Former comrades also attacked him. After the war Joseph J. Bartlett completely reversed his depiction of Slocum at Crampton's Gap, while John A. Logan (or at least one of his

---

6. Charles E. Slocum, *The Life and Services of Major-General Henry Warner Slocum* (I am greatly indebted to this book for the early parts of this current text); *OR* (all citations are to the first series).

supporters) tried to usurp credit for the Battle of Bentonville. Greene provided a more recent example of the attacks Slocum has had to endure. In "A Step All-Important and Essential to Victory," Greene misused Howard's eulogy, treating it as though it should contain claims of professional history. In doing so Greene set an abnormally high standard for Slocum that no one, not even Howard, realistically expected him to reach. When compared to such criteria it is no surprise that Slocum seems to vacillate without explanation. Stephen W. Sears is another avowed Slocum detractor in his book on Gettysburg, where Slocum wavers between being a grumpy coward terrified of acting decisively and an arrogant poseur who foolishly exceeds orders for no apparent reason. Other authors such as Chester Hearn in his book on Harpers Ferry have chimed in on this depiction, but perhaps to a lesser extent.[7]

There is more to Slocum than current history credits. He exhibited a dynamic version of Locke's blank slate. Powerful personalities impressed themselves on Slocum. He tended to absorb the characteristics of his commanding officers and their reputations and then put them to practice in his own style and within his own sphere of influence. This could be either a painful annoyance to the army or a powerful asset. While under McClellan on the Peninsula and Antietam, Slocum became very McClellan-like, excessively nervous over what might happen and focused on protocol and victories by complicated maneuvers. Under "Fighting Joe" Hooker, he became cantankerous and actively undercut Hooker, just as Hooker had Burnside. Finally, while serving under Sherman in the west, Slocum began to live out Sherman's reputation, becoming at times even more aggressive and driving than Sherman himself.

My own interest in Slocum began while I prepared an article on Sherman's March to the Sea, particularly the Army of Georgia's tramp through the small town of Madison. When I searched for information on Slocum, their commander, I discovered that little had been written on him. Unlike most other Civil War army commanders he had no in-print biographies, and even though he commanded one-half of the army under Sherman, most of the books about the march itself did not devote much space to him. Thus my aim in this book is not really to contribute to the

7. Bates, *Battle of Gettysburg*; Report of Col. Joseph J. Bartlett, *OR*, vol. 19, pt. 1, 388–90; Slocum to Sherman, in William F. Fox, *In Memoriam: Henry Warner Slocum*, 109 (Logan); John Priest, *Before Antietam: The Battle for South Mountain*, 272–83; Greene, "A Step All-Important"; Sears, *Gettysburg*, 12, 312; Chester G. Hearn, *Six Years of Hell: Harpers Ferry during the Civil War*, 198.

historiography of Henry Slocum. A "contribution" implies an ongoing conversation, and to this point there is very little being said about Slocum. There are a few scattered paragraphs here and there, but while they may be scholarly they are not comprehensive. Slocum's earlier biographies may have been comprehensive, but they are not remotely scholarly. It is my intention to bring the two sides together, to provide the Slocum thesis that will eventually inspire the first full-length Slocum antithesis in the world of professional Civil War history.

As such, I have laid out this book in a positive form, and though I have researched and utilized much of the existing secondary literature, I have made a general conscious effort to avoid cluttering my text with too many explicit references to other historians. I intend to lay out a full holistic account of Slocum's life, in effect to introduce him really for the first time. As such, I want Slocum himself to appear for who he was, and not necessarily in any of the previous incarnations in which he has been cast. Undoubtedly I will take issue with what other historians have said, but I will do so more by implication than by direct objection. I want Slocum to speak for himself and to enter into the historical record relatively unobscured (as far as this is humanly possible). While I myself will get in the way at times, I have no doubt that intelligent readers will be prepared to see through me and into the man that lies beyond. After all, the ability to discern between fact and interpretation is one of the first skills any good student of history must develop. My interest is not so much whether my readers walk away with a positive or negative impression of the man (though my own is admittedly more or less positive), so long as they base their opinion on the facts of Slocum's life.

The one exception to this general rule is the chapter on Gettysburg. Historians have had more to say about Slocum at Gettysburg than they have had to say about any other time in his military or civilian career. This has affected the way Slocum has been remembered, and it has interfered with our ability to see him as a whole. I will, therefore, enter explicitly into the historiographical fray at this point, not only because it is patently unavoidable but also because I believe that an understanding of the historiography at this point is essential to a proper understanding of how the memory of Henry Slocum became what it is.

In reality Slocum was simply human. He made mistakes, some of which he transcended, some of which haunted him until his death in 1894 and even after, as evidenced by a number of historians. In light of this I submit my effort for the reader's consideration. Most important, I endeavor to provide my readers with a solid, honest, and concise examination of

Slocum's life. He may not have changed the course of the war, but he certainly played a conspicuous and important role in its prosecution.

A Note on Maps

Biographies, especially those of a wartime figure such as Slocum, by definition have some rather extensive requirements regarding maps. Battle or campaign studies (which always require one or two more maps than the author and publisher can deliver) involve relatively short periods of time, anywhere from a few hours to months. An author might be able to scrape by with five or fewer maps if they are organized well. A biography, however, by necessity must often cover a much larger swath of time. I really need several maps for every major battle Slocum fought in, not to mention various snapshots of campaigns and maneuvering. The cost involved in publication makes this a patent impossibility. So, rather than provide only one or two completely insufficient maps, I would simply say this: I strongly suggest that readers pick up one or more of the several excellent Civil War atlases that are available. Doing so will greatly enhance your enjoyment and understanding of this book.

C H A P T E R   1

Early Life

The Speculator Goes to West Point, to Work, and to War

Matthew Barnard Slocum, Henry's father, was born in Marietta, Ohio, in 1788. His family moved east in 1802 to find work and eventually established themselves in New Port, Rhode Island, where Slocums remained prominent through the Civil War. Matthew moved once again in 1812, this time settling in Albany, New York, where he began his lifelong career as a small goods merchant. He married Miss Mary Ostrander on April 9, 1814, and while still in Albany, Mary gave birth to their first two children. Unfortunately, Matthew's business failed in 1817, and the family moved to the tiny village of Delphi Falls, New York, not far from Syracuse, where Matthew opened another shop. At the time, Delphi Falls consisted of little more than a few buildings surrounded by trees and fields. Matthew's shop, Slocum and Marble, stood on the southeastern point of "four corners," as people called the Delphi crossroads. He built the family dwelling, which they named Cheapside, onto the back of his store. Over time he bought the twenty-five acres immediately surrounding the Slocum and Marble shop and acquired a horse, a cow, and other animals that would benefit his family and business.[1]

1. "The Life of Henry Warner Slocum: Program for General Slocum Day," August 11, 1996 (Pompeytown Historical Society and OHA); Charles Slocum, *Life and Services*, 5; "Brilliant Soldier's Record," *New York Times*, April 15, 1894, 16. At the first Battle of Bull Run, for instance, Joshua Slocum commanded the Second Rhode Island Regiment and so had to be both prominent and influential (see *OR*, vol. 2, pt. 1, 383).

Matthew's second son and third child, John Ostrander, joined the family on June 9, 1820. John would later become a surgeon and serve in the Civil War. In early 1827 Mary became pregnant with the couple's sixth child, and on September 24, she gave birth to a boy. The Slocums named him Henry Warner, after a favorite uncle. Mary bore Matthew five more children, making Henry one of eleven siblings. The children scattered far and wide from that small country store over the coming years. William, two years Henry's junior, farmed in the Syracuse area before the war and later moved to California. His brother Barnard became a noted local lawyer in the firm of Slocum and Gifford, maintaining offices in Syracuse. Two of his sisters, Kate and Sarah, became teachers, and two more, Mary and Carrie, married and eventually settled down, Mary in Los Angeles and Carrie in Oswega, New York.[2]

Like other children in the surrounding countryside, Henry attended the Delphi Public School. His teachers kept the sessions short so their students could help with the work at home, and he did his part working at Slocum and Marble. At an early age he displayed a talent for business. He bought and sold sheep, using a portion of his profits to pay for feed. His flock slowly expanded and proved a boon to his family. His numerous successful investments earned him the nickname "Speculator," or simply "Spec" for short. As he grew, Henry became a leader of sorts among the boys in Delphi Falls.[3]

One summer the boys in the community pooled their money and purchased on old cannon, a two-pounder. That Fourth of July, they brought it out and fired it. Afterward they entrusted it to one of their number until the next year. Before the next Fourth came, however, the cannon's guardian

2. Papers of John Ostrander Slocum, "Diploma: Medical School at Castleton," transcribed by Rebekah Ambrose, OHA; Charles Slocum, *Life and Services*, 5–6; Fox, *In Memoriam*, 65. There seems to be some disagreement over whether Slocum was born in 1826 or 1827. The figure of 1826 generally appears in most "official" publications (those sponsored by the state of New York, such as William F. Fox, *New York at Gettysburg*; Fox, *In Memoriam*; and "Monument to the New York Brigade at Lookout Mountain"), and 1827 is claimed in the "unofficial" ones (such as various newspaper articles from around the time of his death). Most authors since the early part of this century pull heavily from Charles Slocum, who in turn relied heavily on Fox, so most of these assume 1826 is correct. At the time of his death in 1894, he was sixty-seven, which would fix the year at 1827. *Winsor's Syracuse City Directory, 1857–1858; Boyd's City Directory, 1859–1860; City Directory for 1862–1863;* "General Slocum," *Syracuse Journal* (hereinafter *Journal*), April 14, 1894. A reference to Carrie at the time of Henry's death only mentions her name as "C." Henry named his first child Carrie, which could imply both her aunt's full first name and that she was one of Henry's favorite siblings.

3. Charles Slocum, *Life and Services*, 6–8.

moved with his family to the nearby town of Woodstock, about five miles from Delphi. Rather than surrender his charge, he took the prized gun with him. When the Delphi boys discovered the theft they held a meeting. After much grumbling and complaining at the injustice, most of the boys wanted to proceed straight to Woodstock and take the cannon back forcibly. Henry, who had been reading a biography of Napoleon, disagreed. He argued that such a direct approach would defeat their entire purpose. To come into Woodstock so openly would surely bring out not only the Woodstock boys intent on keeping the gun, but all their brothers and cousins as well. The Delphi expedition could not hope to succeed against such odds. Instead, he asked them to give him time to devise a plan. Most of the boys agreed, over-ruling whatever minority remained in favor of a frontal assault. They swore themselves to secrecy and the meeting adjourned.[4]

Henry rose early on the morning of July 3 and walked the five miles to Woodstock. Once there he chatted with people about the next day's fes-tivities. He learned that the town planned to fire the gun at sunrise to open their celebrations. Armed with this information he left quietly and made his way back to Delphi. The boys went over Henry's plan and then se-cured a farm wagon and a team of horses. Long before dawn on the morn-ing of the Fourth, Henry snuck out of Cheapside and met his friends outside a nearby barn where they harnessed the horses to the wagon, piled in, and set off toward Woodstock. As they neared the town, they slowed down and one group of boys climbed out. Shortly before dawn, the boys still in the wagon reined in the horses, behind a barn next to the field where the gun would be fired, and waited.

The people of Woodstock began to congregate in the field and brought the two-pounder with them. As the sun broke the horizon, they fired it with a cheer, and the Independence Day revelry began. But before the smoke had even cleared, a commotion broke out at the far end of the field, away from the gun. The first group of Delphi boys had snuck into the crowd as it grew and started a fight. The people, far more interested in a good brawl, forgot completely about everything else. In the confusion the second team from the expedition charged forward in their wagon, grabbed the cannon, and put it into the back. Snapping the reins, they hightailed it

---

4. Ibid. The story is contained in a letter Charles Slocum received from Henry Slocum's brother. It is interesting that Slocum absorbed a reverence for Napoleonic warfare at an early age. He would later exhibit his love for the emperor's preferred approach in the first years of the Civil War and his idolization of McClellanized warfare.

back toward Delphi. The other group took off as well, hoping to make it home before the Woodstock boys realized what had happened.[5]

Time and maturity turned Henry to other pursuits. With the proceeds of his various business ventures he put together enough money to attend Cazenovia Seminary, in nearby Madison County, not far from Woodstock. It was a time that he treasured and, indeed, later in life remembered more vividly than some of his more famous experiences. He had saved enough money to be able to attend the seminary for the fall term and hoped to qualify to teach public school nearby. He wanted to use the money he earned to return that summer. It was a fine plan, but as many students do when first attending college, he ran into some hard realities. Slocum found life at Cazenovia very different from the Delphi public schools. In fact when he began to prepare himself for the examination for his public school teacher's certificate, he began to flounder, wondering, possibly for the first time, if he could actually succeed. His mathematics instructor, Professor Canefield, heard of Henry's woes and invited him to his house for a visit. When Henry arrived, Canefield took him into his study and asked him what was worrying him. Henry poured his heart out to Canefield, telling him his hopes as well as his fears. Canefield responded with kindly encouragement and offered to help him prepare for the exam.[6]

Canefield did not waste his generosity, and in 1843 at the age of seventeen Henry earned a Public School Teacher's Certificate from the county superintendent and took charge of a country school. With his wages he returned to Cazenovia, a fortunate decision, because there he met and became engaged to his future wife, Clara Rice, the daughter of Israel and Dorcas Rice of Woodstock. Henry spent his next four years balancing teaching at a one-room schoolhouse in Woodstock, studying at the State Normal School at Albany, and working at Slocum and Marble during his vacations. After graduation he taught school full-time.[7]

5. Ibid. Henry would have made his first trek on foot, since his father probably had other business for the family's horse. The whole crew must have left very early in the morning to cover the five miles and be in place before the gun was fired at dawn. They would probably have been nervous and rushed their horses. The story has a sad ending. The Delphi boys used their prized weapon in future years, but they eventually overloaded the barrel and it exploded, killing the person closest to it.

6. "First Fifty Years of Cazenovia Seminary, 1825–1875," 319. For this information, I thank John Robert Greene of Cazenovia College.

7. "The Loyal Legion," *Journal*, May 11, 1894, 1–2; Charles Slocum, *Life and Services*, 8, 10; "The Life of Henry Warner Slocum: Program for General Slocum Day"; "Maj. Gen. Henry Warner Slocum"; *New York at Gettysburg*, 1333–34.

The fact that Henry had been reading biographies of Napoleon meant that he had probably fantasized for years about military glory. The outbreak of the Mexican War in 1846 made him one of many who seriously considered a career in the service. He sought and obtained a coveted place at the U.S. Military Academy at West Point. He moved quickly, taking less than a year to gain admission. Daniel F. Gott, an antislavery agitator and congressman from Onondaga, named him the Syracuse district's cadet for the year 1848. Slocum passed the entrance examination and entered West Point on July 1, 1848.[8]

Slocum's decision to attend West Point probably resulted in other plans being put on hold. Although he and Clara had become engaged while he studied at Cazenovia, they postponed their marriage until he could support a family. He probably visited her as often as he could, as he had during his vacations from the State Normal School. She also wrote and visited, sometimes including forget-me-nots she had picked for him.[9]

The West Point that Slocum found waiting for him was sitting on the cusp of change. For decades the academy had been under the influence of long-departed superintendent Sylvanus Thayer and his "spiritual heir" Dennis Hart Mahan. The "Thayer System" would remain in place only two years after Slocum's departure; it was replaced in 1854 by a new system based on the five-year course. For the time being, West Point maintained its very formal, traditional atmosphere, resulting in what has been described as its "golden years." Students spent most of their time reading lessons and learning on their own, though under the guidance of their professors who gave oral exams, called "recitations," on an almost daily basis, and major examinations on each subject twice a year. In terms of what the cadets studied, the curriculum was overwhelmingly weighted toward mathematics, science, and engineering, to which went 71 percent of classroom time during a cadet's four-year stint, leaving only 29 percent for everything else, including French, rhetoric, riding, political science, and drawing. Field tactics and other such military matters were covered in a single class in the cadet's final year. As James L. Morrison Jr. observed:

8. Charles Slocum emphasizes that Slocum's humble beginnings made it difficult for him to gain entrance to West Point, saying it took some time. If his assertion is true, that Slocum had begun to seek the commission only in 1846, then Slocum was not as disadvantaged as Charles makes out. Charles Slocum, *Life and Services*, 8–10. See also "Gen. Henry W. Slocum Dead," *New York Times*, April 15, 1894, 16; Fox, *In Memoriam*, 66; "Gen. Slocum in the War," *Brooklyn Eagle*, Sunday, February 5, 1888, 15.

9. Fox, *In Memoriam*, 74.

"At least the academic board was not guilty of letting the 'military tail wag the academic dog.'"[10]

At twenty years of age Slocum was a few years older than the average cadet, but this lent him maturity that some of the younger men lacked. He had been an advanced student for years by that point and had actually been teaching for the last four. He did not squander his opportunities at West Point, and other students took note and gained from his experience. One of these cadets, a former general store clerk from Ohio who slipped into the academy after another appointee failed the entrance exam, shared a room with Slocum. Beset by behavior problems (one of which would have him expelled from West Point for a year), Philip Sheridan found Slocum's aid indispensable. Sheridan described him as "a cadet whose education was more advanced than mine, and whose studious habits and willingness to aid others benefited me immensely."[11]

Slocum and Sheridan sat up late most nights in their small room, working on their studies. Each night they took a thick blanket and hung it over the single window in the room as taps sounded. They then lit lamps and dug through stacks of algebra, French, and English. Sheridan had trouble with mathematics in particular and gratefully took advantage of Slocum's education and offer of help to prepare for exams. The following January Sheridan approached the examining board with confidence and passed "fairly well." They both could only muddle through French. Slocum himself passed his first year at West Point well enough. He ranked fourteenth out of sixty cadets overall. He scored twelfth in mathematics, fortieth in French, and ninth in English. Over the year he accumulated twenty-three demerits, some no doubt earned when he and Sheridan defied curfew.[12]

The class of 1852 boasted some later Civil War notables, though not as many as the fabled class of 1846, which had included George B. McClellan and Thomas J. "Stonewall" Jackson. Studying alongside Slocum were future Union generals George Crook, Thomas L. Casey, Alexander McCook, and David S. Stanley. Crook would serve extensively in the war, eventually taking command of a corps under Slocum's roommate Sheridan in

10. James L. Morrison Jr., "The Best School in the World": West Point, the Pre–Civil War Years, 1833–1866, 23, 114, 115, 91 (quote); Thomas J. Fleming, West Point: The Men and Times of the United States Military Academy, 53, 126–29.

11. Ezra J. Warner, "Philip Henry Sheridan," Generals in Blue, 437; Philip Sheridan, Personal Memoirs of P. H. Sheridan, 1:10 (quote).

12. Sheridan, Personal Memoirs, 10–11 (quote); West Point Records for Slocum, Henry Warner; Charles Slocum, Life and Services, 9.

the Shenandoah Valley. After the war he ascended to major generalship and spent decades pacifying various Indian tribes on the frontier. Casey, son of another Civil War general, Silas Casey, was a career engineer and officer whose later architectural achievements would include both the Washington monument and the Library of Congress. McCook would become the highest ranking of the fourteen famous "Fighting McCooks," and Stanley would distinguish himself as not only a major general but the only member of the class of 1852 to receive the Congressional Medal of Honor, for action at the Battle of Franklin. There were significantly fewer Confederates in the class of 1852, but among them was George B. Anderson, who would die of wounds received defending the Sunken Road at Antietam. Other Civil War soldiers at West Point during Slocum's time (though not in his class) included James B. McPherson, John M. Schofield, John Bell Hood, William Carlin and Thomas Ruger (both of whom would later serve under Slocum), Jeb Stuart, Stephen D. Lee, Dorsey Pender, Gouverneur K. Warren, Oliver O. Howard, and of course, Sheridan. Slocum just missed studying under Robert E. Lee's administration of West Point, graduating the same year Lee was appointed.[13]

While at West Point Slocum apparently showed little fear of expressing himself on even controversial questions. Like elsewhere in the country, the discussion of abolition and slavery could quickly become heated. One cadet noted that as the debate intensified, the school broke down into two sections, not surprisingly Northern and Southern. Slavery was the primary cause of this mutual dislike, though not the only one. Many Southern cadets resented the better-than-average education of the Northern students, which meant that the Southerners could rarely earn good enough marks to achieve a high standing at the school. This anger sometimes escalated into violence, as evidenced by a bloody confrontation between William L. Crittenden of Kentucky and George H. Derby of Massachusetts in 1847. Crittenden attacked Derby with a drawn sword for no other provocation than that Derby had looked at him. Derby survived with wounds to his head, arm, and shoulder. Crittenden was not expelled, because of his political influence, and survived to die before a Spanish firing squad during a filibustering attempt to invade Cuba in 1851.[14]

13. "Civil War Generals from West Point"; Warner, *Generals in Blue,* 69–70, 102–3, 74–75, 294–95, 470–71, 306–7, 425–26, 415–16, 541–42, 237–38; Ezra J. Warner, *Generals in Gray,* 5–6, 142–43, 183–84, 233–34, 181; "Thomas Lincoln Casey," *Virtual American Biographies;* "Thomas Lincoln Casey," *Dictionary of American Biography, Supplements 1–2 to 1940.*
    14. Fleming, *West Point,* 127–28.

Slocum later noted that during his time the cadets had quickly become separated into numerous social cliques, but the slavery question divided the corps more evenly. Slocum clearly and openly declared himself both antislavery and prounion. This led to arguments with his fellow cadets, the more radically proslavery of whom thoroughly disliked him. Fellow abolitionists, such as Oliver O. Howard, admired his tenacity and honesty and remembered it long afterward.[15]

Any explicit statement Slocum may have made about slavery before the war may well now be lost, but the atmosphere in New York State in the 1840s and 1850s was a hodgepodge of approaches to slavery and black civil rights. Groups like the Liberty Party demanded both emancipation and equal rights for black citizens, most especially suffrage. Other groups tried to ignore the issue altogether, though these dwindled as the decades wore on and it became harder to avoid taking a stand. Many more people—particularly members of the Whig, Democrat, and Free Soil parties—took what they liked to consider a more moderate view: they opposed slavery but also opposed full equality for black men and women. Many New Yorkers were particularly touchy over the idea that blacks should be given voting rights. As James A. Rawley noted: "Racial prejudice conditioned the politics of slavery, which the Civil War generation never forgot was slavery of *negroes*" (emphasis in the original).[16]

Later sources make Slocum's view on slavery much clearer, though to the modern ear his speeches and letters have a schizophrenic tone to them. Depending on what speech or letter is consulted, he looks alternately like a radical abolitionist or a paternalistic racist. This contrast was evident even at the time. Slocum once remarked in a letter to Sherman that, during the war, Democrat (later Republican) John A. Logan feared Slocum would side with the Radical Republicans once the war ended. Slocum did not mince words when discussing the "curse of slavery" and made it very clear that the North fought the war to end slavery. In a speech to the Brooklyn Historical Society, Slocum quoted liberally from Senator James Henry Hammond of South Carolina to show the South's love for slavery, noting that just before the war, "the Institution of Slavery was at its zenith." Hammond had argued that within only a few short years, the South had stopped trying to excuse itself on the issue. Its slaves had dou-

15. In his second class year, Slocum ranked third (Charles Slocum, *Life and Services*, 9); Howard, "Memory of Henry Slocum," 38–41; "Gen. Slocum in the War."

16. Eric Foner, *Politics and Ideology in the Age of the Civil War*, 77–81; James A. Rawley, *The Politics of Union: Northern Politics during the Civil War*, 71.

bled in value as a result. Slocum then responded: "But could the Senator have extended his vision but eight brief years, he would have witnessed a far more wonderful contrast. The prime laborer, who had advanced in value from four hundred dollars in 1828, to eight hundred in 1858, had made a still more surprising advance. The slave of 1858 was the law maker of 1868!" The war, he said, had brought about many "wonderful changes," not the least of which was that it "conferr[ed] on the South free institutions in reality as well as name." He thought this in itself enough to recompense the country for its trouble. While a garrison commander in Vicksburg in 1864 and 1865, Slocum took powerful and positive steps to ensure that blacks received equal treatment under the law, even overturning proclamations by the provisional governor when he thought it necessary. He clearly advocated not only the abolition of slavery but also the extension of at least basic rights of citizenship to black men.[17]

Yet Slocum also routinely referred to blacks as "darkies." In a letter to his wife in 1864, he mentioned the train cars in Atlanta reeking "with the odor peculiar to 'the American of African descent.'" After leaving the army he switched parties specifically because he wanted a brief period of reconstruction that would leave white Southerners much leeway when it came to the civil rights of black Southerners (he naively thought the former masters could be trusted to be fair and humane). So, while not a true radical, he fell toward that side of the moderate camp. Slocum believed in equality for both races, but he was bound by the context of his times and a commitment to what he would probably have called realism.[18]

While maintaining his studies in the midst of a nation in turmoil, Slocum took what work he could and scrupulously saved his money. His father had fallen ill back in Syracuse and found it increasingly difficult to maintain his business at Four Corners. The other children still at home did what they could, and Henry sent as much money back home as his spare time could earn him.[19]

Slocum slowly improved his class standing while at West Point and seems to have learned his lesson regarding demerits after his first year. In

17. Slocum to Sherman, 1868, at Fox, *In Memoriam*, 109; Henry W. Slocum, *Military Lessons Taught by the War*, 4–6 (to historical society).
18. For example, see Slocum's description of the men and women following the Army of Georgia in the wake of Sherman's marches, in Henry W. Slocum, "Sherman's March From Savannah to Bentonville." Another good example is the letter Slocum wrote to his family just before the March to the Sea, where he mentions blacks' alleged odor. Fox, *In Memoriam*, 98 (quote).
19. Charles Slocum, *Life and Services*, 11–12.

his third class year he improved his overall standing to thirteenth and, by his second, had jumped to third place. He did not earn a single demerit in either year, possibly because he had been parted from Sheridan. This performance earned him a spot among the five most distinguished cadets after the annual examination that year. During his final year Slocum slipped back down somewhat, to seventh place in his class, and this is where he graduated in June 1852.[20]

Slocum received a promotion to brevet second lieutenant upon graduation and joined the First U.S. Artillery. If he had hoped for a chance to return to Syracuse and marry Clara, he saw this crumble when the army ordered the First Artillery to south Florida, near Tampa Bay. For years the government had been fighting a series of wars with the Seminole Indians as they came into conflict with land-hungry settlers pushing down out of Georgia. The army had already fought the First and Second Seminole Wars and would soon fight a third and final one in the mid 1850s.[21]

Slocum saw no large-scale action in Florida, but he did experience the rigors of camp life and marching. He also had the opportunity to make the acquaintance of at least one future Confederate general, Ambrose Powell Hill, then a quartermaster stationed at Indian River. What little fighting Slocum may have taken part in against the Seminoles would certainly have been nothing like the Jominian tactics he had learned at West Point. Slocum's company did not stay in Florida for long (they, with their lumbering guns in tow, would have been little use against the very mobile Seminoles), and by the end of 1853, they had been posted to Fort Moultrie in Charleston, South Carolina.[22]

The welcome news of his transfer meant that Slocum and Clara could marry, but sadly there was one family member who would not be in attendance. On August 11, 1853, probably not long before the First Artillery arrived in Charleston, Henry's father, Matthew, died in Scottsville in

---

20. Class years at West Point are counted in descending order. A student's first calendar year there, what many would think of as his freshman year, is his "fourth class year." His second calendar year, or sophomore year, is his "third class" year, and so forth. West Point Records for Slocum, Henry Warner; Charles Slocum, *Life and Services*, 9–10.

21. "Slocum," *Journal*, February 19, 1878; A. J. L. Waskey, "Seminole War, First," "Second," and "Third," in Spencer Tucker, *Encyclopedia of American Military History*, 3:769–72. Much of the following section is indebted to Fox, *In Memoriam*, 67–68; "Gen. Slocum in the War"; and Charles Slocum, *Life and Services*, 10–11.

22. Howard, "Memory of Henry Slocum," 40; *New York at Gettysburg*, 1333; "General Slocum," *Journal*, April 14, 1894; "Third Seminole War," on U-S-History.com; "Billy Bowlegs (Holatta Micco)," The National Portrait Gallery: Native Americans.

Monroe County, just outside Rochester, where he had possibly traveled on business. The elder Slocum was sixty-five at the time, and Henry would not have been able to attend the funeral. Not long after arriving at his new post, Slocum arranged for a house or some small living space for himself apart from the barracks. This done, he petitioned for leave and returned to New York in late January. On February 19, 1854, he and Clara finally married. They enjoyed a short honeymoon before traveling back to South Carolina.[23]

While in Charleston the Slocums enjoyed themselves immensely, taking advantage of the various pleasures available: boating, dancing, fishing, parties, and so on. The long, slow hours of peacetime garrison duty would have allowed the couple much free time. Clara would have had to adjust herself to their new married life in a very different section of the country and to her responsibilities as the lady of the house (however small). Henry had to learn that his life of bachelorhood had finally come to a decisive close. Despite their long engagement they still would have had much to learn about one another and many annoying habits to transcend. Such transitions are rarely completely smooth.

Slocum also began other, less pleasurable pursuits by turning to the study of law. Sometime after he arrived at the post, a flood had forced a number of families living on Sullivan's Island to take refuge in Fort Moultrie. One of these families was that of to a local lawyer, B. C. Presley, who would later serve on South Carolina's Supreme Court. Presley offered to take Slocum into his law firm as a student. Slocum found him a cultured man and worked hard under his tutelage. Slocum's long years as a student and teacher probably led him to throw himself into his studies, which helped pass the time on watch for nonexistent foreign invaders at the decrepit Fort Moultrie.[24]

Slocum, with a confrontational nature and dedication to what he thought true, had ample opportunity to argue over slavery and secession in South Carolina. Although the more moderate states' rights Democrats dominated South Carolina politics for the bulk of the 1850s, Slocum later implied that Charleston exposed him to the more militant wing of the party. He certainly would have had the chance to argue while in Presley's offices. Lawyers there had probably been debating issues such as nullification, slavery, and secession for years and may have baited the Yankee in

23. "Died," *New York Tribune*, August 19, 1853.
24. "Brilliant Soldier's Record," *New York Times*, April 15, 1894, 16; *New York at Gettysburg*, 1334.

their midst. He later credited his prewar services in the South with convincing him of Southern sincerity on the eve of secession and that the Radical Republican Reconstruction agenda could not work. Presley told Slocum that sentiment in the area was so proslavery that most of the federal officers he knew had pledged themselves to resign if Fremont won the election in 1856. In fact, Slocum said he observed some people preparing for open war against the North. Another important change began, however. Slocum grew to appreciate Southerners as both humans and individuals, instead of some monolithic mass of slave-power conspirators. He later remarked that he made the acquaintance of a number of "very fine people" while stationed in Charleston, and so he viewed both masters and slaves in more concrete terms. White Southerners were just as human to Slocum as slaves. As a result, he never developed the abstract loathing for Southerners or for the Southern cultural institutions that supported slavery that many other abolitionists did.[25]

As time passed and his studies advanced, Slocum began to consider resigning from the army. The glory and quick promotions he had anticipated while a young teacher in his one-room schoolhouse had never materialized. What he found he had instead was a low-paying job that could part him from Clara at any time. His worries only mounted when Clara informed him she was pregnant. Why, he may well have asked himself, should he and his family continue to scrape by on a military salary when "Spec" knew he could make much more money as a private citizen? Indeed, he had already made some investments in real estate in Syracuse. Slocum decided to stay, at least temporarily, when he received a promotion to first lieutenant on March 3, 1855. He had not yet finished his law studies and probably wanted to pass the bar examination before giving up his steady income. About this time Clara gave birth to their first child, a daughter, whom they called Caroline (but soon nicknamed Carrie). With this new mouth to feed, Slocum had further incentive to stay in the army. He would regret his decision.[26]

25. "Gen. Slocum in the War" (quote); Wallace Hettle, *The Peculiar Democracy: Southern Democrats in Peace and Civil War,* 104; *Journal* articles "Slocum's Political Pedigree," November 12, 1868, "Tears of the Crocodile," October 25, 1865, "Southern Humanity," October 7, 1865; Slocum, *Military Lessons,* 6. Slocum maintained the antislavery and antisecessionist stand he began at West Point throughout the war and into Reconstruction. His view of Southerners as being human too, however, also meant he expected them to quickly abandon slavery after the war, which was, of course, naive.

26. "Henry W. Slocum," *Onondaga Standard,* October 30, 1858; "Died," *Onondaga Standard,* October 30, 1856.

The summer of 1855 passed very slowly and painfully for Slocum and his family. The weather was hotter than normal, and the steamy climate took its toll on Clara and Carrie. They spent the summer uncomfortable and ill. Also, down in Florida, a U.S. surveying team under Colonel William Harney destroyed the precious crops of a group of Seminoles under Holata Micco, or Billy Bowlegs. The provocation led to open war. In 1856 the army ordered the First Artillery back to Florida.[27]

Slocum decided he could not leave his family and instead must get them back to cooler climes. Clara and Carrie had probably fallen ill again during the summer of 1856, and he knew he must get them away from South Carolina before their illnesses wore them down completely. When news of his new deployment arrived, he submitted his resignation, knowing it would take time to go into effect. In the meantime he organized his affairs with Presley and at Fort Moultrie. Before the end of the fall they would return home to Onondaga County, but he had not acted quickly enough. On October 20, 1856, Carrie died; Slocum's resignation went into effect just eleven days later. Henry and Clara thus returned empty-handed and broken-hearted to Syracuse.[28]

When they arrived home Slocum used what savings they had managed to put away to purchase a pleasant, one-and-a-half-story house on a wooded lot at 91 West Onondaga Street, on the corner of West Onondaga and Russell. The Reverend George H. Huling, who published a local newspaper, the *Religious Recorder,* had built the dwelling just ten years before. Clara set up housekeeping there and mourned the silence. Their second child may well have been on his way by this point, which may have lessened her grief somewhat. She also had help from family when Henry's mother and sister Sarah moved in with them. Slocum's brother Barnard lived nearby at 49 West Onondaga.[29]

Henry, on the other hand, had to find a way to finish his studies and support his family at the same time. One of his sisters had married well and provided him with an important contact. Her husband, LeRoy Morgan, was a prominent Syracuse lawyer who would eventually serve on the New York State Supreme Court. So, in the offices of Hillis, Morgan

27. Waskey, "Third Seminole War"; Howard, "Memory of Henry Slocum," 40.
28. "Died," *Onondaga Standard,* October 30, 1856; "Loyal Legion."
29. "The Slocum House, a Landmark, Is Being Torn Down," *Syracuse Herald,* August 27, 1899. The article lists the adjoining street as Slocum Avenue, but an advertisement concerning the house's later auction in the *Journal,* March 1866, lists the address as Russell; *Winsor's . . . Directory, 1857–1858.*

and Middleton, on Marble Block, off Salina Street, Slocum read law along-side his own nephew, Thomas L. R. Morgan, who was also apprenticing there. In 1857 Slocum and Morgan both stood for the bar examination and passed. The pair decided to set up in business together. On January 25, 1858, either Slocum or Morgan visited the offices of the *Syracuse Daily Courier* and placed an advertisement for the new law offices of Slocum and Morgan at No. 2, Pike Block, in the "Business Cards" section of the paper. They probably also visited the other papers in the area, including the *Journal* and the *Standard*. The first ad appeared a week later on February 2.[30]

Slocum obviously faced more established competition from his brother Barnard, who had served as county clerk from 1853 to 1857 and shared his practice with William H. Gifford nearby. Their offices, at 10 South Salina Street, were opposite Syracuse House, a boardinghouse, and above Pierce's crockery store. Barnard later tried to split off into his own practice in May 1858, moving down the road to 17 South Salina, but he was back together with Gifford by June 10. Barnard may have also diversified his income by opening a picture gallery, "Barnard's Gallery" also opposite Syracuse House on Salina Street, which offered iron-based melainotypes, a process, he assured his prospective patrons, that produced far better results than either the daguerreotype or the ambrotype.[31]

Despite his high marks in philosophy back in the academy, Slocum did not get on very well as a lawyer. After the war he confessed to fellow Syracuse resident William Tracey that the other lawyers in the town "used to hoe around him without much difficulty." In fact he later tried to talk Tracey out of the study of law. Still, he and Morgan must have experienced some success, at least enough to stay in business.[32]

30. "Major-General Henry Warner Slocum," *Syracuse Herald,* September 14, 1902; "General Slocum," *Journal,* April 14, 1894; "Business Cards," *Syracuse Daily Courier* (hereinafter *Courier*), February 2, 1, May 20, 1, both 1858; Howard, "Memory of Henry Slocum," 40; Charles Slocum, *Life and Services,* 11.

31. *Courier* articles "Business Cards," November 19, 1857 (vol. 2, no. 354), 1, "Patent Melainotype," November 25, 1857 (vol. 2), 3, "New Advertisements," May 1, 1858, 2, "Business Cards," May 3, 1858, 1, and June 10, 1858, 1. (Most *Courier* articles are clippings in the Slocum biographic file at the OHA, whereas others were researched on microform from the OHA. These latter are given volume number and sometimes issue number from the masthead of the newspaper and are not in the clippings file. They need to be located independently.)

32. "Loyal Legion," 1 (quote). The evidence seems to contradict Charles Slocum's glowing insistence that his ancestor "soon had a good clientele." Charles Slocum, *Life and Services,* 11.

Whatever Slocum may have lacked as a lawyer he more than made up for as a businessman. Near his house on West Onondaga he had purchased some vacant lots running along Russell Street; now he set about developing them. He leveled the land, installed brick sewers for drainage, and built a house on each plot, varying the design somewhat. He had the area around the houses landscaped and planted with fruit trees. The houses then sold on credit for anywhere from six hundred to twenty-eight hundred dollars. Slocum's mother and two unmarried sisters moved into one at No. 1 Russell Street, giving Clara the run of her own house. As late as 1860 Slocum was still clearing some of the tracts, probably at a small profit, by selling the young trees there for transplanting. People probably took him up on the offer quickly, as he charged them only one-fifth the prices of the local nurseries. The city later changed the name of Russell Street to Slocum Avenue in honor of its developer.[33]

Slocum's largest investment and probably the primary source of his income, by far, lay in what had made Syracuse prosperous from the beginning: salt. The French had been the first to discover the local brine springs. Iroquois leaders had shown them water previously regarded as evil and poisonous. The French and later the British found them singularly profitable (an opinion that the Iroquois quickly came around to as well), and the economy around Syracuse became dedicated to salt manufacturing. Workers would pump brine by hand from any of the large number of wells in the area. The brine then flowed through wooden pipes into salt blocks, large houses of kettles that boiled the brine down into commercial quality salt.[34]

After returning to Syracuse Slocum purchased at least two salt blocks, located at No. 27 and No. 41 in the Liverpool District. He rented these out to local companies for approximately five hundred dollars each. In addition to this, over time he accumulated 360 shares of stock in the Salt Company of Onondaga, and another 30 shares in Sweet, Barnes, and

33. Charles Slocum, *Life and Services,* 12; "Henry W. Slocum," *Onondaga Standard,* October 30, 1858; "The Slocum House" and "Auction Sales," *Journal,* March 20, 1866; (clipping in OHA), *Onondaga Standard,* September 6, 1857; "Houses and Lots for Sale," *Onondaga Standard,* September 6, 1857; *Boyd's City Directory.*

34. E. B. Tustin Jr., "The Development of the Salt Industry in New York," *New-York Historical Society Quarterly* 33 (1949): 40–46; Joseph Hawley Murphy, "The Salt Industry of Syracuse: A Brief Review," *New York History* 30 (July 1949): 304–15; W. Freeman Galpin, "The Genesis of Syracuse," *New York History* 30 (January 1949): 19–32; Valerie Jackson Bell, "The Onondaga New York Salt Works, 1654–1926"; Tom Kise, "Salt in Upstate New York."

Company. By 1859 a local city directory listed him as a businessman providing fine salt. The salt manufacturing of the county was in a state of
transition, however. Years of boiling brine at the salt blocks had stripped
the area of usable wood, and the costs of importing coal from nearby
towns were growing. By 1864 the industry at Syracuse would have completed a forced transition from refining salt by wood and coal to using
solar power. For the moment, though, the Slocums got by quite comfortably on their investments.[35]

At some point after returning to Syracuse Slocum became active in the
local Republican Party. New York was a very busy, passionate theater for
politics during this era. From 1840 to 1860 the state produced a mean voter
turnout of 74.5 percent, the fourth highest of any Northern state. The
political atmosphere of the time would have attracted Slocum to the
Republicans, even if he did not agree with the anti-Southern views of their
more radical members. As Michael Holt noted, by 1860 the Republicans
were seen as the Northern party, in favor of Union and against slavery. In
New York and elsewhere they exploited this to build a winning party, capable of defeating the fragmented Democrats. This meant that by 1858
Republican opposition to slavery was often no longer ideological and did
not have to entail any beliefs in absolute or total racial equality in the
North or South. Republicans simply united on the primacy of the Union
and the need to limit slavery's spread, a cause that everyone from Western
racists to Radicals could support. Slocum's political views fit comfortably
in this very wide berth.[36]

Meanwhile, the local Democrats—led by John A. Green, owner of the
Syracuse Daily Courier, and Thomas Alvord, the Democratic Speaker of the
New York Assembly in 1857—had a problem. By the middle of the 1850s
the Democratic Party as a whole was so fragmented it might not be able
to mount a successful resistance to the upstarts. The Republicans had
swept through Onondaga after their rise in 1856, threatening Green's and
Alvord's comfortable positions in the county. In fact, by the end of 1857,
Green's own paper had sarcastically declared Onondaga the "Citadel of
Black-Republicanism," in the wake of a series of Republican victories. In
the coming months Green's organ bitterly fought the newcomers, but even

35. Bell, "Salt Works"; "Auction Sale," *Journal,* March 20, 1866; "Second Assembly
District" (clipping in OHA, probably the *Journal*); *Boyd's City Directory.*
36. William E. Gienapp, "'Politics Seem to Enter into Everything': Political Culture in
the North, 1840–1860," 22; Michael F. Holt, *The Political Crisis of the 1850s,* 183–85; Rawley,
Politics of Union, 8.

as it insisted that the "Republican party seems to be by the ears and falling out all around," Green knew that something else must be done.[37]

As the election drew near, the Syracuse Democrats knew they needed to ensure that at least one of their men made it into office, where he could then promote Syracuse's salt and canal interests and likely lean them in a way beneficial to Green himself. Things had not gone all that well for Green in particular in recent years, with a mortgage holder from New York repossessing a good deal of property from him in 1857. A man in the assembly could certainly do his part to assuage Green's woes. Green tapped Alvord to run for the seat from the second assembly district of Syracuse. They then approached John L. Schoolcraft of the Republican State Central Committee with a proposition: If Schoolcraft could arrange for a straw man to face Alvord in Syracuse, they would assure Schoolcraft a thousand-vote majority in Syracuse for Republican gubernatorial candidate Edwin D. Morgan. They asked for an unknown Syracuse Republican, Henry Slocum, to be placed on the ballot against Alvord. Slocum had returned to the county less than two years before; Alvord was the incumbent and a well-known, established businessman and politician. They thus expected it to be a sure victory for Alvord.[38]

This idea intrigued Schoolcraft. Morgan had been running a campaign scandalous to the state's Democrats, who were still powerful in some areas. Morgan had claimed at the Republican Convention that year that the U.S. government was nothing more than "the supple instrument of the slave power [conspiracy]" and that it was the Republican Party's sacred duty to destroy it. Morgan meant the slave-power conspiracy, of course, but his poor choice of words lent themselves to Democratic charges of treason. This rhetoric had apparently also unsettled Morgan's own friends enough that he later felt compelled to soften it, claiming that were he to be elected governor, he would respect the rights of both slaveholders and abolitionists

37. Thomas Bailey, *Democrats vs. Republicans: The Continuing Clash,* 63; *Courier* articles "All Hail Onondaga! Honor to Whom Honor Is Due!" November 17, 1857 (vol. 2, no. 352), 3 (first quote), "Heartless Fellow," November 28, 1857 (vol. 2, no. 361; second quote), "Hon. Thomas G. Alvord," November 15, 1857 (vol. 2, no. 351), 3, "African Slavery at the North," December 9, 1857 (vol. 2), 2, "Onondaga County," December 8, 1857 (vol. 2, no. 368), "That Republican State Officer," December 9, 1857 (vol. 2, no. 359), 2, "The Failure of 'Fusion,'" September 15, 1858, 2, and "The Party of Treason Unmasking Its Batteries," September 15, 1858, 2.

38. "Supreme Court," *Courier,* November 18, 1857 (vol. 2, no. 353), 1; "A Story about Slocum," *Journal* (reprinted from the *Albany Knickerbocker*), June 15, 1865; "The Party of Treason Unmasking Its Batteries," *Courier,* September 15, 1858, 2.

alike. It seems that Schoolcraft thought they could afford to give up a single seat in exchange for that extra bit of insurance. He took the offer to Thurlow Weed, a powerful former Whig turned Republican boss who had organized much of the Republican strategy in the state. After a consultation they agreed and sent a man to the Syracuse Republicans to make sure everything went as planned.[39]

The Republicans gathered at the Syracuse city hall on Saturday, October 16, 1858, to nominate a candidate. Not everyone in the local party was as thrilled by the idea of giving away the second district as Schoolcraft and Weed hoped. Some Republicans objected to losing their chance at taking over a traditionally Democratic area. A cadre dedicated to promoting canal interests worked together to defeat Slocum's nomination. They feared, along with the local American Party, that Slocum would neglect the canals currently under construction in favor of railroads. In the end they failed to block him, and the *Syracuse Standard* announced the result in the evening of October 19. Earlier that day, at 2 P.M., the Democrats of the second district had gathered at city hall. They surprised no one when they nominated Thomas Alvord for the Second District.[40]

With the election scheduled for November 2, 1858, both parties got down to some serious last-minute campaigning. For Slocum this meant very little. In fact few of the Syracuse newspapers had much to say about a first-time runner for a single seat in one district of the city. Slocum's campaign managers may have done some legwork and door knocking, but he got very little help from the Republican establishment, and very little attention from the Democrats. The latter in particular seemed to hold Slocum in low regard. And why not? He was their straw man.[41]

When the presses did have anything to say, they generally said the same things but drew opposite conclusions. The Republicans focused on Slocum's

39. "The Party of Treason Unmasking Its Batteries," *Courier*, September 15, 1858, 2 (quote); David Potter, *The Impending Crisis, 1848–1861*, 247; Eric Foner, *Free Soil, Free Labor, Free Men: The Ideology of the Republican Party before the Civil War*, 282; "General Slocum and Mr. Weed," *Journal*, October 25, 1865.

40. "Our Candidate for the Assembly," *Onondaga Standard*, October 19, 1858; "Second Assembly District," *Courier*, October 16, 1858, 2; "Henry W. Slocum," *Onondaga Standard*, October 30, 1858; "Democratic Republican Regular Nominations," *Courier*, November 2, 1858, 2.

41. The *Daily Courier*, for instance, did not run more than one or two articles on Slocum in all of October (though two editions are no longer available). That they had anything to say at all must be deduced from the one or two articles posted in response by the Republican papers.

youth, claiming it lent him energy and drive. Slocum was only thirty-one years old at the time, and the Republicans called his nomination a compliment to one of the brightest young men of the city. They added that those who knew him found him both "capable and honest." The Democrats also pointed to Slocum's age, implying that any man so young as thirty-one years must be unfit for office. How could he hope to compete with experience? They also mentioned Slocum's relative obscurity. As the Democrats had anticipated, Alvord attracted most of the attention of the newspapers, both good and bad. Neither side seemed terribly interested in the remote possibility that Slocum might win.[42]

As the election approached the Democratic press tried to remain calm, but evidences of how desperate the situation had become that year peeked through a cracking veneer. A small article in the *Daily Courier* on the morning of the election shattered the veneer entirely. It screamed, "EVERY DEMOCRATIC VOTER must be brought out" (emphasis in the original). The Democrats even set up a "vigilance committee" to get voters to the polls even if it meant carrying them.[43]

The atmosphere around Syracuse grew increasingly charged on November 2, and rumors of a resounding Republican victory began to make the rounds. The Republicans and the Democrats both threw huge celebrations that night, before the results had even come in. In the days to come, each side's party organ blamed the other for the noise that accompanied the drunken revelry. The counting continued slowly, with the Republicans certain of their victory and the Democrats at the *Courier* watching their thin strand of hope as it gradually withered. Within four days it had finally snapped.[44]

Slocum and the rest of the Republicans had won a string of impressive, if at times slim, victories. Out of 3,615 ballots cast, Slocum defeated Alvord by a thin majority of 143 votes. Alvord won the first three wards of the second district, the first by a single vote, the second by nearly one hundred, and the third by twenty. Slocum won wards five through eight by more decisive margins, taking ward six by a full 115 votes.[45]

42. "Our Candidate for the Assembly," *Onondaga Standard,* October 19, 1858 (quote); "Alvord vs. Sedgwick," *Courier,* October 23, 1858, 2; "Light Wanted," *Courier,* November 2, 1858, 3.

43. "Do You Know," *Courier,* November 2, 1858, 2.

44. *Courier* articles "Let the Eagle Scream," 3, "Assemblymen Probably Elected," 2, and "Stupor," 3, all dated November 6, 1858.

45. "Results in the City," *Courier,* November 5, 1858, 2.

The end result, whatever the margin of victory, was the same: the Democrats of New York had been decimated. In 1857 they had come within a single vote of controlling a majority of the legislature, fifty-four Democrats to fifty-five of other party affiliation. The 1859 legislature would look very different. That year, a mere twenty-five Democrats took their seats in Albany, leaving eighty-four for what the *Courier* lovingly called the "opposition," a furious euphemism for "Republican." All three representatives elected from Syracuse in 1858 would endorse Abraham Lincoln in 1860. As the *Courier* spat out, when all had become clear, "it is hoped that a couple of years' incubation will hatch out a better brood of Democrats than the fledglings that allowed the Black Republican hawks to unfeather their nests."[46]

But how did Slocum, the unknown Republican, upset Tom Alvord? Perhaps it was because, though Slocum may not have had a reputation, Alvord had too much of one. The Republicans brought up charges that Alvord had scammed the city by skimming money off the top of a fund designated for victims of a fire in the first ward. In late 1857 Alvord had been party to a lawsuit that had evicted a number of people from their homes in Syracuse. He ordered everything sold at auction, down to the last barn and outhouse. In a decision fit for the countinghouse of Scrooge and Marley, he scheduled the auction for just less than two weeks before Christmas.[47]

Probably the most tangible millstone around Alvord's neck he had carried over from his previous tenure as assemblyman. Then, Alvord had voted to settle a boundary dispute between Syracuse and the nearby town of DeWitt in favor of DeWitt, which infuriated many voters. In fact even his own Democratic constituency apparently made it clear how unhappy they were; shortly after voting in favor of the measure, Alvord suddenly pledged to overturn it.[48]

A Republican satirist wasted no time in reminding Alvord why he had lost to Slocum. In a dream, he said, the satirist saw a man riding a saw-horse and playing a jews harp, with a ballot for Alvord stamped to his forehead. "Jeems, *whar's* DeWitt?" the man asked forlornly. "My beloved Alvord has gone *thar* and I must follow *arter* and assuage his woe." He

---

46. *Courier* articles "Assemblymen Probably Elected," 2, "Let the Eagle Scream," 3, both November 6, 1858.

47. *Courier* articles "Light Wanted," November 2, 1858, 3, and "Supreme Court," November 24, 1857 (vol. 2, no. 358), 1.

48. "Alvord vs. Sedgwick," *Courier,* October 23, 1858, 2.

added that in the hills of DeWitt, "the lion roareth and the whang-doodle mourneth for her first born." After reprinting nearly the whole article, the *Courier* responded that the Republican star, the "Baldwinsville Comet" as the article named him, had obviously had too much to drink and should go home and sleep it off. No, the *Courier* insisted, the lion did not devour Alvord (much to the whang-doodle's apparent distress), but rather a huge corruption fund of between five and ten thousand dollars had done it. Interestingly enough, the Republicans had already leveled a similar charge at the Democrats.[49]

There were, however, two things never mentioned during the post-election mudslinging, by either side. The first, true to the stereotype of political doublespeak, was evidence. More important here, neither side mentioned Slocum. Even after he had defeated the powerful Democratic incumbent, the spotlight hardly moved to Slocum, even in the Republican press.

Slocum served in the assembly at Albany for the duration of 1859. While there he displayed the same tenacity in his opinions as he had earlier exhibited at West Point. The *Syracuse Journal* characterized him as "industrious, keen, [and] spunky" after watching the young assemblyman question another man's pork barreling. Of more concern to Slocum himself, other legislators repeatedly approached him to get him to participate in any number of schemes. Worse, many of them were fellow Republicans. Slocum refused to go along with them but never forgot the matter, particularly who had asked. The experience shook his faith in the Republican Party. Overall he established a reputation for honesty, one that lasted beyond even his eventual wartime popularity.[50]

The year 1859 saw an increase in sectional tension, and Slocum put his experience as an artillery officer to work with the state militia. When he signed up with the state forces the government awarded him the rank of colonel, and he spent the next two years instructing the militia on the basics of artillery. If this meant working with soldiers of the quality and focus of the guards around Syracuse, it would also have meant frustration for Slocum, if he took his job at all seriously. Antebellum militias, both North

---

49. *Courier* articles "Baldwinsville Comet," 3, "Money vs. The People," 3, both November 9, 1858.

50. *Journal* articles untitled, April 25, 1859 (quote), "Slocum's Political Pedigree," November 12, 1868, "General Slocum and Mr. Weed," October 25, 1865; *New York Times* articles "A Plea for Light," September 9, 4, "The Democratic Candidates," October 23, 4, "A Letter from Major-Gen. Slocum," October 20, 5, all 1865.

and South, nearly always functioned more as social clubs than as fighting units, and the ones in Syracuse were no different. The Grays, the "pride of the city," spent their time and money holding regular socials (dances, during the dancing season) on Wednesdays and renovating their armory. The Grays also put on a "Grand Gift Ball" offering for attendees over 150 warlike prizes such as gold watches, silver spoons, a lady's gold pencil, and a sewing machine. In August 1858 a group from the Light Dragoons turned out in all their finery for the difficult mission of having their pictures taken, a mission that incidentally they failed to complete.[51]

By 1860 Slocum had apparently tired of serving as an assemblyman. His children were growing older, he had continuing business at home, and he had become disgusted with some of the Republican maneuvering in Albany. That year he stood for election as Onondaga county treasurer and won a three-year term. After the election Slocum moved into the treasurer's office in the Onondaga County Savings Bank on the corner of Salina and Genessee streets.[52]

As events moved apace in the larger world Slocum probably observed them with some apprehension. In November 1860 he probably cast his vote for Lincoln and against slavery and secession, though he had fewer doubts than most about how the South would react. When news reached him of Fort Sumter, Slocum arranged for a trip to Albany and a meeting with Governor Morgan. Once there he offered to raise and command a battery of light artillery for the state, if the governor would authorize him to do so. Governor Morgan thanked him for the offer but assured him that the rebellion could be put down without the use of artillery. Morgan then made a counterproposal: he asked Slocum to stay on in the capital as his military adviser. Slocum refused, possibly because his experience told him he would have a better chance at promotion elsewhere.[53]

Slocum instead turned his attention back to Syracuse, as chaos ensued in the statewide scramble for commands. He wrote a letter to the state's

51. Charles Slocum, *Life and Services*, 12; *Courier* articles "Syracuse Grays," November 15, 1857 (vol. 2, no. 351), 3 (quote), "Grand Gift Ball of the Syracuse Grays," May 10, 1858, 3, and "The Light Dragoons," August 17, 1858, 3.

52. S. Gurney Lapham, "Officer Who Reached Highest Rank of Any Syracusian in the Civil War," *Syracuse Herald,* June 11, 1911; *Journal* articles "County Treasurer," September 3, 1861, and "General Slocum and Mr. Weed," October 25, 1865; *City Directory for 1862–1863.*

53. "Loyal Legion"; Fox, *In Memoriam,* 68; Charles B. Fairchild, *History of the 27th Regiment of New York Volunteers;* "Slocum, Soldier and Man," *New York Times,* May 5, 1894, 9; "Gen. Slocum in the War."

adjutant general, offering his services for any position needed, but he received no reply. Someone proposed him as commander of the Fifty-first New York, but the regiment refused him. Then Syracuse itself began raising a regiment of troops. Slocum quietly had some of his friends offer his name for colonel. When it came down to voting, the men passed on the West Point–trained Slocum in favor of a popular local militia officer (who may have been a better dancer).[54] With the comforts and obligations of home beckoning and disgusted by what he had seen, Slocum nearly chose to remain in Syracuse. All his attempts to gain a favorable command had failed. Ironically, one possibility he had no control over played out. A large regiment of men had been raised from the vicinity of Oswego, New York, and were congregating at Elmira. This would eventually become the Twenty-seventh New York Infantry. It had already encountered problems with numbers, but not of the sort regiments would face later in the war. The Elmira regiment had too many companies, and its officers fought hard to get it accepted as a whole.[55]

Meanwhile, Colonel Wood of yet another regiment, the Fourteenth New York, decided he wanted an assistant with military experience. Someone in Albany suggested he contact Henry Slocum of Syracuse. Wood sent word to Slocum that he wanted him for his lieutenant colonel. The *New York Herald*, assuming Slocum would accept, confidently reported the appointment. Unfortunately for the Fourteenth they took too long, and Slocum received an offer from yet another regiment at Elmira (not the soon-to-be Twenty-seventh) to serve as their colonel. When Slocum arrived in town, the men of this third regiment immediately issued a set of demands stating what they expected of him as their colonel. Furious, Slocum refused their terms and returned home to Syracuse. He had not been home long, however, when the Twenty-seventh called him back. They wanted a West Point–trained colonel and offered Slocum command. None of the men knew Slocum personally, and they decided to choose him purely from his reputation in the state militia. They also accepted one of Slocum's chief conditions, that he have absolute power to appoint subordinate officers as he chose. Slocum agreed, sending his apologies to Wood. Slocum received his new commission on May 21, 1861.[56]

54. Fox, *In Memoriam*, 68; "Tender of Individual Services," *Journal*, April 17, 1861.

55. "The Oswego Regiment," *Journal*, May 8, 1861; "Gen. Slocum in the War."

56. *Journal* articles "Col. Slocum Doubly Honored," May 20, and "The Oswega Regiment," May 8, both 1861; "Loyal Legion," 2; H. Seymour Hall, "A Volunteer at First Bull Run," 149; "Gen. Slocum in the War"; Charles Slocum, *Life and Services*, 13.

Slocum then worked quickly to take care of his obligations to county and family before leaving for war. Having no illusions that it would be a short conflict, he had to see to his office as county treasurer. Slocum contacted the previous treasurer, P. H. Agan, who took over the duties at the Onondaga County Savings Bank until more permanent arrangements could be made. Slocum would also have to make provision for his salt-manufacturing and real estate businesses. His nephew Thomas Morgan probably took the clients Slocum still had in his portion of the law firm.[57]

There is no way to know what Clara was thinking as Henry packed his luggage to leave. He had been a military man when she married him, and he became one again with this new crisis. He probably had made certain that she and the children would be provided for while he was away. She could only hope that the war would be short, and that he would come home again. So, with mixed emotions of excitement and fear probably bubbling just below the surface, they said goodbye one May morning, and Henry boarded a train bound for his new regiment, then waiting for him at Elmira.

57. "Gen. Slocum's Accounts," *New York Tribune*, October 26, 1865.

C H A P T E R   2

"I attended services at Manassas last Sunday"

The Battle of Bull Run and After

When Henry Slocum stepped off the train in Elmira for the second or third time in as many months, he had a rude awakening in store for him. The volunteer force would be a very different experience from what he had known as a regular. The new recruits had been trying to force the army to adapt to their wants and wishes, but Slocum knew he must instead make them conform to the army and the rigorous demands that went along with it. He would drill, drill, and drill his men until they learned some semblance of order but at the same time offer his demands in such a way that their sensitive egos could handle it. His approach led to a relatively solid performance at Bull Run, and to promotion, which would give him the chance to drill larger numbers of men with equal passion.

Upon arriving at Elmira, Slocum discovered that his regiment might still be too large for acceptance. The Twenty-seventh had cobbled itself together by taking in companies from all over the state. Each company had arrived late to Elmira and found most of the regiments had already chosen their officers. So, instead of joining regiments where they could have no vote, the men chose to form a new organization. This meant they represented no particular area of the state, and that each company had been recruited according to different standards. Some of the troops had been in Elmira since May 8, 1861, others did not arrive until May 18. They took the name Union Regiment in light of the far-flung origins of their companies.[1]

1. See untitled, *Onondaga Standard*, May 28, 1861; Fairchild, *History of the 27th*, 1–3. All sources agree that the regiment respected Slocum. He himself served as publisher of the

For officers Slocum chose Joseph J. Chambers as lieutenant colonel and Joseph J. Bartlett for major. Chambers, an older man who stuttered when he spoke, was a devout Christian and had been a secretary to former governor Myron Clark. He played a pivotal role in getting the companies of the Twenty-seventh accepted into service. Aside from difficulties with their size, by the time they applied for acceptance Governor Morgan was convinced he did not need any more men. Chambers made the trip to Albany and used his connections to gain an audience with Morgan. When the governor still refused the companies, Chambers barred the door to the governor's office and declared, "B-b-b-by G-G-od! you d-d-d-don't get out of this room t-t-t-till you accept these co-co-co-companies!" Chambers's men from White Plains thus became the first accepted organization in what would become the Twenty-seventh.[2]

Bartlett on the other hand was a younger man, still in his twenties, who had practiced law in Binghamton from 1858 to 1861. He had helped to raise Company C of the regiment. Like Chambers, Bartlett was a novice at military affairs. He had filled his company on April 25 during a meeting at the old Rochester courthouse. Afterward he tried to march them down the street to a nearby oyster saloon for dinner. When they arrived at the door Bartlett did not know the proper command to have his men go inside (a survivor would later note it was "File Left"). It seems that Bartlett disliked Chambers from the beginning, though it remains a mystery as to why. He may have had personal reasons, but perhaps he coveted Chambers's higher-ranking position under Slocum.[3]

Their colonel fell somewhere in between these two opposing figures. Slocum stood at average to slightly above average height. He sported a prominent nose and a very noticeable mustache, which at the time of Bull Run he had complimented with a goatee. He was thin and wiry, carrying

---

Twenty-seventh's history whose author, Charles B. Fairchild, knew Slocum well and, while remaining truthful, probably put a positive spin on even uncomfortable situations. Charles Slocum, *Life and Services*, 13–14; Fox, *In Memoriam*, 69; Hall, "First Bull Run."

2. Fairchild, *History of the 27th*, 1; Hall, "First Bull Run," 148 (quote).

3. See C. A. Wells, speech, at *Seventh and Eighth Annual Reunion Proceedings of the Survivors Association of the 27th Regiment, New York Volunteers, 1st New York Volunteer Cavalry, 33rd Regiment New York Volunteers* (c. 1891; U.S. Army Military History Institute Archives, Carlisle, Pa.), 37–38. When Slocum fell wounded at Bull Run, Bartlett assumed command of the Twenty-seventh. He claimed that Slocum ordered him to, but Hall seems to doubt this claim. Hall, "First Bull Run," 155–56. Later in life Bartlett seems to have become obsessed with promoting himself; although his official report of the Battle of Crampton's Gap gives credit to Slocum, a later recitation gives all the credit to himself.

himself erect as a result of his West Point years. He generally kept his long wavy hair brushed back and anointed it with oil or cream. Slocum did not try to cut a dashing figure but instead calmly kept to himself, unruffled by the chaos around him.[4]

Slocum's calm demeanor served him well, because almost from the beginning the men were out to flout discipline and disobey orders. Many of them looked at their service as wholly dependent upon their own comfort and convenience. War, to them, was a game they were playing for glory, and few anticipated the price many would pay. Most units had elected their officers on the basis of popularity, not military experience, in which case the blind led the blind in the worst manner imaginable. But here the captains of the Twenty-seventh showed themselves more farsighted than others by specifically seeking out a West Point–trained commander in Slocum, and in allowing him to choose his own officers.[5]

Slocum found the whole process of organizing the army revolting. The idea that regiments could haggle over appointments alarmed him. Like Sherman and Grant he distrusted the non–West Pointers and worried about the effectiveness of their units. He found the volunteers themselves naive and entirely too cocksure. They could not appreciate discipline and would not put up with it. They harbored an intense dislike for professional soldiers, and Slocum considered the regulars the only men in the country fitted for what he felt sure lay ahead. How could he fight a war with men like this? He had a battle to win with his own men, before he could hope to fight one against the Rebels.[6]

The regiment gave Slocum no time to get his bearings. Although they had stayed in vacant lots and empty buildings upon arrival, by the end of May the Twenty-seventh had moved to quickly constructed barracks at Southport, across the river from Elmira. Once there they began drilling, guard duty, and grading the parade ground. The men grumbled about the

4. See "Col. Henry Slocum," in Fairchild, *History of the 27th*, 2–4. In the *Syracuse Herald*, September 16, 1902, a letter to the editor objects to an equestrian statue of Slocum erected in Brooklyn, on the grounds that it depicts him with a drawn sword, fiercely leading his troops forward. The writer called this depiction "not true to life," noting that Slocum was "one of the quietest, and most undemonstrative officers."

5. Chaos of this sort was nothing new in America. The same attitudes were clearly demonstrated in every war the United States had fought using the volunteer system. See Lawrence Cress, *Citizens in Arms: The Army and Militia in American Society to the War of 1812* (Chapel Hill: University of North Carolina Press, 1982).

6. Slocum, *Military Lessons*, 6–7. Thomas J. Goss gives a good history of this bickering between volunteers and regulars, stretching back all the way to the Revolution, in *The War within the Union High Command: Politics and Generalship during the Civil War*.

rocks they had to move, but their resistance to the rations caused the most grief and gave Slocum the most headaches.[7]

Upon arriving in Elmira Slocum had not yet had time even to address the troops before he had to reprimand one of them. One evening in the last week of May, the men of Company E from Rochester sat down to dinner in their mess only to discover their meat was undercooked. As they poked it and complained loudly, someone made the suggestion that they had best box it up quickly, otherwise it might escape. They took a large piece and nailed it into a sturdy box. The enterprise quickly grew into a funeral for the beef, and they formed into ranks and bore it to its final resting place to the tune of the Rogue's March. Private Albion W. Tourgee gave a moving eulogy for their lost friend, and they buried the box with full military honors.[8]

Tourgee would himself rise to prominence, though not mainly through military fame. During the war he was wounded twice, captured, and exchanged. Returning to his new regiment, the 105th Ohio, he fought at Tullahoma, Chickamauga, Lookout Mountain, and Missionary Ridge. After his resignation in 1863 he went into the practice of law. He moved to North Carolina during Reconstruction where he became one of the most infamous of the Northern carpetbaggers. He served as a judge, newspaper editor, and utility political partisan for Radical Republican causes but later became better known for his novels of the postbellum South, including *A Fool's Errand, by One of the Fools* (1879), *Figs and Thistles* (1879), *Bricks Without Straw* (1880), and *A Royal Gentleman* (1881). None of his novels is considered of interest for its literary value and polish, but they are appreciated instead as examples of Radical leanings. Of more lasting importance, he argued against the infamous "separate but equal" standard in the case of *Plessy v. Ferguson*, which formalized the system of Southern segregation for the next sixty years. In 1954 the Supreme Court

7. Fairchild, *History of the 27th*, 3.

8. See Hall, "First Bull Run," 150; Fairchild, *History of the 27th*, 3–4. The chronology in this section is based on Fairchild's placing the incident first in his history, but since there is no date given, it could easily have taken place a few weeks later. That this was one of the first incidents is implied by the fact that Slocum would give a speech on June 1 that seemingly tries to settle an ongoing issue. The Thirty-third New York was evidently involved in this incident as well, as their regimental historian also mentions a similar incident involving "all the funeral pomp and ceremony which formerly attended the burial of Euclid at Yale College." It is possible that these are two separate incidents, since neither source mentions the other, and that one simply copied the other. If that is so, it is impossible to tell which, as no date is given for the incident involving the Thirty-third either. See David W. Judd, *The Story of the Thirty Third New York Volunteers*, 32.

acknowledged the justice of his arguments by using his main points to overturn *Plessy*.[9]

Slocum, absent from the camp at the time of Tourgee's oration, heard of the incident upon his return. After indulging in "[s]ome very strong language," he sent for Tourgee who found him, "smoking, not very quietly, and . . . talking to himself quite emphatically," possibly discussing with himself the mess of an army he had landed in. Slocum asked the private if he was involved in "that operation." Tourgee tried to avoid a direct answer, but Slocum wrung it out of him. He asked Tourgee if he "did not know that [his] conduct was derogatory to good discipline and in defiance of authority." Tourgee rather cheekily replied that he "never knew that beef had any particular rank." Slocum, evidently amused by the answer, let the private off with only a lecture. His discipline must not have been very effective, for Tourgee would be arrested twice during the war for what amounted to insubordination.[10]

Overall Slocum adopted a carrot-and-stick approach with his men. He treated the volunteers sternly, but he also took their complaints seriously. After all, discipline or no, these were the men he would have to lead into battle. He had an opportunity to enforce his policies a few days later. On June 1, Companies B and D (from Lyons and Binghamton, respectively) led another protest over the food at dinner. That evening the men returned to the mess and took their places at the long rough-hewn tables. The cooks brought out bowls of steaming, weak soup, and apparently it did not satisfy the Twenty-seventh. Someone gave a signal, and the tables, food, and utensils flew across the room. The frightened cooks quickly put together a meal of mush and milk, and the soup never appeared again.

Slocum, it seems, would combine two bits of advice into one when dealing with his men. One piece of advice probably came from his mother or Clara, the other from Napoleon: The way to a soldier's heart is through his stomach. Slocum took advantage of the disruption to make his first speech to the regiment, and in his speech he established himself as both their disciplinarian and their defender. About an hour after dinner he ordered the

9. "Albion Winegar Tourgee," in *Dictionary of American Biography*; "Albion Winegar Tourgée," in *Encyclopedia of World Biography*. For a sampling of Tourgee's later work, see *A Fool's Errand* (1879; Cambridge: Belknap Press of Harvard University Press, 1961), *Bricks without Straw: A Novel* (1880; Baton Rouge: Louisiana State University Press, 1969), *The Invisible Empire* (1880; Ridgewood, N.J.: Gregg Press, 1968).

10. The story here comes from Hall, "First Bull Run," 150. See also Fairchild, *History of the 27th*, 3–4.

long roll sounded and the regiment turned out into their lines on the parade ground. In the gathering darkness he introduced himself to the regiment and addressed the issue of rations. The men must learn that, while he commanded the regiment, they would have the rations the government provided, but also they "should be served in palatable style." He went on to add that on his watch "no contractor should fill his pockets at the expense of the stomachs of [my] men." More important, Slocum did not allow the matter to rest. While at Elmira, from that day onward, he made frequent appearances in the kitchens. He visibly made sure that the cooks prepared the rations properly and gave his men the best they had. The combination of his attentions and the resulting improvement in rations won him the respect and admiration of his regiment. Similar disruptive incidents steadily declined, though they never fully disappeared, and as Charles B. Fairchild, the Twenty-seventh's historian, put it: "Col. Slocum was idolized."[11]

A similar scenario was taking place all over the country. About the same time Slocum was trying to establish control of the Twenty-seventh New York, Ulysses S. Grant faced a similar situation with his Twenty-first Illinois in the West. The first colonel of the regiment had been run out of camp for trying to maintain discipline. Like Slocum, Grant knew the harsh regular army discipline all too well, and he knew he could not handle the more fragile, volatile volunteer troops as he might a professional regiment. Grant employed a similar approach to the one Slocum used, offering relaxed orders when the men obeyed but punishing disobedience immediately. As with Slocum, Grant found that the men responded well to this treatment, and the reformation began. One notable difference is that, while Slocum insisted the soldiers drill incessantly, Grant relaxed the stringent requirements of his predecessor. In both cases the measures seemed to work.[12]

In any event, if the men of the Twenty-seventh New York themselves seemed to think highly of themselves, their officers certainly shared in similar delusions. Slocum and his officers spent a great deal of time in the city hobnobbing with the upper levels of Elmira society. Bartlett no doubt took full advantage of his position and probably mentioned both his qual-

11. Slocum also knew he would not have to put up with similar incidents for long. Even Fairchild notes that, after the men reached the front, they would gladly have accepted such rations without "kicking." All quotes are from Fairchild, *History of the 27th*, 4.
12. Bruce Catton, *Grant Moves South*, 3–17.

ity and that of the Twenty-seventh to anyone who would listen. After they had forged their command out of remnant companies not wanted by other regiments, the temptation to brag would seem irresistible. This annoyed the other officers so much they dubbed the upper echelon of the Twenty-seventh the "Mutual Admiration Society."[13]

The extra effort to secure the men's goodwill served Slocum well because he was also a strict disciplinarian. From nearly the moment he set foot in camp, he started drilling his troops continually. He kept them busy for eight full hours a day working from Hardee's *Tactics,* maneuvers on the company and regimental level, and at least one day's work on street-fighting techniques. At night they had guard duty, and some of the officers spent their time reading up on army regulations and tactics.[14]

On June 4, Slocum received a welcome visitor. Clara came down to the camp with a group of ladies from Syracuse. With them they brought a fine supper of butter, bread, and cake. Slocum, Clara, and the other visitors ate with the men in the mess, before retiring to their rooms in the city. She and the ladies left soon after, but Slocum probably told her he planned to offer the men a furlough soon in preparation for their march to Washington.[15]

If a casual observer assumed that Slocum's troops had settled down into their routine of drill, drill, and more drill, he would have had a shock on Wednesday, June 12. During the day, a man from Company B, Gibson Dunn, managed somehow to get out of work and into a whiskey bottle. His drunken rambling led him into the camp of the Thirty-third New York, where he came face-to-face with its colonel, Robert F. Taylor. Whatever Dunn in his stupor said to the colonel, it enraged Taylor, who had him thrown into the Thirty-third's guardhouse. Word of Dunn's captivity slowly leaked back to the Twenty-seventh. The regiment's first Wednesday evening prayer service had just got under way when a movement began to free Dunn. Soon the whole camp was astir as men joined the rescue party. Some soldiers even interrupted the preacher, stood up, and left in the middle of the service. With virtually the whole regiment turned out, the Twenty-seventh marched to the camp of the Thirty-third, which then turned out in equal numbers, determined to stop the liberators and defend their own colonel's honor. This may have caused a moral quandary for Company E of the Twenty-seventh, which now found itself facing an entire regiment from its own city of Rochester. Both sides tore

13. Fairchild, *History of the 27th,* 6.
14. Ibid., 5; Hall, "First Bull Run," 151; Charles Slocum, *Life and Services,* 13.
15. Fairchild, *History of the 27th,* 4.

cobblestones up from the roads as they ran and formed into line of battle, as the few officers who remained with the men rode between the lines, calling for calm. As the situation grew worse, the officers managed to send word to Slocum. He had retired to his quarters in the city earlier that day and had not attended the prayer meeting. Slocum mounted and rode hard on the way to his regiment. He made it there in time to prevent the fight. He ordered the long roll sounded, and the men dropped their rocks and obeyed. It must have taken some time for everyone to find their places in the hollow square formation, because by that time it was ten o'clock and nearly totally dark. Slocum lectured the regiment on discipline and good order for quite a while in the ever-deepening evening but assured them that he would have Dunn released. Apparently satisfied, the men dispersed to their tents.[16]

It did not take the authorities in Elmira long to realize that the Twenty-seventh and the Thirty-third should be separated. On June 15, 1861, the Twenty-seventh moved from their Southport barracks to the Elmira Fairground. They had been there ten days when they received their pay for their first full month of service (reckoned by their mustering in to state service on May 21): $8.60. To some of the men, so young they had actually needed notes from their parents before enlisting, it must have seemed a fortune. On June 29, they finally received their first issue of government gear. Company C had been so doubtful this day would ever come they had purchased their own uniforms before marching out of Binghamton. They now discarded these in favor of the stiff, scratchy, government-issue blue. They also received their own knapsacks, haversacks, and canteens. They cut a much more uniform and impressive figure on the parade ground, but their new gear also reminded them that their lives had changed irrevocably.[17]

Slocum then allowed his newly minted soldiers to return home for a few days. On Sunday, June 30, 1861, the new chaplain, D. D. Buck, preached his first sermon to the regiment. After the service Slocum bade most of them goodbye and Godspeed. They had only a week before they

16. Ibid., 5–6; Judd, *Story of the Thirty Third*, 30. I got the story from Fairchild and the colonel's name from Judd, though the incident was apparently not memorable enough for Judd to include. The day of the week was calculated using a universal calendar; it is also implied by the nighttime prayer meeting. The whole scene proved pointless anyway. Dunn's head had cleared while he was sitting in the guardhouse, and he made an escape by removing a board from the building's roof.
17. For the details of the Twenty-seventh's departure, journey, and early days in Washington, see Fairchild, *History of the 27th*, 5–8; Hall, "First Bull Run," 145–46.

had to return. Slocum himself traveled to Syracuse and spent his leave with Clara and his family. While there word reached him that he was to have his regiment in shape and ready to march to Washington before the end of the next week. Slocum returned on July 3 or 4, probably making plans for his regiment and organizing papers. One of the Syracuse newspapers mentioned his trip home in passing.[18]

When the men returned on July 5, the War Department officially mustered the Twenty-seventh New York Volunteer Infantry into U.S. service. The men had signed up for a two-year stint beginning on May 21, 1861. Slocum's own commission as a colonel of volunteers also bore that date. Of the men who returned from leave, seven refused to take the oath and were then discharged and sent home. Not long after, one of the corporals from Company A was found murdered in one of the darker corners of Elmira, where he had gone in search of deserters. Slocum had his body recovered and sent home to White Plains under escort of some men from his company.[19]

Early on the morning of July 10, 1861, Slocum received orders to leave for Washington. He did not feel the regiment was properly prepared, but he had no choice in the matter. When he informed his troops, a mass scurrying and hurrying commenced as they tried to pack everything they had brought with them. Their enthusiasm would bear them up only for a while under the bulk of useless trinkets. Slocum sent Chambers on ahead to Washington to find quarters and food for the Twenty-seventh. The men left their barracks for good at two o'clock in the afternoon and paraded through the city to the cheers of hundreds of onlookers. They arrived at the depot, where they began the arduous process of cramming onto train cars bound for Williamsport, Pennsylvania. By four o'clock they were on their way.[20]

Slocum and his men traveled through a pouring rain for five hours until arriving to a welcome sight in Williamsport. Allowed off the trains for a short rest, they found that the local citizens were expecting them and had prepared what must have seemed a great feast. The ladies of Williamsport had tables of hot food spread out on a green next to the depot and treated the departing tenderfoots like conquering kings. Even years after the incident, with all the war behind them, the men remembered that night as one of the high points of their war experience. In fact one man actually took up

18. "Union Regiment" (clipping in OHA), c. July 5, 1861.
19. Charles Slocum, *Life and Services,* 13.
20. There is some confusion as to exactly when the troops left and arrived. Fairchild marks their departure from Elmira on July 10, but Hall claims that is when they actually arrived in Washington. "Gen. Slocum in the War."

a correspondence with one of the ladies, and a few months later he returned to Williamsport on furlough to marry her.[21]

The regiment's bliss did not last long, though, and by ten o'clock they all had to pile back into the train for a trip that would last the rest of the night. More travel through Pennsylvania, punctuated by brief stops at Harrisburg and York, brought them to a much colder reception in Maryland. Here they saw Union troops guarding bridges and the railroad, but the passage through Baltimore proved the most harrowing event thus far. The city had been racked with sectional tension, and mobs had threatened to riot against troops who had passed through earlier. Maryland was the northernmost slave state on the East Coast, and many within her borders preferred secession to union. Outside Baltimore the regiment had to disembark from their cars and march through the town to reach a train bound for Washington itself. A number of the Twenty-seventh's more nervous officers wanted the men to load their weapons as they neared the city. Slocum refused. He was probably aware of the historical fact that soldiers with loaded guns tend to use them, especially when threatened, but he did order the troops to fix bayonets.[22]

As they approached the city, Slocum could hear the commotion in the streets. Thousands of people had turned out to see the newest batch of troops march through. The Twenty-seventh heard many cheers for the Union, but also hisses and boos. A significant number of people also applauded for Jefferson Davis, the new Confederate president. Slocum kept his men together, and they marched straight through the town without incident, a significant accomplishment with a regiment over one thousand men strong. Relieved to reach the safety of the depot, they soon loaded themselves onto the trains for Washington. After several more hours, between ten and eleven o'clock that night, they began to disembark in the nation's capital.[23]

They arrived in Washington just in time to find enough empty beds for the entire regiment in Camp Anderson, on Franklin Square, northeast of the White House. Unfortunately, Chambers had failed in his mission to collect food, and they found only two barrels of salt pork waiting to feed all ten companies. The men went to bed that night with no supper, furious at Chambers, who apparently had spent the time "refreshing his own inner man." Whether drunk, sleeping, or praying, Chambers had given

21. Fairchild, *History of the 27th*, 6–7.
22. Ibid., 7.
23. Hall, "First Bull Run," 151; Charles Slocum, *Life and Services*, 14.

Bartlett and any other possible opponents a strong argument against his leadership. As Slocum knew, soldiers rarely forget who is to blame when they have to go to bed hungry. The next day the Twenty-seventh was attached to the First Brigade of David Hunter's Second Division in Irvin McDowell's army of thirty-five thousand men. Presumably at this point, they received rations.[24]

McDowell, the man Slocum and Twenty-seventh would follow into their first battle, had been born in Columbus, Ohio, on October 15, 1818. He studied in France before attending West Point, where he graduated in 1838. McDowell later returned there to teach tactics to some of the very same soldiers that now faced him in the Civil War. He performed well during the Mexican War where he served as the adjutant general of the army. He received a brigadier generalship when the war broke out because of the patronage of Secretary of the Treasury Salmon P. Chase, even though he had never commanded a single man in the field. After Robert E. Lee refused command of the Union forces, Lincoln placed McDowell at the head of the army about to move against Richmond.[25]

Slocum kept his men busy with more drilling and camp chores while in Washington, hoping to get them ready in time. On Sunday, July 14, he even drilled his men both before and after worship services. The next day the regiment had the novel experience of actually firing the guns they had carried with them from Elmira. They had been issued .58 caliber Harpers Ferry rifled muskets that "would kick about as hard as a government mule." In fact, one soldier later joked that in battle his firearm "kicked him back over a rail, and kicked him several times after he was down." Slocum arranged for his men each to fire twenty rounds in a vacant lot about a mile from camp. This was the only target practice the regiment managed to get before embarking on the road to Manassas.[26]

Meanwhile the Confederates were scrambling to prepare their own defenses. They managed to put together two small armies to watch their northern frontiers in Virginia. Joseph Johnston sat in the Shenandoah Valley with twelve thousand Confederate soldiers. Facing him, sixty-nine-year-old Robert Patterson, a veteran of the War of 1812, guarded the approaches

24. Fox, *In Memoriam*, 69; Hall, "First Bull Run," 150; Fairchild, *History of the 27th*, 8 (quote).

25. Warner, *Generals in Blue*, 298; Warren W. Hassler, *Commanders of the Army of the Potomac*; Robert S. Harper, *Irvin McDowell and the Battle of Bull Run*.

26. Hall, "First Bull Run," 150; James McPherson, *Ordeal by Fire*, 207; Fairchild, *History of the 27th*, 7–8 (quotes).

north out of the valley with a Union army eighteen thousand strong. Closer to Washington, McDowell stood a mere twenty-five miles from another major Confederate army: Pierre G. T. Beauregard, most recent commandant of West Point, led approximately twenty thousand Confederates near an important rail junction outside the town of Manassas.[27]

If Beauregard or Johnston worried over the possibility of an immediate Union advance, their fears proved temporarily unfounded. McDowell had no intention of taking his untrained and inexperienced army anywhere anytime soon. He distrusted his troops' abilities, given that many of his volunteer units had failed to live up to even the most lax military standards. The antics of the Twenty-seventh give just a taste of the many types of foolishness that for the time being never seemed to cease but that would disappear before the war ended. Unfortunately, an overzealous civilian population and government responded to McDowell's pleas for time by demanding immediate action. When it became known that the Confederate Congress planned to convene in Richmond, Virginia, on July 20, 1861, speakers and newspapers, most notably the commanding New York Tribune, cried, "On to Richmond!" Lincoln, feeling the pressure and still finding his feet in war, added his voice to the cacophony. The pressure annoyed Slocum as much as it did McDowell. Slocum considered Horace Greeley, the Tribune's outspoken editor, "a fool and a meddler, who might better attend to his newspaper than attempt to lead the army!" And so, with its commanders already doubting the outcome, the Union army prepared to advance.[28]

Slocum later remembered McDowell's plan as a good idea that made sound military sense on paper. The army near Washington would march quickly south and west to engage Beauregard, while Patterson would keep Johnston busy in the Shenandoah. Each Union army significantly outnumbered its Confederate counterpart, so if McDowell could fall on Beauregard before Johnston could reach him, he might devour the Confederates in detail. Unfortunately it did not take long before the first grand campaign to end the war degenerated into a comedy of errors.[29]

27. Ethan Rafuse, A Single Grand Victory, 51–66.

28. "The Veterans in This Campaign: Slocum to Burnside," Journal, October 7, 1872 (Slocum quote); Rafuse, Single Grand Victory, 33–66; Maurice Matloff, ed., American Military History, 196–97; McPherson, Ordeal by Fire, 206–7; Keith Dickson, "Civil War, Land Overview," in Tucker, Encyclopedia, 1:194.

29. Rafuse, Single Grand Victory, 51–66; William C. Davis, Battle at Bull Run, 69–70; Matloff, American Military History, 197; McPherson, Ordeal by Fire, 207.

Slocum later observed that most mistakes came simply from inexperience and incompetence at all levels of the army. He lamented the fact that the government had publicly issued the order to advance more than a week early. "Just think of it!" he said after the war. "Three years later there were no military men who would not have laughed at such an order, advising your enemy when you intend to move." He also noted that, on the day they were to break camp, someone handed him, like a railway ticket, a notice detailing the names of the officers and the numbers they commanded. He felt sure "a copy of that would be immediately placed in the hands of the enemy."[30]

The march to Bull Run itself provided plenty of opportunities for self-important ridiculousness. Around noon on July 16, Slocum's regiment received the order to move out. They scrambled to pack everything they had managed to haul with them to Washington, leaving camp between two and three o'clock. While no one professed any concern over the ultimate outcome of the approaching battle, sheer terror of what the Rebels had in store for them slowed the advance to a crawl. McDowell's army marched until midnight, pausing only for supper around six o'clock, and covered about twelve miles. The Twenty-seventh was no exception to the paralyzing fear that pervaded the army (though its historian blamed felled trees for their pace). Slocum noted "the dread on the part of our men of those 'masked batteries' and 'the fierce black horse cavalry,' neither of which ever had any existence, except in the imaginative brains of our newspaper reporters."[31] From the instant they passed out of the safety of Washington, they expected to meet the enemy at any moment. The army inched forward, men and volunteer officers alike terrified of the reports of hidden cannon around every bend. When some noise or odd sight set them off, they stopped and deployed, advancing tentatively in line. The sound of galloping hooves horrified them, as they grew more certain that the ferocious Confederate cavalry would soon bear down on them from behind and leave no survivors. Perhaps hoping to make up for their nervousness with bravado, Slocum's officers requested that he put in a special application for their regiment to be

30. "Gen. Slocum's Recollections," *Syracuse Courier*, April 2, 1879; Slocum, *Military Lessons*.

31. Slocum, *Military Lessons*, 8. The "masked batteries" were supposedly hidden artillery that would lie in wait for approaching troops and suddenly open fire with a devastating volley of canister shot at close range.

included at the front of the attacking column. He is reported to have obliged them.[32]

A second culling of equipment began as the march began to heat up. Slocum's men and many others had been able to ride trains most of the way from their rallying points to Washington, so only the heaviest and bulkiest of burdens had to be left behind. Men now began discarding tents, blankets, rucksacks, and other necessary equipment, a decision they would soon regret. But for now, the Twenty-seventh's H. Seymour Hall found himself following a trail of abandoned artifacts all the way to Manassas.[33]

Along the way an incident took place to cement the self-righteous indignation the volunteers felt toward the regular troops. While in camp one evening, the Twenty-seventh and the Fourteenth New York State Militia heard the regular regiment under Major George Sykes bivouacked next to them called into line. Authorities had caught two men of Sykes's Fourteenth U.S. Infantry attempting to desert and now imposed a penalty the volunteers could not fathom. Each man received thirty lashes on his bare back and had the letter "D" burned into their hips. The neophyte warriors denounced it as "a sickening sight," proclaiming it "was the last case of flogging in the army, as this barbarous style of punishment was soon after abolished." This incident only confirmed the volunteers' disdain for regular service discipline, much to Slocum's chagrin.[34]

Slocum's men did not seem so squeamish when it came to their own depredations, however. Someone, possibly Slocum, had let it be known that foraging the countryside would be allowed. As a result his men "lived well" on the march, but in the process they pillaged houses and burned several barns. This sort of thievery was more common in the First Bull Run Campaign than later Northern accounts would have liked to admit, and it took place while the North had still not really settled on an official policy of conciliation. Other troops, such as those commanded by William T. Sherman, engaged in similar acts. The regiment as a whole professed itself to be "heartily ashamed" of such conduct, but it is interesting to note that, in light of his later exalted position in the March to the Sea with Sherman, from the very beginning of the war Slocum allowed at least some foraging (and the accompanying destruction).[35]

32. Fairchild, *History of the 27th,* 9–11; Hall, "First Bull Run," 151–52; Rafuse, *Single Grand Victory,* 79–83; "Gen. Slocum in the War."

33. Hall, "First Bull Run," 151–52.

34. Fairchild, *History of the 27th,* 7, 10–11 (both quotes).

35. Ibid., 10 (quote); Mark Grimsley, *The Hard Hand of War,* 31, 62.

Unknown to Slocum or any of his commanders, the Confederates did indeed have one significant surprise waiting for them. According to McDowell's plan, the Union army facing Johnston in the Shenandoah had one major job, which was to keep him there. But the elderly Patterson proved past his prime, and Johnston, on orders from Jefferson Davis, managed to get his troops safely to Manassas by rail in time for the battle. Unfortunately for McDowell, Patterson did nothing to prevent it from happening.[36]

After several days on the road, the Twenty-seventh ended July 20 on an ominous and anticipatory note. Slocum ordered his men to draw three days' worth of rations, instead of just one, and to cook them. The men knew this meant they would soon have their first taste of battle. The nearby Marine Corps band struck up the tune of "Home Sweet Home." This seems to have had a sobering effect on Slocum's men, and silence reigned in the camp for the rest of the day.[37]

McDowell arrived across Bull Run Creek from the Confederate army near Manassas Junction and planned to attack its left flank the next morning. Oddly enough Beauregard had exactly the same battle plan in mind. Both sides weakened their left flanks in order to build up their rights for a crushing blow, but McDowell struck first. The Confederates had expected him to try a head-on assault, and accordingly they guarded a stone bridge on the most direct route from McDowell's position. McDowell's troops instead came marching via Sudley's Ford to the north, while two brigades under William T. Sherman and Robert Schenck made a diversion at the bridge. Confederate Colonel Nathan Evans awaited the flanking force with a scant two understrength regiments. Sherman and Schenck made a good deal of noise early in the morning, hoping to cover the real thrust, but by half past seven Evans knew the action at the bridge was just a diversion. McDowell's attack, led by Hunter's division, managed to avoid Confederate intelligence for an hour longer, and when it poured over the ford, barely seven hundred men opposed it. Hunter immediately attacked the Rebels, pressing them backward into an open field at the top of a ridge known as Matthews Hill. Before long he pushed Evans down the far side.[38]

Slocum's regiment was part of the flanking column. He had probably slept very little the night before and had to get his men moving very early

36. Rafuse, *Single Grand Victory*, 117.
37. Hall, "First Bull Run," 152.
38. Rafuse, *Single Grand Victory*, 115–42; William Davis, *Battle at Bull Run*, 162–66.

on the morning of the battle. They left sometime around two o'clock in the morning, following in the rear of a battalion of Marines under Major John J. Reynolds. What should have been a quick march lasted a full eight hours. McDowell's troops encountered a number of problems, but Slocum later recalled one particular incident that brought grief to the Twenty-seventh. Somewhere ahead of them in the morning twilight, a baggage wagon had broken down. The wagon must have carried the supplies of a general, because no one had the sense to move it to the side and allow the army to pass. Instead the entire column of men waited in line for it to be fixed. Also it apparently never occurred to Hunter or any of his subordinates to give the order for the troops to lie down and rest in the meantime. The men simply stood in place for several hours in the damp dawn, wearing themselves out.[39]

With only a few very brief rests allowed, the Twenty-seventh finally arrived on the field near Sudley Church around nine o'clock. As they marched they passed the still-warm remains of numerous campfires and lamented the thought that the Rebels may have retreated without a fight. Almost as soon as they had caught their collective breath and filled their canteens, an aide from brigade commander Andrew Porter's staff arrived with orders for Slocum to advance immediately. When Slocum asked where Porter wanted him to advance, the aide simply waved his hand in the vague direction of the fighting and cried, "You will find the enemy down there somewhere!" Slocum, thinking the Rebels only a short way off, ordered the regiment forward at the double-quick. Thanks to the aide's mistake, the Twenty-seventh jogged roughly a mile before they reached the enemy just "down there."[40]

As they arrived at the crest of Matthews Hill Slocum dismounted, deployed the regiment into line of battle, and advanced down the hill into the fight without stopping. On their way they passed the gray-clad soldiers of the Eighth New York tending their wounded. A disorganized group of Confederate infantry tried to make a stand near the Stone House

39. Report of Maj. J. J. Bartlett, *OR*, 2:388; "Gen. Slocum's Recollections," *Syracuse Courier*, April 2, 1879.

40. "Gen. Slocum in the War" (quote). Hall mentions taking a short rest, while Bartlett and Fairchild (who may well have been relying on Bartlett's report) say they went from two o'clock and into the battle without rest. While it is probably fair to say they did not have much rest, they did halt on the march and were not constantly moving all that time. For the following account of the first battle at Bull Run, I rely heavily on Fairchild, *History of the 27th*, 11–14; Report of Maj. J. J. Bartlett, *OR*, 2:388–90; Hall, "First Bull Run," 153–59; and Rafuse, *Single Grand Victory*, 146–47.

at the bottom of the hill, under cover of John Imboden's artillery. Imboden was stationed partway up the Henry House Hill on the other side of the valley. The Twenty-seventh charged the infantry and drove them away. Slocum then began to advance to Imboden's position. After the Twenty-seventh attacked the battery, Imboden withdrew back toward the newly formed position on Henry House Hill. Slocum ordered the color guard to a position to the left and rear of the Stone House in order to close up his regiment before he attacked again.[41]

Up to this point in the battle, the Twenty-seventh had performed as well as could be expected but had not yet tested themselves against a serious formation of enemy troops. Unfortunately for Slocum, that opportunity came presaged by the confusion for which First Bull Run is famous. As the regiment regrouped a unit of soldiers in gray uniforms approached through a ravine vaguely in the direction of the Twenty-seventh's rear, its colors furled. This threw Slocum's ranks into chaos. Some men shouted that the newcomers were enemies and began firing. Others screamed they were the Eighth New York or a Massachusetts regiment coming to their support and begged that the shooting cease. The odd regiment had not yet either opened fire or declared themselves friendly. Instead they marched into line near the Twenty-seventh, using deep brush in the area for cover. While Slocum tried to regain control, a man sprinted up to him and claimed that the "regiment yonder wanted to surrender." Slocum drew his sword and threatened the man, but the man insisted. Still not convinced, Slocum ordered his adjutant to investigate. The man, waving an improvised flag of truce, called on the group to identify itself.[42]

The response came quickly. Wade Hampton's men unfurled their flag and loosed a volley into the Twenty-seventh's right flank. Slocum immediately mounted his horse and rode down the line, crying, "Give it to them, boys!" Not all of the men heard him, though, and some still refused to shoot. Those who realized what had happened returned fire, and Lieutenant Colonel Chambers encouraged them with all sorts of scriptural injunctions: "G-g-g-give it to 'em, b-b-boys; God l-l-loves a cheerful g-g-g-giver!"[43]

This brief firefight proved the high-water mark of the Twenty-seventh at Bull Run. Slocum tried his best to rally his men, but they did not recover from the shock and confusion. Bartlett tried to find reinforcements but succeeded only in gathering about two hundred exhausted men from the

41. Report of Col. Andrew Porter, *OR*, 2:384.
42. Fairchild, *History of the 27th*, 13.
43. Hall, "First Bull Run," 155.

Eighth New York who were willing to follow him forward. So Slocum gave the order to fall back up Matthews Hill, where he could draw on the support of other friendly regiments that had remained behind. During the retreat Slocum reeled over in pain and may have fallen out of the saddle, with blood spurting from a wound in his right thigh. The regiment carried him with them back up the hill, but his wound was serious enough they soon had to lay him down and call surgeons from the rear to attend to him. Chambers had also fallen during the attack, leaving Bartlett in command of the regiment.[44]

The surgeons worked quickly to try and stop the copious bleeding by applying a tourniquet. On the far hill Confederate gunners considered the group an excellent target, and shells began landing far too close for comfort. Four men carried Slocum farther to the rear, struggling with the ineffectual tourniquet as they ran. They soon set him down again and tried to stanch the wound a second time. Again Confederate guns took aim and made them move. This time they loaded Slocum onto an ambulance, accompanied by a lieutenant from the regiment who had steadfastly refused to kill the enemy (he had stood his ground and fired into the air). The surgeons moved Slocum six times before finding an oasis of relative calm at the Sudley Church where they finally brought the bleeding under control. After they had properly dressed his injuries, doctors set him in an ambulance headed for Fairfax Station. From there he would depart to Washington, where he hoped to hear news of a Union victory.[45]

Slocum probably would not have been away from Sudley Ford long before his hopes for word of success would have been dashed. As he lay in the jolting ambulance with other wounded, his head swimming with pain and exhaustion, Slocum would soon have seen the first elements of McDowell's army begin to overtake them. Slocum never explicitly detailed what he saw that day, but he seems to have observed some of the worst of the panicking. After the war he remarked that William H. Russell's account of the battle "was not greatly exaggerated." He doubtless worried over what had become of his own regiment in the mass of terrified boy-soldiers crowding around him.[46]

44. *New York Times*, July 24, 1861, p. 1 col. 3; Bartlett commanded the Twenty-seventh through the remainder of the battle and wrote the after-action report. At least Hall seems to think Bartlett's claim may have been a little specious. Those interested in Bartlett might enjoy reading his report, which is filled with all sorts of exact military terminology, coming from a man who only two months before had not known how to "file left."
45. "Col. Slocum's Experience after He Was Wounded," *Journal*, July 30, 1861.
46. Slocum, *Military Lessons*, 9.

What had happened to them? After taking command, Bartlett pulled the Twenty-seventh into the woods to rest and refill their cartridge boxes. They reformed on the top of Matthew's Hill and marched toward Henry House Hill, where the fighting now raged. Confederate reinforcements had arrived just in time to stem the flow of McDowell's assault, and the Rebels made a stand on the crest of the hill. Unknown to Bartlett, Johnston's arrival from the valley had already turned the tide. The Twenty-seventh passed the Stone House again, making its way up toward the Henry House. They reached the crest just in time to see the Union line crumble for the final time that day.[47]

The Twenty-seventh retired in an orderly fashion amid the chaos until it passed the Sudley Church, where the regiment became swamped in a mass of men, horses, wagons, and field pieces, and it disintegrated almost completely. In an infamous case of bad timing, someone raised the cry "Black Horse Cavalry!" just as a group of frightened Union troopers thundered their way through the Twenty-seventh's ranks. After this nothing the officers could do could prevent the men from stampeding. Several companies managed to stay together, but many of the Twenty-seventh's soldiers became lost in the throng of frightened men and animals. Over the next few days the fragmented group made its way back to its camp at Franklin Square in Washington.

Members of the Twenty-seventh, Slocum included, carefully insisted both during and after the war that their regiment managed to quit the actual field of battle in an orderly fashion. Slocum perhaps may be excused for a bit of exaggeration, as he had to rely on the reports of others for his version. Although the men of the Twenty-seventh had little to be ashamed of, neither did they have much to brag about. Their first attack went well, but when presented with the odd regiment on their flank, they lost order and had to retreat. Bartlett, for whatever reason, did not get them back into the battle until late afternoon, just in time to retreat safely. Their coherence lasted only for a short while, after which their organization fell apart, like that of the rest of the army.

Slocum's own conduct was solid and presaged his battlefield demeanor for the rest of the war. Unlike other generals, he did not try to lead through pomp and dash, nor did he indulge in much screaming and shouting. His troops remembered most of all his calm cool bearing, and Bull Run seems to have been no different. One testimony to this is the fact that very little is

---

47. Rafuse, *Single Grand Victory,* 143–89.

said in the *Official Records* about Slocum's leadership either one way or the other. He did not either impress his superiors or warrant their condemnation. Slocum himself never completed an after-battle report for Bull Run, and it is not surprising that the one filed by Bartlett mentions Slocum's wound only in passing. Bartlett preferred to focus on his own role in the battle and on events seen from his own perspective.[48]

Back in Syracuse a worried Clara awaited word from her husband. The first news came in the form of a telegram from Bartlett informing her that Slocum had been wounded. Bartlett assured her that Slocum's wounds were no cause for concern and that he should be home soon. Unfortunately for Clara this seemingly straightforward telegram would be the beginning of a nervous and frustrating few days.[49] The confusion had to do with another man in McDowell's army, Colonel John S. Slocum (possibly a distant relative), who commanded the Second Rhode Island at Bull Run. This John Slocum received numerous accolades for his bravery under fire, but unfortunately they were all posthumous because he was killed directing skirmishers into line. John A. Green's newspaper, the Democratic *Daily Courier*, printed a telegram that mentioned the death of a Colonel Slocum, and of course Syracuse assumed this meant Henry Warner. What was worse, when the official casualty lists came out soon after, they made no mention of either Slocum.[50]

An understandably confused and upset Clara telegraphed the army to try to find out his real condition. Before she could hear anything back from the army, a letter from Slocum himself reached her. On July 25, he managed to have himself propped up in bed well enough to write. After letting her know he had "attended services at Manassas last Sunday," he described himself "as happy as a clam in high water." He said the Twenty-seventh distinguished itself as "one of the first in, and last out." He denied that his wound hurt him much and assured her he would be up and about again very soon. Clara sent the letter to the *Syracuse Journal* before quickly departing for Washington to be with her husband. Ironically it took the *Courier* nearly a week to print a retraction. Clara would have been with her husband another week beyond that before the army established that he

48. Report of Maj. J. J. Bartlett, *OR*, 2:388–89; Report of Col. Andrew Porter, *OR*, 2:385–87.
49. "Col. Slocum Wounded," *Journal*, July 22, 1861.
50. No. 41 Report of Lt. Col. Frank Wheaton, Second Rhode Island Infantry, *OR*, 2:400; "Condition of General Slocum," *Courier*, July 30, 1861; "Letter concerning Slocum's status after Bull Run," Veterans Records for Henry Warner Slocum, NA.

was indeed alive and should be added to the list of wounded from Porter's brigade.[51]

News of Slocum's wound made him an instant hero in Syracuse. Even his old enemies at the *Daily Courier* began to call him "*our* colonel Slocum" (emphasis in the original). Several prominent Syracuse residents embarked for Washington almost immediately, some of them bearing expensive gifts such as fine wine. On July 29, Slocum received C. B. Sedgwick, Judge Spencer, J. J. Belden, and S. F. Smith of Syracuse. They tried to make arrangements to have him transferred to the expensive Willard's Hotel for the remainder of his convalescence, but his surgeon would not allow him to be moved (an indication that his wound was perhaps more serious than he or Bartlett told Clara). They expected him to recover in roughly four weeks, and Slocum hoped to spend at least some of that time back home in Syracuse.[52]

In the midst of all the comings and goings Slocum received one very important visitor. New York congressman Richard Fanchot, of the Oswego District, arrived at his bedside soon after the battle. He found Slocum still confined to bed but sitting up, laughing, and chatting easily. Fanchot was looking for New York names for promotion and must have liked what he saw in Slocum. A few days later, when the New York congressional delegation met to discuss their suggestions for promotion to brigadier general, Fanchot and another powerful New York Republican, Alexander S. Diven, put forward Slocum's name. Although Slocum came in second behind a three-way tie for first place, Fanchot and Diven managed to get his name on the list for promotion.[53]

51. Slocum to Clara, July 25, 1861, in Charles Slocum, *Life and Services,* 15–16; "Direct from Col. Slocum," *Journal,* c. July 25, 1861; "Condition of General Slocum," *Courier,* July 30, 1861; "Letter concerning Slocum's status after Bull Run." There is also some confusion as to exactly where he received his wound. Bartlett in his official report said it was in his right thigh, but Fairchild in the regiment's official history claims the bullet passed through his hip. A Syracuse newspaper at the time called it a "flesh wound in the calf of his leg." One of Slocum's men, Hall, is safe in noting simply that he received "a bullet through the leg." It is doubtful Slocum was wounded so high as the hip, as such a wound would no doubt have been permanently debilitating, and Slocum healed completely. It was probably a flesh wound, since he did not have his leg amputated. It is also likely that he took it in the thigh, not the calf, given that after the battle he reported having trouble sitting up and indeed needed to be "propped up."

52. "Condition of General Slocum," *Courier,* July 30, 1861; *Journal* articles "Col. Slocum's Condition," August 4, "Col. Slocum's Condition," c. August 13, "Letter from General Slocum," August 15, all 1861.

53. *Journal* articles "A Bit of War History," May 17, 1894, 3, and "Vote of the Congressional Delegation," August 7, 1861.

Slocum's wound healed rapidly. On Friday, August 9, 1861, he rode out for the first time, and it is not surprising that he immediately intended to visit his own regiment. He rode in a carriage, probably provided by one of the several citizens of Syracuse who accompanied him. He found the Twenty-seventh, still under Bartlett, stationed in temporary housing in the city. When Slocum arrived he still had to rely on crutches, and although sitting up may not have posed a problem, he found walking painful. The men immediately rushed over to greet him. Soon they had hoisted Slocum onto their shoulders and carried him into a nearby house, where he could sit more comfortably. He spent the afternoon shaking hundreds of hands.[54]

Rumors had already begun to spread concerning Slocum's promotion to brigadier general. By the time he was ready to return to Syracuse for a brief stay, the rumors had become reality. He stopped to visit the Twenty-seventh again one more time before leaving. He called the regiment together and gave a speech announcing his promotion and disappointing those who had speculated he might decline the nomination in order to stay with the Twenty-seventh. He informed them he did not feel he could decline, but that he knew the Twenty-seventh, not himself, had brought about the honor. Afterward he made his way to the train station.[55]

Back in Syracuse word spread that he had been promoted and was planning to come home, but no one knew exactly when to expect him. Slocum himself had written to the *Journal* that he had accepted his commission and expected to be assigned a brigade as soon as he was well enough to take the field. He apparently did not anticipate any sort of official welcome, so he did not bother to mention his travel plans. There were others with quite different intentions, however. When it became known that Syracuse could now count a general to its name and that this new general was coming home, the Citizens Corps went to work. They put together a grand reception for Slocum, planning to pounce upon him the moment he stepped onto the train platform. But when to have it ready? The problem was solved on August 20, when someone traveling with Slocum—and apparently without his knowledge—sent a priority telegram around eleven o'clock from Albany that Slocum had arrived there and expected

54. "News from Col. (Gen.) H. W. Slocum," *Courier,* August 14, 1861; *Journal* articles "The Condition of General Slocum," August 13, and "Gen Slocum's Visit to the Union Regiment," August 14, 1861.
55. *Journal* articles "Will Col. Slocum Accept?" August 19, and "The Condition of General Slocum," August 13, 1861.

to take an express train to Syracuse about noon. This would put him back at home around five o'clock that evening. The Citizens Corps had less than six hours to pull the reception together.[56]

They succeeded, of course, and with style. As Slocum's car pulled into the crowded station near the office of the *Daily Journal* on Warren Street, a large group of citizens, Sutherland's brass band, and the mayor all awaited him. As he hobbled out of the car on crutches with Brigadier General John Peck and the mayor of Syracuse, the Citizens Corps went to present arms and Sutherland's band struck up "Hail to the Chief." The crowd of thousands huzzahed as Slocum, still looking somewhat pale and haggard, waved his hat. He tried to make a response, but the crowds drowned him out. The mayor took the lead, giving Slocum a rousing welcome-home speech, and this time Slocum replied he was too tired to attempt another speech just then. The mayor helped him down to an expensive carriage, draped in the flag, and drawn by four black horses.[57]

In the midst of all the commotion, another soldier wounded at Bull Run also arrived home on the same train and stepped out onto the platform. The Citizens Corps did not include him in their merriment, and Slocum, understandably distracted by all of the celebrations, did not notice him. The only person waiting for him was his sister, who helped him limp home. Reporters for the *Syracuse Daily Courier* paid heed, though.[58]

The crowd cheered Slocum as he drove away. A number of the ladies of Syracuse leaned out of the windows of nearby buildings, watching and cheering. One even dropped a bouquet of flowers into the carriage as it passed. The whole of Syracuse had bedecked itself in red, white, and blue, as if preparing for the Fourth of July. They escorted Slocum through the streets with the band playing and flags flying, before finally depositing him at the home of his brother-in-law, LeRoy Morgan, on James Street. Here Slocum made a short speech, thanking the people for their attentions

56. *Journal* articles "Will Col. Slocum Accept?" August 19, "The Condition of General Slocum," August 13, "Gen. Slocum at Home," *Journal,* Wednesday Evening, August 21, 1861. The temptation is nearly irresistible here for the cynical historian (an august body the present author holds in high regard) to assume that Slocum was intentionally playing the innocent hero for political gain. The current evidence provides no clear proof of this sort of skullduggery, however. So until contrary proof comes to light, we must give Slocum the benefit of the doubt.

57. *Journal* articles "Will Col. Slocum Accept?" August 19, "The Condition of General Slocum," August 13, "Gen. Slocum at Home," *Journal,* Wednesday evening, August 21, 1861; "Reception of Brigadier General Slocum," *Courier,* August 21, 1861.

58. "A Contrast," *Courier,* August 24, 1861.

and repeating how much of a surprise the reception had been. He then retired into the house to rest from the enthusiastic greeting. The town kept
celebrating, however, and the day culminated with an artillery salute at
nine in the evening.[59]

If Slocum had been relatively unknown in the town before leaving, as
his critics at the time of his election to the state legislature claimed, he had
plenty of fame to enjoy from now on. The next day, the *Journal* lauded him
in verse:

> Let the shout of welcome pierce the sky,
> for Onondaga's favorite son!
> His worthy name shall yet adorn,
> the true historian's brightest page
> and thronging millions yet unborn,
> shall chant his fame from age to age![60]

The newspapers began to report Slocum sightings, as they kept track of his
whereabouts in town. Around midnight on August 23, the Slocum house-
hold turned out to hear a group of German singers accompanied by a
brass band who had arrived with other members of the citizenry to take
part in a surprise serenade. They played several selections under a bright
white full moon, and afterward Slocum shook hands with a number of
the participants.[61]

Others were less than happy that Slocum received so much attention.
The *Daily Courier* had been using the defeat at Bull Run as an argument
against the war. While too afraid to attack the war hero outright, John A.
Green and his editors did get in some veiled criticism. On August 24, after
making certain to say that Slocum deserved all the laurels the people
could throw, they brought out the story of the lonely soldier on the platform. Although they noted that Slocum had been visibly taken aback by
his reception, surely, they said, this other soldier deserved just as much attention. The supposed hypocrisy of the situation certainly must reflect
badly on the Syracuse "Black Republicans."[62]

59. "Gen. Slocum at Home," *Journal,* Wednesday evening, and "Reception of Brigadier
General Slocum," *Courier,* both August 21, 1861.

60. E. W. Jones, "Welcome Home the Brave," *Journal,* August 22, 1861.

61. "Serenade to Gen. Slocum," *Journal,* August 23, 1861; "Brigadier General Slocum,"
Courier, August 24, 1861. The term "Slocum sighting" is my own and is, of course, intended tongue-in-cheek.

62. "Gen. Slocum at Home," *Journal,* c. August 23, "A Contrast," *Courier,* August 24,
both 1861.

While other Republicans in Syracuse may have simply brushed the criticism off, one of them did not. Slocum was an avid newspaper reader, and his list obviously included the *Daily Courier* because he encountered the article and took it to heart. From this point forward he consciously tried to avoid receptions of the sort he received on this trip. He would abruptly change his plans or the timing of them, or come in at odd hours. At the end of the war he credited the *Courier*'s article with causing this change.[63]

There were other issues that needed dealing with while he healed. Knowing the war would be more than a brief interlude, he took this opportunity to set his affairs into more permanent order. Aside from any business or personal issues, he needed to take care of his unexpired term as county treasurer. He arranged with Dudley Phelps, treasurer of the Onondaga County Savings Bank, to finish out the remainder of his term. With Slocum's departure date rapidly approaching, on September 2, 1861, the two men made a hasty examination of the books, and in the process they overlooked a mistake. Slocum had evidently taken out a voucher from the county and recorded the transaction twice. As a result, unknown to Slocum or Phelps, when the new general returned to war he did so with roughly nine thousand dollars of Onondaga's money. When his successor looked into the books and discovered the mistake he contacted Slocum immediately, and Slocum paid the money back in full on one of his next visits home to Syracuse.[64]

As the time approached for him to depart, festivities began anew. In the waning days of August and the first few days of September, Slocum attended at least two occasions in his honor. At the first, citizens presented him with a pair of specially made epaulets. A few days later, probably on the eve of his departure, James J. Belden and Robert Greer gave him a dress saber and sash that they considered equal to his rank. In the evening of September 2, 1861, Slocum boarded a train headed for Binghamton. Although a large number of personal friends saw him off, his departure

63. "A Talk with Gen. Slocum," *Syracuse Daily Standard,* March 17, 1884; "The Position of General Slocum," *Journal,* October 3, 1865. For an example of his future surreptitious returns see *Journal* articles "The Committee Heard From" and "Arrival of General Slocum," both September 28, 1865.

64. "County Treasurer," *Journal,* September 3, 1861; "Gen. Slocum's Accounts," *New York Tribune,* October 26, 1865. It might be tempting to assume this was intentional, but again the evidence currently available points to the contrary. To tip the balance and remove any remaining doubt, when this incident was used against Slocum in his quest for the position of secretary of state of New York, Phelps (who opposed Slocum's election) wrote a letter to the editor clearing Slocum of any wrongdoing.

did not garner nearly the same attention as his arrival. There seem to have been no speeches, no bands, and no official send-off. It may be that he left when he did specifically hoping to avoid another ostentatious display. So, still using a cane for support, Slocum waved goodbye to family and friends and went to join his brigade, then at Washington.[65]

The days leading up to Bull Run and the battle itself awoke Slocum to the realities of life in a volunteer army, and he demonstrated the intelligence and ability to adapt himself to the situation. He found the proper balance between coddling his men and demanding too much of them. Once he had arrived at this balance, he could whip his men into shape without appearing either soft or too much like an arbitrary tyrant.

Slocum's wound also proved of the best possible kind, as far as those things go. Although initially the bleeding made it serious, he was able to recover quickly and be ready to take the field again. In the interim, the time in the spotlight it afforded him (as well as the opportunity to take advantage of it) undoubtedly played a role in both his newfound popularity as well as his promotion. He did not suffer any long-term debility as a result of his wound and would be just as physically active with his new brigade. Successfully taking control of that brigade would be another matter entirely.

65. *Journal* articles "Departure of General Slocum," September 3, "Presents to General Slocum," September 4, "Gen. Slocum at Elmira," September 6, all 1861; "Brigadier General Slocum," *Onondaga Standard*, September 9, 1861; Fox, *In Memoriam*, 70.

C H A P T E R   3

Principles, Party, and Promotions

From Bull Run to Antietam

If Slocum reveled at all in his promotions and popularity, he would have still more reason to rejoice in the coming months. George Brinton McClellan, his preferred commander, would soon fall from favor, but Slocum's own rise to higher command had only just begun. He had already claimed a brigade, and in 1862 he would receive his own division and then a corps in relatively quick succession. Each promotion gave Slocum the opportunity to demonstrate all over again his love for discipline and drill. He also began to exhibit other behaviors that, for the moment at least, suited him less. Beginning with his appointment under George B. McClellan, Slocum would often unconsciously emulate the army commanders under whom he served, sometimes living out their reputations more consistently even than they did themselves. To borrow a phrase from Sir Arthur Conan Doyle, Slocum was not himself luminous, but he was a conductor of light.[1] Under Joseph Hooker, for instance, Slocum became both petty and contentious, characteristics that generally were absent from his military character before his association with Hooker. Under Sherman, he became driving and unorthodox, attributes he rarely displayed earlier in the war, at least not to the extent he would in 1864. But a conductor of light can be only as bright as its

---

1. Sir Arthur Conan Doyle, *The Hound of the Baskervilles*.

source, and from Bull Run through Antietam, the only light he had the opportunity to reflect came from McClellan.

While Slocum convalesced in the wake of the debacle at Bull Run, Lincoln appointed McClellan to command the army around Washington. Like Slocum, McClellan was not an elderly man. He had been born to a prominent family in Philadelphia on December 3, 1826, less than a year before Slocum. He graduated from West Point in 1846, second in a class that produced twenty Civil War generals. During the Mexican War he served on Winfield Scott's staff and garnered a good deal of attention for his gallantry and his engineering ability. After spending three years as an instructor at West Point he traveled overseas to observe the armies of Europe in the Crimean War. Everything about the man seemed to point to a great destiny, which earned him the nickname Little Napoleon. An arrogant man by long habit, McClellan carried himself in a manner that conveyed confidence and assurance.[2]

McClellan's most difficult and most pressing job proved the reformation of the masses of men coalescing around the capital after the defeat at Bull Run. He organized the camps, made sure they were clean, and re-equipped the men with standard arms and uniforms. He constantly drilled his troops, parading them in their new gear and giving them rousing speeches. The food improved notably. Soon the men began to feel like soldiers again, and the officers in particular grew to idolize McClellan. He gave his force the name it would be known by from then on: the Army of the Potomac.[3]

Slocum's trip from Syracuse to Washington was uneventful. Whether he knew it or not, the press back home (and elsewhere) followed his every move, even noting which boardinghouses he patronized. Taking control of his brigade proved challenging. Slocum arrived in Washington on Saturday, September 7, 1861. His new brigade was the same one he and the Twenty-seventh had served in at Bull Run. It would soon be designated the Second Brigade of William Franklin's division in the Fourth Corps. His command encompassed the Fifth Maine, the Sixteenth, Twenty-sixth, and Twenty-seventh New York Volunteers, the Ninety-sixth Pennsylvania, a company of cavalry, and a battery of artillery con-

2. Warner, *Generals in Blue*, 290–91.
3. Stephen W. Sears, *To the Gates of Richmond: The Peninsula Campaign*, 3–9; Matloff, *American Military History*, 204–5; McPherson, *Ordeal by Fire*, 211–15; Dickson, "Civil War, Land Overview," 194–95.

Major General George B. McClellan, whom Slocum imitated and strongly supported. Library of Congress, Prints & Photographs Division, Civil War Photographs

sisting of six pieces. All told, Slocum's brigade boasted just over five thousand men.[4]

Other brigade commanders in the division were George W. Taylor and John Newton, and Slocum worked well with both of them. It was Franklin himself who seemed to leave the biggest impression on Slocum. Franklin was an old friend of McClellan's and later became one of the most "McClellanized" of all the Army of the Potomac. He was such a defender of the "Little Napoleon" that later, when Joseph Hooker took command of the army, Hooker wisely made sure that Franklin would top the list of officers to be relieved, thereby freeing the army somewhat from its creator's shadow. Slocum knew and trusted Franklin, and through him he received an impression of McClellan that was thoroughly positive. Paired with his tendency to emulate commanders, this meant that Slocum's performance as commander would suffer for some time to come.

In the chaos of the army's reorganization, the brigade's quality had degraded, especially since Slocum had been absent while recovering. Sanitation in particular had grown lax, so it is not surprising they had the highest rate of sickness in the division, roughly double the sickness rate of the others. Some fifteen hundred men still had not received vaccinations against smallpox. Unfortunately Slocum had virtually no time to get the brigade cleaned up before it faced its first review by the commanding general. Only a few days after Slocum arrived, McClellan himself came for a review. Overall, McClellan did not like what he saw. Slocum's own Twenty-seventh had maintained its discipline, and McClellan gave it a passing grade. He made it clear to Slocum that he needed the rest of the brigade brought up to the quality of the Twenty-seventh, and as quickly as possible.[5]

4. "Brigadier General Slocum," *Onondaga Standard*, September 9, 1861; *Journal* articles "Departure of General Slocum," September 3, "Gen. Slocum at Elmira," September 6, "Gen. Slocum's Brigade," September 9, 1861; No. 1. Extract from McClellan's Report from July 27, 1861, to November 9, 1862, *OR*, 5:16; Report of Surg. Charles S. Tripler, *OR*, 5:85; Correspondence, orders, and returns relating specially to operations in Maryland, Northern Virginia, and West Virginia from August 1, 1861, to March 17, 1862, *OR*, 5:719.

5. "Slocum's Brigade," *Journal*, September 14, 1861; Correspondence, orders, and returns relating specially to operations in Maryland, Northern Virginia, and West Virginia from August 1, 1861, to March 17, 1862, *OR*, 5:719. The fact that Slocum's brigade was the largest can account only partially for this increased sick rate (double that of either Newton's or Kearny's brigade); Report of Surg. Charles S. Tripler, *OR*, 5:85; "Gen. Slocum's Command," *Journal*, September 10, 1861. The dates and days of the week in this section of text were calculated using a universal calendar and information given in these cited sources. The state of the brigade is inferred by a report that McClellan wanted the entire unit brought up to the standards of the Twenty-seventh. This would mean the other regiments were lacking somewhat, and that Slocum had not been lax in his own original command. Fairchild, *History of the 27th*; Fox, *In Memoriam*, 70–71.

Slocum had worked with his men for only two weeks before he tested them against a small detachment of Confederate cavalry. On October 3, 1861, he learned that a group of the enemy was encamped nearby at Pohick Church. (The church, just south-southwest of Washington near Lorton, Virginia, had a long history reaching back to about 1695. George Washington, George Mason, and many other famous figures had worshiped there.) The best estimates Slocum had available claimed there could not be much more than fifty men. He called Colonel William Christian of the Twenty-sixth New York into his headquarters and gave him detailed verbal instructions that would soon be followed up with written orders. Christian was to take a detachment of 300 soldiers and march out at six o'clock the next morning. Slocum would personally take 225 men and sneak into the camp's rear. The remaining 75 soldiers would advance straight on Pohick the next morning, in theory driving the cavalry into Christian's waiting arms.[6]

Nothing of the sort actually took place. Slocum later claimed to have heard that Christian ignored his orders. Blatant disregard of orders notwithstanding, Slocum had asked too much of his men. Like Washington himself at Princeton, Slocum had ordered multiple columns of relatively inexperienced men to converge on a single point early in the morning. Later in the war such a plan would have been executed easily, but for now even simple maneuvers could be too much for the volunteers. Whatever the case, the expedition proved a failure. Not only did the Confederates escape, but Christian did not keep his men in order on the return. Instead he allowed them to disperse into the countryside where they "converted into a band of marauders, who plundered alike friend and foe." It is doubtful this destruction amounted to much by later standards of the war, but it was enough to concern Slocum, who had been forced to deal with the same problem on the march to Bull Run.[7]

This would especially be the case given the general shift in policy since McClellan gained command of the army. As Mark Grimsley notes in his authoritative treatment of the evolution of Union military policy, *The Hard Hand of War*, McClellan combined the approaches of both Winfield Scott (with his extremely cautious Anaconda Plan) and Lincoln (who knew the Anaconda Plan would take too long). The resulting hybrid led McClellan to advocate a strict policy of conciliation toward Southern civilians combined with overwhelming military force. While he rebuilt his army, McClellan insisted that his men refrain from annoying Southerners and abided scrupulously by the

6. "Expedition to Pohick Church, Virginia," *OR*, 5:236–37, at http://www.pohick.org/history.html.
7. Ibid. (quote); Fairchild, *History of the 27th*.

laws of the various localities. Slocum himself quickly adopted this view as his own, and the conduct of his men in the Pohick Church debacle seemed a serious violation of McClellan's principles and plans.[8]

In response Slocum wrote a report of the incident and forwarded it to McClellan's headquarters, calling for a court of inquiry. There is no evidence one ever took place. Next he issued stringent orders throughout his brigade against depredations toward civilian property (a very McClellanesque action). Deserved or not, this decision resulted in a small-scale revolt among his officers, especially those whose regiments had not been involved in the incident. Eighteen officers of the Sixteenth New York objected vocally and "respectfully demanded" (a contradiction in terms, from Slocum's point of view) that he revoke it. Slocum took this as a direct challenge to his authority and arrested each signatory, and ordered them to be confined to their tents. The desired reformation took a day or two, but eventually the apologies began pouring into brigade headquarters. As Slocum put it, "it had a most wonderful effect."[9]

Later in the fall Slocum did what he could to help out the Republican ticket back in Syracuse. While his brigade resided in Camp Franklin near Alexandria, Slocum wrote a letter home to the Republicans of Onondaga County, which he undoubtedly intended for publication. In fact the letter may well have been solicited. Dated October 26, 1861, the papers printed a notable quote from it three days later: "If I were at home, I should join with you most cordially in support of the Republican State and County tickets, for I have yet to learn what good reason any Republican can have for deserting either his principles or his party." He also included what the papers described as a "liberal" contribution to the Republican cause. It was a small thing, and not surprising given Slocum's newfound fame, but the whole episode would cause him serious trouble later on.[10]

A month earlier, on September 30, Frederick F. Wead had received a note while he sat at mess with his fellow officers of the Sixteenth New York. Possibly written in Slocum's own characteristic scribble, it officially informed him of his appointment as Slocum's aide-de-camp. Slocum ordered Wead to report for duty the next morning at nine. Wead looked forward to serving with Slocum, especially because were he to take another assignment it would "deprive my future years of the satisfaction of hav-

8. Grimsley, *Hard Hand of War*, 31–35.

9. Slocum quoted from Fox, *In Memoriam*, 70–71.

10. "Gen. Slocum's Position," *Journal*, October 29 (quote), "True as Steel," *Onondaga Standard*, November 6, 1861.

ing been present at the death blow . . . of the Slaveholder's Revolt." He wrote to his family on October 10 that Slocum was "altogether . . . one of the most admirable men whom I personally know."[11]

It is clear from Wead's correspondence that Slocum and the rest of the army thought they had to be ready to go on the offensive at any moment. On the same night that Wead received notice of his appointment, he also mentioned that the whole brigade had been warned to have their haversacks packed and rations cooked, ready to move instantly. McClellan's oratory regularly promised dramatic action, which meant that many of his soldiers, Slocum included, naively expected it.[12]

While he mirrored many of McClellan's less desirable traits, Slocum also proved ready to do something McClellan could do only by reputation, which was fight. For Slocum this meant he must push his brigade to get it into fighting shape, and once again he drilled his men incessantly. In this respect he hardly needed McClellan's encouragement. Wead wrote home, "Every pleasant day (and that means nearly every day . . .) we have out our four battalions and the General puts them through the most complicated evolutions of the line for two or three hours." In the afternoon, while Wead and Slocum departed on various other chores, Slocum undoubtedly had his colonels fill the time with practice on the regimental level and camp duties. They would have had to get their camps into better order after their bouts of sickness, something Slocum did not overlook. The army's medical director made certain to get them the missing vaccinations, administered by the brigade's surgeons. Occasionally General Franklin called the entire division out to take part in maneuvers. This rarely happened, as the division's entire drill ground covered only about one-half a square mile and did not allow for much movement on that scale.[13]

McClellan stayed in the vicinity of Washington for what seemed an eternity to Lincoln. The president and Congress were growing restless with the inactivity. At one point the president reportedly even suggested to McClellan that, if the general was not using the army, Lincoln would like to borrow it for a while. Finally Lincoln forced McClellan's hand, and the Little Napoleon had no choice but to deliver some sort of action.[14]

11. F. F. Wead to Father, September 30, October 10, 1861, F. F. Wead Papers.

12. Sears, *Gates of Richmond*, 3–9.

13. Wead to Parents, January 11, 1861, Wead Papers; Report of Surg. Charles S. Tripler, *OR*, 5:85.

14. Sears, *Gates of Richmond*, 3–39. For the story in the following paragraphs, from Washington to Yorktown, I am indebted to ibid., 3–86.

Slocum's brigade received more false marching alarms before the army actually moved anywhere. Several of Wead's letters mention being under orders to pack and be ready to move. This might explain why the first real order apparently caught Slocum by surprise. When it arrived at his headquarters on the night of March 11, 1862, he had gone into Washington. Wead wired him but got no reply. Wead then rode into town in search of him. He found Slocum on the corner of Fourteenth Street and Pennsylvania Avenue near the famous Willard Hotel, and the pair started immediately to the stable where, to their frustration, they discovered Slocum's horse was missing. The general managed to find a buggy and get to his brigade in time.[15]

For all Slocum's haste he would have missed nothing important. They marched south toward Manassas but discovered the Confederates had already retreated. The army then turned around and marched back to Washington whence it came. McClellan eventually returned to an earlier proposed plan of operations, later known as the Peninsula Campaign. Instead of advancing on Richmond from the north, as everyone expected, he would transport his entire army by boat to the far end of the peninsula on which the Confederate capital sat. They already had a safe landing zone at Fort Monroe. The Army of the Potomac currently numbered around one hundred thousand, and to this McClellan hoped to add another thirty thousand under McDowell, whom Lincoln had kept in the vicinity of Washington until he felt it safe to release them. When Lincoln approved the plan, it then became a question of getting the army to Fort Monroe.[16]

When the next real order came to move, Slocum marched his men onto transports, and they made the trip to Fort Monroe. Once there, on April 22, 1862, they took up positions in front of Confederate General John B. Magruder's troops. Magruder occupied a series of defenses around Yorktown, including some of those originally held by the Continental army in 1781. Magruder had only about ten thousand men to confront McClellan's rapidly multiplying thousands. If reinforcements were not sent soon Magruder would find himself in the unenviable position of confronting an army roughly ten times the size of his own. In order to stave off the attack he felt sure would soon be coming, Magruder staged a show

15. Wead to Father, January 1862, and Journal of the March of the Army of the Potomac, Wead Papers.
16. Matloff, *American Military History,* 204–5; McPherson, *Ordeal by Fire,* 211–15; Dickson, "Civil War, Land Overview," 194–95.

of strength. He paraded units back and forth across his defenses, had officers shouting orders to nonexistent regiments, and had trains act as if more reinforcements arrived by the hour.[17]

McClellan swallowed the performance. Allen Pinkerton, of Pinkerton's Detective Agency, served as McClellan's chief spy. Unfortunately he managed only to prove that his intelligence (in any sense of the word) was not entirely to be trusted. His flawed information-gathering techniques greatly exaggerated Magruder's strength, feeding misconceptions that McClellan had already come up with entirely by himself. As a result McClellan moved very carefully. He was convinced Magruder outnumbered him at least two to one. He besieged Washington with requests that McDowell be sent without delay, before the massive Confederate war machine came alive and crushed his tiny force. Instead of immediately attacking the Yorktown defenses, McClellan laid siege. He called up his heavy guns and ordered miles of crisscross trenches built. The Army of the Potomac would spend weeks preparing to take lightly held Yorktown.

These days must have passed very slowly for Slocum and his brigade. They passed the time in simple siege operations, which for any army in any time is boring at best: a slow buildup of anticipation to a bloody and deadly climax. Here there would be no such culmination, bloody or otherwise. Just as McClellan's noose seemed about to snap tight, Magruder withdrew. Slocum along with the rest of Franklin's division followed him up the Peninsula.

Along the way McClellan made one half-hearted attempt to cut off the retreat by using the York River. He hoped to throw Franklin's division into the Confederate rear, maybe striking a killing blow against Magruder. He sent Franklin to West Point by boat, but unknown to McClellan, Franklin, or Slocum, this movement came two days too late. Before the Federals had even begun loading onto transports the Confederates had already escaped. Franklin disembarked his division at Eltham plantation on May 7, 1862, arraying it across the open fields. He also posted skirmishers in the woods surrounding his position.[18]

Joseph E. Johnston, now in overall command of Confederate forces on the Peninsula, was aware of Franklin's presence and somewhat worried that he might threaten the few remaining wagon trains in the area. Johnston sent John Bell Hood with his Texas Brigade and an assortment of supporting regiments to keep watch on Franklin and prevent any mischief.

17. Charles Slocum, *Life and Services*, 21.
18. Report of Brig. Gen. Henry W. Slocum, *OR*, vol. 11, pt. 1, 622.

Hood was a bear of a man who loved a good fight, and he took this as license to deal with the situation as he saw fit, so long as he neutralized Franklin. He pushed his troops into the woods around the landing and drove in Franklin's pickets. A general firing broke out, primarily on Franklin's right, held by John Newton's Third Brigade. Slocum, who saw little of the fighting personally, dispatched two of his regiments to Newton's assistance, but this gesture proved futile. After multiple charges and countercharges, several of Newton's regiments, fearful that Hood had flanked them, broke for the rear. They managed to reform closer to the landing and stave off total defeat. Franklin lost around 186 men as opposed to Hood's 48. The battle was of little importance overall, but it was effective in quashing McClellan's feeble flanking attempt.[19]

Eltham's Landing ranks as little more than a large-scale skirmish, and Slocum's brigade saw little of the fighting. In fact Slocum would take part in almost no real combat as a brigade commander before receiving yet another promotion. When Franklin took command of the newly formed Sixth Corps, Slocum succeeded him in command of the First Division, though he did not receive a higher rank. This promotion did little to alter the relationships he had already established, and in particular, he remained in the same position relative to Franklin. Less than a year from the interview with New York's governor in which Slocum asked for a captaincy and permission to raise and equip a small battery of artillery, he found himself at the head of three brigades totaling over nine thousand men. Things could hardly have looked better as the Army of the Potomac moved forward, straddling the Chickahominy River just outside the capital. Slocum could hear Richmond's clocks chime the hour. "We got near enough to Richmond to see the steeples," he would later remark.[20]

McClellan tended to see enemies where none existed. Pinkerton and Magruder had helped him conjure up a huge army of phantom Confederates, and Stonewall Jackson helped him to create traitors on his own side. As McClellan's army approached Richmond, Jackson's Shenandoah Valley Campaign shocked the North, energized the South, and worried Lincoln. Concerned that Jackson might be powerful enough to march on Washington itself, Lincoln ordered McDowell to remain in the vicinity of the capital. This proved a fatal blow to McClellan's sensitivities. The promised addition of McDowell's corps had been McClellan's one hope of marshalling an army large enough to challenge Johnston's hypothetical

19. Ibid.
20. Charles Slocum, *Life and Services,* 24; "Gen. Slocum in the War" (quote).

hordes. McClellan now strongly believed he no longer had a chance to overcome the odds he thought he faced. In a few short hours after he heard the news, the Little Napoleon's grand scheme changed from a careful attempt to take Richmond to a desperate search for an excuse to retreat and still have it look good. After all, if McClellan had lost his campaign (which in reality he had not), then the defeat must become as spectacular as any victory could have been.[21]

In Slocum's case there is little evidence to suggest what he thought. Contextual inferences suggest he wholeheartedly followed McClellan's lead. First, Slocum served directly under Franklin, who was one of McClellan's most trusted subordinates. Virtually every bit of information Slocum received would have been filtered through Franklin, skewing it in McClellan's favor. It is also clear that Slocum became as dedicated to McClellan as anyone else in the army, and he continued to believe in him long after McClellan had been fired by Lincoln. As late as 1864 McClellan thought Slocum "strong in my favor" during McClellan's Democratic presidential bid, even though he acknowledged Slocum to be a Republican.[22]

A look into Wead's letters is revealing and allows historians to come the closest to Slocum himself. Given that Wead almost idolized Slocum and was serving on his staff at this time, it is likely that his opinions reflect the feeling around Slocum's headquarters during spring and summer 1862. When the army reached Harrison's Landing after the campaign, Wead wrote several letters home to explain the series of disastrous events that had got them there. The defense he crafted in one letter in particular could very well have come from the pen of McClellan himself:

> Beyond doubt the Rebels have over 200,000 men about Richmond . . . [other matters being equal] their central position makes their 200,000 equal to 300,000. . . . To counter this advantage of "interior lines" we must have one half more troops than they have. To get there, even if the dullard of the War Dept. can be driven to see the necessity of such augmentation . . . is a work of long time, as McClellan will not risk anything on so critical a juncture. . . .

21. Robert G. Tanner, *Stonewall in the Valley*, 239; James MacPherson, *Ordeal by Fire*, 242; David G. Martin, *Jackson's Valley Campaign*, 68.

22. McClellan to Samuel Barlow, 1864, in Stephen W. Sears, ed., *The Civil War Papers of George B. McClellan*, 600–601. McClellan's remark that Slocum would favor him in the army must also be reconsidered. Unlike many other McClellanites, Slocum not only survived Joe Hooker's culling but rose to command an entire army. So he must not have been so radical in McClellan's favor, or so like him in his incompetence, that it marked him for the fate of men such as Franklin.

> Yet, we are in a desperate position, there is no disguising that we are here
> against McClellan's judgment and protest.

Even so, Wead maintained, "We have a wonderful army." He openly admitted he got a great deal of his information from Franklin, and though he does not explicitly mention Slocum, he probably would have noted if his patron's views differed from Franklin's.[23]

Although McClellan had not yet officially settled on the decision to retreat, his advance on Richmond, slow to begin with, became a crawl. Had he really been facing an opponent as large and as powerful as he imagined, this care might have been justified, but under the actual circumstances, it simply meant the Confederates had ample time to prepare and rush reinforcements to the scene. McClellan approached Richmond from the east and placed his forces along a north–south line, bending around the city to the north and west. The Chickahominy River flowed through his lines, effectively dividing his army in two. The ever-careful McClellan had no intention of allowing Johnston's multitude to devour him in detail, so he ordered several bridges built over the river to ensure his wings could reinforce each other. He then gingerly worked his way forward toward Johnston's entrenchments and began the arduous process of once again bringing his heavy siege weapons up from the rear.[24]

McClellan seemed to think he had plenty of time, but Jefferson Davis grew frustrated with Johnston's inaction. Although Davis had originally ordered Johnston to defend Richmond by fighting on the peninsula, Johnston had retreated time and again, hardly firing a shot. Once they arrived on the very outskirts of Richmond, Johnston finally launched a major assault on McClellan's corps south of the river. McClellan's men managed to repulse him in what came to be called the Battle of Seven Pines or Fair Oaks. As Johnston rode forward to observe the fighting, he fell wounded by a piece of shrapnel. In his place Davis appointed his own personal advisor, Robert E. Lee.

McClellan did not react to the change with any particular vigor, giving Lee plenty of time to reorganize his army. The armies were now almost evenly matched, with McClellan possibly enjoying a slight advantage in numbers. Lee had no intention of allowing McClellan to retain the initiative in the campaign. He wanted to hit the Union army hard, using the river to

23. Wead to Parents, July 7, 1862, Wead Papers.

24. For the following story, along with individual sources cited, I am indebted to Sears, *Gates of Richmond*, 87–177, 181–248; McPherson, *Ordeal by Fire*, 238–39, 242–50; and Matloff, *American Military History*, 218–25.

divide it. His plan called for a powerful assault on the corps north of the Chickahominy, with the hope of destroying a significant portion of McClellan's force. If all went well, Lee planned not only to push McClellan away from Richmond but to annihilate him completely. At the Battle of Mechanicsville, Lee attacked the single corps remaining north of the Chickahominy, the Fifth. His plan fell apart because of its complexity and the inactivity of the normally hard-driving Jackson. When the smoke cleared Lee's men pulled back defeated, and McClellan remained unmoved.

If Slocum's division had wanted a further chance to "see the elephant" as Civil War soldiers often put it, these events had left them disappointed. When Johnston attacked at Seven Pines, Slocum was posted north of the river and sat out the battle safely. Not long afterward, McClellan ordered Slocum's division to march south of the river, so they missed the Battle of Mechanicsville. Whatever Slocum may have thought, McClellan had seen enough fighting around Richmond. He had no tangible reason to believe his siege had been broken (his forces had in fact repulsed Lee with heavy losses), but McClellan began his retreat. He preferred more daring terminology to describe it (a change of base from the York River to the James, all in the face of the enemy), but a retreat by any other name is still a retreat. He began to pull his troops—including those Lee had attacked at Mechanicsville—over to the south bank of the Chickahominy. Lee had no reason to expect anything of the sort, and finding the Federal works empty the next day came as a surprise. When he discovered that McClellan was moving away south of the river, Lee acted without delay and inaugurated the second of the Seven Days battles. Lee ordered the attack to go in on June 27, 1862, resulting in the Battle of Gaines Mill.

The Army of Northern Virginia quickly caught up to the Union rearguard, commanded by Major General Fitz John Porter who was charged with guarding the bridges over the river until the army had made it safely across. Porter arranged his troops into a semicircle behind marshy ground, with his flanks resting on the river. By early afternoon that Friday, Lee began probing Porter's lines and soon followed up with full attacks involving heavy formations of infantry. They pressed Porter uniformly across his broad front and, after he had thrown his few reserves into the fray, he dared not weaken any part of his line to reinforce another. He quickly sent a request to McClellan for aid. McClellan ordered Slocum's division north of the river to Porter's rescue.[25]

25. Reports of Brig. Gen. Fitz John Porter, OR, vol. 11, pt. 2, 221–32; Report of Maj. Gen. George B. McClellan, ibid., 21.

Earlier in the day Slocum had resupplied his men and moved his division closer to the Chickahominy, as McClellan had originally intended his men to go to the immediate support of Porter. Before they actually crossed the river, McClellan recalled them, afraid Franklin might stretch his own lines too thin and invite attack. So Slocum's men relaxed in the shade and enjoyed lunch until afternoon, listening to the sounds of cannon echoing from across the river. Not long after they finished eating, around two o'clock, word came from General Franklin for Slocum to detach one brigade to support Porter north of the river. Slocum ordered John Newton's brigade to march immediately via Alexander's Bridge. They had scarcely started when, at two-thirty, one of McClellan's staff galloped madly up to Slocum, shouted a few hurried words at him, and dashed off again. Slocum had put George Taylor's men on the march by three, and his final brigade, now under Bartlett, followed closer to four.[26]

The help could not have come at a better time for Porter. The attacks had nearly broken through in a number of places. Newton's brigade, the first to arrive, marched into line in the center, immediately to the right of Brigadier General Charles Griffin's command. Taylor followed him, falling in on Newton's left. Slocum started to direct Bartlett's brigade into a position on the far left to extend the lines, but orders came from Porter to send the brigade to the far right to bolster Sykes's division. The brigades then broke up into individual regiments as they replaced exhausted troops at the front. As a result many of Slocum's regiments did not know the regiments next to them.[27]

At some point during the course of the fighting, Slocum slumped over on his horse and slid to the ground, vomiting heavily. Several nearby staff members came to his aid and helped him into the shade. They tried to convince him to retire from the field. He refused, but he did stay in the shade for the remainder of the day. A letter from Slocum to Clara a little more than a week later mentioned that he had felt ill on the 26th, which he blamed on the stresses of the campaign.[28] The weather had been excessively hot, and the swamps offered the men little good water but quite a bit of sickness and disease. He worried excessively over what was going on. No doubt his belief in McClellan's estimates of Lee's strength affected him

26. Reports of Brig. Gen. Henry W. Slocum, *OR*, vol. 11, pt. 2, 432; William Westervelt, diary, in Charles Slocum, *Life and Services*, 26–27.

27. Reports of Brig. Gen. Henry W. Slocum, *OR*, vol. 11, pt. 2, 432–33; Reports of Brig. Gen. Fitz John Porter, ibid., 229; Sears, *Gates of Richmond*, 215–16, map on 230.

28. Henry Slocum, quoted in Charles Slocum, *Life and Services*, 30.

Franklin's staff at Cumberland Landing on May 14, 1862. The child in the fore-
ground is possibly Pete, whom one Syracuse newspaper says served Slocum as a
servant. Library of Congress, Prints & Photographs Division, Civil War Photographs

seriously, leading himself and others to think they would be overwhelmed
at any moment unless they maintained perfect discipline and control. In
this Slocum once again exemplified McClellan. Gaines Mill was also
Slocum's first battle as a division commander, and the thought of being responsible for the lives of so many men could not have been easy for him.

Another account bears mention here but must be assessed more carefully than others. According to one Syracuse newspaper, at some point
during the campaign, a small slave boy, Pete, had arrived at Slocum's
headquarters. Pete was undoubtedly one of many "contrabands" who had
entered Federal lines in a bid for freedom and is possibly the child sitting
at the feet of Franklin in the picture above. There is no way of knowing
what happened to his parents, but the Sixth Corps adopted him. He accompanied them on the march to Richmond as Slocum's servant, according to the *Daily Journal.* In the lull between Seven Pines and the Seven

Days, Pete fell ill. Slocum had become very attached to Pete and had sat up late the three nights previous with him. Unfortunately Pete died, and the vigil exhausted Slocum. It could easily be that the illness that killed Pete also afflicted Slocum at Gaines Mill, and the fatigue of sitting up with the child wore him down further. The excessive heat on the field that day could only have made matters worse and may have been a primary cause of his condition, completely apart from the somewhat idealized depiction of his love for Pete. There was also the possibility of illness due to diseases carried by mosquitoes and bad water in the swamps in the area. In any case Slocum's condition obviously limited his effectiveness on the field that day.[29]

Fortunately for Slocum, Porter's decision to break up the division so thoroughly restricted the possible negative effects of the illness on the battle. With no real coherent brigade to command, Slocum became little more than a nauseated spectator. As night fell, Lee finally achieved the breakthrough he had been seeking all day long. In fact he managed to create several almost simultaneously. Porter was too busy on all fronts to retaliate effectively in any single trouble spot. His line disintegrated, and he had no choice but to retreat in the most orderly fashion possible. He rapidly pulled his forces back toward the crossings.[30]

Here Porter paid for his decision to break up Slocum's command. Because his men had been scattered across the entire field, Slocum could be of little practical help in directing the retreat. He certainly could not be expected to exert any sort of reasonable control over his men, even if he had recovered enough to command them effectively. All the division and brigade drills he had pounded into their heads became instantly useless, and his men simply had to fight where they stood. In the ensuing confusion, entire regiments became lost and separated. Had Slocum been able to lead his division in any kind of coherent fashion, Lee would still have won, but Porter's retreat could have been slower and more orderly. Luckily for Porter, darkness finally put an end to the fighting, saving him from possible annihilation.[31]

Slocum's division paid a heavy price at Gaines Mill. Of the 8,000 men in his division who had crossed the bridge in Porter's support, the list of killed, wounded, and missing came to 2,021. Slocum later reported he had

29. "Gen. Slocum," *Journal*, July 5, 1862. This account claims to be based on a direct report from Slocum himself.

30. Reports of Brig. Gen. Fitz John Porter, *OR*, vol. 11, pt. 2, 226–27.

31. Sears, *Gates of Richmond*, 242–48 (esp. 247).

lost half his regimental commanders and a quarter of all other officers. Still, the right wing of the Army of the Potomac managed to cross the river to safety and McClellan immediately resumed his retreat.[32]

Lee made another attempt to destroy McClellan at the Battle of Savage's Station, but the Army of the Potomac's rearguard held him off. Lee's next chance came on June 30, 1862, at Glendale, an important road crossing. While Jackson continued to press McClellan's rear, Lee threw James Longstreet and A. P. Hill at the center of the Army of the Potomac. If successful he could split McClellan in two and destroy the halves one at a time.

Slocum had not had time to recover from his illness before Glendale. His division had finally quit the Gaines Mill field about eleven o'clock on the night of the battle, June 27. The Confederates pushed their artillery forward and forced Franklin to move Slocum's men to a place where they could more safely rest. They had not been at this place long when orders arrived for them to move to Savage's Station. They began this march at eleven o'clock on the night of June 28 but, because of roads clogged with men and wagons, did not finally complete it until five in the morning on June 29. At Savage's Station, McClellan himself arrived to order Slocum to move across White Oak Swamp. Slocum held the far right flank of the Union line facing west in this battle, guarding the northwestern approaches to Glendale. An open space separated him from the rest of Franklin's corps, which faced Jackson's forces to the north.[33]

As soon as Slocum arrived, he threw out half his force as advanced skirmishers and finally went to bed. As Slocum dreamed fitfully of a feast spread out before him, Colonel Calvin E. Pratt of the Thirty-first New York stumbled into the general's tent. Pratt had been wounded two days earlier at Gaines Mill and left for dead. He had managed to find his way back to the division, covered in his own blood. When he heard of Slocum's condition, he insisted that the general eat something. Pratt woke him, gave him a tube of French soup to eat, and then left. Pratt somehow made it to the hospital, where he spent the rest of the Seven Days recovering. Slocum did not recognize Pratt at the time but later said he preferred the soup even to his dream.[34]

32. Ibid.; Reports of Brig. Gen. Henry W. Slocum, *OR*, vol. 11, pt. 2, 433–34.

33. Reports of Brig. Gen. Henry W. Slocum, *OR*, vol. 11, pt. 2, 434–35; Sears, *Gates of Richmond*, map on 297; Charles Slocum, *Life and Services*, 30.

34. Charles Slocum, *Life and Services*, 30; Warner, *Generals in Blue*, 385; Reports of Brig. Gen. Henry W. Slocum, Report of Brig. Gen. John Newton, *OR*, vol. 11, pt. 2, 434, 457.

When Slocum woke the next morning he might have been somewhat refreshed, but far from recovered. He still had preparations to make, and being so distant from Franklin, he practically exercised an independent command. As he said later, "I did it my own way," and he made careful use of his artillery. In addition to the three batteries attached to his division, he also had another two loaned him from the Fifth Corps. Benjamin Huger, whom Lee had picked to lead off the assault, faced Slocum down the Charles City Road. Huger commanded the largest, freshest Confederate division on the field that day. When the battle opened, Huger moved so slowly that his men did not even come into direct contact with Slocum, who had ordered dozens of trees felled to block his path. Instead of clearing the road Huger tried to cut a new one, which proved such an arduous undertaking that it was late afternoon before he even came close enough to lob artillery shells into Slocum's lines. Rather than press on with an infantry attack, Huger decided to bring up his two batteries. Slocum would have none of this. As the first few rounds fell, he posted all five of his batteries against Huger's two, giving the Confederates the worst of it. This clearly points to Slocum's original training in artillery, and he would continue to demonstrate an appreciation and effective use of artillery for the rest of the war. Slocum later loaned Bartlett's brigade to Philip Kearny, and it participated in the final push on Kearny's front, but no more of his infantry was engaged.[35]

That night Slocum, with his men low on ammunition and without rations, got permission to march his troops to McClellan's position on Malvern Hill, where McClellan had drawn his army up into an impressive defensive position. When they arrived, Slocum (who by now had probably given up on more sleep until they reached Harrison's Landing on the James) kept his troops under arms and building field fortifications. His preparations were unnecessary. His division, placed on the back of the hill, saw no action at all in Lee's last, desperate assault the next day.[36]

Slocum arrived at Harrison's Landing sick and exhausted. His division had made it through the Seven Days intact and arrived at the James in good order. While at the landing, Slocum received news of his promotion to major general, effective July 4, 1862. Fox notes that this was because of

35. Sears, *Gates of Richmond*, 280–81, 284–85, 303; Reports of Brig. Gen. Henry W. Slocum, *OR*, vol. 11, pt. 2, 434–35; Slocum to Clara, Harrison's Landing, Virginia, July 10, 1862, in Charles Slocum, *Life and Services*, 31.
36. Sears, *Gates of Richmond*, 308–36; Reports of Brig. Gen. Henry W. Slocum, *OR*, vol. 11, pt. 2, 436.

"conspicuous services rendered by him at Gaines Mill and in the movement to the James," and he is the closest any source comes to explaining the reasoning behind Slocum's promotion. Slocum had demonstrated his abilities as a competent officer but had not acquitted himself spectacularly. At Gaines Mill he had fallen ill and then had his division ordered out from under him by Porter. He could not have rendered such significant services to make Congress decide to grant him a near-instantaneous promotion. He had handled the affair at Glendale well, but Huger's timidity ensured that Slocum missed the bulk of the fighting. His men had spent Malvern Hill digging entrenchments they would never use. New York politics and a need to appoint major generals probably influenced Congress more than anything else.[37]

It took Slocum nearly a week to recover, now that he could rest. Around July 7, 1862, he wrote to Clara that he had actually gotten worse. "My last letter," he said in a separate note penned on July 10, "was rather blue I think. I had then been here a day or two and the reaction from the excitement of the previous ten days weighed heavily upon me." He had been worried over Lee's constant attacks and the thought that the army was in imminent danger of destruction. McClellan himself could hardly have said it better. With a gift for understatement Slocum added, "this army is safe, I do not think the prospect of an early and successful termination of the war is bright." For the first few nights after reaching the safety of Harrison's Landing, dreams of still "being on the march, of losing wagons, artillery, etc." troubled his nights. He worried excessively over the state of the army and what they faced. Although he insisted to Clara that he had not been really ill, and that he was only "rather worn and nervous," his own description sounds to a certain extent like the beginnings of depression, brought on at least in part by exhaustion and sleep deprivation. This was Slocum's first sustained exposure to large-scale battle. When the adrenaline finally stopped flowing he found himself descending into a state of shock and exhaustion. He had seen little of the carnage at Bull Run and had missed both the major battles before Gaines Mill. His induction to massive slaughter was a trial by fire where he not only had to contend with the horror of what was going on around him but was given no opportunity to recover emotionally or physically until they reached Harrison's Landing. Slocum began to improve when he found a way to

37. Reports of Brig. Gen. Henry W. Slocum, *OR*, vol. 11, pt. 2, 434–36; "Promotion of General Slocum," *Journal*, August 6, 1862; Fox, *In Memoriam*, 71 (quote).

adapt emotionally. He came to the realization that he could not affect the outcome of events in any substantial way now they were no longer on the move, and so he made the conscious choice to relax. "Things must take their course," he philosophized. "I made up my mind to get a good novel and try to forget everything here." It seems to have worked because, by July 10, Slocum could report to Clara, "I feel better today than I have in several days."[38]

As McClellan hovered near the river, events moved apace to the north. The force remaining with McDowell received a new commander, John Pope, a successful Union general in the western theater, who began building another army just outside Washington. Pope's Army of Virginia prepared to march on Richmond directly, posing another threat that Lee could not afford to ignore. Lincoln, tired of McClellan but unable to remove him because of his popularity with the troops, took a different tack. If he could not actually throw McClellan out, he would pull his army out from under him. He began breaking off groups of men from the Army of the Potomac and attaching them to the Army of Virginia. With luck McClellan would be a commander without an army, and Pope would be in Richmond before year's end. Unfortunately for Lincoln and Pope, Lee learned of this plan after J. E. B. Stuart and his cavalry captured Pope's dispatch case on August 22, 1862. Lee decided he must act quickly to crush Pope before McClellan's reinforcements arrived. Lee sent Jackson to keep Pope busy until he could come with the rest of the army.[39]

Slocum's turn to be parted from McClellan came soon enough. On August 16, he marched away from Harrison's Landing and five days later reached Newport News. The next day the division boarded transports bound for the wharves at Aquia Creek, but somewhere along the way it was diverted to Alexandria, Virginia, where it disembarked on August 24. Pope had already begun his advance on Manassas where he hoped to catch Jackson's isolated command before Lee joined him. Henry Halleck, overall commander of the Union armies, was concerned for Pope's safety. Knowing Confederate forces were somewhere in the area, Halleck ordered Slocum to send a brigade through to Centreville to search out the enemy. On August 27, Slocum moved Taylor's brigade across Bull Run Bridge,

---

38. Slocum to Clara, July 7, 10, 1862, in Fox, *In Memoriam*, 71–72; Charles Slocum, *Life and Services*, 31.
39. McPherson, *Ordeal by Fire*, 254–60; Justin D. Murphy, "Bull Run / Manassas, Second Battle of," 1:132–34; Matloff, *American Military History*, 224–27; John J. Hennessy, *Return to Bull Run: The Campaign and Battle of Second Manassas*.

and two miles beyond the bridge his men collided with a portion of Jackson's forces. Badly outnumbered, Slocum's troops endured a murderous artillery barrage before retreating. Taylor himself was killed, and his brigade suffered significant casualties.[40]

Only two days after mauling Taylor, Jackson met Pope on the battlefield of First Bull Run. Jackson had given his opponent quite the runaround, hiding from him, even destroying Pope's supply depot at Manassas. Jackson managed to hold off Pope's attacks long enough for Lee and the rest of the army to arrive on the Union flank. The ensuing attack crushed Pope, and his badly beaten forces once again withdrew toward Washington, though in better order than McDowell's had a year and a month before.[41]

Slocum and his division missed the actual battle. In accordance to orders, he had moved his division to a position south of Fairfax Courthouse on August 29, on the route to Manassas Junction. They spent the day of August 30 astride the Warrenton Pike, acting as a net to catch the many stragglers streaming back from Pope's army. Although Slocum does not mention it, the sheer number of stragglers must have seemed overwhelming. Franklin noted that his corps stopped more than seven thousand men in less than half an hour. While Franklin quickly gave up on this idea, Slocum's division stayed in place into the night, after which he fell back into the fortifications around Centreville. From there Slocum and his division would return once more to Washington.[42]

Lincoln now faced a frustrating decision. With Pope's humiliating defeat Lee seized the initiative, launching his first invasion of the North. For Lincoln this meant he must appoint a new commander immediately. No Western commander could reach the capital in time, and with no other Eastern generals he trusted to handle the job, Lincoln had to turn to McClellan. At the very least he knew McClellan had the ability to get the defeated army back into fighting shape. Lee planned for the Army of Northern Virginia to move into Maryland, reducing the garrison at Harper's Ferry. He would then send forces to hold the various passes along the Shenandoah Valley, using it as a protected supply line. Lee knew

40. No. 117. Itinerary of the First Division, Sixth Army Corps, Brig. Gen. Henry W. Slocum commanding, August 16–31 [1862], *OR*, vol. 12, pt. 2, 536; Charles Slocum, *Life and Services*, 38–39.

41. McPherson, *Ordeal by Fire*, 254–60; Murphy, "Bull Run/Manassas," 1:132–34; Matloff, *American Military History*, 224–27.

42. Itinerary of the First Division, *OR*, vol. 12, pt. 2, 536; Report of Maj. Gen. William B. Franklin, ibid., 536.

that once he set foot onto free soil McClellan had to attack him. Lee would fortify and then wait for the sea of blue uniforms to dash themselves against the rock upon which his army stood. With the Northern army destroyed, Lee hoped negotiations would soon follow. At the very least, the armies would be away from Virginia for a time, giving the Old Dominion a chance to recover.[43]

At first everything went according to Lee's plan. He marched straight into Maryland and also laid siege to Harpers Ferry, Virginia. McClellan had succeeded in pulling his army back together but, true to form, followed Lee almost grudgingly. By the time the Army of the Potomac reached Frederick, Maryland, Lee's army had already been gone for two days. At Frederick, however, an outstanding stroke of fortune came McClellan's way when his troops discovered a complete copy of Lee's plan of campaign. McClellan now knew exactly where Lee was going and what he was aiming to do. The Little Napoleon actually began to move. McClellan's normally plodding pace was key to Lee's plan, and now that McClellan was moving faster than Lee anticipated it derailed his plans. Lee was expecting the Army of the Potomac to be demoralized after its defeat at Second Bull Run. He had not reckoned on McClellan's ability to inspire them. Realizing something had happened, Lee tried to block McClellan's pursuit temporarily by holding passes through South Mountain, one of them near Burkittsville, Maryland. It fell to Franklin's Sixth Corps to force this one, the southernmost, called Crampton's Gap. Franklin arrived at the approaches to the gap in the morning of September 14, 1862.

Several Confederate commanders held different parts of the field, including Howell Cobb and Thomas Munford of Lafayette McLaws's division. Although they did not take the time to entrench, Cobb and Munford enjoyed a strong position protected by a number of both natural and man-made obstacles. They set what infantry they had at the base of the mountain along a stone wall and placed their artillery roughly parallel to the wall about halfway up the slope. They had an excellent view from the side of the mountain, and the Sixth Corps had very little cover as they approached. As Franklin drew near, Confederate artillery opened on them but then discovered their guns did not have the necessary range. To rem-

43. For this and the next paragraph, I am indebted to McPherson, *Ordeal by Fire,* 280–88; Matloff, *American Military History,* 227–29; Bruce Tap, "Antietam/Sharpsburg, Battle of," in Tucker, *Encyclopedia,* 1:49–52; Stephen W. Sears, *Landscape Turned Red: The Battle of Antietam,* 65; Perry D. Jamieson, *Death in September;* Reports of Maj. Gen. William B. Franklin, *OR,* vol. 19, pt. 1, 375.

edy this they moved a pair of Napoleons to the top of the slope. Two dismounted regiments of cavalry took up positions to the left and right of the road through the pass.[44]

Slocum drove Confederate pickets from Burkittsville itself in preparation for the assault. His old brigade under Bartlett pursued the pickets back to the mountain where the brigade came under fire from the Confederate batteries on the crest. Slocum gave the order to halt in order to mass his troops. Years after the engagement Bartlett reported that Franklin and his division commanders met behind a building in town to enjoy a few cigars and discuss matters. A disagreement arose over which side of the road they should use to attack the position. Franklin settled this by ordering the assault made on the right, but he planned to hold off until the following morning or for further orders before making the attack.[45]

Slocum, Bartlett, and Newton apparently saw no reason to wait. Despite Franklin's timidity they planned a head-on charge to take place that very afternoon. In the meantime the men took cover in the woods nearer to town, and the artillery worked to soften up the Rebels. The men formed into two lines, one behind the other. Each line was one regiment wide. Bartlett led his brigade from the front, followed by Newton's troops. Between three and four o'clock Slocum gave the nod and his men went forward. As they approached, the Confederates put up a horrendous fire. Bartlett found himself marching through the middle of crossfire from the guns mounted on both the left and right slopes of the mountain and the infantry behind the stone wall immediately to his front. He threw out a strong line of skirmishers and developed the enemy line. The opposing infantry hammered each other for approximately forty-five minutes, with

---

44. Reports of Col. Thomas Munford, *OR*, vol. 19, pt. 1, 826–27; "Gen. Slocum's Division in Battle," *Journal*, September 19, 1862.

45. Reports of Maj. Gen. William B. Franklin, *OR*, vol. 19, pt. 1, 375; Sears, *Landscape Turned Red*, 147; Priest, *Before Antietam*, 272–83 (Bartlett, years after the engagement). This last source provides a very different, very negative depiction of Slocum. In 1889 Bartlett wrote a more detailed account of the battle for the *National Tribune*, where he claimed credit for the battle plan and its execution. He shows Slocum, feeling slighted by Franklin when Franklin deferred to Bartlett, almost pouting and refusing to take active control of his own division. Bartlett's two accounts are contradictory and mutually exclusive in more than a few ways. For instance, in his official report, he specifically gave credit to Slocum for the "masterly arrangement" of the troops. Twenty-seven years later he says that he, not Slocum, was responsible. Here it seems safe to say that his earlier account is probably more accurate, though why he changed his story later is unknown. Report of Col. Joseph J. Bartlett, *OR*, vol. 19, pt. 1, 388; Priest, *Before Antietam*, 272–83.

Bartlett losing almost one hundred men. When he looked for his support he found Newton's brigade had not followed as planned. It remained on the far edge of the field, out of harm's way. Seeing the situation Slocum himself began ordering troops up to the front. Eventually, when his troops revealed the full extent of the position, Bartlett withdrew his skirmishers and gave the order to charge at the double-quick.[46]

The men surged forward with a cry, leapt over the stone wall, and put McLaws's men to flight. Most Confederates, seeing there would be no stopping the attack, hardly paused as they ran, though some of the more stubborn ones turned it into a semblance of a fighting retreat. Slocum's men chased their enemies all the way through the pass and down into the valley below in one sustained charge. Slocum's command captured three stands of colors, over seven hundred rifles, three hundred prisoners, and a great many knapsacks and blankets. His division lost five officers killed and sixteen wounded. Of the enlisted men, 109 were killed while 381 fell wounded. The Union totals for the day were 114 killed and 397 wounded for an aggregate loss of 511.[47]

What some found most impressive about this battle was the precise manner in which Slocum's men executed the orders. Slocum himself noted that, though under fire, "the troops advanced steadily, every line in the entire column preserving its alignment with as much accuracy as could have been expected at a drill or review." Franklin called the advance one of "admirable steadiness through a well directed fire." Bartlett also made note of this in his report, mentioning that clearly written orders had much to do with it, calling the plans a "masterly arrangement." Still, Bartlett himself noted an exception to this glowing account. The second line of attack followed much farther back than was intended, so far back in fact that it could hardly support the first.[48] In the end this posed no serious problem. Slocum told his friend Joseph Howland that it was "the most complete victory of the war [to that point]."[49]

Slocum and Howland kept up a correspondence for the next few years, providing a rare window into Slocum's mind and emotions. Howland came from a prominent merchant family in New York City and had once

46. Sears, *Landscape Turned Red,* 147–49; Reports of Maj. Gen. Henry W. Slocum, Report of Col. Joseph J. Bartlett, *OR,* vol. 19, pt. 1, 380, 388–89; Priest, *Before Antietam,* 272–83.

47. Reports of Col. Joseph J. Bartlett and Maj. Gen. Henry W. Slocum, *OR,* vol. 19, pt. 1, 388, 380.

48. Reports of Maj. Gen. Henry W. Slocum, Maj. Gen. William B. Franklin, Col. Joseph J. Bartlett, *OR,* vol. 19, pt. 1, 380, 375, 388.

49. Slocum to Joseph Howland, September 28, 1862, NYHS.

considered becoming a minister. When the war broke out he enlisted with the Sixteenth New York as an adjutant, and when Slocum came into brigade command, he chose Howland as his chief of staff. The two worked closely together in the coming months, and their families also became acquainted. At Gaines Mill Howland was in command of the Sixteenth, and while he was directing his troops into line a ball struck him in the left thigh. Amazingly, he stayed in the saddle and kept his horse under control. He refused to leave the field, and he stayed with his regiment throughout the fight, leaving only when the regiment retired. While the Sixteenth New York report claimed he would be kept out of action only for several weeks, in reality the wound ended Howland's military career. Slocum expected him to eventually return to active duty and the two kept in touch with each other. Howland even made a point of writing to Clara Slocum from his sickbed to make sure she knew Slocum had not been injured in the fighting.[50]

After the battle Slocum remained at Crampton's Gap. Franklin pushed tentatively toward Harper's Ferry with the rest of his corps, and several Confederate brigades involved in the siege of Harpers Ferry turned to oppose him. Franklin moved no farther. Meanwhile McClellan had finally caught up to Lee at Antietam Creek, near Sharpsburg, and prepared to attack. Lee's army made a stand along a low line of hills behind the creek, but a significant number of his troops, notably an entire division under A. P. Hill, had not yet reached the field. The Potomac River ran across Lee's rear, and he knew of only one small ford through which he could escape if necessary. If his lines broke here, Lee knew it would be the end of his army. McClellan attacked on September 17, 1862. Although he greatly outnumbered Lee, his attacks went in one at a time on three separate fronts, which gave Lee time to shift men from one trouble spot to the other.[51]

After Franklin's halting movement toward Harpers Ferry, Slocum's division stayed still for three days before marching to join the rest of McClellan's army. Franklin considered them damaged too badly in their recent assault to use again so soon. Slocum reached the field about noon on September 17, 1862, and took up a position near the Dunkard Church on

50. Mark M. Boatner III, "Howland, Joseph," in *Civil War Dictionary*, 415; Slocum to Howland, July 19, 1862, NYHS; Report of Maj. Joel J. Seaver, Sixteenth New York Infantry, of the Battle of Gaines Mill, *OR*, vol. 11, pt. 2, 451–52; "General Joseph Howland" at http://www.howlandculturalcenter.org/General.html.

51. McPherson, *Ordeal by Fire*, 280–88; Matloff, *American Military History*, 227–29; Tap, "Antietam/Sharpsburg"; Stephen Sears, *Landscape Turned Red*; Jamieson, *Death in September*.

the north end of the field, relieving a portion of General Edwin "Bull" Sumner's Second Corps. Slocum's division had not fought since Crampton's Gap and was one of several powerful, relatively fresh and un-bloodied forces that McClellan had on hand but ignored. Had Slocum's division pressed forward now, he would most certainly have demolished Lee's left flank. Historians ever since have pointed out McClellan's lost opportunity. By late afternoon the fighting on this end of the line had spent itself, and so the Sixth Corps did not actively engage the enemy but rested on their arms in line of battle for more than forty hours, during which time Confederate artillery hammered their position. Although Slocum's men did little that day, the barrage wore greatly on their nerves.[52]

While the infantry had little to do, Slocum's artillery had its hands full. All of the First Division's batteries engaged the enemy, though they only succeeded in silencing the Confederate guns for two short intervals. Slocum also mentions that they "[held] in check a large force of . . . infantry."[53] As Lee's army was in no condition to attack by this time, Slocum no doubt misinterpreted what he saw, once again demonstrating how much he had come to think like McClellan. Lee certainly did not have a substantial number of fresh infantry massing on his left. He had diverted all his reinforcements at that time to his right, where he had to fight off Burnside. There was no danger of a Confederate advance on Slocum's front, but he had developed a tendency to worry more about what Lee was planning than about what he and his men needed to do.

When it was all over, Lee's army was holding on by the thinnest of threads, but it had still repulsed McClellan at every point. The Army of the Potomac was well able to renew the battle the next day, especially given its reserves, but once again McClellan did nothing. Afterward Lee retreated back across the Potomac to rest and refit his army. As Lee marched south McClellan made a small show of pursuit but did not get very far.[54]

When Slocum's division reached Hagerstown on October 15, 1862, news of his latest promotion reached him: command of the Twelfth Corps. Slocum, already a major general, had distinguished himself as a competent and professional officer with Old Army training and had just won a

52. McPherson, *Ordeal by Fire*, 280–88; Matloff, *American Military History*, 227–29; Tap, "Antietam/Sharpsburg"; Jamieson, *Death in September*; Sears, *Landscape Turned Red*, 155, 256, 257, 271; Report of Maj. Gen. Henry W. Slocum, *OR*, vol. 19, pt. 1, 382.

53. Report of Maj. Gen. Henry W. Slocum, *OR*, vol. 19, pt. 1, 382.

54. McPherson, *Ordeal by Fire*, 285–88; Matloff, *American Military History*, 227–29; Tap, "Antietam/Sharpsburg."

very one-sided victory at the (admittedly small) battle of Crampton's Gap. His political allies from Onondaga probably made up for what Crampton's Gap lacked in size. As for his new corps, the Twelfth's history up to this point in the war had not been particularly successful or glorious. Though not yet designated a corps, its troops had served under General Patterson in his non-attempt to keep Johnston from reinforcing Beauregard in the First Bull Run Campaign. Afterward it had been a part of Nathaniel P. Banks's forces, which he had led into a series of humiliating defeats against Jackson in the Shenandoah Valley. When the army moved on Lee at Antietam, Joseph Mansfield had taken the reins, but Mansfield, a strong and competent officer, would only be in active command for two days before his death. Also, because one division remained perpetually detached, the Twelfth was the smallest corps in the army. Its field strength consisted of two divisions, but it had in its favor a number of West Point–educated officers and a great number of veteran troops. Unfortunately, since these troops had been on the receiving end of some of the worst setbacks of the entire war, their morale would be a serious concern indeed.[55]

A number of important developments took place in Slocum's life between Bull Run and Antietam. He received a rapid string of promotions, but McClellan imprinted himself so strongly on Slocum's mentality that it would take an equally powerful personality to remove his influence. Since Slocum would not serve under such a person until late in the summer of 1864, McClellanism would haunt him, as it did the rest of the army, for some time to come.

Yet there are limits to how far this criticism can legitimately be carried. For all of the negative aspects of the McClellan stereotype he absorbed, Slocum also picked up a few good ones. For instance, unlike the real McClellan, Slocum would and did actually fight. McClellan himself was in theory supposed to be capable of this, and he fooled his soldiers (and possibly himself) into thinking it was always some uncontrollable external circumstance that prevented him. Slocum simply led his troops into battle when the situation called for it, even if he did both worry himself sick over what might happen and also greatly overestimate the odds he faced. He continued to develop independently of McClellan in other ways as well. His devotion to drill and duty, which he continued to improve

55. Fox, *In Memoriam*, 74; Warner, *Generals in Blue*, 309.

and apply with zest to each new level of command, predated his association with McClellan. His use of fieldworks at Malvern Hill and elsewhere not only did not come from McClellan but actually prefigured developments in the western theater.

Slocum's new appointment began an association that would leave its mark on both himself and his new command. Oddly enough Slocum would be better known to history for his command of this, the least of all corps in the East, than he would be for commanding entire armies in the West. As time passed, the general and the corps became so closely linked that Oliver O. Howard would later remark, "even in the records to say, 'The Twelfth Corps,' is to say, 'General Slocum.'"[56]

56. Howard, "Memory of Henry Slocum," 40.

CHAPTER 4

Corps Command and Controversy
Harpers Ferry, the Mud March, and Chancellorsville

No one could really accuse the Twelfth of being the crack corps of the army when Slocum assumed command in the fall of 1862. It would be up to him to find some way to make them into a group of fighting men worthy of respect, and Slocum, the strict disciplinarian, would be well suited to the job. While he had developed his dedication to discipline independently from McClellan, he undoubtedly got better at it while serving under him. If McClellan could do anything it was build up a broken army, and in little over a year Slocum had watched him do it twice. Slocum now had to accomplish a similar task in microcosm with his own corps. Fortunately he had been assigned to the reserve, which would give him an opportunity to work in detail with the Twelfth.

Unfortunately Slocum's fortunes as a conductor of light did not improve much. His newest commanders, Burnside and Hooker, would prove not much brighter than McClellan, and when Slocum compared "Fighting Joe" Hooker's arrogance with his failings it would produce an abiding hatred between the two. Unfortunately Hooker's most prominent characteristic, which Slocum as conductor would pick up on, was his contentious lobbying both in the army and outside it. Hooker's leadership seemed to make Slocum somewhat more aggressive on the battlefield, but Slocum would also distinguish himself for his furious fight to have Hooker removed from command just as Hooker had fought Burnside before him.

In the wake of Antietam Lincoln finally had had enough of McClellan. In his place he wanted to promote Ambrose Burnside who possessed a

charming personality and had become a favorite after some early suc-
cesses. Lincoln had arranged for Burnside to head an expedition along the
North Carolina coast. Thoroughly successful, it brought the Union a base
of operations early in the war and Burnside a promotion to major general
of volunteers. He commanded the Ninth Corps at Antietam, where he
wallowed in mediocrity along with the rest of the army. Executing his orders with painstaking precision, Burnside delayed his assault against
Lee's extremely weak right. Instead of dealing a deathblow he allowed
Lee time to reinforce and thereby lost a grand opportunity. When Lincoln
offered it Burnside took command of the Union army from McClellan only
reluctantly. Although arguably a decent corps commander, he did not feel
up to the job of leading an army.[1]

Burnside quickly split his army up into what he called "grand divisions"
made up of two corps each and placed each division under the command
of one of his top generals. Franz Sigel, a German-speaking politician, took
the Reserve Grand Division, which was made up of the Eleventh and
Twelfth corps. Sigel had been an unsuccessful but very popular general in
the German Revolutionary movement of 1848 in Europe. After being
crushed by the Prussians he went into exile but remained a loud voice for
his own lost cause. When he arrived in America his fame was already well
established among the German community. Unfortunately his habit of mas-
terfully losing battles continued unabated in the Civil War though his par-
adoxical popularity with German Americans remained a strong asset to the
Lincoln administration.[2]

When the Army of the Potomac moved after Lee on November 1, 1862,
they left Slocum and the Twelfth behind, isolated in Harpers Ferry. There
is not much information available for historians to determine Slocum's attitudes and thoughts during this time. He did not like the grand divisions,
and he probably disliked serving under Sigel. He seems to have taken particular exception to being grouped with the Eleventh Corps. One of the
eleventh's division commanders, Carl Schurz mentioned Slocum's dislike
of the Eleventh later the next year in a letter to Lincoln, but if this dislike
was the result of either an anti-German or an anti-immigrant bias, this
was not apparent to the German citizens of Syracuse who had honored
him with a serenade the previous year. Slocum probably appreciated the
chance to get his corps into shape. This would have led to further frus-

1. William Marvel, *Burnside*, 159–60; Warner, *Generals in Blue*, 57; David Coffey,
"Burnside, Ambrose E.," in Tucker, *Encyclopedia*, 1:137–38.
2. Stephen Engle, *Yankee Dutchman: The Life of Franz Sigel*, xviii, 151.

tration, though, when the War Department began detaching his brigades to aid Burnside but left him all the while at Harpers Ferry. He could not condition a corps he did not have with him.[3]

Whatever he may have thought, Slocum did not have an insubstantial command; it totaled over fifteen thousand men in and around the town. Nearby Major General George Morell commanded another five thousand men. Together Slocum and Morell chased roving bands of guerrillas active in the valley, but they had little success in sweeping them from the Shenandoah because Slocum's best efforts were focused elsewhere. He noted with regret that the Twelfth "was not much like the old Division" and so set to work on it with a vengeance. He appointed a board of officers to examine the corps, weeding out inferior officers and court-martialing those he considered guilty of egregious transgressions. As he put it, "all the most approved appliances [are] in full blast." By January 6, 1863, he proudly stated that the Twelfth had shown much improvement. Even after those few months, however, he found himself casting his mind longingly back to his former division, not feeling quite at home with the Twelfth Corps.[4]

Burnside planned for the rest of the army, now nearing 120,000 strong, to march quickly on Fredericksburg, Virginia. Once safely across the Rappahannock River he would lead his men rapidly down onto Richmond's defenses before Lee could react. Burnside planned to use all his superior numbers at once, something Lincoln thought key to success. It was a good plan. Yet, as for other Union commanders both before and after him, the trouble came when he tried to execute it. The Fredericksburg Campaign began with great promise for the Union. Burnside managed to reach the river crossing before Lee, but someone's failure to bring the army's pontoon bridges ensured Lee had time to arrive and contest the crossing. Once the army finally reached the far bank of the river and secured it, Burnside chose to use a head-on attack, in keeping with his plan to exploit his superior numbers. Unfortunately he chose to focus his assault toward a virtually impregnable section of Lee's line. Union soldiers fell by the hundreds on one of the best fields of defensive fire known to military history. As the sun set, most of the remaining attackers scrambled back into Fredericksburg

3. Carl Schurz to Lincoln, August 8, 1863 (Breaking up of 11th Corps), Lincoln Papers; Warner, *Generals in Blue*, 447–48; Special Orders No. 282, U.S. War Department, *OR*, vol. 19, pt. 2, 431; Hearn, *Six Years*, 198.

4. Hearn, *Six Years*, 198; Slocum to Howland, November 17, 1862 (two quotes), January 6, 1863, NYHS.

while others piled up the dead bodies in a desperate attempt at makeshift breastworks. For the day Burnside lost over twelve thousand men as compared to Lee's figure of less than six thousand.[5]

Burnside called for the Reserve Grand Division to join him as things went wrong at Fredericksburg. He bypassed Sigel and ordered Slocum to move the entire Twelfth Corps to the east, with the exception of troops in the permanent entrenchments. Burnside then sent word to Morell to fill the gap left by the Twelfth Corps. The desperate Burnside hoped for Slocum to reach Hillsborough that very night.[6]

Morell, though warned of this movement at the same time Burnside notified Slocum, seemed surprised. Objecting to the sudden withdrawal of so many men, Morell pushed forward two regiments to fill the gap, which stretched the lines around Harpers Ferry dangerously thin. In *Six Years of Hell*, historian Chester Hearn criticizes Slocum's abrupt departure, saying he left so quickly he did not ensure that the city and arsenal would remain secure. While this is technically true, Hearn is wrong to lay the blame on Slocum, who left in such a hurry because ordered to do so by Burnside. Slocum knew very well what this meant for the defense of Harpers Ferry, but he obeyed orders: "My command has left this place, by order of General Burnside. . . . This place is not sufficiently protected."[7]

As Slocum and his men marched through Chantilly he began to hear from Sigel, who had joined Burnside's chorus. Slocum asked for a day to shoe his weary horses, which had been performing sweeps down the Shenandoah, but Sigel insisted he press on, even if it meant his cavalry should fall behind a day's march. Neither Sigel nor Slocum mentioned artillery, which seems to imply Slocum had little if any along with him. What he had he most likely left in Harpers Ferry to man the redoubts. Meanwhile Burnside interjected that they must move even faster. Slocum stripped down his command and drove his men onward. With all due

5. George C. Rable, *Fredericksburg! Fredericksburg!*; Marvel, *Burnside*, 151–217; McPherson, *Ordeal by Fire*, 303–4; Bruce Tap, "Fredericksburg, Battle of," in Tucker, *Encyclopedia*, 1:329–32; Matloff, *American Military History*, 230–32.

6. Reports of Maj. Gen. Ambrose E. Burnside, *OR*, 21:62. It is notable that Burnside continued to send orders directly to Slocum and not through Sigel. This might imply the most practical objection some of Burnside's contemporaries had against the grand divisions, which is that Burnside did not use them. He continued, at least to some extent, to treat his army as a group of individual corps. This would negate the value of the Grand Divisions, in effect creating an extra set of useless middlemen. When Sherman used this same basic scheme on the March to the Sea, he kept the meddling to a minimum, and Slocum had no further objections.

7. Hearn, *Six Years*, 198; Slocum to Halleck, Morell to Cullum, both at *OR*, 21:847.

haste he did not (and could not) make it to Fredericksburg before the bat-tle culminated in a devastating loss. If they had been able to arrive in time, their presence would have made little difference in the outcome. Burnside initially thought to renew the attack the following day, but his subordi-nates managed to talk him out of it. As the Army of the Potomac retreated back across the river, the Twelfth settled down on the north bank, in the vicinity of Stafford, Virginia.[8]

Burnside, the fate of his slow-moving friend McClellan still fresh in his mind, knew he must keep on the move. He ordered another march in late January 1863, this time back up the Rappahannock. General Orders No. 7, which announced the movement, exhibited a bravado that must have sounded both hypocritical and melodramatic considering recent events. The Rebels had been "divided and weakened" by actions in North Carolina, Tennessee, and Arkansas, and the "auspicious moment" had ar-rived to "strike a great and mortal blow to the rebellion." In fact Burnside said that, if "the gallant soldiers of so many brilliant battle-fields accom-plish this achievement, . . . a fame the most glorious awaits them."[9]

Unfortunately for the demoralized Army of the Potomac, they found nothing of the sort on this new end-the-war campaign. Whereas a combi-nation of ineptitude and Lee's army had foiled the Fredericksburg Campaign, it seemed that Burnside now must deal with God as well. As the march commenced, so did a rainstorm of biblical proportions. The Army of the Potomac, already metaphorically swamped in a deep gloom brought on by the Fredericksburg fiasco, started literally sinking into the Virginia mud. Wagons mired to their hubs, and men sank down to their knees. Artillerymen struggled for hour upon weary hour with their pieces, eventually having to leave some buried to their axles in muck. An icy January wind bit into their flesh, and the rain kept coming. The men re-membered it simply as the "Mud March." It proved the death knell of Burnside's tenure as commander of the Army of the Potomac.[10]

Slocum's Twelfth Corps arrived just in time to join this abortive campaign. The First Division, under Alpheus Williams, reported no real difficulties dur-ing the first two days' march. By January 20, they had made it back to Dumfries, Virginia. On the next day, however, they found themselves able to

8. Sigel to Burnside (Slocum), Park to Sigel (Burnside), both at *OR,* 21:850; Fox, *In Memoriam,* 74.

9. General Orders No. 7, *OR,* 21:127.

10. Rable, *Fredericksburg!* 408–23; Marvel, *Burnside,* 211–17; McPherson, *Ordeal by Fire,* 317–19; Warner, *Generals in Blue,* 58.

move only about three miles. Chopawamsic Creek overran its banks with storm water, and the men settled in as best they could while the engineers constructed a bridge. When they made it to Aquia Creek, they found it flooded as well. Williams's men bivouacked again, but this time without food or shelter. The supply wagons remained three or four miles to the rear, stuck in the mud. Finally, on January 23, they managed to cross the creek and make it to Stafford Courthouse. John W. Geary's Second Division met similar difficulties and took a few days longer to complete the trip. Unlike Williams, who advanced in a straight line, Geary found himself marching and countermarching from creek to creek. Most days the Second Division covered only three or four miles. After Burnside canceled the campaign, the entire Twelfth Corps settled in for the remainder of the month at Stafford Courthouse.[11]

Slocum wrote to Howland later that the roads were in awful condition and noted that the Twelfth Corps lost many good horses and mules along the way. His men "bore up well and appeared cheerful to the last." Here, their absence from the bloody field at Fredericksburg was clearly demonstrated, since, as George Rable observes, the morale of the vast majority of the army was in truly dire straits. Staying with the rearguard to see to the safety of the train, Slocum entered Stafford Courthouse exhausted and covered with mud. He noted to Howland with some amazement Thomas L. Kane's brigade of Williams's division out at drill "appearing as clean as if they had never seen any mud." Actually Kane had arrived the previous evening and at once set his brigade to cleaning up, afterward heading straight back to drill.[12]

Major General Joseph Hooker, commanding the Center Grand Division, quickly exploited Burnside's humiliation. Using his political connections Hooker tried to have Burnside thrown out of command. Hooker had long ago earned a reputation for this sort of skullduggery, which stretched back to testimony against Winfield Scott in the Mexican War. Early in his life Hooker had acquired an enviable reputation in the regular army. In the Mexican War he participated in both Winfield Scott's campaign and that of Zachary Taylor. He won brevets for gallant service for all the ranks from first lieutenant to lieutenant colonel. By 1853 he had apparently tired of peacetime army life and resigned his commission to take up farming in

11. Extracts from Records of Events, *OR*, 21:754–55.
12. Slocum to Howland, February 4, 1863, NYHS. See also Rable, *Fredericksburg!* 408–23.

Joseph J. "Fighting Joe" Hooker, with whom Slocum feuded bitterly during the war. Library of Congress, Prints & Photographs Division, Civil War Photographs

California, but his fortunes rapidly declined, leaving him so impoverished that when the Civil War started he had to borrow money to head east to accept his commission as a brigadier general of volunteers.[13]

Hooker had a solid record for the current war as well. He commanded a division on the Peninsula, where he acquired his nickname of "Fighting Joe" because of a widely circulated newspaper error. (A journalist had sent

13. Warner, *Generals in Blue*, 233–34; Walter H. Hebert, *Fighting Joe Hooker*, 21–35; McPherson, *Ordeal by Fire*, 318–19; Roger Caraway, "Hooker, Joseph," in Tucker, *Encyclopedia*, 2:400–402.

a dispatch from the front, in which he intended to write "Fighting—Joe Hooker," but he accidentally left out the dash, which resulted in "Fighting Joe.") Hooker also gave good showings at Second Bull Run, Antietam, and Fredericksburg. His personal life caused the most controversy. At one point he declared that the United States could use a good dictator. He spent much of his spare time drunk, sometimes exploding into fits of rage in which he flung out obscenities thick enough to stick to walls and ceiling. A notorious womanizer, he spent a great deal of time in Washington's red-light district, and because of both this and his management policies while stationed in the city, that section became known as "Hooker's Division." If Lincoln had any moral qualms concerning Hooker's character, they did not prevent him from giving Hooker the job. In all probability Hooker's association with Secretary of the Treasury Salmon P. Chase and an excellent war record off-set his personal liabilities and political views.[14]

When Fighting Joe took command of the demoralized Army of the Potomac in the winter of 1863, Slocum was his youngest corps com-mander. Hooker's attacks on Burnside worried Slocum. He told Howland that "all this must stop or we are ruined." Consequently, he did not trust Hooker at first but decided to talk to him before passing a final judgment. Whatever the two men said in the meeting, Fighting Joe must have im-pressed his subordinate, for Slocum confided to Howland afterward, "I am willing to follow him. My confidence has greatly increased with him." Slocum's greatest hope for the immediate future was that Hooker would disband the grand divisions, which would free him from his disagreeable service under Sigel.[15]

In light of the hatred the two men later developed for each other, it is important to take note of Hooker and Slocum's meeting. Although his opinion of the man was "greatly increased," Slocum still had nothing more enthusiastic to say than he was "willing to follow" Hooker. From this it is not difficult to infer that his initial opinion must have been low indeed. Slocum held any new Eastern commanders to the abnormally high standard he thought McClellan capable of reaching. Yet this can not go very far in explaining Slocum's opinion. He later stated, "Hooker was a worthless loafer in the Republican Army, an oaf and vagabond in civil

14. For the journalist, see http://www.civilwarhome.com/hookbio.htm (incidentally, Hooker hated the nickname). Warner, *Generals in Blue*, 234–35; Caraway, "Hooker, Joseph."

15. Allen C. Guelzo, *Abraham Lincoln: Redeemer President*, 360–61; Daniel E. Sutherland, *Fredericksburg and Chancellorsville: The Dare Mark Campaign*, 99. Quotes are from Slocum to Howland, February 4, 1863, NYHS.

life, a braggadocio and drunkard in our present army." He wrote this to Howland in October 1863, when the feud had already developed for some time, so it must be taken in the context of Chancellorsville. It is perhaps not too much to suppose that Slocum had deeper, moral qualms about Hooker before the debacle in the Wilderness. While there may have been some hope for their relationship after their talk, subsequent events only reinforced his initial opinion.[16]

Hooker knew the first order of business was to convince both the Lincoln administration and his own men that he could live up to his claims. Washington as always continued not-so-gently to demand action, but its newest commander refused to be hurried. Hooker knew he needed to rebuild the Army of the Potomac yet again, and this would take time. He instituted a series of reforms to resurrect the army's morale from the depths to which Fredericksburg and the Mud March had buried it. Desertion had reached monumental proportions. As of February 15, 1863, Hooker reported over eighty-five thousand officers and men absent without leave. To curtail this, he instituted a program of liberal furloughs and cracked down harshly on stragglers. In order both to give his men something to be proud of and to improve the ease with which they could be identified, he started a system of corps insignia. The Twelfth Corps received a five-pointed star. Over time the men grew intensely loyal to these bits of fabric. Hooker ordered the weekly ration spiced up with onions, potatoes, and soft bread, issued several times a week. He saw to it that the camps were better policed and kept sanitary. As a result the army's overall health improved, and the men began to return to camp. Drills improved efficiency, making the men act like soldiers again. Gradually, the troops began to believe that Hooker really could deliver on his promises. More important, they began believing in themselves again.[17]

Hooker also made many changes in organization. He discontinued Burnside's grand divisions and split them back into their component corps, with Slocum remaining at the helm of the Twelfth. He also made other changes that Slocum liked less. He cleaned out quite a few of the top-level generals who had served (and some might say still did) under McClellan. Three of the most notable were William F. "Baldy" Smith, Edwin "Bull" Sumner, and William B. Franklin, Slocum's former corps

16. "To Samuel L. M. Barlow, Sept 24, 1864," in Sears, *George B. McClellan*, 600–601. Quotes are from Slocum to Howland, October 22, 1863, NYHS.

17. Stephen W. Sears, *Chancellorsville*, 54–82; Edward J. Stackpole, *Chancellorsville: Lee's Greatest Battle*, 13–36; McPherson, *Ordeal by Fire*, 319; John Hennessy, "We Shall Make Richmond Howl," 1–2, 9–13.

commander. In some cases, particularly Smith's, Slocum saw the removals as simply the result of each officer's own stupidity. As he said, "I have lost my confidence in [Smith] and think the Government will be justified in removing him." On the other hand Slocum felt that Franklin would soon be cleared of any charges brought against him. Overall, he perceived a relatively clear division between the "old . . . [and] new order of things." For the moment he gave it his nodding approval.[18]

Hooker's rearrangements brought Slocum back into closer contact with the general circle of corps commanders, which his previously isolated position in the Reserve Grand Division had prevented. In the new, improved Army of the Potomac, Slocum found himself serving with a number of officers whom he respected and others he had little use for. In the former category fell First Corps commander John F. Reynolds, Second Corps commander Darius N. Couch, Fifth Corps commander George Meade, and Sixth Corps commander John Sedgwick. All these men were professional soldiers, and Slocum worked well with them, though he may have felt some irritation at Sedgwick who occupied the position Slocum thought should still belong to Franklin. The remaining commanders, Daniel E. Sickles of the Third and Oliver O. Howard of the Eleventh, probably pleased him less. Only a few months later Slocum would lump Sickles in with what he called Hooker's "gang," though he may still have been relatively well disposed toward him at this point. What Slocum thought of Howard in particular is not known, but he had previously established a reputation for disliking the Eleventh Corps in general.

Also during this time Slocum had occasion to visit the men of his old commands. Around February 1, 1863, he had to travel to general head-quarters, perhaps on his way to his meeting with Hooker. Learning that Bartlett's brigade was camped nearby, he told Howland, he stopped in to see them. He found Bartlett more than happy with the ascension of Joe Hooker, something that Slocum himself was still not sure of. While he was chatting with Bartlett, word got out into the brigade that Slocum was in camp. Led by the Twenty-seventh New York, the regiments of the brigade turned out in front of Bartlett's headquarters. When Slocum, Bartlett, and Bartlett's staff emerged, the men gave three loud cheers for their "old commander." Slocum tried to reply, but the brigade repeated the cheers several times before he could begin. He made a short speech thanking the men for

18. Summary of Principal Events, OR, vol. 25, pt. 1, 1; McPherson, Ordeal by Fire, 319; Hennessy, "We Shall Make Richmond Howl," 16. Quotes are from Slocum to Howland, February 4, 1863, NYHS.

"making me who I am" and then mounted his horse. As he rode through their lines they cheered him again, leading one admiring reporter to remark, "he is their *friend* as well as their *commander*, and that he would not needlessly sacrifice the life of the meanest soldier under him, sooner than he would his own" (emphasis in the original). A few weeks later, Slocum returned to Syracuse for ten days' leave. The papers also monitored this visit but with notably less interest and enthusiasm than before. Apparently the novelty of having a major general about town had begun to wear off.[19]

Hooker spent over a month rebuilding the army. Lincoln as always felt the campaign must get under way. He visited the camp with his family on April 5, 1863, and caught Hooker carousing at his headquarters. Hooker had not expected the president's arrival and was entertaining several women, probably recruited from his Washington-based division. Lincoln surprised Hooker so suddenly that he had to send his playmates scampering out the back, while Lincoln and his family approached from the front. The Lincolns stayed for five days, reviewing the army and consulting with Hooker and his officers. Hooker had done a thorough job; the finely tuned machine presented to the president barely resembled the demoralized mess Burnside had left behind in January. Lincoln also did what he could to light a fire under Hooker, making it clear that Lee was the target, not Richmond, and that he expected Hooker, unlike McClellan, to commit all his overwhelming numbers at once. This said, the First Family returned to Washington.[20]

Less than a week after the president's departure, Slocum wrote Clara about the visit: "I received a beautiful bouquet this morning from Mary [Todd Lincoln]. The flowers are all from the President's garden. It is beautiful. . . . I thought Mary would remember me. I take back all I have said unless she has sent one to all the other generals." The letter also reveals his romantic side, as he knew what his wife may think of another woman sending him flowers: "I do not think I was as happy over this bouquet of rare flowers from the wife of the President as I was over a single blue forget-me-not received by me while in Albany from a young country girl."[21]

Apparently Slocum had made the acquaintance of Mary Todd earlier in life, and well enough for them to be on a first-name basis. Mrs. Lincoln may have failed to speak to Slocum while the family visited the army, leading

19. Slocum to Howland, February 4, 1863, NYHS; *Journal* articles "Compliment to Maj. Gen. Slocum: A Short Speech in Response," February 6 (quotes), "Gen. Slocum at Home," February 16, "Gen. Slocum's Return," February 23, all 1863.
20. Sutherland, *Fredericksburg*, 126–27; Sears, *Chancellorsville*, 114–17.
21. Slocum to Clara, April 19, 1863, in Fox, *In Memoriam*, 74.

him to vent his frustrations to Clara. Mrs. Lincoln must have recognized Slocum during the visit but for one reason or another had failed to speak to him. After returning to Washington, she sent Slocum the bouquet as penance for ignoring him. Where they met or how this association may have benefited Slocum during the war remains open to speculation.

After the First Family left, Hooker wasted no time. The next day he put his preliminary plans onto paper and fired them off to the president. He did not outline a specific tactical plan, but he stated he would move directly against the Army of Northern Virginia. He intended to march part of his force quickly to the west, cross the river, and turn Lee's left while leaving an equally powerful force at Fredericksburg to hold him there. True to boastful form, Hooker's only fear was that Lee might get away toward Richmond before the Army of the Potomac could trap and destroy him. In order to prevent Lee's escape, Hooker ordered almost all of his cavalry away, trying to interject them between Lee and Richmond. He hoped to cut off both Lee's communications as well as his line of retreat. That Lee might just turn around and maul the Army of the Potomac does not seem to have been a real consideration. Lincoln approved the plan and did what he could to speed it along.[22]

Once Hooker got under way, Lee failed to give the Federal movements the appropriate attention. Thinking Hooker would stay on the defensive for a while longer, Lee continued to rebuild his own army. Hooker encouraged this inactivity by feeding Lee's signal officers a steady stream of misinformation. From the fake intelligence, Lee believed that George Stoneman and his cavalry were headed out to the Shenandoah Valley. This would only make sense if Hooker intended to stay where he was and therefore needed no cavalry screen or reconnaissance. It would soon turn out that Lee was both right and wrong at the same time. Hooker would indeed move in short order, but he would come to rue sending his cavalry on what would turn out to be a useless errand.[23]

This policy of miscommunication applied as much to Hooker's own corps commanders as it did to Lee. Hooker moved with such secrecy that he informed virtually no one of his plans for Stoneman. He realized that Slocum and Sickles would know about the movement from their positions in the line, but he tried to cover this up by sending them both a vague no-

22. Hooker to Lincoln, *OR*, vol. 25, pt. 2, 199–200; Michael Smith, "Chancellorsville, Battle of," in Tucker, *Encyclopedia*, 1:162–63; Stackpole, *Chancellorsville*, 92–98.
23. Sutherland, *Fredericksburg*, 129; Stackpole, *Chancellorsville*, 99–102; McPherson, *Ordeal by Fire*, 320; Smith, "Chancellorsville," 162–63.

tification that the cavalry had "gone in the direction of the Shenandoah." Hooker added that they would be "absent some days." This meant that, although they quickly figured out this was only true in the strictest sense, a majority of his corps commanders, even Sickles and Slocum, had no real idea how few cavalry Hooker had or how blind the army was. Most probably these officers would assume Hooker's intelligence was reliable.[24]

Hooker's decision accents some of the key aspects of his generalship that would greatly contribute to the eventual rebellion of his own corps commanders. In the wake of Burnside, Hooker offered the army a level of self-confidence that was as healing to its morale as it was insanely centered on Hooker. His boundless confidence in his own abilities was infectious, and it set a very high standard that he now had to attain. When he spoke of having no mercy on "Bobby" Lee, leaving the distinct impression that the battle would be so easily won he could afford to joke about it, he tied his own reputation and support intimately into his fortunes on the battlefield. If he failed to deliver on his promises, it could easily be perceived not just as another loss but as broken faith. Any loss would look much worse in such a light.[25]

Before embarking on his great flanking movement Hooker ordered Sedgwick and his Sixth Corps to stay in the immediate vicinity of Fredericksburg and occupy Lee's attention. After Hooker had flanked Lee, he wanted Sedgwick to push through Fredericksburg and press Lee's lines. In this manner Hooker could take advantage of his numbers, as the president insisted. He could come at Lee from multiple directions, and no single unit would be small enough for Lee to defeat in detail, theoretically. Even if Lee discovered Hooker's plan, he could not react with impunity. If Lee attacked Hooker's column, Sedgwick would be in his rear. If he remained at Fredericksburg, Hooker would be on his flank. If he retreated, he would run into Stoneman's throng of cavalry and have the entire army right behind him.

Hooker's advantage proved greater than even he imagined. Lee, assuming his opponent planned on dallying north of the river, had dispatched General James Longstreet with two divisions to Suffolk, Virginia, to gather much-needed supplies and deal with an anticipated thrust from Burnside, who had transferred there with the Ninth Corps. Once away, Longstreet beleaguered Lee with all sorts of schemes for how the war

---

24. Hooker quoted from Edwin Fishel, *The Secret War for the Union,* 346–47.
25. Stephen W. Sears, *Controversies and Commanders: Dispatches from the Army of the Potomac,* 137.

should be run, many of which Lee heeded. As a result Longstreet remained absent for the bulk of the upcoming battle. With him he kept an
aggregate of thirteen thousand desperately needed men, depleting Lee's
army substantially. Hooker's main thrust on Lee's flank involved some
sixty thousand men, Sedgwick's holding force comprised just less than
that number, while Stoneman would command around ten thousand in
Lee's rear. After Longstreet's departure, Lee and Jackson had to face this
lumbering behemoth with just over forty thousand men. If ever an opportunity had presented itself to crush Lee outright, this was it.[26]

Hooker ordered the Eleventh and Twelfth corps to move on April 27,
1863. He wanted them to reach Kelly's Ford on the Rappahannock and
camp as soon and as quietly as possible. Both corps had to be in place by
the next day. Hooker insisted the men be kept in camp when they arrived,
threatening to hold the corps commanders themselves responsible for any
indiscretions. Slocum got as far as Hardwood Church. He continued onward the next day and reached Kelly's Ford at four in the afternoon. Here
word came for him take command of not only the Twelfth Corps but the
Eleventh as well. He proceeded over the Rappahannock and headed toward the Rapidan River. As he did so, he fought a series of running battles with Confederate cavalry and small cadres of infantry. The advance
hardly slowed at all. As Slocum's men approached Germanna Ford on the
Rapidan, they encountered their stiffest resistance, which was still far from
significant. A small body of infantry, Slocum thought them to be about 125
in number, opened fire as he approached the crossing. Sometime earlier the
bridge over the ford had been destroyed, but local builders had assembled piles of heavy timber on the bank for repairs. Some Confederate engineers were still hard at work when the Twelfth arrived. The few troops
protecting them, mostly from a Louisiana regiment, took advantage of the
piles for ready-made breastworks, and a nearby mill served as a snipers'
nest. Slocum reacted by deploying the Second Massachusetts and Third
Wisconsin volunteers. They quickly enveloped the tiny line, taking the defenders prisoner. Slocum ordered his men to wade the current while
Federal engineers picked up on the bridge where the Confederates had
left off.[27]

26. Sutherland, *Fredericksburg,* 129; Stackpole, *Chancellorsville,* 76, 92–93; McPherson,
Ordeal by Fire, 319–20; Smith, "Chancellorsville," 162–63; Sears, *Chancellorsville,* 96–97.
27. "To Commanding Officers, Eleventh and Twelfth Corps," *OR,* vol. 25, pt. 2, 255–
56; Report of Maj. Gen. Henry Slocum, ibid., pt. 1, 669; Report of William A. Daniels,
ibid., pt. 1, 699; "An Important Command," *Journal,* May 4, 1863; "Crossing the
Rappahannock," *Journal,* May 5, 1863.

During the march Joe Hooker unleashed his infamous temper on the Twelfth. After scolding Geary for not keeping the gap between his division and the First closed up, Hooker descended on Slocum with a similar complaint. He accused him of holding up the Fifth Corps by lagging behind the Eleventh and, as Alpheus Williams said, "seemed full of dire anger, swearing heavily at somebody or something [on] which he was not very clear headed." Williams's division, the head of the Twelfth Corps column, had in fact been delayed by the rearguard of the Eleventh, and Williams sent forward for them to hurry up.[28]

At two o'clock on April 30, 1863, Slocum reached Chancellorsville, to be met by Major General George G. Meade and the Fifth Corps. Meade had crossed the river at a different ford, arriving before Slocum and his two corps. With him Meade herded more than three hundred prisoners captured by the Fifth along the way. The three corps then assumed a solid front, the Twelfth Corps in the middle, the Fifth on the left, and the Eleventh on the right. When Hooker arrived later in the evening and took over, Slocum returned to the Twelfth Corps.[29]

Events had thus far vindicated Hooker's offensive. Meade wanted an immediate advance. "This is splendid Slocum," he said when the New Yorker's column joined the Fifth Corps, "hurrah for old Joe! We are on Lee's flank and he does not know it." Whether Slocum himself thought it a good idea, he had informed the ecstatic Meade they could go nowhere. Although the plan had originally been to push forward, Slocum reportedly had received personal instructions from Hooker altering his orders just before the march. Instead of attacking, the three corps set themselves to digging entrenchments. Everyone expected to take up the offensive in the morning.[30]

The area they settled into was one of the worst possible places Hooker could have chosen. Known as the Wilderness, it was covered with a dense forest that would impede troop movements and be a positive nightmare for cannon crews. The men could not see their enemy, and in an age that still relied on visual targeting this effectively neutralized Hooker's substantial advantage in artillery. To understand the terrain, it is helpful to visualize what most people in modern America think of as regular unimproved

28. Alpheus Williams, *From the Cannon's Mouth,* 180.

29. Report of Maj. Gen. Henry Slocum, *OR,* vol. 25, pt. 1, 669; Report of Adj. Gen. William A. Daniels, ibid., 699; Report of Maj. Gen. George G. Meade, ibid., 505; Report of Brig. Gen. Alpheus S. Williams, ibid., 676; Williams, *Cannon's Mouth,* 179; "An Important Command," *Journal,* May 4, 1863.

30. Sutherland, *Fredericksburg,* 136 (Meade); Stackpole, *Chancellorsville,* 145; Fox, *In Memoriam,* 75.

woodland. Saplings, briars, and underbrush grew up thick but were far from impenetrable. It appeared abnormally dense to the soldiers by comparison. Due to fence-out laws, which protected crops, most areas in nineteenth-century America allowed livestock to range where they liked. Thousands upon thousands of cattle and hogs roamed the woods, grazing down the scrub. In places like these, troops could maneuver with relative ease and see the ground for hundreds of yards in front of them. This was not the case in the Wilderness. Although a few individuals could walk through it fairly easily, it would be difficult to maintain the huge tactical formations that had dominated the battlefield since before the days of Napoleon. The vegetation limited visibility to only a few yards. Overall, the Wilderness would be a major boon to Lee in the upcoming battle, making his job much easier.[31]

The next morning around eleven o'clock Slocum sent the Twelfth Corps forward on Hooker's orders. His men followed the Plank Road toward Fredericksburg. Hitting a few skirmishers about a mile from their original position, they formed a line of battle and began driving the Rebels before them. As they approached a series of entrenchments Slocum's troops were in high spirits. Like Meade the day before, they could feel they finally had Lee on the run. They needed only to push on to Fredericksburg and finish the war once and for all. Then another verbal order arrived from Hooker, via an orderly, directing them to fall back into the breastworks they had left just that morning. This shocked Slocum. He felt something must be wrong, the message had to be an accident. At first he flatly refused to believe the messenger: "I told the bearer of this order that I could not believe that General Hooker wished me to fall back, and I would require a written order before doing so." Hooker's decision also sent a wave of consternation and frustration through the ranks of the Twelfth Corps. They were desperate to press on. According to Williams, "the men went back disappointed, not without grumbling, and it really required some policy to satisfy them that there was not mismanagement somewhere." They reached their original positions with minimal loss, only ten casualties. Once there Slocum immediately ordered the men to get back to work on their entrenchments. They spent the remainder of Friday and all of Saturday morning so engaged.[32]

For the remainder of the battle the whole army, most corps commanders included, seemed unable to reconcile themselves to the fact that, after

31. Stackpole, *Chancellorsville*, 98–102.

32. Williams, *Cannon's Mouth*, 186–87; Report of Maj. Gen. Henry Slocum, *OR*, vol. 25, pt. 1, 670; "Gen. Slocum in the War" (quote).

all his offensive bluster, Hooker had suddenly gone on the defensive. As Edward Stackpole put it, regarding one set of orders, Hooker thought "statically" while his corps commanders thought "dynamically." Hooker had handed his opponent the initiative on a platter. Lee took it graciously, handing the plate back in short order, this time with Hooker's head on it.[33]

While the Union entrenched, Lee ordered Longstreet to return, left a screening force to watch Sedgwick in Fredericksburg, and moved to meet Hooker in the Wilderness. As he approached, his cavalry discovered an important fact. Hooker's position resembled a large horseshoe with its open end facing the fords of the Rapidan and Rappahannock Rivers. Unknown to even Hooker himself, his right lay "in the air," which meant that no geographical feature prevented it from being attacked. Oliver O. Howard who commanded the Eleventh Corps, which formed the end of the line, had not even refused his flank. With the help of some local boys serving in the Army of Northern Virginia, Lee and Jackson acted on this intelligence on May 2. In a daring move Lee stripped his already sparse lines even further, giving Jackson 33,000 men and 108 guns. Stonewall then marched his force across Hooker's front.[34]

Completely unaware of what Lee and Jackson were doing, Hooker did, however, have some inkling of the danger to Howard's flank. At half past nine in the morning on May 2, Hooker sent a communication to both Slocum and Howard that his advocates have waved ever since. It came by way of his adjutant, J. H. Van Howard: "I am directed by the major-general commanding to say that the disposition you have made of your corps has been with a view to a front attack by the enemy. If he should throw himself upon your flank, he wishes you to examine the ground and determine upon the positions you will take in that event, in order that you may be prepared for him in whatever direction he advances." Van Howard went on to say that Hooker was not pleased with the disposition of Howard's force in particular and wanted it changed. Hooker thought that Lee might try moving against the right. This did not really affect Slocum, as the Third Corps covered his right and left him with no open flank to attack. Howard felt that the brush and scrub at the end of his line grew so thick no army could pass through it and kept his position as it was.[35]

33. Stackpole, *Chancellorsville*, 175–76.

34. A commander occupying the end of a line would often bend a short section of it back to a ninety-degree angle to fend off any attacks that might come from that way. This was called "refusing" his line. Sears, *Chancellorsville*, 225–64 (esp. 64); McPherson, *Ordeal by Fire*, 320–21; Smith, "Chancellorsville," 163–64.

35. J. H. Van Howard to Howard and Slocum, *OR*, vol. 25, pt. 2, 360.

Meanwhile Jackson's flanking force drew dangerously close. His column passed so near Hooker's men it could easily be seen and heard. At Hazel Grove the road turned southward, moving away. Here some of Third Corps commander Daniel E. Sickles's men observed Jackson, apparently heading off the field. The news convinced Sickles, who occupied the line between Slocum and Howard, that Lee was in fact retreating. Geary's men also observed this movement, firing a few volleys at Jackson's men as they passed. Sickles sent a steady stream of reports to Hooker's headquarters claiming he had Lee on the run, urging that an attack get under way at once. Hooker, with no cavalry to tell him otherwise, broadcast this faulty intelligence throughout his whole army, reinforcing the idea that they would soon take up the offensive again. He let Sickles loose after his prey, also sending Slocum forward to support him.

By the time Sickles finally moved, the rear of Jackson's column was almost out of sight. Still, he collided solidly with Jackson's rearguard and began to push them heartily. Fierce fighting erupted around Catharine Furnace, which kept the overconfident Sickles busy while Jackson finished his march. The Third Corps pressed some of these men, Georgians, back into an unfinished railroad cut. Soon, Sickles's men flanked the Rebels out of this position, taking around three hundred prisoners.[36]

Geary personally led a part of his Second Division forward about five o'clock that afternoon. Hooker wanted him to get in among what he felt must be Lee's supply train, cutting it off from the main Confederate army if possible. Lee, however, did not have retreat in mind, and Geary ran straight into a well-entrenched, well-manned line of battle. Its fire wreaked havoc with his exposed artillery, which he soon sent to the rear. He continued his attack until ordered by Slocum to retire. Two of his regiments failed to fall back and received a pounding for it.[37]

Slocum's First Division, under Williams, also advanced. They moved in direct conjunction with Sickles's men, intending to sweep the Plank Road clean of enemy rifle pits. Sickles thought that by doing so they would lay bare Lee's retreat, leaving him open to a crushing blow. Yet the evils of the Wilderness soon took effect, and Williams's lines became entangled in the dense thicket. While in the process of cleaning up the mess, Williams received the order to return to his works. Slocum, a little more wary than Hooker or Sickles, was apparently still unconvinced of Lee's retreat. Instead

---

36. Sutherland, *Fredericksburg*, 151–52; McPherson, *Ordeal by Fire*, 321; Smith, "Chancellorsville," 163–64.
37. Report of John W. Geary, *OR*, vol. 25, pt. 1, 730.

of an all-out attack, he sent forward the entire First Division but only a portion of the Second in an attempt to ascertain Lee's position. When he found that the Confederates in fact had gone nowhere, he ordered his men back into their trenches.[38]

Hooker had finally taken some sort of action, but it was only a glimmer of what he could have done. Lee had stripped his already-thin position bare to give Jackson the men he needed. Hooker could have called for a general advance, a sensible action if his enemy really was in retreat. If he had, he almost certainly would have punched through the farce of a line, shattering Lee's army. It could have changed the whole demeanor of the battle and possibly even the course of the war. In the end he did much too little much too late. Hooker did call on Sedgwick to cross the Rappahannock at Fredericksburg. Just after four o'clock that afternoon, Hooker dispatched a message informing Sedgwick he had Lee in full retreat. Now, Hooker thought, the time had come to take Fredericksburg and press Lee as hard as possible. Something delayed the message, however, and Sedgwick did not receive it until after six that evening. Even if he had received it earlier, and if Hooker's orders had actually been followed, Sedgwick could have done little at that time. Hooker had ordered him to take up his pontoon bridges over fourteen hours before, an order Sedgwick had ignored.[39]

Along the Orange Plank Road, Howard's Eleventh Corps had settled in to enjoy supper after a hard day of ditch digging. Some relaxed for a few games of poker, others probably wrote letters home. Suddenly dozens of animals poured out of the woods on their right flank. Deer, turkeys, and rabbits scattered this way and that, in a frantic attempt to get away from something coming through the woods. It was an eerily accurate portrayal of what the Eleventh Corps themselves would soon be doing. Only a moment or so passed before Howard's men found themselves facing thousands of yelling Rebels charging out of the woods. The Eleventh broke and ran, some regiments not even bothering to fire a shot. Quite a few kept going until they had fled the field completely, making for the fords on the Rapidan and Rappahannock rivers, hoping to find ultimate safety.[40]

38. Report of Brig. Gen. Alpheus S. Williams, ibid., 679; Report of Maj. Gen. Henry Slocum, ibid., 670.

39. Sutherland, *Fredericksburg*, 154.

40. Ibid.

Jackson's attack threw Hooker's headquarters at the Chancellor House into chaos. Orderlies darted this way and that, carrying reports from and orders for various commanders. Stragglers from the Eleventh Corps quickly surrounded the building, which stood only half a mile away from Jackson's advance. The air filled with shouts and cries, a mixture of German and English, many bearing tall tales of complete defeat. Forcibly stirred out of his complacency Hooker scrambled to plug the hole, throwing any troops he came across into the breach. One of these was Williams's division of Slocum's Twelfth Corps, which was falling back into position at that very moment.[41]

Williams had been quietly returning to his lines when sounds of pitched battle erupted on the Union right. Hoping to stem the tide of Jackson's advance, Slocum sent for Williams and Geary to hurry. Williams knew nothing of the retreat of the Eleventh Corps and unintentionally led his men into a firestorm. Jackson had quickly driven the Eleventh and the Third corps in, taking the right of Williams's former line near the Plank Road. This gave Jackson's men an element of surprise, and they poured devastating volleys into Williams's men as they drew near. One regiment, the 128th Pennsylvania, lost its colonel, lieutenant colonel, and over 150 men when it suddenly found itself partially enveloped. Williams successfully reoccupied the left of his original position and set about stopping the stragglers. Those who rallied he armed and put into line of battle, but the sight of the Confederates proved too great a strain on the reformed line. As Jackson's men approached they left Williams where he stood and ran farther into the darkness and away from the howling gray hoard. Jackson's troops had become disorganized in their rapid advance, however, and fresh Union reinforcements arrived by the moment. In the growing darkness Jackson's assault ground to a halt.[42]

Having embarrassed himself earlier in the day by insisting Lee was in full retreat, Sickles now felt compelled to try and salvage both his career and his reputation. Not willing to wait for morning, he planned to launch a night assault to dislodge Jackson. He wanted his men to go in between ten and midnight and accordingly sent messages to the other corps commanders. Slocum's men now held the ground immediately to Sickles's left, and Sickles wanted Williams to cooperate with him in the attack. One of Sickles's staff officers found Williams, but Slocum still had not returned

41. Stackpole, *Chancellorsville*, 244–46.
42. Report of Maj. Gen. Henry Slocum, *OR*, vol. 25, pt. 1, 670; Report of Brig. Gen. Alpheus S. Williams, ibid., 679.

to corps headquarters. Williams asked that the movement be deferred until Slocum could make it back. The aide left, but soon afterward, Sickles decided against holding off and opened his attack anyway.[43]

Night battles in the Civil War were few and almost always dismal failures. Sickles's attack at Chancellorsville was no exception. Slocum himself knew nothing of the plan until he heard firing in front of Williams's division. He had been out walking his lines and apparently did not credit Sickles with enough foolishness to send his men bumbling around in the dark. Thinking Jackson had renewed the battle, Slocum ordered his artillery to open on the spot. One large group of guns contained as many as thirty-four cannon. All these converged blindly on the sound of Sickles's firing. As Slocum put it, "I have no information as to the damage suffered by our troops from our own fire, but fear that our losses must have been severe," while Williams later declared that the damage done by friendly fire was insignificant.[44]

The next day, Sunday, May 3, Rebel troops attacked again, even without their beloved Stonewall who had been mortally wounded the night before. The large battery Slocum and his artillery chief had assembled during the night fired on them as they approached. Most of the line held, but one division of Sickles's corps fell back, losing a battery and causing confusion as they raced back into Williams's line. The Confederates soon moved against the flank and rear of Geary's division, attacking his artillery with dreadful results. By eight o'clock Slocum and Williams informed Hooker that Williams's men had nearly run out of ammunition and needed assistance. Hooker gruffly replied Williams must furnish his own. Fortunately, as this was impossible, Hooker sent forward some of Sickles's men as relief. Eventually, with Sickles's line faltering and a great slaughter commencing as the Confederates pushed their infantry against the artillery, Slocum withdrew his troops. He took up a position along the extreme left of the Union line, where his men began fortifying with a vengeance. Even though he still had the power to fight Lee, Hooker simply curled up and waited for help to come.[45]

43. Williams, *Cannon's Mouth*, 194; Reports of Maj. Gen. Daniel E. Sickles, *OR*, vol. 25, pt. 1, 389–91.

44. Report of Maj. Gen. Henry Slocum, Report of Brig. Gen. Alpheus S. Williams, *OR*, vol. 25, pt. 1, 670, 679.

45. Jackson had fallen to the fire of his own men the night before while riding his lines. Slocum considered this loss tantamount to Lee losing an entire corps. He believed Jackson would have succeeded where Ewell and Longstreet failed on Culp's Hill at Gettysburg. "Gen. Slocum in the War"; Williams, *Cannon's Mouth*, 198; Report of Maj. Gen. Henry Slocum, *OR*, vol. 25, pt. 1, 671; Stackpole, *Chancellorsville*, 302.

In Fredericksburg Sedgwick had crossed the Rappahannock in order to press Lee's "retreat." He sent his men in to take Jubal Early's position on Marye's Heights by direct assault, as Burnside had done the previous December, and this time it worked. Early evacuated his force, placing it between Sedgwick and Lee. When Lee heard of Early's retreat from Fredericksburg, he made an even more daring move. For the third and final time in the campaign, Lee split his forces. Leaving an insignificant force to watch the cowering Hooker, he marched the remainder of his army toward Fredericksburg and pounced on Sedgwick at Salem Church, between Fredericksburg and Chancellorsville. Over the next two days Lee boxed Sedgwick up against the Rappahannock, taking a large number of prisoners. Sedgwick finally managed to pull his corps back over the river intact on May 5. With that threat taken care of, Lee turned back to face "Fighting Joe."[46]

All this time Hooker had waited patiently for Sedgwick to reach the field and save him. Instead he found Lee marching from Fredericksburg, ready to attack him again. Hooker had already held a council of war on the night of May 4, the only time he consulted his generals in the entire campaign. Slocum, with the farthest to ride, did not arrive until the meeting had already broken up, but the result was clear. Whatever his officers might say, Hooker would retreat. Lee attacked Hooker's position all day on May 6, but Hooker had already begun his withdrawal. On Tuesday night, the Twelfth Corps recrossed the Rapidan and on Wednesday made its way back to its former camps. The brilliant campaign of Fighting Joe Hooker ended in failure, made all the more humiliating and inexplicable by its very promising start.[47]

The battle had devastated Slocum's corps. The Twelfth still had only two small divisions, and both divisions suffered about equally. Slocum counted 158 officers and 2,725 enlisted men killed, wounded, or missing for a total of 2,883 casualties. As Slocum noted in his report, this represented roughly 30 percent of his entire command. Like the rest of the army, he was depressed after defeat, even ill. He harbored no doubts whatsoever as to who was responsible for it all. As he put it to Howland: "It was a sad failure, a bitter disappointment to us all. Our movements up to the arrival

46. Sutherland, *Fredericksburg*, 165–77; McPherson, *Ordeal by Fire*, 321–22; Smith, "Chancellorsville," 164.

47. Sutherland, *Fredericksburg*, 165–77; McPherson, *Ordeal by Fire*, 321–22; Smith, "Chancellorsville," 164; Stackpole, *Chancellorsville*, 344–53. Slocum's Gettysburg report contains a backhanded reference to this when he explicitly praises Meade for supporting his units and not allowing troops to sit idly by while others are attacked.

at Chancellorsville were very successful & were unflawed. Everything after that went wrong, and fighting Joe sunk into a poor driveling cur. The fact is whisky, boasting, and vilification have been his stock and trade. Sickles and Butterfield are his boon companions, and everything is conducted as might be expected with such leaders."[48]

Hooker and Slocum's personalities clearly clashed, especially when Slocum still saw all commanders in shades of McClellan. Hooker had been treading on Slocum's sensibilities since at least before the battle, as evidenced by the cursing he received on the road to Chancellorsville. More to the point, Slocum felt that Hooker abandoned the Twelfth Corps, exposing it to the brutal mauling it received. When pressed for help during the ordeal of Williams's division, Hooker had curtly rebuffed them, then only grudgingly sent troops but after the need was past. In short, Slocum not only thought Hooker had failed to meet McClellan's standard, he held Hooker personally responsible for the loss of so many men in the Twelfth Corps.[49]

From this point on Slocum was Hooker's enemy. It is ironic that, after complaining about other commanders speaking against their superiors, Slocum now added a portion of Hooker's own persona to what he had already absorbed from McClellan. Slocum became openly critical and started maneuvering to oust Hooker from command. As Slocum wrote to Howland, "Hooker knows my hatred of himself and all his gang. I have not even attempted to disguise my disgust." Slocum seems to have been a mirror for some of the worst aspects of his commanding general.[50]

In keeping with the tradition of politicking in the Army of the Potomac for which Hooker himself was renowned, Slocum, Darius Couch, and other corps commanders set plans in motion to get rid of "Fighting Joe." Sears notes that for ten months prior to Chancellorsville, there had been a general revolutionary state of affairs in the high command of the army. The participating generals varied from time to time, as did the object of their discontent, but politicking as a method of problem solving was by this time a well-established trend, one that seemed to have no end. Hooker's spectacular failure, coming on the heels of so many specific and grandiose promises, left his corps commanders the impression that he had also betrayed them. His secrecy—particularly his attempts to mislead his

48. Report of Maj. Gen. Henry Slocum, *OR*, vol. 25, pt. 1, 672–74; Slocum to Howland, May 29, 1863, NYHS.
49. Charles Slocum, *Life and Services*, 84.
50. Slocum to Howland, May 29, 1863, NYHS.

own corps commanders—added to the view that he was untrustworthy and deceitful at worst, weak and cowardly at best.[51]

Slocum was clearly one of the major forces behind this new revolt, and it was his idea to secure the support of the other corps commanders against Hooker. He planned to approach Lincoln himself with the signed petition when the president visited the army. No doubt it took some degree of cynicism on Slocum's part to ignore the hypocrisy of the situation, given his previous views that this sort of subterfuge should be avoided. Their choice for successor, Meade, was junior to all the other corps commanders, but each of them sent him word of being willing to serve under him. The one snag in the plan was Meade himself. Although he implied he would vote to remove Hooker if it came to it, he would not allow his name to be used by the cabal. This being the case, Sears states that Slocum remained silent and allowed the president's visit to pass uneventfully.[52]

Other officers in Hooker's army apparently did manage a word or two with Lincoln. Lincoln and Hooker held a meeting on the evening of May 13, but Lincoln said nothing to him at the time about the growing discontent over Chancellorsville. The next day, however, Lincoln wrote Hooker he had "some painful intimations that some of your corps and Division Commanders are not giving you their entire confidence. This would be ruinous, if true; and you should therefore, first of all, ascertain the real facts beyond all possibility of doubt."[53]

Slocum proved a bit slower than some others but was still doggedly determined to be heard. Although he missed an opportunity in camp, he created another when he contacted Secretary of State William Seward who, on May 19, informed Lincoln via telegraph that Slocum wished to consult with him. The actual meeting in Washington took place sometime before May 23. During the meeting Slocum told the president the "whole story," probably dwelling on his critique of Hooker as a "driveling cur." In a later letter to Seward, Slocum reminded him that, at this encounter, he "implored [the president] for the sake of the Army and the Country, that [Hooker] should be relieved from the command of that Army." He had stated to Howland, "I have no faith whatever in Hooker's ability as a military man, in his integrity, or honor. Nearly all his officers feel towards him as I do and several have already left the army. Others will do so. I am strongly tempted to do it."

51. Sears, *Controversies*, 133–35, and esp. 158–59.

52. George Gordon Meade, *The Life and Letters of George Gordon Meade*, 373; Sears, *Chancellorsville*, 435, and *Controversies*, 158–63.

53. Hooker to Lincoln, May 13, 1863 (Telegram concerning a meeting with Lincoln), Lincoln to Hooker, May 14, 1863 (Army of the Potomac; quote), Lincoln Papers.

Slocum did not report to anyone what Lincoln said in reply, but obviously Slocum found it sufficient to keep him from resigning. Although Lincoln had not yet decided to replace Hooker, he certainly would not like to lose a veteran corps commander over an issue that might be solved in short order. It also may be that Slocum's acquaintance with Mary Todd influenced Lincoln. Lincoln did not tell Slocum that Hooker would be replaced, as Slocum was still wrestling with the idea of serving under him when he wrote his letter to Howland on May 29. Lincoln probably acknowledged Slocum's complaint but stopped short of committing to anything.[54]

Despite all that had happened Slocum still believed in the Union cause. It was the prosecution of the war that bothered him. "I believe . . . that in the end we shall be successful," he said, once again echoing the voice of McClellan. "It cannot be otherwise, but how dearly we are paying for our folly, for the folly of our administration." At the time of Chancellorsville, Slocum was still a Republican. Yet, for the past two years he had dealt with an ever-increasing number of ignorant politicians and generals. Every one of these men (except McClellan, who was a Democrat), whether meddlers from Congress or failures like Burnside and Hooker, came to the field as arms of Republican policy. It was also a Republican administration that had removed McClellan, whom Slocum still thought the best-fitted for command. He resented what looked like a boatload of fools guiding the ship of state through the tumultuous waters of rebellion. This may have lessened his attachment to his party, but he was not about to switch to another at this time. He wanted the war prosecuted vigorously, and for all their failures the Republicans supported this seriously. The Democrats on the other hand were overrun with Copperheads.[55]

If Slocum had indeed wanted to ponder his party affiliation, he had little time to do so. The army kept him busy in the months after Chancellorsville, and he desperately needed to build the Twelfth Corps back up. On May 14, 1863, he called his officers and men together at Falmouth, Virginia, to address their latest defeat at Lee's hands. Slocum thanked them for their bravery and dedication. He mentioned that the recent accounts of the battle had not done justice to the Twelfth's part in it. He assured them the truth would come out in time. A reporter called his remarks "quite lengthy" but also noted that they ended with deafening cheers for both himself and Williams.

---

54. Seward to Lincoln, May 19, 1863 (Meeting with General Slocum), Lincoln Papers; Slocum to Howland, May 29, 1863, NYHS; Slocum to Seward, November 14, 1863 (Does not want to serve under Hooker), Lincoln Papers; David Donald, *Lincoln*, 440.

55. Slocum to Seward, November 14, 1863 (Does not want to serve under Hooker), Lincoln Papers.

In the rush of the upcoming campaign, Slocum also found the time to respond in writing to a committee from Binghamton. The Twenty-seventh New York would be mustered out before the end of the month, and he apologized for not being present.[56]

By June 1863 Slocum had demonstrated that his emphasis on hard-core drilling and discipline worked on every level from regiment to corps. He had taken the Twelfth Corps and completed their transformation into a solid, if small, fighting force. More important, he had proved himself willing to use it. His casualty figures demonstrate that a reputation as an overly cautious commander would clearly be undeserved. Slocum did worry almost incessantly, but this did not stop him from fighting when the need arose. His McClellan-like frustrations and concerns unfortunately seemed to mount as his corps took appalling losses in its first battle. The Twelfth also became a temporary plateau at which his meteoric rise to fame came to a sudden halt. All that was left was army command, and Slocum had shown no inclination of ascending to that level (which at this point would probably have only resulted in incompetence). Contrary to later charges, he had not actively sought command when the opportunity presented itself. Instead he specifically agreed to serve under Meade.

Slocum had also chosen for himself someone on his own side he could hate as thoroughly as he might any Confederate. Even though Hooker later seemed willing to let his rivalry with Slocum go, at least temporarily, Slocum would continue to despise Hooker with such a passion it would actually get in the way of his ability to fight the war. In fact Slocum seemed to be acting more like the supposed Joe Hooker than Hooker himself. It is this aspect of Slocum's personality that is both fascinating and also necessarily elusive. Hooker would be the last powerful personality to leave his mark on Slocum for the next year, as Slocum would soon be shuffled from commander to commander, none of whom he stayed under long enough to make much of a difference. As Chancellorsville led into Gettysburg, Slocum found himself at the helm of a diminishing command and quickly became unhappy with both the Republicans and Joe Hooker. His command decisions at Gettysburg, often overlooked by subsequent historians, would prove themselves as necessary to Union victory as they were unspectacular, and at times questionable. He made good decisions, though not the best or the flashiest.

56. *Journal* articles "Maj. Gen. Henry W. Slocum," May 14 (quote), "Letter from Gen. Slocum," May 28, 1863.

CHAPTER 5

"Stay and fight it out"
McClellan at Gettysburg by Proxy

At Gettysburg, Slocum seemed to hover constantly on the periphery of famous events, just missing the fame that would be gained by other generals. His corps would see heavy action—but never in the right places or at the right times to gain much attention. This, and the fact that historians have known so little about him for so long, means that his decisions on those three days have at times not been judged fairly or accurately. Also, in the absence of a fuller picture of Slocum, many historians remember him for what would later turn out to be the last prominent gasp of his inherited paranoia and over-cautiousness. This results in a caricature of Slocum, indignant, vacillating, and terrified of the responsibility he could have exercised. In many ways Slocum became the stereotype of McClellan himself. Historians, familiar with this Slocum at Gettysburg, then read the same man into other places and times. As A. Wilson Greene noted, Slocum had never acted this way before and never would again, but his performance here stands as a mark against him.[1]

Upon deeper consideration we can see that, in spite of his McClellan-esque proclivities, in the Gettysburg Campaign Slocum made good choices based on the information he had available to him. It is true he could have made better decisions, even based on the little he knew at the time, but as the cliché goes, "hindsight is always twenty-twenty." This said, we should

1. Greene, "A Step All-Important," 101.

also be cautious not to exaggerate. His performance might have been solid but it was unspectacular.

After consolidating and resupplying his army, Lee decided the time had come for another invasion of the North. With his brilliant victories at Fredericksburg and Chancellorsville behind him, Lee hoped winning a major battle on Northern soil would convince its people the war could never be won. If so, then victory through negotiation—or at least survival—would be a real possibility. The Army of Northern Virginia moved westward into the Shenandoah in June 1863. From there Lee planned to move past Harpers Ferry, across the Potomac into Maryland, and into Pennsylvania's fertile Cumberland Valley. He wanted all this to take place long before anyone had an inkling his army was on the move.[2]

Meanwhile, Joe Hooker remained commander of the Army of the Potomac. He needed to know where Lee was and what he planned for the upcoming summer. In order to find out, Hooker sent his horsemen south of the Rappahannock to gather intelligence and to head off what he thought was a large cavalry raid. As Lee started to move quickly west to the sheltering walls of the Shenandoah, Lee fully expected his own excellent cavalry would screen the movement from prying Yankee eyes. The Southerners had ridden circles around their inept Northern counterparts earlier in the war. Yet, as time had progressed, Northern cavalry had grown steadily better, which an overconfident J. E. B. Stuart, Lee's cavalry commander, discovered for himself when they attacked him at Brandy Station. There, while the rest of Lee's men marched west, Hooker's cavalry hit Stuart so hard they forced him to call up infantry for support. Stuart's failure showed that Lee was moving, and in what direction he was headed. Fighting Joe and the Army of the Potomac scrambled to catch up with Lee, though Hooker still had no real plans in mind.[3]

During Hooker's pursuit Slocum took up the difficult question of dealing with deserters. Several corps commanders, including Slocum, met sometime before June 20, 1863, to discuss how to bring the problem under control. They hoped to deal with the bounty-jumping problem in particular. A bounty jumper was a man who enlisted in a regiment, took the thousand-dollar signing bonus offered by the government, then deserted, to reenlist under a new name in a different city, collecting the money again. Some men deserted several times, and the practice had a devastating effect

2. Brian Melton, "Gettysburg, Battle of," in Tucker, *Encyclopedia*, 2:347.
3. Ibid.

on morale when more honest soldiers began to encounter the same individual offenders over and again, each time in a different regiment. Slocum's approach was both simple and brutally effective: shoot convicted bounty jumpers. Slocum had in fact tried to do so before, but much to his annoyance, Lincoln often intervened with a pardon before the order could be carried out. Feeling that the tender-hearted president was unintentionally hurting the army, Slocum and some of the other commanders determined finally to go through with some executions before Lincoln could intervene.[4]

Shortly after the meeting, a court-martial found several men of Slocum's command guilty of bounty jumping. As the Twelfth Corps approached Leesburg, Virginia, Slocum acted quickly, knowing it would not be long before the signal corps established telegraph communications with Washington. At nine o'clock in the morning his men rolled out and dug graves. At ten minutes to twelve, the convicted men knelt at the edge of the holes. Slocum noted that his men were betting five to one the executions would not be carried out. The betting men lost their money when at noon sharp Slocum gave the order to fire. Sure enough, when the operators set up the telegraph, Lincoln wired for the men to be spared if his message was not already too late.[5]

While Lee marched and Slocum dealt with deserters, Hooker tried to set another plan in motion. He had previously attempted several other halting responses to Lee's march, but none had yet come to fruition. This time Hooker hoped to use Lee's plan of campaign against him and to trap him north of the Potomac. He ordered Slocum to move the Twelfth Corps to Williamsport, Maryland, where Lee had crossed the Potomac only a few days before. He asked Halleck that Slocum be given command of the ten thousand remaining troops at Harpers Ferry. This force paired with the Twelfth Corps would bring Slocum's command to nearly twenty thousand strong. Isolated and planted firmly in Lee's line of communication and supply, Slocum was thus to become the bait for Lee. Hooker assumed the Army of Northern Virginia would turn on Slocum as it had on Hooker himself at Chancellorsville. Slocum would have enough men to hold Lee off for a short time, giving Hooker the chance to assemble his army. After this, Hooker could sweep in with overwhelming force and destroy the weakened Lee.[6]

4. "Gen. Slocum's Recollections," *Syracuse Courier,* April 2, 1879; Slocum to Butterfield, *OR,* vol. 27, pt. 3, 223.

5. "Gen. Slocum's Recollections," *Syracuse Courier,* April 2, 1879; Lincoln to Slocum, June 25, 1863, in Abraham Lincoln, *The Collected Works of Abraham Lincoln,* 6:295. Slocum's dispatch to Butterfield says the execution took place at one o'clock.

6. Coddington, *Gettysburg Campaign,* 128–33; Fox, *In Memoriam,* 76.

The fact that Hooker chose Slocum to occupy such a key position demonstrates an interesting dynamic in the relationship between them. Slocum hated Hooker, and it was common knowledge he was engaged actively in trying to remove Hooker from command. Slocum knew that Hooker understood what was happening, and he apparently feared retribution of some sort. It is notable then that Hooker still trusted Slocum with such a key position. Lincoln's secretary John Hay wrote later that year that "Hooker does not speak unkindly of Slocum while he [Slocum] never mentions Hooker but to attack him," noting that Lincoln thought he could rely on "Hooker's magnanimity" in situations like this.[7] Why Hooker chose Slocum in particular is less obvious. It certainly was not out of convenience or sheer practicality. Slocum's corps, the smallest in the army, was one of the farthest away from Williamsport. Perhaps Hooker placed Slocum in command of his daring movement because he honestly felt Slocum best suited for the job, or perhaps Hooker simply made the decision based on seniority. In any event Hooker obviously remained willing to work with Slocum, if only Slocum could contain his righteous indignation.

Whether the plan would have worked is another matter. Lee, who was raiding and not likely to put much stock in a line of supply he did not depend on, might not have acted as Hooker expected. In order to find out Hooker had to put his plans into action, and to get at the troops in Harpers Ferry he had to have Halleck's approval. Unfortunately for Hooker, Halleck's approval proved an insurmountable obstacle. Hooker, even after all this time, failed to appreciate the value of diplomatic manners when dealing with anyone other than Lincoln himself. He phrased his "request" to Halleck as a demand: Halleck had to release the troops at Harpers Ferry or Hooker would resign. Having his own long-standing feud with Hooker, Halleck refused to bow to the pressure. Offended, Hooker asked to be relieved of command, abandoning the movement to Williamsport. As Lee pushed deeper into Union territory, Lincoln quickly honored Hooker's request—as it turned out, only two days before the Battle of Gettysburg. No doubt this surprised Hooker, who probably thought that, given the circumstances, he could be more demanding than usual. In Hooker's place the president appointed the man Slocum's cabal had originally asked for: George G. Meade.[8]

7. Carl Sandburg, *Abraham Lincoln: The War Years*, 2:428.

8. Coddington, *Gettysburg Campaign*, 128–33; Fox, *In Memoriam*, 76; Summary of Principal Events, *OR*, vol. 27, pt. 1, 4.

Meade had been born on the last day of 1815, in Cadiz, Spain, where his father lost most of his money supporting Spain in the Napoleonic Wars. Most of his brothers and sisters returned to the United States and married well, but Meade chose West Point. He graduated in 1835, ranking nineteenth out of a class of fifty-six. After a short stint in the army, he tried civilian engineering but gave it up and after less than ten years went back into the service. With brief asides in Mexico, Meade spent the years from his reenlistment until the Civil War working with the Army Corps of Engineers. In 1861 he received an appointment from the governor of Pennsylvania as a brigadier general of volunteers, commanding a newly formed brigade. He led his men through the Peninsula Campaign and was severely wounded at Glendale. After recovering, he commanded them again at Second Bull Run, South Mountain, and Antietam. He took charge of a division for the Battle of Fredericksburg, and a few days after the battle he succeeded to command of the Fifth Corps. After the infamous campaign of Fighting Joe, Meade suddenly found himself in command of the entire army.[9]

Meade had no time to get accustomed to command. He put his army in motion immediately. Even if he had little opportunity to put together an overall strategy, common sense (not to mention Lincoln and Halleck) told him he must keep between Lee and Washington. Meanwhile Lee had spread his army out and was moving fast. At one point Lee had elements strung across three states, with the most advanced units actually in Carlisle, Pennsylvania, threatening the state capital at Harrisburg. Such long thin lines put Lee in a vulnerable position. If Meade could concentrate and attack before Lee had a chance to round up his scattered forces, he might end the war in the East by destroying the Army of Northern Virginia.[10]

His first and foremost difficulty would be to gain control of the far-flung Army of the Potomac. The army had recovered surprisingly quickly from Hooker's embarrassing loss at Chancellorsville, and it was still a powerful—if somewhat cynical—force. Its seven corps were led by men of varying ability. John Reynolds of the First Corps, for instance, was a first-rate soldier who could well have occupied Meade's own position as army commander, whereas Daniel Sickles, commander of the Third Corps, had distinguished himself thus far for being a somewhat inept

9. Freeman Cleeves, *Meade of Gettysburg*, 3–126; Warner, *Generals in Blue*, 315–16; Mark Calandra, "Meade, George Gordon," in Tucker, *Encyclopedia*, 2:553–54.

10. For the next stretch, along with specific references, I am indebted to McPherson, *Ordeal by Fire*, 324–26; Melton, "Gettysburg, Battle of," 348.

political general and the first man to be acquitted of murder by reason of temporary insanity. Oliver O. Howard, smarting from Chancellorsville, still led the Eleventh Corps but remained on the low end of the learning curve as a corps commander. He was learning from his mistakes and was improving, though. Slocum's performance was average when compared with the extremes. His corps was the smallest in the army and had suffered heavily at Chancellorsville.

Lee remained ignorant of his peril, as the bulk of his cavalry had recently embarked on a wide, wheeling raid around the Northern army. Unlike Hooker's use of cavalry before Chancellorsville, this had not been part of Lee's plan. Stung by his near defeat at Brandy Station, Stuart decided to make up for embarrassment with daring, and he had taken advantage of Lee's very generously worded orders. Unfortunately for Stuart, the Union cavalry kept pace with him, and he would not reach Lee until late in the second day of the upcoming battle. The first indication of trouble reached Lee through a spy, Henry T. Harrison, who was later made famous by his prominent role in the Pulitzer Prize–winning book *The Killer Angels*. Once impressed with the full danger of his position, Lee recalled his scattered forces to Cashtown, Pennsylvania, east of Gettysburg and not far north from the Maryland border. Lee knew that if Meade attacked in force before the Army of Northern Virginia could be concentrated, the results could be disastrous.

Meade acted with cautious deliberation as he moved the Army of the Potomac from Frederick, Maryland, toward Lee. He wanted to ensure an excellent chance of success before he brought on a general battle with the increasingly legendary General Lee. Hearing that Lee had abandoned his attempt to take Harrisburg, Meade did not order an immediate concentration for an attack, knowing that any defeat north of the Mason-Dixon Line, even a minor one, could have a ruinous effect on Union morale and therefore on the overall war effort. On the evening of June 30, 1863, after receiving various scouting reports, he issued what came to be called the Pipe Creek Circular.[11]

Meade wanted to find out more of what Lee had in mind before taking any decisive action, and the circular reflected this. He left Reynolds's First Corps, Howard's Eleventh, and Buford's cavalry in an advanced position near Gettysburg. The rest of the army hung back a short distance. Meade, like Lee, also issued orders for his men to avoid a general engagement. If

11. Pipe Creek Circular, *OR*, vol. 27, pt. 3, 458–59.

Lee acted aggressively, Meade wanted his army to retire to a prepared defensive line along Pipe Clay Creek. Thus, Meade kept his options open without committing himself to a specific course of action. If an opportunity to strike presented itself, Meade had an entire corps under his most competent commander, Reynolds, close enough to act. Reynolds had at his disposal over twenty-one thousand troops, with another nine thousand in the form of Slocum's Twelfth Corps nearby. Otherwise, the Army of the Potomac could easily fall back to an excellent prepared position, where Meade hoped Lee might exhaust himself attacking them. If the circular went into effect, Reynolds would assume command of the left wing and Slocum the right. Slocum therefore would have received responsibility for the Fifth Corps, situated at Hanover. The circular did not arrive at Slocum's headquarters until near midnight on June 30, so he had practically no time to communicate with the Fifth's commander, George Sykes, before the chaos of Gettysburg's first day.[12]

The next morning Henry Heth's division of Lee's army made its way toward Gettysburg, looking for anything but a fight. According to some stories, the footsore soldiers just wanted to get their hands on a large number of shoes that rumor had placed there. Instead, they found John Buford's cavalry ready to receive them. Buford had not received a copy of the Pipe Creek Circular, so he took a more aggressive stance than Meade intended. Buford had posted his men on a road northwest of town, determined to resist any Confederate advance until help could arrive. From Heth's perspective, this normally would have posed no real problem. Infantry could nearly always put cavalry to flight very quickly, and once Heth's entire division reached the field, he would outnumber Buford substantially. Heth thought he would easily be able to brush the Federals aside and get to his prize, thereby staying true to Lee's orders of not bringing on a general engagement. When Buford's men surprised him and held fast, a frustrated Heth kept escalating the fight.

As the attack began that morning, Reynolds and Howard still had miles to go before they could reach the field. Buford's stubbornness bought Reynolds, in particular, the time he needed to get there. Just when it appeared that Buford's men would give way, Heth ran headlong into the Iron Brigade of the First Corps. The battle quickly outgrew either side's ability to control it. When Reynolds fell, not long after reaching the field, Howard took overall command. A. P. Hill soon arrived with more Confederate reinforcements. By midday the Federals had fought brilliantly and managed

12. Coddington, *Gettysburg Campaign*, 237–41.

to blunt Heth's push from the west. The battle slowed down into an uneasy calm around noon. The lull would not last more than a few hours, however. Richard Ewell, commanding Jackson's old corps, approached from the north, arriving on Howard's flank. Though not at all pleased that Heth had engaged against his wishes, Lee ordered his army to converge on Gettysburg when the battle began to go his way. Howard's men could not hope to hold out against such superior numbers. The Federal lines began to break, and Howard retreated through town. The Army of the Potomac eventually settled onto a line of hills south of Gettysburg called Cemetery Ridge.[13]

While the battle opened to the northwest of Gettysburg, Slocum and the Twelfth Corps set out on their appointed march for the day. They did not have far to go, so they did not hurry. The fight had fallen into its mid-day lull by the time they arrived at Two Taverns and settled down for a rest. This tiny settlement lay about five miles southeast of Gettysburg in a fertile valley surrounded by fields. Hills to the northwest blocked any view Slocum might otherwise have had of the action on the far side. Although Howard had been heavily engaged at Gettysburg, exactly how much Slocum knew of this is still open to question. It is clear he did not move immediately to the sound of the guns, which is odd. Though not a notoriously aggressive commander like Sickles, Slocum had never shirked his combat responsibility before, so to delay at all was certainly out of character for him. As strange as it may seem, however, Slocum apparently could not hear what was happening close by and so did not immediately know about the battle. He stated that "On the march and while at Two Taverns, some firing was heard, but the sounds did not indicate a great battle." His division commanders heard very little of it also, only muffled booms that many wrote off as a cavalry scuffle.[14]

Other eyewitness accounts serve only to confuse matters further. John Hill of the 107th New York said that, after they had begun the morning's march, "heavy cannonading was soon heard in the front." A soldier of the Third Wisconsin claimed that, though they could hear some skirmishing, he could not tell whether it was an important battle. Charles F. Morse of the Second Massachusetts reported hearing a "heavy and continuous firing" but did not note any delay in marching. Slocum historian George Fox explained this strange silence as the result of a phenomenon called an

13. Pfanz, *Gettysburg,* 31–70.

14. Henry Slocum, Letter to T. H. Davis and Co., publishers of Bates, *Battle of Gettysburg* (quote); Pfanz, *Gettysburg,* 92; Greene, "A Step All-Important," 95.

acoustic shadow, in which geographic features such as hills and ridges deflect sound over or away from a potential observer. This most probably afflicted Joseph E. Johnston at the Battle of Seven Pines and Don Carlos Buell at Perryville. The terrain between Two Taverns and Gettysburg makes this a possibility.[15]

In all likelihood Slocum's failure to hear a major battle at Gettysburg resulted from a number of factors. First, the Twelfth Corps arrived at Two Taverns around noon. They probably did not hear much because there was not much to hear at that time. The battle had slacked off considerably since about eleven o'clock. What little cannonading and firing could be heard would have sounded like a smaller skirmish. Given the time of day, Slocum probably availed himself of lunch inside somewhere, and being indoors meant he would have heard even less. Any acoustic effects would have made it virtually impossible to know what was going on at Gettysburg. In any case it would not be the last curious thing to happen with Slocum on what would turn out to be a peculiarly unimpressive day.[16]

As the situation deteriorated, Howard sent Slocum several messages asking him to push the Twelfth Corps forward and take command. With Reynolds down and Meade too far away, Slocum would have been the most senior man nearby. The first message left via courier around one o'clock and doubtless reached Slocum not long after two. It stated simply: "The general commanding directs me to inform you that Ewell's corps is advancing from York. The left wing of the Army of the Potomac is engaged with A. P. Hill's corps." Slocum apparently took no action.[17]

At three o'clock Howard sent Captain Daniel Hall to locate Slocum again and find out if the Twelfth Corps was on its way. Hall delivered Howard's message and briefed Slocum on the situation, but he found Slocum's response somewhat lacking. Although Hall did not explain himself, he stated, "[Slocum's] conduct on that occasion was anything but honorable, soldierly, or patriotic." Slocum finally got his men moving by half past three that afternoon. Not long after Hall delivered his message, a dispatch arrived from Meade, in which Meade noted Reynolds's death and appointed Winfield Scott Hancock to take his place. This could be the first time Slocum learned of Reynolds's demise, but he probably had

15. John Hill, July 5, 1863, folder NY-107, GNMP; Hinkley Letter, folder 6-W3–3rd Wisconsin, GNMP; Charles F. Morse, "History of the Second Massachusetts Regiment of Infantry," 6; Fox, *In Memoriam*, 77n; Greene, "A Step All-Important," 96.

16. Fox, *In Memoriam*, 175n.

17. Meysenburg (for Howard) to Slocum, Sickles to Howard, both at *OR*, vol. 27, pt. 3, 463. Reynolds may have known nothing of the Pipe Creek Circular.

heard of it already from Hall. A third message from Howard reached him while en route.[18]

According to Slocum, he had no real indication of how big the fight had become before a civilian came down the pike about one o'clock. Some officers casually asked the man what news he had. The man replied, "a great battle was being fought on the hills beyond Gettysburgh." Slocum's officers sent him word, and he dispatched Major Eugene Guindon to ride ahead and discover the truth. He probably wanted to make sure the man had not overstated the case; even a small fight can look like a "great battle" to a civilian with no military experience. Guindon returned in a few hours with news that a large engagement was indeed raging only a short distance away. Slocum got the corps moving immediately. As he later said, "I was not summoned by Gen. Howard or any other person, but marched of my own volition, the instant I knew help was needed."[19]

From the bare facts of the matter, it is easy to see how historians could question both Slocum's performance and his motives. While the Eleventh and First corps fought for their lives a mere five miles away, Slocum spent the morning on a leisurely stroll and in the fields around Two Taverns with his men relaxing. Even if it is granted that he could not hear the battle (something most people found hard to believe), he ignored one note from Howard and then gave what Hall called a dishonorable, unpatriotic response to another. Reynolds had been killed, and yet Slocum did not rush forward to take command. Slocum then makes a claim that looks like little more than a bold-faced lie. How—knowing that Howard sent him the messages, knowing that it was proved he had received them—could he still claim to have "marched of my own volition"? A cursory examination would seem to leave historians with two mutually exclusive propositions: If Slocum is telling the truth, everyone else must be lying, or vice versa. A closer look shows that reality split the horns of this dilemma.

The main, but not only, reason Slocum's hesitation looks so bad here is because it is seen in the shadow of the now infallible martyr Reynolds as represented in the Gettysburg Paradigm. Reynolds and Howard unwittingly disobeyed a direct order from Meade, but because the battle was Gettysburg, if the error is even mentioned at all they are not held accountable for it. In fact Reynolds, in particular, actually garnered a good deal of post mortem praise for his part in accidentally subverting Meade's

18. Hall quoted in Pfanz, *Gettysburg*, 94.
19. Slocum, Letter to T. H. Davis and Co., 7–8.

circular. Since everyone knows that Gettysburg was the war's most famous battle, the logic seems to run, how could anyone have dared delay?

Unlike Reynolds and Howard, however, Slocum had received the Pipe
Creek Circular. He had also received extra instructions from Meade that
reiterated the commanding general's strong desire to fall back on that line
rather than bring on a major engagement. Through Butterfield, Meade
stated:

> You will also be prepared to commence the movement indicated in the in-
> closed [sic] circular upon receipt of intelligence from General Reynolds that
> he has uncovered Two Taverns. You will, if in good position for the pur-
> poses of the circular inclosed, halt your command where this order reaches
> you, and, in communicating to General Sykes, halt his advance in a similar
> manner, and give him the instructions necessary for a proper compliance
> with the circular order inclosed in case intimations from General Reynolds
> render it necessary.[20]

From Meade's wording it is clear he expected this to be the course of action Reynolds would take. It was not a question of if Reynolds might decide to uncover Slocum's position; rather Slocum must be ready for when
it happened. Slocum, therefore, would judge everything that took place
that morning by the retreat outlined in Meade's circular and would prepare Sykes and the Fifth Corps to do the same.

All the criticisms of Slocum's performance, both on the first day and
later, are contained in Samuel P. Bates's history of the battle. Historians
since that time, knowingly or otherwise, have simply parroted the essence
of Bates's attacks:

> Marched a short distance; passed Two Taverns; formed in line of battle; hear-
> ing firing in front; a report that the 1st and 11th corps are engaged with the
> enemy. The roar of battle was constantly resounding. But here the corps re-
> mained all day. . . .
>
> But why so tardy in his movements? It is of little moment at what hour
> Howard summoned him—if he summoned him at all. The guns of the
> enemy had been resounding all day long. . . .
>
> Both Slocum and Sickles were morally culpable for not going to the as-
> sistance of the forces engaged at Gettysburgh on the first day; Slocum hav-
> ing full warrant for doing so in the orders and circular of General Meade.[21]

20. Butterfield to Slocum, *OR*, vol. 27, pt. 3, 462.
21. Bates, *Battle of Gettysburg*, 93, 185–86.

Slocum himself believed that "If there was any semblance of truth in the[se] statement[s], I should consider Mr. Bates treatment of the subject, by far too generous."[22]

Slocum's time at Two Taverns needs putting in perspective. Although Bates and others imply that the Twelfth Corps puttered about their camp all day, the actual time in question is much shorter. The Twelfth arrived at Two Taverns around noon and got moving again before half past three that afternoon. In the worst-case scenario, Slocum could not have stayed in place for more than a few hours. The rest of the day he spent marching, first to Two Taverns and then to Gettysburg itself. In any case, it is a far cry from wasting an entire day.

While Slocum may have appreciated Bates's restrained treatment, others are not so generous with the subject. One of these is Greene, in "A Step All-Important and Essential to Victory," who portrays Slocum as a waffler, deathly afraid to take responsibility for the fight, calling up every excuse imaginable to keep his troops and therefore himself away from the field. Greene confesses to be somewhat confounded by Slocum's behavior, since nothing in Slocum's life before or after seemed to explain it. Greene also states that the Twelfth's relative anonymity at Gettysburg has led to a general neglect that has prevented more round condemnations of Slocum's performance. This may be true, but it is also true that lack of attention has led to the dichotomy of Slocum being either a coward or a hero at Gettysburg, with no middle ground. With the exception of Harry Pfanz, there are not many nuanced perspectives.[23]

What historians see in Slocum at Gettysburg is not so much a failure of nerve (though it could be described as such) but, rather, the triumphant moment of his McClellanism. Slocum, with his tendency to absorb the philosophies of his powerful superiors, displayed conduct on day one and two of Gettysburg that looks like McClellan in microcosm. He was absorbed with maneuver, over-cautious, focused on retreat, and scrupulously concerned with orders and the chain of command (sometimes conveniently so). Like McClellan on the Peninsula, he found excuses that kept him away from the fight, and therefore the responsibility. Like McClellan during the Seven Days, he overestimated the size of his enemy and was prepared not to act, but to retreat (in Slocum's defense this is what Meade had ordered him to do). And like McClellan at Antietam, he moved too slowly to make a difference.

22. Slocum, Letter to T. H. Davis and Co., 2.
23. Greene, "A Step All-Important," 87–135; Pfanz, *Gettysburg*.

Acting as Howard and Reynolds had—which proved justifiable under the circumstances—was not really something Slocum was prepared to do at this point in the war, and the fact that he hesitated should not be surprising. It probably seemed to Slocum that Reynolds and Howard were actively disobeying orders, and when it finally became clear (if it ever really did) what Howard wanted, they now asked Slocum to knowingly do the same. From a McClellanesque perspective, this would make little sense.

Slocum also did not want to take command, and this probably demonstrates the fact that, for some generals, experience in the Army of the Potomac resulted in more political acumen than tactical ability. As he told Lt. Col. Charles H. Morgan of Hancock's staff, Slocum had no interest in stepping into a position "which might make him responsible for a condition of affairs over which he had no control." Pfanz implies that this is simply common sense, though it was irresponsible given the circumstances. If he was not in control, he should have ridden forward and taken it forcibly. Slocum had no apparent intention of becoming the scapegoat for a lost, politically important fight someone else started against standing orders. Like McClellan he knew well what that could mean in such an atmosphere, and like McClellan, he instinctively used whatever semi-legitimate excuse he could to get out of it.[24]

It is important to note that none of this points to inherent cowardice or willful negligence. Slocum found himself acting from learned behavior, which he had previously absorbed and other commanders had positively encouraged as the way to run an army. While it is indeed true that he should have known and done better, it is also easy to understand how he could have conceived of his own actions as being more than cowardice and how historians can see them as far less than stellar. Due to his early war experiences, he simply was the wrong man in the wrong place at the wrong time, and he acted accordingly.

The most difficult issue for historians, as well as for Slocum himself, is how to deal with the question of Howard's messages. An acoustic shadow at least has a precedent, and there is some evidence to suggest it may have happened in this case. Yet if Slocum received Howard's messages, which he did, the case for cowardice and particular conniving is strengthened notably. The first message clearly made its way into Slocum's hands before he got his corps moving. The second one, at three o'clock, probably arrived as he prepared to move, and the final one reached him as he was on the way to Gettysburg. So the latter two are not too important, but taken

24. Pfanz, *Gettysburg*, 97.

as a whole, they seem to leave two mutually exclusive propositions (mentioned before), and the result is invariable: Slocum must have lied.

Reconstructing the events of the day from Slocum's perspective dramatically clears up the issue, however. Events during the early part of the morning are not in question. Slocum received Meade's Pipe Creek Circular—along with extra, more explicit, instructions from Butterfield—around midnight the night before. With only a short distance to march, Slocum allowed his men to sleep in and then make their way easily to Two Taverns. The army had been engaged in a great deal of hard marching recently, and Slocum would have jumped at the chance to give his men some extra rest when the opportunity presented itself. They arrived around noon, and Slocum ordered the corps into the fields to take their lunch, warning them to remain alert and ready to march. The battle up ahead slowed down considerably around eleven o'clock, before Slocum reached his destination. By the time his men dispersed into camp, the lull was a full hour old and would last for a few more. Aside from the muffling effect of the hills between Two Taverns and Gettysburg, Slocum therefore did not hear a large battle for the simple reason that no one was fighting one. By the time the battle started up again, around two o'clock that afternoon, Slocum had received other reports concerning it. Under the circumstances listening for sounds of battle could profit Slocum little or nothing.[25]

Around one o'clock the civilian came down the pike with information on the fighting. It would have taken a short time for the report to reach Slocum himself, but when it did, he dispatched Guindon to determine its veracity. Guindon had around six miles to cover to top the hills and get a clear view of what was going on. Given that a good horse could ride that distance one way in about an hour, this meant the trip probably took him no less than about two, possibly more.

Sometime after two in the afternoon, Howard's first message arrived. This one, the only one of the three in question to be reproduced in the *Official Records,* is simple: "The general commanding directs me to inform you that Ewell's corps is advancing from York. The left wing of the Army of the Potomac is engaged with A. P. Hill's corps." It is important to note that Howard did not mention Reynolds's death, and he did not ask for any assistance, though in retrospect we can see this is undoubtedly what he intended. Slocum, who by now had probably seen the first of the Eleventh Corps stragglers, interpreted the short dispatch in light of the Pipe Creek Circular (with McClellan's influence). Howard and Reynolds

25. Slocum, Letter to T. H. Davis and Co.

should fall back, probably on Slocum's position, rather than bring on a full-fledged battle. So Slocum moved nowhere. Sickles and the Third Corps had also taken a little time to sort things out but had started marching. Sickles had proved himself a notoriously aggressive commander, however, not overly concerned with orders or military sense, as the second day at Gettysburg would further demonstrate.[26]

Guindon probably returned with his report sometime between half past two and three in the afternoon. He told Slocum what he had seen, confirming the citizen's report, and probably pointed out that Howard showed no signs of the withdrawal expected by Slocum. Finally realizing the desperateness of the situation, Slocum gave the order to move around three, which is evident from the fact that Slocum's corps was on the move by half past three (to allow thirty minutes for the execution of the order is only reasonable).

Assuming Slocum made the decision to move before the other dispatches reached him, it is notable that he told the truth about marching on his own. Howard did not call him to the field, at least not in the message of one o'clock. If Slocum thought that Howard would fall back toward Pipe Creek as ordered, then the first, short, message alone would not necessarily be enough to stir him to action. The left wing could have joined at least three other corps before Lee's pincers closed. When it became apparent that Howard had no such intentions, and given he now had Guindon's report, Slocum decided to move on his own, before the second, more explicit, message reached him.

Howard sent this second message around three, so Slocum probably received it as his corps got seriously under way. Given Slocum's emphasis on the propriety of retreat, following orders, and his bias against the Eleventh Corps, he would have been upset with Howard for acting as he did. Slocum could be openly and loudly critical, as Hooker had learned. The news had put Slocum in a foul, uncomfortable mood, and he probably let Hall know exactly what he thought of their actions. If Slocum had criticized Reynolds's and Howard's conduct, this might explain what Captain Hall referred to when he called Slocum's behavior unpatriotic. Howard later acknowledged that Slocum's main problem rested in the perceived disregard for orders.[27]

Slocum himself laid a heavy emphasis on standing orders in his letter on the subject to T. H. Davis, the publisher of Bates's history of Gettysburg.

26. Howard to Slocum and Sickles, Sickles to Howard, both at *OR*, vol. 27, pt. 2, 463.
27. Pfanz, *Gettysburg*, 98.

His fury can also explain why he did not want command. The army once again seemed headed for defeat, in Slocum's mind, mainly because its commanders would not obey orders. Now, it seemed, Howard and Hancock wanted to give the command away as soon as possible and thereby avoid the brunt of the blame. Even if their intentions were wholly pure, from all appearances they asked Slocum to jump on as captain just in time to go down with the ship. As Pfanz points out, any normal person would have objected to this, and a McClellanized general without a doubt would have objected. No matter how noble a beast the general may have been, common sense dictates that the proposition should give him pause.[28]

In the end all that historians are left with, barring new information, is reasoned speculation. Slocum steadfastly maintained that he answered no calls from Howard. The convenient approach would be to accuse him of cowardice, but the evidence simply does not support it. Howard, who had the strongest complaint against him, said just that: "I think he did wrong to delay, and was hardly justified under the circumstances, even by the written orders of General Meade; still in all his previous history and subsequent lengthy service by my side in the West and South he showed himself a patriot in spirit, a brave man, and an able commander." Slocum dallied, much to the astonishment of those who served with him. Howard's brother wrote bitterly a week later that Slocum had earned his name: "slow come."[29]

No matter what his reasons, Slocum missed an opportunity to play an important role in the most famous battle ever fought on this continent. Acoustic shadows and conflicting orders kept him away from the fighting when other corps desperately needed him. Instead of covering himself with glory on that day, the best he can hope for is to be quietly excused. What makes matters worse is that the Battle of Gettysburg has provided some of the most detailed information about Slocum (as far as it goes). So students of the war, especially those who see Gettysburg as its totality, have since judged all of Slocum's actions, both before and after, with one ear turned toward the far side of Culp's Hill. His mediocre performance there on July 1, 1863, would become the lens through which his entire career was viewed.

Sometime during the afternoon, most likely in his second message, Howard apprised Slocum of the situation on the field. Slocum replied that he would bring the Twelfth Corps up about a mile to the right of

28. Ibid., 97; Slocum, Letter to T. H. Davis and Co.
29. Pfanz, *Gettysburg,* 97.

Gettysburg. This seems an odd decision at best, plain foolishness at worst. If he had marched straight up the Baltimore Pike, he would have reached the field earlier. Yet Slocum chose this approach because, as other historians have pointed out, his most recent intelligence placed the left wing still on the far side of Gettysburg, with Early bearing down on them from the north. In this case it made more sense for Slocum to move to its right and extend the Northern flank. Finally Slocum arrived and took command on the evening of July 1. About seven o'clock, an insulted Howard received a belated order from Meade giving command of the left wing to Hancock. Crestfallen, Howard relinquished his charge to Hancock, who in turn gave it to Slocum when he arrived. Slocum paused a moment to inform Meade of the situation. He notified him that he had amended his earlier order and placed Williams's division on the right, with Geary's on the far left. He said things had not gone well, but that he hoped their work was done for the day.[30]

Meade arrived early in the morning of July 2, 1863, and shifted the Twelfth Corps around briefly as he solidified his lines, finally posting it to a position on a ridge just east-southeast of the north end of Cemetery Hill, known as Culp's Hill. The Union army now occupied a long position that stretched along Seminary Ridge up to Cemetery Hill, where it bent backward, running through a few low spots and onto Culp's Hill. Thus the Twelfth formed the barbed end of what became known as "the fish hook." As soon as they came to rest, Slocum's men got to work yet again building entrenchments. It is notable that they built the only substantial breastworks at Gettysburg, a feature of Slocum's generalship that seems quite peculiar when compared with other Eastern corps commanders. This quirk of his would prove especially important during the next day and night.[31]

The morning and afternoon passed relatively quietly for Slocum, with the exception of a contemplated spoiling attack on Lee. Meade issued orders for the attack, which he thought would come from the corps on Culp's and Cemetery hills, and placed Slocum in command of the right wing to carry it out. This caused a necessary reshuffling of the Twelfth Corps's command structure. With Slocum temporarily promoted, Alpheus Williams took command of the Twelfth. In the First Division, Thomas Ruger stood in for Williams. The adjustments did not directly affect Geary's Second

30. Slocum to Howard or Hancock, Meade to Howard or Doubleday, Slocum to Meade, all at *OR*, vol. 27, pt. 2, 462–63.

31. Report of Maj. Gen. Henry W. Slocum, ibid., pt. 1, 759.

Division. Later Meade canceled the attack but failed to explicitly rescind the entire order, expecting Slocum to return to command of the Twelfth Corps by default. He did not. Instead Slocum assumed that only the attack had been canceled and that he still commanded the right wing. Ironically, he continued to act like it throughout the rest of the battle. This left Slocum in an interesting position, a sort of command limbo. Williams actively commanded the Twelfth (though he took Slocum's orders), while Slocum did not try to exercise his authority over other corps. So, oddly enough, the confusion meant that Meade had a phantom wing commander he knew nothing about, while Slocum commanded a wing that did not exist.[32]

The relative quiet enjoyed by the Twelfth came to a deadly halt when an artillery bombardment from Confederate major Joseph Latimer's cannon rained down on their heads in the afternoon. Union artillery replied, with various widespread guns converging on Latimer's exposed position. Although Latimer's guns did some damage, Federal artillery proved more effective, and eventually Latimer himself fell mortally wounded. The effectiveness of the guns probably points in part to Slocum's original training as an artillery officer. He took care that his lines were always well supported with more than enough guns and ammunition. Latimer's successor withdrew the remaining Confederate pieces around half past six that evening. Skirmishers also traded sniper fire on a regular basis, but in comparison to the left flank of the army, Slocum's men had it easy.[33]

While Slocum had been resting and then dealing with Latimer, Lee resumed his offensive, this time against Meade's left. He ordered his "Old War Horse" James Longstreet to lead a flanking movement to the south. Due to mismanagement of orders Longstreet and his men ended up marching and countermarching in a vain attempt to remain concealed, and as a result, the morning attack took place in the afternoon. As Longstreet advanced, much to his shock and dismay, he stumbled over Union troops where there should have been none. Earlier that day, Sickles, whose Third Corps occupied a low portion of Cemetery Ridge and was the left flank of the army, had asked if he could move his men into an advanced position. It seemed to him the ground in front of him was infinitely superior to what he then occupied; it was higher and had a good field of fire. Meade, knowing that Sickles held the extreme left of the line, denied his request. So Sickles did it anyway. In doing so he isolated his

---

32. Union Correspondence, ibid., pt. 3, 486–87.
33. Greene, "A Step All-Important," 112–13.

corps from the rest of the army and exposed its flank. There was no time to order them back before Longstreet's assault hit them.[34]

Vicious fighting raged all afternoon on the southern end of the line. While the Union managed to take and hold the all-important Little Round Top, they also faced a daunting challenge in the area known as the Wheat Field, where the battle swayed back and forth as both sides brought in reinforcements. Finally, late in the day, Longstreet committed Lafayette McLaws's division, which he had previously kept out of the fray. Sickles's line wavered, then broke, and the Third Corps began a hasty retreat back into Meade's main line. Longstreet's exhausted men followed as fast as they could. Unless Meade acted quickly, Lee might well win the dramatic victory he sought.

Meade wasted no time. He had noticed the relative quiet in Slocum's sector and ordered Slocum to reinforce the left wing. The dispatch itself no longer exists, but Slocum obviously interpreted it as a request for his entire corps. He discussed the matter with Williams in his assumed role as commander of the Twelfth Corps. Both of them expected Meade to amend the order when made aware of the situation on Culp's Hill. They had Edward Johnson's large Confederate division facing them, and they did not outnumber the Rebels by much. Weakening the right wing's defenses would invite disaster. If the Twelfth lost its fortified line, Lee would have a strong position on high ground, within easy striking distance of assets Meade could not afford to lose.[35]

Slocum ordered Williams to get the First Division moving immediately, while the Second, under Geary, remained in place. Slocum appealed to Meade through his adjutant, Hiram C. Rogers, who found Meade and explained the situation, but Meade insisted the real danger was on the left. Meade would allow Slocum the option of retaining a single brigade, if he felt it necessary. Slocum accepted this without further argument and ordered Brigadier General George S. Greene to hold all of the Twelfth's earthworks with his single brigade by stretching its lines thin. The rest of Geary's troops he sent after Williams. Johnson now enjoyed a better than two-to-one advantage over Greene.[36]

34. McPherson, *Ordeal by Fire*, 328–30; Melton, "Gettysburg, Battle of," 347–49.

35. Coddington, *Gettysburg Campaign*, 433–34; Pfanz, *Gettysburg*, 284; Report of Maj. Gen. Henry W. Slocum, *OR*, vol. 27, pt. 1, 760.

36. Pfanz, *Gettysburg*, 194–96; Bruce Catton, *Gettysburg: The Final Fury*, 45; Fox, *In Memoriam*, 62.

Meade never discussed the questionable dispatch in any detail after the battle. Some of Meade's proponents have argued that the order could not have asked for an entire corps and that the decision to send so many must have been Slocum's. Meade's son, for instance, stated it called for only a division, thereby shifting to Slocum some of the blame for what would happen next. After the war, however, Slocum insisted that Meade ordered him to send the entire corps. Howard, Williams, and Abner Doubleday also contradict Meade's defenders and sustain Slocum.[37]

It is evident from context that the order asked for more than a division. If it had not, why would Slocum have complained to Meade at all? He had already sent a division at the same time he dispatched Rogers. Had this really been all that Meade wanted, the order would have been fulfilled without the need for an appeal. It is unlikely that Meade could have misunderstood this, as Rogers had to tell him what Slocum had done. If Slocum had misunderstood and Meade had wanted only a single division, then he could easily have made that clear to Rogers. Geary would not have needed to move anywhere. Rogers's appeal gave Meade every opportunity to correct any confusion or to rein in a suddenly and inexplicably overzealous Slocum.[38]

Several historians have argued that Slocum should have refused to follow this order or at least should have modified it significantly. It was indeed a foolish move. Both Slocum and Williams remarked on it at the time. Bates, Pfanz, and Greene all agree that Slocum should have done something to correct such a serious oversight. If Meade's orders had spared Slocum any initiative, he could have repaired the error. Sears makes Slocum appear culpable by quickly passing over Slocum's appeal to Meade and blaming Slocum alone for the decision to move the whole corps.[39]

Yet Slocum did indeed try to correct the order. He, Howard, and Doubleday all mention his attempts to sway Meade. This is also implied by the fact that the Second Division delayed their departure by an hour after the First. Slocum left Geary in place until Rogers had found Meade and returned with his decision. Had Slocum himself desired to send all of the Twelfth, or even most of it, nothing would have stopped him from

37. Meade, *Life and Letters*, 2:87; Slocum, Letter to T. H. Davis and Co.; Abner Doubleday, *Chancellorsville and Gettysburg*; Coddington, *Gettysburg Campaign*, 433; Pfanz, *Gettysburg*, 195; Fox, *In Memoriam*, 62.

38. It is more likely that Meade and Rogers thought Slocum exaggerated the danger and did not take his pleas seriously. See Pfanz, *Gettysburg*, 439 n. 8.

39. Slocum, Letter to T. H. Davis and Co.; Pfanz, *Gettysburg*, 195; Greene, "A Step All-Important," 88–90; Sears, *Gettysburg*, 312.

doing so without delay. Slocum's appeal also demonstrates that Meade left him no initiative, despite what some historians have alleged. Slocum tried to amend the order, Meade insisted. He clearly gave Slocum no choice in the matter.[40]

It comes down to an issue of military principle. Should a soldier refuse to follow an explicit order from a superior officer if he thinks that order will endanger the army? Slocum would say he should obey. After the war he argued that the "first duty of a subordinate is to obey the orders of his superior; and this is particularly true when an army is engaged," and that he could "hardly conceive of any excuse that would justify" any denials. He had done all he ethically could by making Meade aware of the facts and by suggesting he reconsider. History has borne out this principle, as the destructive antics of the Confederate Army of Tennessee's high command demonstrate. In reality Meade's decision could have cost him the entire battle. Paired with Slocum's poor performance on the first day, however, it cost Slocum much of his historical reputation.[41]

Williams led the Twelfth's First Division and an independent brigade of Pennsylvania men, that of Henry Lockwood, in repulsing the very last of Longstreet's assault. In the end they probably were not really needed. The Confederates, exhausted from an entire day of marching and fighting, had already lost their momentum. Geary's division, on the other hand, managed to take a wrong turn. Instead of heading toward the fighting, Geary marched away from it. His path led him into the rear of the army, back down the Baltimore Pike in the direction of Two Taverns. Williams later said

40. Slocum, Letter to T. H. Davis and Co.; Doubleday, *Chancellorsville and Gettysburg,* 180. Ruger reports leaving Culp's Hill at six o'clock, while Geary notes they left at seven. Reports of Thomas H. Ruger, John W. Geary, Brig. Gen. Alpheus S. Williams, *OR,* vol. 27, pt. 1, 778, 826, 774. Sears's argument in this case is fallacious. He points out that Williams recorded he received an order to "detach all [he] could spare, at least one division," and from this statement Sears infers the order must have reflected Meade's language. In doing so Sears overlooks the fact that any orders Meade sent would have passed through Slocum first and would no doubt reflect Slocum's own attempt to modify them while he appealed to Meade. In fact, in his official report on the battle, Williams states explicitly that the orders to move came directly from Slocum, not Meade. It is therefore highly probable that Williams's wording reflects the conversation he and Slocum had on the subject, not the verbatim text of Meade's message, which would have been delivered to Slocum personally.

41. Slocum, Letter to T. H. Davis and Co. (quotes). Only historians and armchair generals (both with the benefit of hindsight) have the luxury of speculating when an order can be "responsibly" disobeyed. Most corps commanders would understand they must balance their own initiative with the knowledge that they are not in possession of the full facts of the whole battlefield.

that Geary blamed the mistake on bad directions from some stragglers they met on the way, but there is no excuse for how Geary handled the situation. Once he and his officers finally realized that they had no idea where they were, instead of turning around or sending out staff officers to find the way back, Geary actually ordered his division to encamp. After Longstreet's repulse, half of Slocum's corps seemed to have disappeared into thin air. Despite desperate searches no one found Geary for hours. When someone finally did, Slocum ordered them back into position immediately.[42]

Back on Culp's Hill Slocum's and Williams's worst fears were realized when the single brigade remaining in position came under heavy assault from Johnson's division. Lee had intended this attack to serve as a diversion for Longstreet's, but Johnson had been delayed. Now, due to Meade's error, Johnson had a chance to accomplish what Longstreet had failed to achieve.[43]

George S. Greene, the commander of Slocum's lone remaining brigade, was one of the oldest field officers in the Union army. Born on May 6, 1801, he graduated second in his class at West Point and then pursued a career as an engineer, both inside and outside the army. He reentered the military in 1862 as a colonel in the Washington defenses until his promotion to brigadier general. Prior to Gettysburg he had served at Cedar Mountain, Antietam, and Chancellorsville. Greene had not had time to extend his line throughout all of the Twelfth's breastworks before Johnson struck. If he had, his lines would probably have been pulled so thin Johnson could have broken them. Instead Greene found that he and his men now shared their hill with the Confederates, who had simply walked into the empty trenches. Knowing he could not hold the entire position against the numbers Johnson had sent, Greene withdrew into the northern section of his works and refused his flank. The Twelfth's entrenchments gave Greene his most important advantage but also magnified the potential effects of Meade's mistake. Greene had a chance to hold out until dark against a vastly superior force, but if he failed, Johnson would be more difficult to drive off.[44]

42. Pfanz, *Gettysburg*, 194–204; Coddington, *Gettysburg Campaign*, 418–20, 433; Report of Maj. Gen. Henry W. Slocum, *OR*, vol. 27, pt. 1, 760. The fact it took so long to find Geary addresses the dynamics of a very odd situation. The most likely reason they could not find Geary was that he had marched to where he was least likely to be. A search for a general whose bravery no one questioned would not begin directly in the rear of the army nowhere near where he had been ordered to go. The advancing night also quickly transformed everything to a mess of dust, smoke, campfires, and shouting, making already similar bodies of men even harder to distinguish.

43. Pfanz, *Gettysburg*, 205; Catton, *Final Fury*, 45; Fox, *In Memoriam*, 62–63.

44. Warner, *Generals in Blue*, 187; Pfanz, *Gettysburg*, 211; Coddington, *Gettysburg Campaign*, 430–32; Fox, *In Memoriam*, 62–63; Catton, *Final Fury*, 45.

A rendition in oil of Johnson's attacks on Culp's Hill at Gettysburg. Library of Congress, Prints & Photographs Division, Civil War Photographs

Once Greene settled in for the fight, he called on what meager reinforcements he could from the nearby First and Eleventh corps and then refused to budge. Wave after wave of Confederates broke against Greene's stubborn defenses, but to no avail. Soon the darkness that frustrated the search for Geary also brought an end to the fighting. Greene remained unmoved, but Johnson still held in force the fortifications south of him. Returning from the repulse of Longstreet, an infuriated Williams heard about what had happened. Both he and Slocum had expected Meade to order Geary to remain, so the Second Division's absence came as a shock. Williams could not think where Geary had gone. By midnight, however, the entire Twelfth Corps had been relocated and set back in place around Culp's Hill, frustrating any easy attempt by Johnson to exploit the foothold he had gained. When Williams informed Slocum of the exact nature of the situation after the council of war that night, Slocum replied, "Well, drive them out at daylight." Williams, Ruger, and Geary immediately began preparations in earnest for the coming of first light.[45]

At the close of the fighting on the second day, Meade called his commanders together to discuss whether he should stay or retreat closer to his supply lines. All of them expressed similar sentiments that Meade should

---

45. Pfanz, *Gettysburg*, 234 (quote); Report of Maj. Gen. Henry W. Slocum, *OR*, vol. 27, pt. 1, 760.

stay, but Slocum's reply became the most famous: "Stay and fight it out." As Pfanz notes, "This epigram was one of the finest of the war; it represented Slocum at his best." These are certainly not the words of a coward not wanting to risk his men in a fight. At the time of the council Slocum knew all that had occurred on Culp's Hill. Had he wanted to retreat and thereby avoid battle and responsibility, he had every opportunity to advise Meade to pull back. Whatever later historians may make of his motivations on the first day, it is clear Slocum was still a fighter, and perhaps this meeting marks the beginning of a change in his military fortunes.[46]

This change also demonstrates another interesting aspect of Slocum at Gettysburg, which would denote the zenith of McClellan's influence. There would still be times in the next year when Slocum would act following the example of his former leader, but the reformation had begun. Slocum would soon be divorced from the familiar, comfortable environment of the East that fostered his worship of McClellan. He would find himself thrust into the rough, hard-nosed atmosphere of the West. The resulting change, presaged in Slocum's advice to Meade on the night of July 2, 1863, would result in a more effective Slocum, one that his friends from the early days would hardly be able to recognize.

For the moment, though, Slocum left the tactical planning for the upcoming fight to Williams, Geary, and Ruger. Mostly the brainchild of Williams, the plan was that Geary would attack after the Federal artillery had softened the Confederates. Geary occupied a position on Culp's Hill to the right of Greene's steadfast brigade. Ruger and the First Division remained off to the right, hovering on Johnson's flank. From there Williams hoped they could exploit some weakness while at the same time preventing Johnson from moving around them. Everyone knew well that the brunt of the fighting would fall on Geary. At half past four the next morning, the roar of Slocum's cannons startled Howard awake over on nearby Cemetery Hill. After the bombardment slowed but before Williams could give the order to attack, Johnson launched his own assault. Lee hoped this would serve as another diversion in favor of Longstreet, but this time Johnson was early whereas Longstreet was late. Overnight Johnson and his corps commander, Richard Ewell, had roughly doubled the number of men holding Slocum's old lines, in preparation for the attack, even sending in the famous Stonewall Brigade.[47]

---

46. Reports of Maj. Gen. George G. Meade, *OR*, vol. 27, pt. 1, 73; Pfanz, *Gettysburg*, 200.

47. Pfanz, *Gettysburg*, 284–85; Coddington, *Gettysburg Campaign*, 465–76.

The Confederates raced straight up the side of the hill, aiming for the same positions they had tried to take the night before. Geary had planned for this, weakening his right flank somewhat by shifting troops to the left. The first attempt broke against Greene's prickly front. Johnson reformed his lines and launched a second attack at the same positions. This, too, met with failure. Finally, probably at Ewell's suggestion, Johnson gave it one last supreme effort. This time he pulled several brigades out of line, sending them to his left to extend the attack. Once again they could not penetrate Geary's lines. Finally, around half past ten that morning, Johnson withdrew his spent command as Slocum's men pressed forward. Long before Pickett's Charge was even ready, Ewell had attacked and failed. The Twelfth Corps finally possessed its entire line once again. The fighting at Culp's Hill had been vicious. The Twelfth had received 1,082 casualties. Although only 204 men actually died, for the moment Slocum had lost roughly 10 percent of the Twelfth's effective force. After the 30 percent losses taken at Chancellorsville but a few months before, Slocum could count himself lucky he still had a corps to command.[48]

Shedding reality for a moment, what was really at stake that evening on Culp's Hill? Historians cannot reasonably expect Slocum to have disobeyed a direct order from the commanding general. What if he had simply forwarded the entire Twelfth Corps on, as Meade clearly wanted? In all likelihood Johnson's blow would have fallen on thin air. His troops would have occupied all of Culp's Hill with little or no resistance. As Pfanz notes, Culp's Hill was one of several keys to the Union position on Cemetery Ridge. Coddington agrees, calling the fight there an "overlooked or underrated" one that could win a "rich prize." With an entire division occupying the only substantial works on the field, Lee might have reconsidered his options. Johnson's division would be situated in the rear of the Union army, within easy striking distance of Meade's main line of supply and retreat. Even if the Union troops posted behind a nearby stone wall had been able to rebuff attempts to take the pike, Lee would probably have been able to roll up Meade's entire line on Cemetery Ridge. Instead of repulsing Pickett's Charge, Meade would have been forced to withdraw in a tactical defeat before this could happen. Such a turn of events would have been disastrous for Union morale, even if probably not fatal. Slocum himself remarked on this after the war.[49]

48. Pfanz, *Gettysburg*, 310–52; Coddington, *Gettysburg Campaign*, 465–92.

49. Pfanz, *Gettysburg*, 25; Coddington, *Gettysburg Campaign*, 465–66; Henry Slocum, "Gen. Slocum's Recollections," *Syracuse Courier*, April 2, 1879.

Why, then, do so many normally careful historians attack Slocum for such an effective disaster-averting performance? Primarily, in light of his performance on the first day, negative assumptions are easy to make. But there is another important reason, and it is found in the use, or rather misuse, some historians have made of a eulogy to Slocum made by Howard. In 1894 Howard delivered a speech concerning Slocum's wartime exploits, at the famous Plymouth Church, in Brooklyn, New York, where he called the fighting at Culp's Hill the "most impressive incident of the great battle of Gettysburg" and "a step all-important and essential to victory." He even went so far as to claim that Slocum "prevented Meade from losing the Battle of Gettysburg."[50]

As we have noted so often before, published information on Slocum is a relative rarity in the world of Civil War history. Whereas other generals, even his subordinates, often have any number of recent biographies in print, Slocum's are out of print, limited in utility, and predate the First World War. With nothing else easily available many authors use Howard's eulogy, particularly after an edited version appeared in *Civil War Times Illustrated* in 1982.[51]

Was Slocum as important to the outcome of the battle as Howard seemed to think? Of course not. Were historians to call up Howard's shade, he would be quick to point out that the speech he gave in that Brooklyn church was a memorial delivered to grieving family, not professional history. What Howard was getting at was not so much that Slocum changed the course of the battle but, rather, that he prevented it from changing. In the sense that Slocum's decision and appeal moderated Meade's decision, it was an important step toward ultimate Union victory. Howard should be excused if, given the circumstances, he embellished the tale. Some historians cannot be let off so easily, however. By treating Howard's eulogy as something it made no claims to be, they set an unreasonably high standard for Slocum's performance, and in so doing, they predestine Slocum to failure.[52]

Although Slocum would have access to a wealth of battlefield intelligence, after Meade moved into the right wing's headquarters to escape Confederate shelling, most of Slocum's men saw little of the rest of the

50. Howard, "Memory of Henry Slocum," 40.
51. For example, see Fox, *In Memoriam;* Charles Slocum, *Life and Services;* Howard, "Memory of Henry Slocum." Greene, "A Step All-Important," provides an example of one historical account that uses Howard to frame an entire discussion.
52. Howard, "Memory of Henry Slocum," 39, and Greene, "A Step All-Important," 88–89.

battle. When Pickett thrust for the heart of the Union army later that day, Meade called for Slocum's First Division only. Williams moved them posthaste, but they only stood by, watching Hancock's men repulse Pickett without their help. Slocum later noted that no one on Culp's Hill, officer or enlisted man, could see anything of the attack.[53]

The Army of Northern Virginia stayed in place an entire drizzly day before retreating. Lincoln rode Meade, pressing for him to follow up on his success, but Meade gave chase at a slow careful pace that almost made McClellan look fast. Lee, though harassed by cavalry, managed to stay ahead of his pursuers, finally reaching his crossing point at Williamsport in safety. Once there he discovered his pontoon bridges had been destroyed, leaving him with no way to cross the river. Yet Meade moved so deliberately that Lee had time to construct makeshift bridges and slip across the Potomac before he was caught.

Not long after the end of the engagement at Culp's Hill, Slocum's men undertook the morbid task of dealing with Confederate dead on the field. They had buried over nine hundred when their marching orders reached them and they departed, leaving a large number of corpses to the tender mercies of animals, the elements, or the desperate ministrations of the citizens of Gettysburg. On July 5, 1863, the Twelfth Corps moved to Littlestown, in the opposite direction of Lee's retreat. Slocum and his men remained there until ordered to move on at four o'clock on the morning of July 7, when they turned south, now parallel to Lee. They marched through Frederick, Maryland, on July 8, camping on the far side of town. Next day they passed through Crampton's Gap at South Mountain, site of Slocum's earlier victory in the Antietam Campaign. Slocum arrived in Williamsport on July 12, where Meade had Lee bottled up against the Potomac. Slocum rode ahead of his men to attend Meade's council of war that night. The rest of the Twelfth Corps did not arrive at the town until the next day. According to Slocum, Meade had already made up his mind not to attack. Before polling his commanders, Meade emphasized the fact that he had been unable to find out much about Lee's position. He then asked if they wanted to attack anyway, without any further intelligence gathering. Hearing the matter phrased that way, Slocum said, he and the other corps commanders refused to attack. Meade then said that, in general, they should do something and then retired for the night. While

---

53. Catton, *Final Fury,* 76; Henry Slocum, "Gettysburg, Thirty Years After," *North American Review,* 140.

Meade and his generals debated, Lee slipped back across the river. The Gettysburg Campaign had ended.[54]

How did Slocum feel about the campaign? In his official report he focused more on their victory than anything else. McClellan's influence peeked out just once when he noted "every one felt convinced that we were greatly [Lee's] inferior in point of numbers." He praised Meade for shifting forces around rather than letting Lee attack one portion of the army while the others sat by idly. This was probably another backhanded criticism of Hooker at Chancellorsville.[55]

Slocum would write about the battle later, but by that time he was more concerned that Meade ignored his role as wing commander and Williams's service at the head of the Twelfth Corps. One thing had already become apparent: Slocum realized very early on how important the Battle of Gettysburg was and had himself to some extent fallen prey to the Gettysburg Paradigm. He called the battle "the most important contest of modern times" and certainly wanted his place in it to be remembered well. As he said in a letter to Meade: "Your report is the official history of this important battle, and to this report reference will always be made by our Government, our people and the Historians, as the most reliable & accurate account of the services of each Corps, Division, and Brigade of your army." Ironically, it would have served Slocum far better to stake his reputation elsewhere. For a general to quibble before winning the war is pointless. So at least for the moment, Slocum had to turn himself back toward the task at hand.[56]

Quite a few historians have mistakenly taken Slocum's performance on July 1 as a view of his career in microcosm. This is not true over all. Slocum gave much greater performances on many other fields of the war. He certainly failed to cover himself with glory at Two Taverns, even though a close examination of the facts reveals he made the best decisions he could have done given what he knew about the situation, the orders he received, and his own absorption of McClellan's style of warfare. He was not equipped to face the situation when he faced it. Ironically, by the time he

54. See Fox, *In Memoriam*, 82; Report of Maj. Gen. Henry W. Slocum, *OR*, vol. 27, pt. 1, 761–62; Slocum to Morgan, January 2, 1864, in Charles Slocum, *Life and Services*, 135–36; Jacob Hoke, *The Great Invasion*, 466.

55. Report of Maj. Gen. Henry W. Slocum, *OR*, vol. 27, pt. 1, 762–63.

56. Slocum to Greene, December 30, 1863, NYHS; Slocum to Morgan, in Charles Slocum, *Life and Services*, 134. Quotes from Slocum to Meade, December 1863 ("Slocum [General] H. W. War 1861–65, Box 7, NYHS).

had shed enough McClellanism to have done well on the first day of Gettysburg, the war would practically be over.

While there is very little that can be said for his performance on July 1, in the confusion and turmoil that characterized so much of the fighting on Culp's Hill, Slocum made good decisions, and those choices played a definite role in ensuring the security of the entire army. By no means was he the hero of Gettysburg. Instead, he was one of thousands who did their jobs the best they could and prevented a Confederate breakthrough. In doing so, as a whole, the army pushed Lee toward the now-famous Pickett's Charge. Slocum's success contributed his mite to victory, ensuring that millions of later Americans would visit the Bloody Angle chiefly, and Culp's Hill mostly as an afterthought, if at all. It is ironic that, in doing so, he would also help to doom himself as little more than a footnote in Civil War history.

CHAPTER 6

"Where is Slocum?"
Tennessee, Vicksburg, and Atlanta

A McClellanized Henry Slocum, with more than a dash of Joe Hooker, had accustomed himself to life in the Army of the Potomac. He had fought in the East since the First Battle of Bull Run and probably would have preferred to stay right where he was. Washington had other plans, however, which ensured that Slocum would go west and find a brighter light to reflect than could be offered by McClellan, Hooker, or Meade. In the short run, Slocum's transfer brought with it both good and bad effects. With his talent for handling business affairs and his hard-nosed discipline, he quickly distinguished himself as a capable administrator in occupied areas. But his continuing bitter conflict with Hooker gave him the chance to demonstrate those skills by landing him in the rear, and the same feud would bring him back to the front line only when Hooker had scuttled his own career near Atlanta.

After Lee recrossed the Rappahannock in July 1863, both armies stayed in place for several weeks, on opposite banks of the river. It could be said that during the pursuit Meade was still reeling from his victory. That he had finally beaten Lee almost proved too much for him. Meade's apparent lethargy frustrated Lincoln. As he wrote to Howard on July 21, "I was deeply mortified by the escape of Lee across the Potomac, because the substantial destruction of his army would have ended the war, and because I believed such destruction was perfectly easy." Lincoln had for some time thought that, if handled properly, any movement north of the

Potomac would annihilate Lee. After a few days' reflection, though, he said he was "now profoundly grateful for what was done, without criticism for what was not done." Meade still had his confidence, he said. Still, if Lincoln had finally found someone who would not let Lee simply walk away with yet another dramatic victory, he had not found the man to best him. When Lincoln called Meade to Washington, Slocum, by virtue of seniority, took temporary command of the Army of the Potomac. He occupied Meade's headquarters, but nothing untoward occurred. After Meade returned, Slocum left for Syracuse around September 1, 1863, for a few days of rest.[1]

The story of the Twelfth Corps's operations in the months immediately following Gettysburg is singularly uninteresting when compared to other times. But then again, after Chancellorsville and Gettysburg, Slocum's corps could hardly stand any more excitement. The armies moved from place to place, but neither side accomplished anything. Williams described the time as being taken up mostly by marching and camping. Pickets and cavalry saw some action, but the bulk of the army had to find other ways to pass the time. Slocum remained a strict disciplinarian for the course of the war and probably took advantage of the lull to drill his men. Only the occasional visit of foreign dignitaries or the execution of deserters disturbed their monotonous life.[2]

An execution took place on Friday, September 18, 1863, on the Rapidan River. The day dawned with a gale, the wind whipped through the trees, and rain came down in torrents. When the storm let up around noon, Williams called the First Division into line to witness the execution. As they proceeded, it began to pour again, which Williams thought provided an appropriate setting for such dark duty. The man sat down on the edge of his coffin, apparently without a struggle. Perhaps he simply realized he had no hope of escape (Williams had seen to that) and so had resigned himself to die well. The man had deserted twice, and the army had extended mercy to him the first time, but none now remained. The man's former comrades loosed the fatal volley and he fell dead in his coffin. Although he hoped displays like this would cut down on desertion, Williams expected to lose twenty or so of his men to the executioner's metaphorical axe.[3]

1. Lincoln to Howard, July 21, 1863, Lincoln, *Complete Works*, 2:373 (quotes); Guelzo, *Redeemer President*, 366–67; Fox, *In Memoriam*, 87–88; "Gen. Slocum at Home," *Journal*, September 1, 1863.
2. McPherson, *Ordeal by Fire*, 331–32.
3. Williams, *Cannon's Mouth*, 257.

Not everything proved so serious. Slocum prided himself on being approachable by his soldiers, but at the same time his strict sense of discipline limited the ways in which he would let them act toward him. One afternoon in early September, one of his men pushed him too far. Slocum's headquarters guard, the Tenth Maine Battalion, had broken camp with Slocum as they moved to a campsite near Raccoon Ford. Slocum and his staff had stopped for lunch when a drunken lieutenant of the artillery rode up. Upon seeing Slocum, he dismounted immediately and threw his arms around the general's neck, exclaiming, "O! Sloky! You're a hunkey boy!" Slocum disentangled himself and had the man arrested immediately, where he remained until he apologized. News of the "Hunkey Boy" affair slipped quietly through the Tenth Maine and then filtered down into the rest of Slocum's corps. The men would often call him by his new unwanted nickname, intending it as a compliment. Slocum thought it beneath the dignity of a corps commander to be known by such a silly moniker, so the historian of the Tenth Maine also notes that they called him Hunkey Boy "at a little distance."[4]

Meanwhile events had moved apace in the western theater. The Union's rising star, Ulysses S. Grant, had been striving in Tennessee and Mississippi to open the "Father of Waters" since the beginning of the war. As Lee in the East dispatched one Federal general after another, Grant in the West had done the same with his opponents. Starting with his successful assaults on Fort Henry and Fort Donelson, Grant drove progressively deeper into the heart of Dixie. He suffered setbacks such as the Battle of Shiloh, where Confederate General Albert Sidney Johnston caught him by surprise and could have destroyed his army. Yet, thanks to Grant's legendary tenacity, the Union army not only survived but forced Johnston's replacement into retreat. After the fall of New Orleans in 1862, Grant knew the key to the Mississippi lay in the Confederate stronghold at Vicksburg, and he turned his attentions there. Opposed by John C. Pemberton and Joseph E. Johnston, not to mention difficult terrain and long supply lines, Grant nevertheless managed to meet and defeat Pemberton's army at Champion's Hill. After the battle, Pemberton retreated back into Vicksburg while Johnston hovered nearby, crying for reinforcements. Grant invested the city and, after his direct assault failed miserably, settled

4. *Journal* articles "Compliment to Maj. Gen. Slocum: A Short Speech in Response," February 6, 1863, "Gen. Slocum's Kindness and Urbanity," undated; John M. Gould with Leonard G. Jordan, *History of the First-Tenth-Twenty-ninth Maine Regiment,* 358–59 (quote); Charles Slocum, *Life and Services,* 138–39. It is interesting to note that Charles Slocum corrects the soldier's diction and replaces "Sloky" with "Slocum."

in for a siege. On July 4, 1863, as the Eastern armies sat exhausted in Pennsylvania, the half-starved garrison at Vicksburg surrendered. With the fall of Port Hudson five days later, the Union finally possessed all of the Mississippi River.[5]

In Tennessee, Confederate General Braxton Bragg unknowingly conspired to relieve the Twelfth Corps of its boredom. As Grant dueled his way south toward Vicksburg, Bragg faced off with Union General William S. Rosecrans. Bragg had steadily fallen back in the face of the Union's superior numbers. Rosecrans followed Bragg slowly but steadily through Tennessee and into the far northwestern corner of Georgia where Bragg attacked at Chickamauga Creek, hoping to bottle up Rosecrans and destroy him. Fortunately for Rosecrans he detected the movement just in time, and the two armies met on more even terms than Bragg would have liked. At first the Federals held their own, but then Rosecrans bungled an order, which left a gaping hole in his lines at the worst possible moment. Just as men scrambled to plug the gap, Longstreet (on loan from Lee) sent in an assault. Rosecrans's entire right wing disintegrated around him as Confederates poured through the break. The Union left, under the command of George H. Thomas, managed to hold on and cover the retreat, preventing greater destruction. Rosecrans pulled his forces back into Chattanooga, Tennessee, where Bragg laid siege. Broken worse than his army by the defeat, Rosecrans simply hunkered down and waited for the killing stroke. Around him his men began to starve. Unlike Hooker cowering against the Rapidan after Chancellorsville, however, Rosecrans could count on a rescue. Lincoln, Grant, and Sherman had full intentions of relieving the forces in Chattanooga. They made a number of plans, and some of these would have a direct influence on Slocum and the Twelfth Corps.[6]

After word reached Washington of the disaster in Georgia, Secretary of War Stanton called a meeting on the night of September 23–24, 1863. Lincoln was out of the city and had to return quickly. According to Stanton, Rosecrans desperately needed reinforcements and could stave off Bragg for no more than ten days. Stanton argued that if troops were detached

5. McPherson, *Ordeal by Fire*, 221–35, 332–44; Dickson, "Civil War, Land Overview," 194–97; David Coffey, "Grant, Ulysses S.," and Steven E. Woodworth, "Vicksburg, Campaign and Siege of," in Tucker, *Encyclopedia*, 2:357–58, 3:887–90.

6. Steven E. Woodworth, *Six Armies in Tennessee*; McPherson, *Ordeal by Fire*, 332–41; Curtis King, "Stones River/Murfreesboro, Battle of," in Tucker, *Encyclopedia*, 3:821–22; Dickson, "Civil War, Land Overview," 194–97; Steven E. Woodworth, "Chickamauga Creek, Battle of," and "Chattanooga, Battle of," in Tucker, *Encyclopedia*, 1:183–84, 172–74; Guelzo, *Redeemer President*, 369.

from Meade (who was accomplishing nothing in particular at that point) they could ride the rails through Kentucky and Tennessee and reach Rosecrans in five days. Lincoln, possibly tired from his return journey and certainly soured after three years of brilliant failures, openly doubted the troops could even reach Washington in five days, but Stanton convinced the group to try it. They authorized the immediate transfer of the Eleventh and Twelfth corps to Tennessee and placed both under the command of Joe Hooker. This ended up being part of a greater effort, the end result of which, Lincoln promised Rosecrans at ten o'clock the next morning, "shall get you from forty to sixty thousand additional men." About twenty thousand were eventually transferred from Virginia.[7]

Lincoln also took other very important steps to aid the army besieged in Chattanooga. Foremost among these was that he appointed Grant to command of the new Military Division of the Mississippi. This division combined several previously unconnected departments, including the Ohio, the Tennessee, and the Cumberland. In short order, but not before Slocum arrived, Lincoln also would replace Rosecrans. His choice for this job would be Thomas, now known as the "Rock of Chickamauga."[8]

On September 24, 1863, only two days after Chickamauga, Williams received orders to march. He expected to attack the flank of Lee's army, but he was wrong. For the rest of the war the men of both the Eleventh and the Twelfth corps were to campaign in the West. Slocum first heard of the appointment when Hooker's initial orders arrived on the morning of September 25. Hooker gave him very specific and detailed instructions on the Twelfth's departure for Tennessee, as if afraid to leave Slocum any room for discretion. Hooker went further, implying that, were Slocum to suffer any desertions in the movement west, it could "only proceed from inattention and neglect," and that the "public exigencies demand the labor and vigilance of every one," again implying that Slocum might not take sufficient care on his own.[9]

While Hooker may have intended all of this to apply to Howard, his orders reopened Slocum's wounded sensibilities, which had festered since

7. Donald, *Lincoln,* 457–58; Lincoln to Rosecrans, September 24, 1863, in Lincoln, *Complete Works,* 2:412.

8. Donald, *Lincoln,* 458.

9. Williams, *Cannon's Mouth,* 237–60; Howard, "Memory of Henry Slocum," 40; Summary of Principal Events, *OR,* vol. 29, pt. 1, 3; Guelzo, *Redeemer President,* 369; Transfer of the Eleventh and Twelfth Army Corps from the Army of the Potomac to the Army of the Cumberland, *OR,* vol. 29, pt. 1, 151–52 (quote).

Chancellorsville. Immediately upon receiving Hooker's orders, Slocum fired off a letter of resignation to Lincoln. He stated bluntly:

> My opinion of General Hooker both as an officer and a gentleman is too well known to make it necessary for me to refer to it in this communication. The public service cannot be promoted by placing under his command an officer who has so little confidence in his ability as I have. Our relations are such that it would be degrading if made to accept any position under him. I have therefore to respectfully tender the resignation of my commission as major-general of volunteers.[10]

It is unclear whether he feared Hooker might finally retaliate against him for his vitriolic attacks or he simply felt he could not honorably accept such a situation. Both may well have been true. It is clear this was no mere bluff on Slocum's part. He set the Twelfth Corps moving in short order and then, without informing Hooker, left for Washington with a portion of his staff. Such actions imply he fully expected not to come back.[11]

Slocum arrived in Washington at the end of September and stayed for about a week. His meeting with Lincoln took place on September 28, 1863. Exactly what Lincoln knew of the situation from Hooker's perspective no source directly reveals. Hooker had met with Lincoln back on the evening of May 13, but they obviously did not discuss the growing wave of criticism for Chancellorsville.[12]

Lincoln displayed little patience with other complaints from some generals, but here he apparently understood Slocum's position. Slocum's acquaintance with the president's wife may have helped him once again, or it could also have been that, since they were operating with such a tight time limit, Lincoln said what he thought was necessary to pacify Slocum as quickly as possible and get him back on his way. Whatever the reason, instead of sending the general packing for Syracuse, Lincoln proposed a compromise. If he would take the Twelfth Corps into Tennessee, Slocum would not be placed under Hooker's command once they arrived. In addition to

---

10. Slocum to Lincoln, *OR*, vol. 29, pt. 2, 156; "Gen. Slocum's Resignation," *Journal*, September 29, 1863.

11. The timing is clear from the fact that a correspondent to the *Journal* places Slocum in Washington for three days around Friday, October 2. "Gen. Slocum's Resignation Not Accepted," *Journal*, October 10, 1863. But by October 4, Hooker had not heard from Slocum and, by the next day, was reduced to sending dispatches aimed only at "Senior officer, Twelfth Corps."

12. Hooker to Lincoln, May 13, 1863 (Telegram concerning a meeting with Lincoln), Lincoln to Hooker, May 14, 1863 (Army of the Potomac), Lincoln Papers.

this Lincoln assured Slocum he would be assigned to a command of equal importance, away from Hooker, as soon as possible. In Slocum's presence Lincoln composed, read, and mailed a letter to Rosecrans on the subject. He noted that he was sending Rosecrans "two small corps" and that

> Unfortunately relations between Generals Hooker and Slocum are not such as to promise good . . . . Therefore, let me beg—almost enjoin upon you— that on their reaching you, you will make a transposition by which General Slocum with his corps may pass from under the command of General Hooker . . . . It is important for this to be done, though we could not arrange it here. Please do it.[13]

Lincoln could hardly have been clearer had he taken a train to Chattanooga and seen Rosecrans personally. Slocum accepted this arrangement and withdrew his resignation, and when he left, he rightly felt confident that "I should be relieved from serving under General Hooker." This may have settled the matter for the moment, but it did not provide an ultimate solution. Lincoln's compromise would hold back the tempest only for a short time.[14]

Probably at this meeting Lincoln brought up the issue of the executions Slocum had carried out hastily at Leesburg during the Gettysburg Campaign. Calling it an occurrence that "caused me more pain than almost any incident that had occurred during the whole war," Lincoln asked Slocum if he remembered it. Slocum said he had already forgotten the circumstance. The president, though, could not. The wife and sister of one of the men had come to Washington to plead for their loved one's life. Slocum's telegram announcing the execution arrived while Lincoln was speaking with them in the Oval Office, where Lincoln opened it and had to read it to them.[15]

After the interview Slocum did as asked and returned to the Twelfth Corps, which was already on the march. His prophecy of trouble under Hooker proved self-fulfilling. Hooker, who had moved his headquarters to Stevenson, Alabama, had assigned Slocum to protect the stretch of rail-

13. Abraham Lincoln to William S. Rosecrans, September 28, 1863 (Rosecrans to receive 11th and 12th Corps under Hooker's command), Lincoln Papers.

14. "Gen. Slocum's Recollections," *Syracuse Courier*, April 2, 1879 (quote); Fox, *In Memoriam*, 89; Slocum to Howland, October 22, 1863, NYHS.

15. "Gen. Slocum's Recollections," *Syracuse Courier*, April 2, 1879 (quote); Slocum to Butterfield, *OR*, vol. 27, pt. 3, 223; *Journal* articles "Gen. Slocum's Resignation Not Accepted," October 10, "Gen. Slocum's Resignation," October 3, 1863; Slocum to Rosecrans, in Ulysses Grant, *The Papers of Ulysses S. Grant*, 9:322n.

road from Wartrace to Tantalon. He had been vainly trying to communicate with Slocum in a flurry of detailed telegrams and dispatches and found the stony silence on Slocum's end unnerving. Hooker had heard nothing from the Twelfth since it had left the Army of the Potomac back on September 25, and he did not even know its approximate location. By October 6, a frustrated Fighting Joe had been reduced to vaguely sending his dispatches to the "Senior Officer of Twelfth Corps" at "Tullahoma, Decherd, or Wartrace."[16]

Slocum had arrived in Nashville by October 5 but still showed little interest in cooperating with Hooker or with his chief of staff, Daniel Butterfield, whom he had long ago tossed in with Hooker's "gang." By that day, officers in Kentucky and Tennessee mentioned Slocum issuing orders concerning the situation around Nashville, but he still had not bothered to report his location or progress to Hooker. To make matters worse, at approximately the same time Slocum arrived in Nashville, guerrillas cut the railroad south of town in several important places and laid waste to the city's telegraph wires. On his side of the breach, Slocum had only two brigades, but on October 6 he telegraphed Butterfield curtly from Nashville that he would use them to occupy the line Hooker wanted.[17]

All this had been too much for Hooker's patience, and he had already assigned Butterfield himself to command the Twelfth Corps south of the breach. Butterfield marched and countermarched, but he succeeded in doing little more than cataloguing the success of rebel saboteurs along the railroad. Butterfield commanded the Twelfth for about four days before finally meeting up with Slocum on October 10 and turning it over. By this time the unfortunate Williams, caught in the middle between an irate Slocum and an inept Butterfield, had grown tired of pointless marching. As he reported to Slocum, "The late movements of troops has been arduous and not eminently fruitful." Slocum finally settled down with Williams's division and took charge of the railroad from Murfreesboro (where he finally established his headquarters) to Tantalon. Hooker would, on occasion, have Slocum marching up and down the line, but he stayed in this general area until transferred. The majority of the official

16. Correspondence, orders, and returns relating to operations in Kentucky, southwest Virginia, Tennessee, Mississippi, north Alabama, and north Georgia, from August 11, 1863, to October 19, 1863, Union correspondence, etc. no. 4, *OR*, vol. 30, pt. 4, 92–95, 136–37.

17. Transfer of the Eleventh and Twelfth army corps from the Army of the Potomac to the Army of the Cumberland, *OR*, vol. 29, pt. 1, 191–92; Correspondence, *OR*, vol. 30, pt. 4, 137.

communications from this point forward are composed of brief orders
from Hooker to Slocum via Butterfield, who repeatedly warned Slocum of
reports of Rebels operating in the area and instructed him on how to deal
with them. Most of the important action in the area took place farther to
the south, though Slocum's pickets and cavalry certainly kept busy.[18]

Slocum began to institute changes to civilian affairs around Tullahoma.
When he had finally arrived in Tennessee, he found "thousands of 'poor
white trash' eating up the supplies of the government" and the railroad
broken in several places nearly every day. In particular, a number of
Northern officers objected to having the families of known Rebels depending upon them for supplies. The previous commanders had issued
permits to buy and sell liberally, so one could easily be obtained, even by
the wife of a local bank manager who had run off with all the bank's funds
upon the approach of the army. Why, they asked, would anyone feel compelled to take a new oath of allegiance to the United States, if they could
live just as well without?[19]

In the winter of 1863–1864, Slocum took stern action to lift the burden
off his own troops and place it on the backs of secessionist civilians. He
reasoned simply that since "the natural protectors of these women and
children now applying for support, are now in the ranks of the rebel
army—and as in most instances they have been brought there through the
influence of their wealthy secession neighbors these women and children,
have upon such neighbors, a much more equitable claim for support than
they have upon the United States Government." In order to enforce this
claim, Slocum established a camp at Fayetteville, Lincoln County, and put
Colonel William Hawley of the Third Wisconsin Volunteers in charge of it.
All refugees, women, and children in the vicinity of Federal posts that
could "with propriety" be moved from their homes were to be sent to the
new camp. Slocum authorized Colonel Hawley to send out foraging parties to compel all wealthy secessionists within twenty miles to provide
whatever supplies the refugees needed. Those people who could not be
moved could remain at home but could not draw government rations.
Instead, he ordered the post commanders to appoint a "worthy and com-
passionate" officer to impress supplies from secessionists around the base.

18. Woodworth, *Six Armies in Tennessee,* 142; Report of Maj. Gen. Daniel Butterfield,
OR, vol. 30, pt. 2, 713–19; Williams from Union correspondence from August 11 to
October 19, 1863, *OR,* vol. 30, pt. 4, 228, 266, 344; Butterfield to Slocum, *OR,* vol. 30, pt.
4, 94.
19. "Gen. Slocum in Tennessee," *Journal,* undated (quote); Sturdevant to Rogers, *OR,*
vol. 32, pt. 2, 258–59.

By concentrating the refugees into one area, Slocum made the civilians easier to control and supply. Also, by forcing local secessionists to pay for the camp's upkeep, Slocum freed up more government supplies to go forward to the armies.[20]

Slocum displayed little patience with violence against Unionists. When he arrived at the post, guerrillas attacked loyal citizens attempting to take cotton to market on a regular basis. If lucky, the loyalist escaped with only his cotton burnt, but all too often he lost his life as well. Slocum attempted to end these attacks in the same order by which he established the refugee camps. If a property holder who had cotton destroyed proved his loyalty, he could apply to Slocum for help. If Slocum approved, Federal authorities would then requisition an appropriate amount of undamaged goods from nearby secessionists. If the Rebels refused, the provost marshal of the post would confiscate the needed assets, which would then be put up for public auction. He made it abundantly clear he wanted wealthy Rebels to bear this burden.[21]

Slocum also took part in assessing damages against civilians for attacks on Union troops. Late in the evening of December 23, 1863, a wagon became separated from a foraging expedition moving through Mulberry, Tennessee. Before the wagon could catch up with the rest of the group, guerrillas attacked and took the men prisoner. The Rebels moved them rapidly through the woods to avoid the roads, stopping just after midnight to set up camp where they bound the prisoners' hands, robbed, and then shot them. Two men survived the encounter. This murderous spree, of course, infuriated Thomas, by then commanding the department. On January 6, 1864, he ordered Slocum to forcibly collect thirty thousand dollars from nearby secessionists and distribute the sum among the dead men's families.[22]

Slocum's men departed on their task in early February 1864, and they had returned by February 16. He placed Colonel John H. Ketchum of the 150th New York in charge of the expedition, ordering him to encamp in the area of Mulberry until the entire sum had been raised. Ketchum performed his job with zeal and had soon accumulated $5,654.57 more than the required $30,000. On the return march, though, some of Ketchum's men got careless. Two of them, without orders, rode ahead while the rest of the command ate dinner. They had gone only about a quarter or a half

20. "Assessing the Secesh," *Journal,* undated.

21. *Journal* articles "Gen. Slocum in Tennessee," undated, and "Assessing the Secesh," undated.

22. General Orders No. 6, *OR,* vol. 32, pt. 2, 37–38.

a mile when the 150th heard the reports of several rifles. On investigating they found their comrades dead. A cavalry detachment caught up with the bushwhackers later but did not capture them. Upon their return to camp, Slocum sent the thirty thousand dollars on to the respective recipients but then had to decide what to do with the remaining money. Ketchum approached him for permission to divide the funds between the families of the two slain soldiers. Slocum agreed, but with a slight caveat. He would return $654.57 to several civilians who should not have been charged and then send Ketchum home to New York with the remainder. He applied to Thomas for permission to do so. Thomas granted Slocum his chance, stipulating that Ketchum be back in thirty days' time.[23]

Overall, Slocum's conduct as a civilian administrator is intriguing. He ordered the forcible removal of civilians into a refugee camp and then forced other civilians in a war-torn area to support them with little or no government help. While there is no evidence currently available to show that any sort of mistreatment occurred, the very idea seems harsh by more recent standards. It is tempting to view Slocum, serving later under Sherman's gigantic shadow, as completely unoriginal when it comes to hard-war policies, mechanically putting Sherman's ideas into action. Slocum's tendency to imitate his commander would lend credence to this interpretation, especially in light of Sherman's very powerful personality. Slocum's conduct in Tullahoma and later in Vicksburg points to a different conclusion. There is no evidence to suggest the two men had experienced any extended contact up to this point. Yet Slocum's approach to the administration of Tullahoma might be a page taken straight out of Sherman's manual on war. It is notable that Slocum evolved his opinions on the treatment of civilians separately from Sherman. In a way he prefigured Sherman, and this is undoubtedly one reason why the two worked together so well.

Meanwhile, Slocum's injured honor had received no salve. Contrary to Lincoln's promise, Rosecrans did nothing to alleviate the tension. In response to Lincoln's very detailed letter, Rosecrans stated lamely that he could not give any substantial commands to Eastern generals because "Any attempt to mingle them [Western soldiers] with Potomac troops by placing them under Potomac Generals would kindle a flame of jealousy and dislike."[24]

23. Wooddin Letters, *Poughkeepsie Daily Eagle*, February 22, 1864 (special thanks to Mike Peets for this reference); Slocum to Whipple, *OR*, vol. 32, pt. 2, 405–8.

24. Rosecrans to Lincoln, October 13, 1863 (Consolidation of the XX and XXI Corps), Lincoln Papers.

Flames of dislike, at least, were soon blazing between Slocum and Hooker once again. On October 12, 1863, the day before Rosecrans refused to do anything about Slocum's command, Hooker made known his opinion on the subject. He wrote a letter to President Lincoln in the hopes of ridding himself of Slocum and at the same time strengthening his own hand. The letter dripped polite condescension and thinly veiled disdain:

> Permit me to make a suggestion with reference to my command . . . . It is that General Slocum may be tendered a command in Missouri or somewhere else . . . . Unless he gives more satisfaction in the discharge of his duties, he will soon find himself in deeper water than he has been wading in . . . . I shall act very deliberately with him . . . [as] [h]e now appears to be swayed entirely by passion in the exercise of his office. I hear that his grievances are hostility to myself . . . and disrespect shown his rank in detailing him for this service . . . . It seems that he aspired to the command of the Army of the Potomac, and that mortal offense was given in not naming him first. Of these you probably know more than myself.[25]

If the president decided to honor Hooker's request, Hooker would both be rid of Slocum and be able to place his faithful crony Butterfield in command of the Twelfth Corps. From his perspective this would be an ideal solution.

The letter implies that Hooker had not spoken of the situation extensively with Lincoln before, but that he did know Slocum had met with Lincoln after Chancellorsville. He could have inferred this from Lincoln's letter of May 14, 1863. There would have been no reason for Hooker to mention it prior to this time. His spat with Slocum was personal, and he would not want to accent the fact that half his command hated him. Hooker wanted to put the specter of Chancellorsville behind him, and acknowledging Slocum would do him no good in that respect. At any rate Hooker seemed to feel he should feign ignorance of the situation. It was not the first time Hooker tried this sort of subterfuge against Slocum, but he aimed his earlier attempts at his immediate superiors. For instance, he mentioned he had placed the matter before Rosecrans as well, who refused to remove Slocum from command. Lincoln also took no action and let the situation stand as it was for the moment.[26]

An interesting point here reveals something of Lincoln himself. It is certain that Slocum at least had revealed to Lincoln the full extent of the ill

25. Hooker to Lincoln, *OR*, vol. 30, pt. 4, 322.
26. Ibid.; Lincoln to Hooker, May 14, 1863 (Army of the Potomac), Lincoln Papers.

will between himself and Hooker; Darius Couch certainly intended to follow suit, Reynolds definitely had already done so in an interview with the president, and other generals may well have done the same. Yet Lincoln apparently never told Hooker explicitly of Slocum's more recent meeting with him. Had he done so, it certainly would have altered the tone of Hooker's letter. As it stands, Lincoln probably read the dispatch with at least some amusement. Hooker condescended to inform him of a continuing squabble that Lincoln already knew all about. In this case as in others, Lincoln listened more than he spoke and proved the wiser for it.

Slocum's conduct had given Hooker an ample case against him. First, instead of accompanying the Twelfth Corps to Tennessee immediately, Slocum had departed for Washington, without informing Hooker. Then, when Lincoln convinced him to stay on, he gave Hooker a minimum of cooperation. It was true that Slocum was furious at him for his failure at Chancellorsville and his tendencies toward drinking and bragging. This much Slocum made abundantly clear in his letter to Lincoln as well as in those he wrote to Howland. Slocum apparently had few qualms about letting people know exactly what he thought. He made it obvious before he accepted his current position that he did not think he could offer Hooker even the most basic faith. The fact that no one less than the president of the United States had promised Slocum he would not be put in this very situation only made matters worse.

For all that may have been true, Hooker's letter also contains vagaries and outright lies that would continue to haunt Slocum for years to come. Even here Hooker coats the falsehoods with a believable veneer of truth. Slocum did connive to get command of the Army of the Potomac away from Hooker, but he did not put himself forward for the command. Lincoln knew of this firsthand, as this had been the whole point of Slocum's visit to him back in early May. It seemed no secret in the army that Slocum and Couch masterminded the plot. At least Meade and apparently several other corps commanders all knew about it. Slocum had stated explicitly to Meade that he was willing to serve under him. The charge that he resented being snubbed for command of the army had no substance, but it was easy to make, and Slocum would have to deal with it again. As a corps commander, the most senior, he would be expected to want command. In fact it is somewhat surprising that he apparently did not.

Whether Slocum knew of Hooker's communication with Lincoln, he embarked upon his own letter-writing campaign later that month. He had earlier written a letter to Rosecrans flatly stating, "under no circumstances would I take my men into action under an officer in whom I had so little confidence as I had in Hooker." In this letter he did not offer to resign, as previously, but he did emphasize his former position as the senior commander in the Army of the Potomac and the record of the Twelfth Corps, and he asked that neither be disrespected by forcible service under Hooker. Rosecrans replied on October 24, 1863, that he had shown Lincoln's letter to Thomas but had decided against heeding it. This time Rosecrans pleaded the excuse of his own troops having suffered the traumatic experience of the merging of the Twentieth and Twenty-first corps. Slocum had attempted to see Rosecrans personally on the subject. Based on his replies and constantly changing excuses as to why he could not honor Lincoln's request, it seems Rosecrans was trying to avoid him.[27]

Rosecrans's stonewalling did not put off Slocum, who sent what Grant later called a "very disorderly communication, stating that when he came here it was under promise that he should not have to serve under Hooker, whom he neither regards with confidence as an officer nor respects as a man." This letter is reproduced in Grant's published papers. Its recipient differed; instead of Rosencrans, he addressed it to Thomas, who had now taken command of the Army of the Cumberland. Slocum repeated his request to be relieved. Thomas forwarded the request to Grant, and Grant added his endorsement on October 24, asking that Slocum be relieved from duty since Hooker had been personally appointed by Lincoln. It certainly bothered Grant, whom Lincoln had just placed in command of the entire theater. Grant placed a premium on harmony and loyalty among his officers. Whatever Grant's opinion of Hooker, Slocum's attacks defied the chain of command and the government's orders. Still, Washington did nothing.[28]

Rather than let the controversy die, on November 14, 1863, Slocum wrote a long detailed letter to Seward, which Lincoln himself later endorsed. Slocum probably approached Seward because of their mutual New York political connections. Slocum informed Seward that upon his arrival he had waited a month before asking Rosecrans to honor Lincoln's letter, only to be brushed aside. He settled for a command in the rear mainly to avoid contact with Hooker, but now, as Grant proceeded with his plans to relieve Chattanooga, it appeared the Twelfth Corps might be headed back into action. Slocum would be expected to cooperate with

27. Slocum to Rosecrans, at Grant, *Papers*, 9:322n; Rosecrans to Slocum, *OR*, vol. 31, pt. 1, 715.

28. Dana to Stanton, *OR*, vol. 31, pt. 1, 73; Endorsement of Slocum's resignation letter, ibid., 740; Slocum to Howland, October 22, 1863, NYHS; Slocum to Thomas, in Grant, *Papers*, 9:322n.

Hooker, and this he could not bear. He therefore, once again, tendered his resignation:

> It is now apparent to me that my Corps will soon take the field—that it is the intention, notwithstanding my entire lack of confidence in Hooker as an officer—notwithstanding my utter detestation of him as a man, absolutely to force me to lead my men into battle under him . . . . My own reputation is not only endangered by it—but the interest of the country cannot but be injuriously effected [*sic*] by it.

Slocum hurled down his gauntlet over and again, challenging anyone who thought otherwise to hear him present the facts of his case against Hooker, even to the point of a board of inquiry.[29]

While Slocum could rightly insist that Lincoln's promise to him be honored, for a subordinate so unashamedly to criticize his superior officer was clearly irresponsible. Slocum, knowing his principles and opinions would not allow him to serve under Hooker, had warned of this situation and hoped to avoid it in his letter and visit to Lincoln. Both Lincoln and Slocum share the blame for the stresses that occurred. Hooker cannot be faulted at this point, though his reactions did nothing to soothe Slocum. No matter what Hooker tried, Slocum would still despise him. Lincoln did not ensure his promise was kept nor did he simply let Slocum head back into civilian life. As for Slocum, from the very beginning he had made it very clear that he would not serve quietly under Hooker. He even left his corps in the field, with the expectation he would be relieved. When he agreed to stay, Slocum did not keep his complaints to himself. In pushing the subject to the point he did, he became guilty of insubordination bordering at times on dereliction of duty. His duty called him to serve Hooker, not necessarily idolize him. That Slocum proved incapable of the former, even when he knew the importance of teamwork, points to a definite flaw in his military character. Such weakness could have caused a great deal more harm than it actually did, had circumstances fallen into place a little differently.

Hooker's letter accomplished nothing, but Slocum's barrage finally brought action. Thomas dealt with the situation in a temporary manner. He had Slocum take his First Division, under Williams, and guard the railroad between Murfreesboro and Bridgeport, well away from Hooker,

---

29. Slocum also mentions that "the President thought proper to refer this matter to you when my resignation was presented—and the interest which you were kind enough to manifest in it." Slocum to Seward, November 14, 1863 (Does not want to serve under Hooker), Lincoln Papers.

while Geary's division stayed with Hooker and the Eleventh Corps. Becoming one of the few officers to observe the chain of command in this affair, Thomas passed Slocum's newest resignation on to Grant. Thomas then ordered Slocum to report directly to his headquarters in Chattanooga, thereby sufficiently altering the command structure that so irked Slocum.[30]

Nothing changed during the climactic battles around Chattanooga. In fact, under Hooker, Geary's division played a conspicuous role in the Battle Above the Clouds at Lookout Mountain. Earlier, Grant had managed to open a line of supply into the city, breaking Bragg's stranglehold on Chattanooga. Bragg had dispatched Longstreet to attack Burnside, who occupied Knoxville. Unfortunately for Bragg, Longstreet neither took Knoxville nor returned in time. After ferrying in more troops and supplies, Grant launched a series of attacks that dislodged large portions of a reputedly impregnable Confederate position along Missionary Ridge. Bragg managed to leave the field with his army intact and retreat back into Georgia.[31]

Another small controversy erupted in December 1863, this time between the high command of the Twelfth Corps and their former commander George Meade, whose report of Gettysburg had finally been published. Williams read a copy and, finding quite a few errors in it, forwarded it along with his complaints to Slocum, who had also read the report. Slocum then fired off a long letter to Meade on the subject, sending along the reports of Ruger's division, which had only recently been completed. The War Department had called Williams and Ruger away immediately after the battle to help quell riots raging through New York City, so these reports had been long delayed. Slocum next wrote to General Greene, sending him a copy of the letter and asking him to broach the subject personally with Meade. He mailed both letters on December 30, 1863. Slocum also brought up the subject on January 3, 1864, with LeRoy Morgan, back in Syracuse, saying he felt compelled to explain himself. He had earlier given Morgan his own account of the battle and wished to explain the discrepancies between his report and Meade's. Slocum, Williams, and apparently Greene as well, all felt they had a good deal at stake in how people remembered this, "the most important contest of modern times."[32]

---

30. Thomas to Slocum, Butterfield to Williams, *OR*, vol. 31, pt. 1, 741.

31. Woodworth, *Six Armies in Tennessee,* 180–218.

32. Slocum to Meade, December 1863 (quote), Slocum to Greene, December 30, 1863, NYHS; Williams, *Cannon's Mouth,* 279–91 (Slocum to Morgan at 284).

They essentially objected that in his official report Meade had neglected the First Division of the Twelfth Corps or mistakenly given others recognition for the role it had played in the battle. While crediting Lockwood's brigade with great service on the afternoon of the second, Meade mistakenly assigned it to the First Corps. This omission particularly irked Williams, who had personally led the brigade into the fight. Next, Meade did not explicitly mention Greene's name in connection with the dramatic night battle on Culp's Hill. Greene had preserved the entire Union right while Williams, Ruger, and Geary were away, and Slocum thought this worthy of mention. Slocum also charged that Meade had ignored Williams's movement in support of the left that night, while acknowledging Geary's, which had ended so comically. Next, he objected to the fact that Meade had not credited Williams with command of the Twelfth Corps nor himself with that of the right wing. He pointedly reminded Meade that he had in his possession the order placing him in this position.[33]

Meade replied to these charges much later than Slocum would have liked. He said he had been ill and away from his headquarters when the letter arrived and pleaded this as an excuse. He immediately wrote a revised report and forwarded it on to the War Department, fixing some of the mistakes that Slocum had pointed out. He sent a copy of the new report to Slocum along with a letter of apology that admitted some errors and denied others. In general Meade blamed his blunder on the fact that he had prepared the report hurriedly, at a time when several of his corps commanders had not submitted their accounts. Responding point by point, he at first stated that Slocum was right about Lockwood's brigade, though he gave no reason why this error occurred in the first place. He would not apologize for the fact that he had overlooked Greene's battle and Williams's First Division, for the reason that he aimed to produce a general account of the battle. He could not mention the services of every single brigade and division in the army, though he admitted that, had he known Greene's full story, he certainly would have included it.[34]

Meade steadfastly refused to acknowledge Williams's and Slocum's positions as corps and wing commander respectively. Meade said he had not included this because he had no idea they had served in those capacities. He remembered the order to which Slocum referred. In it Meade had placed Slocum in command of the Twelfth, First, and Sixth corps with the idea of attacking Lee. Although Meade later called off the attack, he never re-

33. Slocum to Meade, December 1863, NYHS.
34. Meade to Slocum, *OR*, vol. 27, pt. 1, 769–70.

scinded the entire order. So even when Meade ordered the Fifth and Sixth corps away later, Slocum thought he remained in command of the wing for the duration of the battle and acted accordingly. Williams retained command of the Twelfth, and Ruger of the First Division. Instead, Meade stated, he simply assumed that Slocum had realized Meade intended him to return to the command of his corps. He thought the departure of the other corps would be another hint. In fact, he said, he wondered why Williams attended the council of war but said nothing out of politeness.[35]

This whole confusing situation demonstrates the chaos that the Battle of Gettysburg had the potential to become. Meade had been in command of the Army of the Potomac for only a few days and in reality had not fully come to grips with it. He did not inform Slocum more fully of his intentions. It seemed a besetting sin of generals on both sides to think their subordinates possessed a capacity to read minds. From Slocum's perspective, Meade placed him in command and never took him back out. It is not surprising that he continued to think as he did in the press of battle. Even the Pipe Creek Circular had a clause showing that Meade intended Slocum to assume the role of wing commander in any upcoming battle. As was his general rule, Slocum did exactly what his superior told him, no more or less. From a historical perspective, there may not be an easy way to categorize this strange event, though it might be safe simply to call Slocum a non-acting wing commander, while noting that Meade had no real idea what was going on in his own army. Historians have generally given Meade a good rating for the Battle of Gettysburg, as they should. Many commanders cannot keep track of their own armies even after being in command for months, so Meade's small failure is not surprising.

Meanwhile Grant remained unsure of what to do with Slocum and Hooker, but he wanted to solve the situation for good. Grant had little patience for either man. Hooker "ha[d] behaved badly ever since his arrival" and had thoroughly disgusted him. Grant thought Hooker's position in command of two tiny corps "rather embarrasses the service."[36] His appointment by President Lincoln made Grant hesitant to remove him, however. Grant's main problem with Slocum seems to spring from Slocum's vocal opposition to Hooker. The "disorderly communication" had bothered Grant in particular. Immediately upon reading Slocum's latest letter, he asked for Slocum to be relieved and Hooker placed in his stead as commander of the Twelfth. After his temper had cooled Grant changed his mind. He wanted simply to

35. Ibid.
36. Endorsement of Slocum letter of resignation, *OR,* vol. 31, pt. 1, 740.

transfer them both out of his command, as he felt "that their presence [was] replete with both trouble and danger." He proposed that the War Department consolidate the Eleventh and Twelfth under Howard.[37]

Time would mellow Grant's opinion of Slocum, and as the winter progressed, Grant actually began to side with him in his campaign against Hooker. On February 2, 1864, Slocum mailed yet another letter, this time following the chain of command through Thomas. It passed through to the War Department, gathering endorsements from Hooker himself, Thomas, and Grant. This time Slocum tried a different tactic. He dissected the command scheme that kept him under Hooker, comparing it to Burnside's grand divisions, pointing out that Hooker himself had disliked them. Slocum objected that, although he was one of the most senior men in the field, he in reality occupied the position of a division or brigade commander. He then asked that the system be either discontinued or made general. Grant added his endorsement on February 9, adding that Hooker's position was "embarrassing to the service and I think injurious" and suggested that the Eleventh and Twelfth corps be filled up from new levies, left with Howard and Slocum, while Hooker be transferred to a state like Ohio.[38]

Whatever the case, Grant knew the situation must be dealt with soon. After his success at Chattanooga, Lincoln had appointed Grant commander in chief of all Union armies. As the months dragged on and the 1864 campaigning season bore down, Grant planned to launch a coordinated offensive that he hoped would finally end the war by November. While he remained in Virginia to deal with Lee, he planned for several other armies—Sherman's the most important—to advance at once. The ultimate goal of the campaigns was to ensure the destruction of the Confederate armies. Grant stated to Meade: "Wherever Lee goes, there you will go also." To Sherman he made it clear he was to "move against Johnston's army, to break it up, and to get into the interior of the enemy's country as far as you can, inflicting all the damage you can." Other generals with smaller commands such as Benjamin Butler, Nathaniel Banks, and Franz Sigel were to move too. As Lincoln so classically put it: "Those not skinning can hold a leg." This meant it would be of paramount importance to arrive at the end of the Slocum-Hooker feud quickly and finally before Sherman embarked on his campaign against Johnston.[39]

37. Grant to Halleck, and Dana to Stanton, ibid., vol. 31, pt. 1, 740, 73.
38. Slocum to Whipple and Endorsements, *OR*, vol. 32, pt. 2, 313–15; Grant to Halleck, endorsing Slocum's letter, at Grant, *Papers*, 10:95.
39. James McPherson, *Battle Cry of Freedom: The Civil War Era*, 722; Grant to Meade, *OR*, vol. 33, pt. 3, 827–28; Grant to Sherman, *OR*, vol. 32, pt. 3, 245–46.

Grant got mixed results. The War Department eventually settled on the idea of consolidating the two corps into one, originally to be called the First Corps. Howard would not be as strong a candidate for the new corps because of the criticism he had garnered at Chancellorsville and Gettysburg. Grant also could not be rid of Hooker so easily. He had fought well in Tennessee, but his arrogant nature prevented him from cooperating smoothly with anyone who would not kowtow to him on a personal level. But Hooker enjoyed the president's continued support. Slocum's sensibilities prevented him from working well with Hooker, and Slocum had caused the most visible trouble. So the War Department consolidated the Eleventh and Twelfth into a new corps, the Twentieth, and placed it under Hooker's command. This displaced Slocum; Grant now had to decide what to do with him.[40]

Whatever he thought of Slocum's abilities as a general, Grant needed to get him away from Hooker as quickly as possible. To leave the two operating in the same general vicinity was asking for trouble since no one could guarantee they might not be forced to cooperate in some future crisis. After some internal discussion of the situation, Grant and Sherman sent Slocum to guard one of the Union's most prized possessions: Vicksburg. Sherman issued the order in accordance with General Orders No. 5 from Huntsville, Alabama, when Slocum reported there on April 12, 1864. Slocum started for Vicksburg on the morning of April 18 after meeting personally with Sherman. Most agreed that Slocum was well suited for his new command. He had "acquired an enviable reputation in [Tennessee], on account of the system of economy . . . in the issuing of rations to indigent citizens." Sherman stated simply: "Slocum will be a good commander for Vicksburg and Natchez." James B. McPherson, former commander of the post, replied that he thought "the assignment of Major-General Slocum to the command of the District of Vicksburg an excellent arrangement." McPherson, a graduate of the West Point class of 1853, probably knew Slocum personally. His vote of confidence would have been important to Sherman, since Sherman looked on McPherson as a protégé and expected him to succeed to command of the Army of the Tennessee, when the opportunity arose.[41]

40. General Orders No. 5, *OR*, vol. 32, pt. 3, 268.

41. General Orders No. 3 (referencing no. 5), ibid., 339; Sherman to McPherson, ibid., 400; "Maj. Gen Slocum," *Journal*, April 20, 1864 (quote; this article mentions that a member of Slocum's staff keeps the *Journal* updated on his affairs); Sherman to McPherson, McPherson to Sherman, *OR*, vol. 32, pt. 3, 276 (quote), 296.

Grant also echoed this confidence in Slocum's abilities when he stated to Halleck later that one of the reasons he sent Slocum there in the first place was to take care of rampant corruption and mismanagement on the Mississippi. Grant doubtless hoped Slocum's same rigid standards that had caused the friction with Hooker would be put to good use in the new position. Lincoln and Stanton also liked the appointment on the grounds that Slocum, an avowed prewar abolitionist, would be better suited for organizing and commanding the various regiments of colored troops that were still forming. Grant noted to Sherman that "Slocum will take an active interest in this work which the President and Secretary of War fear [John] Newton . . . [a Southerner] will not." Also, Slocum's reputation as a disciplinarian was probably well-known.[42]

Grant had good reason to be concerned about Vicksburg. The siege had left it a mess of craters, blackened rubble, and half-starved citizens. The city had been steadily recovering for almost a year and had made some significant progress. Its economy, aided by the inherently corrupt system of trade imposed by the Treasury Department, had made an even more startling recovery. If anything, the trade in cotton had grown to monumental proportions, nearly all of it based on corruption. A brisk business in forged commerce authorizations (not to mention semi-legitimate ones obtained by bribery) ensured that the cotton speculators would have it all their own way.[43]

Slocum's charge in Mississippi proved anything but the military backwater Hooker would have been happy to see him in. The Department of Vicksburg embraced all the land between the mouth of the Arkansas River to the west and the Tallahatchie River on the east, from Tennessee down to the Department of the Gulf. Slocum's command consisted of more troops than some army corps, more than double the Twelfth, totaling in excess of nineteen thousand soldiers both present and absent. Of these nearly half were African American. Slocum's official returns reported in July 1864 note that, of sixteen thousand troops present for duty, nearly six thousand clearly were U.S. Colored Troops (USCT). His largest single organization (at 5,335 present) was African American. Six thousand is in fact a deceptively low figure, since colored regiments made up a sizable percentage of the brigades, and detachments are listed only generally.

42. Grant to Halleck, *OR*, vol. 34, pt. 4, 527; Grant to Sherman, April 4, 1864, in Grant, *Papers*, 10:255.

43. Peter Walker, *Vicksburg: A People at War, 1860–1865*, 215; James Currie, *Enclave: Vicksburg and Her Plantations*, 3–32.

Maltby's brigade, for instance, had a strong USCT presence, as did the cavalry in the area. The Natchez defenses also contained a significant number of African American regiments.[44]

What seems more impressive is that Grant and Sherman chose to trust their hard-earned prize to Slocum's keeping. Sherman actually worried little over the city itself. His later correspondence with Slocum shows he cared a great deal for the interior of the state and expected Slocum to keep it secure. He stated: "Vicksburg and its people are no use to us unless used offensively against the interior of Mississippi." Slocum tried to look at his position in this light, and to use what troops he could spare to march into the interior as much as he could. His immediate goal was to draw the attention of Stephen D. Lee's Confederate cavalry, keeping them away from "that devil" Nathan Bedford Forrest. Overall Slocum tried to wreak as much havoc as he could with any Rebel force that reared its head within his district boundaries.[45]

Slocum made several small expeditions from Vicksburg over the course of his tenure there. He headed one expedition—composed of twenty-eight hundred men and six artillery pieces from the Seventeenth Corps—and destroyed the bridge over the Pearl River. He moved on and encountered Lee's cavalry about three miles from Jackson. Slocum attacked, forcing Lee back after two hours of fighting. Later, on July 10–17, 1864, he led another incursion through Port Gibson and Grand Gulf, pushing back the Confederates in both places. He also organized a force that moved from Yazoo City to threaten Grenada.[46]

Almost from the beginning, however, Slocum found himself caught in the midst of a group of competing authority figures, which limited the effectiveness of his raiding. He had seniority over both the commander of the Sixteenth Corps at Memphis, Stephen A. Hurlbut, and the commander the entire Military Division of West Mississippi, Edward R. S. Canby. Sherman and McPherson realized this and, in the case of Hurlbut, actually exploited it to a certain extent. A man who thrived on the very corruption Slocum had been sent to combat, Hurlbut had been appointed by Lincoln

44. McPherson to Washburn, *OR*, vol. 32, pt. 3, 430; Abstract from returns of the Department of the Tennessee, ibid., 561, and ibid., vol. 38, pt. 5, 318, 744. A breakdown of the regiments at Vicksburg from October 1864, which probably closely resembles what Slocum would have commanded only two months before, is found at District of Vicksburg, *OR*, vol. 39, pt. 3, 568.

45. Sherman to Slocum, *OR*, vol. 34, pt. 2, 151; Sherman to McPherson, McPherson to Hurlbut, McPherson to Washburn, *OR*, vol. 32, pt. 3, 383, 415, 430.

46. Fox, *In Memoriam*, 92–93; Slocum to Sherman, *OR*, vol. 39, pt. 2, 160–61.

himself to the command of the Sixteenth Corps. Sherman and McPherson hoped to use Slocum's appointment as part of a plan to render Hurlbut impotent. By appointing Slocum to Vicksburg and shifting other troops out of Hurlbut's reach, they effectively removed the Sixteenth Corps from under him. As it turned out, Hurlbut's incompetence asserted itself dramatically in the form of the Fort Pillow Massacre, and Grant relieved him of command, effective the same day Sherman appointed Slocum to Vicksburg. They did nothing about Slocum's relationship with Canby for the moment, even when Canby ordered Slocum to keep two thousand troops in constant reserve, waiting on Canby's call. With most of his command tied up with garrison duties, this hamstrung Slocum and prevented him from sending out any more expeditions into the interior.[47]

On the civil front, Slocum dealt primarily with unbridled fraud and depredations against the freedmen. Writing home about this time, Williams commented that he thought Slocum well suited for the job, being a "hard nut to corrupt." In General Orders No. 4, Slocum cracked down on fraud. Only goods essential to loyal government lessees could be sent across district lines. He required provost marshals to keep detailed and accurate records of all passes issued. He outlawed all trade taking place outside a town garrisoned by at least one regiment, and no one could use a landing that did not fall immediately under the guns of either Federal troops or river gunboats. Anyone caught violating this order had his stock immediately confiscated. Slocum enforced these measures ruthlessly, leading one exasperated plantation lessee to write Lincoln in the hopes of getting Slocum to make exceptions.[48]

The corrupt officials resided primarily in the Treasury Department, though Assistant Secretary of War Charles Dana noted that they also included the commissioner of abandoned plantations, and Lorenzo Thomas, Jr., the son of one of the adjutant generals of the U.S. Army. An investigation by Major General Napoleon J. T. Dana, who would succeed Slocum at Vicksburg, revealed that Thomas stole numerous government supplies, which he then forwarded to his brother, who in sheer coincidence hap-

47. Jeffrey N. Lash, *A Politician Turned General: The Civil War Career of Stephen Augustus Hurlbut*, 142–43; Warner, *Generals in Blue*, 67–68, 244–45; McPherson to Sherman, *OR*, vol. 32, pt. 3, 297–98; Canby to Slocum, *OR*, vol. 34, pt. 4, 59–60; Clinton to Slocum, Slocum to Sherman, *OR*, vol. 39, pt. 2, 126, 160–61.

48. Williams, *Cannon's Mouth*, 319; Fox, *In Memoriam*, 94; Thomas A. Marshall to Lincoln, May 27, 1864 (Requests Lincoln to write letter on his behalf to General Slocum), Lincoln Papers (in this case online at http://lcweb2.loc.gov/cgi-bin/query/r?ammem/mal:@field(DOCID+@lit(d3334800)).

pened to be leasing one of the most prosperous plantations in the entire district. Thomas had also forged numerous signatures, even claiming at one point to be the secretary of war. Thomas was caught and sent to Slocum's headquarters under arrest by his commanding officer along with a detailed explanation of the charges. When he arrived, however, Slocum was in the field commanding an expedition. A cohort of Thomas's on Slocum's staff released the culprit and apparently destroyed the letter containing the charges.[49]

Mixed reports of Slocum's success against all this corruption—not to mention his desire to succeed—floated back to the government in the East. Halleck, for instance, sent a rather confused message to Grant in late June, stating that though he "hear[d] no complaints of . . . General Slocum at Vicksburg," he still thought Slocum had somehow become involved in the corruption he had been sent to clean up. Perhaps Halleck thought, after hearing so many complaints about men like Hurlbut, that silence indicated something sinister as well. Grant responded that independent information he believed reliable indicated Slocum was in fact "making war on a den of thieves" in the town, and that he wanted Slocum left alone.[50]

Other problems arose sometime before May 18, 1864, this time with the colored troops under Slocum's command. John Bobb, a Vicksburg citizen, returned home one day to find a group of black troops rummaging through his house and garden. First he called on them to stop, but when they ignored him, he chased them off his property. He reportedly even went so far as to hit one of them with a brick. According to one version of the story, they shot and killed him on the spot. According to another story, they came back later and bayoneted him. In either case Bobb was killed by members of Slocum's colored infantry.[51]

Slocum responded with General Orders No. 7. He denounced the breach in discipline. He reminded the officers in charge of the colored troops that they were involved in a program that was very new and very worthwhile, but they must prevent such violence. If not, history would

49. Halleck to Grant, *OR*, vol. 39, pt. 4, 568; Dana to Stanton, *OR*, vol. 36, pt. 1, 96; Dana to Christensen, *OR*, vol. 39, pt. 2, 190–93. That the adjutant must have hidden or destroyed the order is implied by the fact that Slocum never replied to it. This takes as a tacit assumption that Slocum had no reason to ignore the letter. This is a logical possibility, but in the absence of evidence to put it beyond reasonable doubt, the author has decided to give Slocum the benefit.

50. Halleck to Grant, *OR*, vol. 39, pt. 4, 568; Grant from Dana to Stanton, *OR*, vol. 36, pt. 1, 96.

51. "Gen. Slocum on Negro Difficulties," *Journal*, June 16, 1864; Currie, *Enclave*, 26.

remember them as a stain on the project rather than pioneers. He went on to state:

> if, in teaching the colored man that he is free, and that in becoming a soldier he has become the equal of his former master, we forget to teach him the first duty of a soldier, that of obedience to law and to those appointed over him—if we encourage him in rushing for his arms and coolly murdering citizens for every fancied insult, nothing but disgrace and dishonor can befall all connected with the organization.

He ended the order with a stern yet tempered reminder: "Every wrong done to the colored soldiers can and shall be punished, but he must not be permitted to take the law into his own hands." Rather than simply discipline individual soldiers, an easy way out that would have made sure few whites were punished, Slocum intended to hold the white officers accountable for any crime that "brought disgrace upon the colored troops."[52]

Slocum spoke out against slavery both before and after the war, but this incident shook his faith in the black troops under his command. Doubtless, white troops committed similar atrocities, but the newness of the idea of black troops in the army probably led Slocum to treat them differently. One of his officers, Colonel Joseph Stockton, remarked that during one expedition, his unit was, on July 13, "Rear guard again. General Slocum, fearing an attack on our train and not having as much confidence in the colored troops as in the two white regiments, kept us in the rear all the balance of the march."[53] Clearly, integration of the armed forces had a long way to go.

Slocum aimed a second order at guerilla bands attacking government-leased property. He promoted a policy that took an eye for an eye in the individual localities. If guerrillas destroyed a lessee's crops, troops harvested produce of a similar kind from nearby disloyal plantations and gave it to the victim as payment. If guerrillas killed a lessee, an assessment of ten thousand dollars was immediately levied upon all Rebels within thirty miles of the place. He required that full reports of all seizures be sent directly to his headquarters, hoping to cut off the layers of corrupt bureaucracy that had built up in the post prior to his arrival. Whatever Halleck might think, the resulting reports in the press cast Slocum in a favorable light. The *Syracuse Journal* stated that since "he took command there he has made a raid upon the swindling contractors and rascally

52. General Orders No. 7, *OR*, vol. 39, pt. 2, 38.
53. Joseph Stockton, *War Diary*, entry for July 13, 1864.

traders with the enemy, and his energetic and thorough measures have produced a new, wholesome, and credible state of things in his department." While this is surely overstating the case, Slocum apparently did his best to ensure that law and order returned to the city.[54]

A sad note from back home probably reached Slocum in late June or early July. One of his unmarried sisters, Sarah, had traveled to Jacksonville, Florida, to teach in a school for freed slaves. In early May, she fell ill and had to give up her teaching. One of the other ladies took care of her, but her condition did not improve. After several weeks her doctors decided there was no hope, but they did not tell Sarah, who continued to make a great many plans for what to do after her recovery. As she sank, she became delirious and passed away on May 28, 1864. Her friends buried her the next day.[55]

In the Eastern theater, Sherman and Grant prepared to embark on two campaigns that would lead to the fall of the Confederacy. Grant stayed with the Army of the Potomac to the north and faced Lee, while Sherman headed an army group made up of the armies of the Ohio, Cumberland, and Tennessee in Chattanooga. Slocum's old command, still under Hooker, had become part of Schofield's Army of the Ohio. Waiting for Sherman at Dalton, Georgia, the Army of Tennessee continued to entrench itself. In the wake of his loss on Missionary Ridge, Bragg asked to be relieved, and Jefferson Davis replaced him with Joseph E. Johnston. Johnston had spent the winter preparing to give Sherman a very warm welcome when the time came for the spring campaigns. Grant, having taken command of all Union armies, had a new plan in mind for that year. Instead of the armies moving piecemeal, left to the whims of their individual commanders, Grant ordered all Union forces to move together, which he hoped would prevent the Rebels from shifting troops to the area of greatest need, as they had done so often before. Grant and Meade would use Richmond to pin down the Army of Northern Virginia. Grant ordered Sherman to do the same to Johnston in Georgia, using Atlanta as the bait. Neither general could abandon either city, so Grant planned to use the Union's superior numbers and firepower to smash Lee and Johnston against their own strongholds.[56]

The campaigns began on May 1, 1864. Instead of attacking Johnston outright (a suicidal idea), Sherman flanked him, hoping to cut off his retreat

54. "Gen. Slocum's Administration at Vicksburg," *Journal*, May 28, 1864.
55. "The Death of Miss Sarah E. Slocum at Fernandina, Fla.," *Journal*, June 11, 1864.
56. McPherson, *Ordeal by Fire*, 410–12.

and force a surrender. Johnston recognized the significance of the move-ment and managed to pull his army out in time. Sherman followed, flank-ing Johnston again and again. Johnston kept retreating until, by the end of June, he occupied a series of prepared works along the side of Kennesaw Mountain just outside Marietta. There, Sherman switched tactics after Johnston checked yet another flanking attempt at Kolb's Farm. Hoping to catch Johnston by surprise, Sherman ordered a direct assault on a bulge in the center of the Confederate lines. After a short time, Johnston repulsed the attacks, inflicting heavy casualties on Sherman's men. Still, a feint to the south succeeded in seizing an important road junction, and Johnston re-treated again.[57]

Sherman, as overall Western commander, paid close attention to Slocum in Vicksburg. He had fought hard for the state and wanted to be certain the Confederates never took it back. The day after his failure at Kennesaw, Sherman vented some of his frustrations at Slocum in a dispatch. Sherman probably knew that McPherson had sent a number of suggestive dis-patches to Slocum, trying to prod him into action. Slocum could not obey, because of Canby's conflicting orders, but he had said nothing to Sherman or McPherson about it. On June 23, 1864, an Atlanta newspaper of a few days earlier had come to hand, and a dismayed Sherman read that the Confederates had begun to rebuild the railroad bridge at Jackson, Mississippi. Furious, Sherman warned Slocum that if he permitted this to continue, he could "expect no military favors from General Grant or my-self." He then issued orders for a weekly expedition against the railroad, adding that "unless all the negro troops have disappeared," Slocum should have enough men to do the job.[58]

Put off by Sherman's language, Slocum sent him an icy reply on July 2, 1864. He mentioned one of his earlier expeditions against the railroad, noting that while it was still out, Canby had issued his order that pre-vented Slocum from obeying Sherman's. When Sherman's dispatch ar-rived, Slocum ordered these men out, as requested. Less than a week later, Slocum received an order from Canby to forward him the troops held in reserve, then out on Sherman's orders. Slocum laid all this before Sherman, stating he had not mentioned it because Sherman had other, more important concerns on his mind. Slocum also made certain to point out he did not enjoy receiving orders from Canby, his junior, especially

57. Stephen Davis, *Atlanta Will Fall*, 73–91.
58. McPherson to Slocum (two communications), *OR*, vol. 39, pt. 2, 151, 74; Sherman to Slocum, *OR*, vol. 34, pt. 2, 151.

Major General William T. Sherman, under whom Slocum excelled. Library of Congress, Prints & Photographs Division, Civil War Photographs

when they contradicted others from Sherman. He ended his reply with a quote from Sherman:

> If I fail to accomplish what you suggest I am, in the language of your dispatch, "to expect no military favors from yourself or General Grant." The penalty which General Canby proposes to inflict has not yet been announced. Without any particular desire to secure favors from yourself or any other person, I shall continue faithfully in the discharge of my duty, which, I think, you readily perceive a very disagreeable and difficult one when you compare the different orders issued to me by General Canby with those issued by yourself.

Far from becoming angry over this letter, Sherman offered Slocum an apology, a promise, and what would prove a hint of things to come. He started by saying, "I fear you were more affected by the words of my telegram than I designed." He had not meant to offend Slocum by his choice of words, only to impress upon him how strongly he felt about affairs on the Mississippi, which he called "the spinal column of America." Also, since Sherman had sent the telegram the day after the slaughter at Kennesaw Mountain, he may not have been thinking clearly. He told Slocum to obey Canby's orders if conflicts continued, on the grounds that Canby knew more of the situation in Mississippi than he did. Sherman would attempt to keep better informed in the future. Next, to prove his goodwill, Sherman told him, "Be assured of my sincere respect." If Slocum would try his best to ensure that the road stayed broken, Sherman promised him he could "count on my personal and official support."[59]

Sherman also informed Slocum of McPherson's death. In the time it had taken for these communications to pass back and forth, Sherman had chased Johnston all the way back into Atlanta. Fearing Johnston might give up the city, Davis appointed yet another commander for the Confederate Army of Tennessee. The fiery Texan John Bell Hood knew he got his position in order to do one thing: fight. And fight he did. On July 20, 1864, he attacked an isolated Union army at Peachtree Creek, which included Slocum's former men, now under Hooker. The attack failed, and Hood sustained a great many casualties. He tried again on July 22, 1864, in what became known as the Battle of Atlanta.[60]

Sherman reported that McPherson had been directing some of his units into line when he encountered a group of advanced Confederate skirmishers. Before he could ride away, they shot him in the breast. His horse staggered to the side of the road, where McPherson fell off dead. His men managed to recover the body, which the army then sent north for burial. Sherman greatly rued the loss, describing his friend as "a noble, gallant gentlemen, and the best hope for as great a soldier that I had in my mind's eye." More important for Slocum, Sherman was not sure what would come of the inevitable shuffling of generals that would follow. As he put it, "General [John A.] Logan is in command of the army [of the Tennessee] in the field, but the President must name his successor. In the meantime execute his general orders, and in all matters of detail your own good

59. Slocum to Sherman, Sherman to Slocum, *OR,* vol. 34, pt. 2, 160–61, 202–3.
60. Castel, *Decision in the West;* Stephen Davis, *Atlanta Will Fall,* 129–47; Steven E. Woodworth, "McPherson, James B.," in Tucker, *Encyclopedia,* 2:552–53.

sense must direct." Neither Sherman nor Slocum knew it yet, but McPherson's fall would soon lead to Slocum's return to the front line.[61]

When the time came for a successor to be named, several generals remained hopeful. Historian John Marszalek notes in *A Soldier's Passion for Order* that Sherman used Thomas's hatred of Logan as an excuse to look for a West Point–trained officer. Of the more or less professional officers, Hooker had the most seniority, so he expected to receive the appointment by default. He did not realize exactly how well he had succeeded in disgusting Sherman, who chose Howard to be the new commander. When news of Sherman's decision reached him, Hooker flew into a rage. As Sherman put it, "Hooker, [went] off offended because he was not made McPherson's successor." Hooker indignantly offered to resign, a card that other generals, including Slocum, had successfully played on other occasions. Unfortunately for Fighting Joe, he had so worn on Sherman's and Grant's nerves that even the favor of the president himself did not prevent them from accepting his resignation. In fact, when questioned on the matter by Lincoln, Sherman respectfully stated that "[Hooker] is welcome to my place if the President awards, but I cannot name him to so important a command." With the Twentieth Corps now without a commander, Thomas suggested Sherman call Slocum from Vicksburg to take the helm of the corps.[62]

Sherman had told Halleck that "no indignity was offered nor intended," but Hooker, already smarting from Howard's appointment, must have been furious to hear Slocum would receive the command he had just relinquished. No one acquainted with the two men could fail to appreciate its meaning. Less than a year from the time Hooker had lobbied to dispatch his rival to Missouri, Slocum had returned and replaced him at the head of the corps "made up for [Hooker's] special accommodation." Sherman and Thomas, on the other hand, thought it an excellent and just arrangement. Slocum had lost his position during the consolidation process, so it seemed only right to them that he have the opportunity. Sherman sent for Slocum and placed N. J. T. Dana in command of Vicksburg.[63]

61. Sherman to Slocum, *OR*, vol. 34, pt. 2, 202–3.

62. Reports of Maj. Gen. William T. Sherman, *OR*, vol. 38, pt. 1, 78; Sherman to Washburn, *OR*, vol. 41, pt. 2, 533 (quote); Sherman to Halleck, *OR*, vol. 38, pt. 2, 271 (quote); John F. Marszalek, *Sherman: A Soldier's Passion for Order*, 279.

63. Sherman to Halleck, *OR*, vol. 38, pt. 3, 523 (quotes); Dana to Christensen, *OR*, vol. 39, pt. 2, 190–93; "Gen. Slocum's New Command" (clipping in OHA), c. August 1864; Dana to Howard, *OR*, vol. 39, pt. 2, 271; Marszalek, *Sherman*, 279. Ironically for any frustrated parties in Vicksburg, Dana was even more inflexible than Slocum.

Slocum arrived in Georgia and took command of his corps on August 27, 1864. The veterans of the Twelfth received him with loud cheering, as they looked forward to the prospect of serving under him again. One man Slocum worried about meeting again was Alpheus Williams, who, much to his own chagrin, had made a career out of being a brigadier general. Slocum was concerned it might bother Williams to be passed over for command once again. Williams, on the other hand, wanted no more of corps command for the moment and gladly turned it over to Slocum when he arrived.[64]

The Army of the Cumberland, of which the Twentieth remained a part after its consolidation, was still led by George Thomas, who obviously had respect for Slocum's abilities. Aside from the Twentieth, Thomas also commanded the Fourth Corps (now under Oliver O. Howard) and the Fourteenth Corps (commanded by Jefferson C. Davis, after Richard W. Johnson was wounded at New Hope Church). The Twentieth itself had quite a few familiar faces in it. When the Eleventh and Twelfth had merged, the elements of the Eleventh had been broken up and hung on the existing Twelfth Corps in order to fill it out. Both Williams and Geary had kept command of their divisions and a third was created. Not surprisingly, Hooker saw to it that Butterfield received this command. He led the Third Division through most of the Atlanta Campaign but eventually was relieved, on June 29, due to sickness. This was before Slocum took command. In his place William T. Ward, an Eleventh Corps veteran and leader of the First Brigade, ascended to command. So Slocum took over a corps that was mainly a modification of the one he had led for so long. In general, even those like Ward who had not been in the Twelfth at least knew him from the eastern theater. This helped ensure that the transition from Hooker would be relatively painless and that few, if any, of Hooker's proponents would be ranked high enough to worry Slocum.[65]

After the Battle of Atlanta, Hood tried one last time to break Sherman's tightening stranglehold on the city. At Ezra Church to the west of the city, he threw his army at another isolated portion of Sherman's troops. Bloodily repulsed yet again, Hood withdrew into Atlanta's defenses, leaving Sherman to decide exactly how to move the Army of Tennessee from its perch. At first Sherman opted for wholesale bombardment of the city, as Hood's defenses had been laid out long before and seemed impregnable.

---

64. Williams, *Cannon's Mouth*, 342.
65. Hebert, *Fighting Joe Hooker*, 271, 284; Warner, *Generals in Blue*, 538; Mark M. Boatner III, *The Civil War Dictionary*, 212; "The Atlanta Campaign, Order of Battle."

When the roar of the cannon failed to bring Hood out of Atlanta, Sherman considered other options. Attacking Atlanta head-on would prove suicidal. Instead Sherman decided to take his army on a great wheeling raid around the entire city in order to cut all of Hood's railroad supply lines. Once Sherman accomplished this, Hood would have to either retreat or starve. Either option would suit Sherman. When the rest of the army moved south unopposed, Slocum remained behind guarding the frail supply route along the Chattahoochee River. With the destruction of Hood's lines near Jonesboro, Sherman cut the last rail link supplying the Confederates, and Hood began preparations to abandon the city.[66]

To the north Sherman put Slocum on alert. When it became clear that Hood intended to evacuate, the Twentieth Corps stood ready to seize the city at the first practical moment. Because of the vulnerability of the railroad he protected, Slocum would have to be sure of Hood's location before he moved anywhere. On the night of September 1, 1864, Slocum and his men heard a huge series of explosions. Hood's ammunition trains had not left the city on schedule, and he was forced to destroy them. The conflagration made so much noise that many of the men north of the city thought Sherman had attacked, and ironically, Sherman's men south of town thought Slocum had made an assault. The next morning Slocum sent a strong detachment toward the city. They met a small party under a white flag led by the mayor of the town, James M. Calhoun, who surrendered the city. Slocum arrived sometime around two in the afternoon and established his headquarters at the Trout House. Shortly thereafter he dispatched a courier to Sherman to tell him of the conquest. He also sent a short telegram to Washington, stating simply, "General Sherman has taken Atlanta."[67]

Slocum had spent the year since Gettysburg embroiled in low-level controversies and apparent stagnation. His hatred for Hooker nearly accomplished his resignation, caused him to defy orders, and tried the patience of Grant, Sherman, and Lincoln. It ensured he would spend roughly the first nine months with parts of his command minding supply trains in Tennessee, and the next five months chasing corrupt carpetbaggers

66. Summary of Principal Events, *OR*, vol. 38, pt. 2, 54; Fox, *In Memoriam,* 97; Stephen Davis, *Atlanta Will Fall,* 148–72, 173–90.

67. Castel, *Decision in the West,* 527–29; Marszalek, *Sherman,* 287; Slocum to Halleck, *OR*, vol. 38, pt. 2, 763 (quote); Reports of Maj. Gen. William T. Sherman, *OR,* vol. 38, pt. 1, 82; "Gen. Slocum at Atlanta" (clipping in OHA), c. September 1864.

around Vicksburg, far away from the front-line commands he preferred. In all this, though, he still proved his worth to Grant and Sherman, which led to greater opportunities once Hooker resigned. One significant point stands out above all others, though. For all that he had absorbed from McClellan and Hooker, he had also begun to innovate some hard-war developments himself. This meant that, while he still had much to learn from Sherman, in this instance he was far from a blank slate. In many ways he prefigured his time as a western hard war commander, which meant he would work well with his new light: Sherman.

CHAPTER 7

"Sherman's mud-sills of the North"
To Savannah and Bentonville

Slocum would not be in Atlanta long before a marked change in his attitude and personality began to manifest. Under McClellan he had shown himself overly dedicated to caution and complex maneuvers. Under Joe Hooker he added to this a tendency to complain and an obstructive personal grudge. Under Sherman all the chaff quickly burned away. Although he had always been willing to fight when necessary, Slocum now became more aggressive and demonstrated a drive to hurt the enemy he had rarely displayed earlier. While the army was at Atlanta and Savannah, Sherman himself had to rein in Slocum's new aggressive persona. In the newborn Slocum, Sherman found one of his most useful and most trusted subordinates. His time under Sherman brought Slocum to the peak of his military prowess, and just in time: he would play a vital role in the successful attempt to march from Atlanta to the sea.

At first Sherman heard only rumors that Slocum had taken control of Atlanta. He sent couriers to find out the truth. When he ascertained that Slocum had indeed occupied the city, Sherman sent word for him to hold the existing entrenchments while the rest of the army regrouped and dealt with Hood. The Army of Tennessee had been bloodied and weakened by the battles that lost Atlanta: Hood now commanded less than forty thousand men, while Sherman still had more than eighty-five thousand. Yet, for all his failures, Hood was now doing what Jefferson Davis and the Confederate government thought most important, which was to take action. His army was still mobile and could easily keep Sherman's

175

more ponderous formations on the move for the foreseeable future. Hood moved his army north toward Tennessee and Alabama, hoping Sherman would follow him away from the heartland of Georgia. Hood intended to embark on a new campaign in which he would control the initiative. If Sherman wanted to destroy Hood's army, he had no choice but to follow, thereby ensuring that the rest of Georgia would remain safe. Also, if all went well, Hood could restore Tennessee to the Confederacy. At first Sherman obliged, following Hood north. Grant's plan called for the destruction of the Rebel armies, so even though he did not know it, Hood had every reason to expect pursuit. It seemed completely contrary to both commonsense and the laws of war to ignore a large enemy force heading into recently secured territory.[1]

Before leaving the area Sherman gave more thought to Atlanta's safety, placing Slocum officially in command and leaving the Twentieth Corps with him. In the vicinity Slocum would be responsible for tons of Union and captured Confederate stores, over 5,000 mules and horses, 80 pieces of artillery, and 12,700 sick and wounded soldiers. Both Sherman and Slocum knew that Hood's army was the only substantial enemy force in the area, but Sherman worried that Hood might slip away and turn south before he could respond. If so, Hood could throw the bulk of his force onto Slocum and the lone Twentieth Corps in Atlanta. Sherman therefore encouraged Slocum to contract his lines, fortify, and guard his supplies with care. The Twentieth Corps would be occupying a major enemy city that dangled tenuously on the end of a single railroad, deep in the heart of the Confederacy. As in the case with Vicksburg, Sherman had fought hard to capture the city and wanted to be certain it remained firmly under Union control.[2]

Sherman seemed honestly impressed with Slocum and kept his promise to support him. Slocum's anticipation of Western tactics and hard-war strategies made him fit into his new command much more readily than some other Eastern generals might. The men of both theaters saw a sharp distinction between themselves, and each group thought itself far superior to the other. The Western armies tended to think Eastern men arrogant and ineffective, while the Eastern armies thought the Western dirty and

1. Boatner, *The Civil War Dictionary*, 33 (Atlanta Campaign); Allan Nevins, *The War for the Union: The Organized War to Victory, 1864–1865*, 172; Sherman to Howard, *OR*, vol. 38, pt. 5, 771; Special Field Orders Nos. 245, 83, *OR*, vol. 39, pt. 2, 805, 43; Anne J. Bailey, *The Chessboard of War: Sherman and Hood in the Autumn Campaigns of 1864*, 13–47.

2. Stanley P. Hirshson, *The White Tecumseh: A Biography of General William T. Sherman*, 245; Sherman to Slocum, *OR*, vol. 39, pt. 2, 69; Reports of Maj. Gen. Henry Slocum, *OR*, 44:157; Marszalek, *Sherman*, 290–91.

uncultured. Rosecrans, for instance, felt that Western soldiers were so biased against their Eastern counterparts they would refuse to serve under an Eastern general. Despite the influence of McClellan and Hooker, Slocum did not have the learning curve that others, such as Franklin, might have faced. He had demonstrated Western tendencies before he ever fell under Sherman's discerning eye, so he more or less plugged into his new theater with few difficulties. Still, Slocum had not fully developed his Western persona while under McClellan, Hooker, and Meade. The hard-driving, effective aspects of his generalship were already there, but muted. Sherman's oversight would soon let Slocum reach his full potential. It should come as no surprise to hear Slocum inviting his friend Howland to come see him, noting that "you will not lose any of the good opinion you have always entertained of our noble army by the visit."[3]

As Sherman began his march northwest, he kept in regular contact with Slocum, appraising him of the overall situation. Sherman also offered warnings and thoughts on what Slocum might face. When Slocum received Sherman's first dispatches in Atlanta, he assured Sherman there was little to worry about. Slocum's troops were already working on a new set of contracted entrenchments that would be ready in short order. None of the patrols had seen the enemy within five miles of Atlanta, and any they encountered farther out appeared only in small groups.

Until Slocum finished his own works he ordered his men to hold the ones around the city built by the Rebels. This could prove difficult, since the original trenches were built to house a much larger army. Slocum ordered each division of the Twentieth Corps to hold a separate section of the line thinly, Williams's division with only one-third of its men. Slocum then ordered the remainder to join him and the Department of the Cumberland staff and guards in the center of town, near Slocum's headquarters on the city square. If attacked, Slocum planned to throw this reserve quickly at the section under assault. Slocum sent his artillery to cover the redoubts above and around his farthest lines. He positioned cannons throughout the breastworks, so they could pour an effective fire into any approaching enemy. The Union troops had also managed to capture fourteen working cannon left behind by Hood when he abandoned the city; no doubt Slocum used these to bolster his own artillery.[4]

3. Rosecrans to Lincoln, October 13, 1863 (Consolidation of the XX and XXI Corps), Lincoln Papers; Slocum to Howland, October 22, 1863, NYHS.

4. Slocum to Sherman, Signal from Slocum, *OR*, vol. 39, pt. 2, 69; Circular, Headquarters, Twentieth Corps, ibid.; Reports of Maj. Gen. Henry Slocum, ibid., vol. 38, pt. 2, 20.

Slocum's temporary arrangement seems a good one, though he never had the opportunity to prove it. If the Twentieth could not hold the entire front, then Slocum must be able to react quickly with sufficient force to any threat. By spreading out a thin line over the whole length of the works he essentially created a gigantic skirmish line. If the Confederates attacked in any strength, Slocum hoped the few men manning the works and supporting artillery would slow the advance enough for the rest of the corps to respond. The Twentieth's men camped in the center of town could therefore move quickly wherever he needed them most. Slocum would be hard-pressed to hold out against a foe attacking from more than one direction, however. In that case he could only trust that Sherman would indeed keep the majority of Hood's army in check; anything less, Slocum could handle tolerably well. He felt confident, as even the largest and most exaggerated indications placed only one corps of Confederate troops still south of the Chattahoochee.[5]

On October 9, 1864, Slocum reported that his men had repaired the bridge over the Chattahoochee and were guarding it in force. Trains to and from Chattanooga rumbled in and out again, at least temporarily. Slocum would have to do without the railroad on several occasions during his stay in Atlanta, as enemy cavalry broke the road repeatedly farther north. Although the Twentieth Corps had a good supply of food, Slocum expressed concern over the amount of forage available. By the time Sherman took the city, the armies of both sides had been marching and countermarching in the area for almost half a year. Although each army had maintained lines of supply, they often supplemented them with forage from the countryside. If this were not enough, Confederate impressment agents had scoured the area for supplies for Lee. Taken in total, five armies had stripped the vicinity clean. "I have not a pound for my own private horse," Slocum remarked. In order to secure enough for himself and his men, Slocum wanted to send out a foraging party as soon as possible. Sherman had no objection to sending a strong force south of Atlanta, a division at least. He thought one hundred wagons enough. Slocum sent out a column the same day he received Sherman's reply. It encompassed every available wagon in his command, with Geary leading.[6]

Slocum's final wartime transition had begun in earnest. Only a year ago, a McClellanized Henry Slocum would hardly have imagined such

5. Circular, Twentieth Corps Headquarters, ibid., vol. 39, pt. 2, 70.

6. Slocum to Sherman, Sherman to Slocum, ibid., 163 (quote), 178; Circular, Headquarters, Twentieth Corps, ibid., 179.

an aggressive foraging expedition. Previously, even though Hood was much less of a threat than Lee, Slocum probably would have magnified Hood's numbers ad infinitum, as McClellan had so often done before. He would probably have thought it foolhardy to dispatch so many men on the errand, given that he barely had enough to ensure his defenses would work if necessary. This time, however, he thought of the situation as Sherman himself might. He knew the location and realistic size of Hood's army, more or less, including the corps rumored to have stayed behind near Atlanta. More important, Slocum knew that Sherman's own forces sat squarely between Hood and Atlanta. This would leave only a small force of cavalry to the south to endanger the city, and Slocum's new lines were rapidly nearing completion. When they were finished, Atlanta could be defended successfully with a greatly reduced force. Also, necessity forced Slocum's hand. If they had so little forage that Slocum could not even provide for his own horse, then a new supply must be secured immediately before the army's animals suffered. Slocum, therefore, gave less thought to what McClellan would have said, and he acted more aggressively than he ever had before.

By October 14, 1864, he had finished his new lines. Having sent out cavalry patrols, he once again reassured Sherman everything was quiet. His men encountered only small groups of horsemen, and this was not often. Sensing the obvious power vacuum and inspired by Sherman's example, Slocum shed even more of his McClellanism as he began consciously to exceed orders. Instead of the one hundred wagons suggested by Sherman, Slocum soon informed him he expected the return of the four hundred he had sent out, well guarded, that evening. "If they come in sanely," he reported, "I shall send again at once. Our new line is well advanced and very strong." Sherman seemed pleased and ordered him to repeat the process, accumulating all the provisions he could.[7]

Meanwhile Hood failed to regain control of North Georgia. Sherman caught up with him but could not bring him to bay. Both generals continued to maneuver for the next month, but neither could gain the advantage. Hood hoped to keep Sherman boxing the air for the next few months at least. An increasingly frustrated Sherman began to turn his mind to other plans, not the least of which was that of a long march through the very center of Georgia itself.[8]

7. Slocum to Sherman, Dayton to Slocum, ibid., 242, 270.
8. Bailey, *Chessboard of War,* 13–47; McPherson, *Ordeal by Fire,* 460.

Left in Atlanta, Slocum had grown anxious to do something worthwhile for the war effort. He asked Sherman on several occasions if there was not something he could do to aid the army moving toward Tennessee and Alabama or even if he could simply send out more foraging parties. The great success of his supply operations convinced Slocum he could penetrate Georgia's interior. The new Slocum wanted to take full advantage of Georgia's weakness.[9] On October 18, 1864, Slocum requested Sherman's permission to go forward with an idea he had been considering. Confident that a single division could hold his new position, Slocum wanted to embark on a sort of proto-march to the sea. He planned to leave one division to hold Atlanta and strike out for Milledgeville and Macon with the other two. His aims were simple. "I believe I can go through the State with two good divisions," he wrote. "I can get a new outfit of horses and mules and damage the enemy seriously by destroying the railroad, &c., even if I fail in capturing either Macon or Milledgeville. I am positive they have no force in this section of the State except Iverson's cavalry." Although eager to get under way, Slocum did temper his request. He would only attempt it if Hood chose to remain at Blue Mountain during the winter, with Sherman keeping him in check. As Slocum said, "Let me try it. I will return if I become satisfied I am hazarding too much."[10]

There have been many claims laid as to who first formulated the idea for the march to the sea. It was a brilliant concept and would be an intellectual feather in the cap of any man whose historian could prove that he—not Sherman—had come up with it. And there has been no shortage of potential claimants: George Thomas in 1864 (who wanted to destroy the prison at Andersonville), Ambrose Burnside in 1863 (who proposed a march to relieve Chattanooga), and even Montgomery Blair (who Sherman noted wanted to march from Kentucky to the Gulf using only five thousand men armed with broomsticks). Sherman himself noted that talk of this sort of march was common campfire fare well before he proposed anything to Grant. Slocum made no postwar attempts to convince anyone he gave Sherman the idea, but at least he could say that he and Sherman thought alike, since he proposed a very similar plan to Sherman about the same time that Sherman proposed it to Grant.[11]

Slocum had learned well from his raids in Mississippi. He had more men to spare in Atlanta than he had in Vicksburg, and with Hood's army

9. Slocum to Sherman, *OR,* vol. 39, pt. 2, 106, 125.
10. Slocum to Sherman, ibid., 347–48.
11. Hirshson, *White Tecumseh,* 248–49.

occupied by Sherman, he faced even less opposition. The rough style of generalship he had encountered in the West had loosened him up. His time in Vicksburg and Tullahoma had probably contributed to his ability to see an opportunity like this one long before most of his fellow officers, many of whom remained reflexively focused on Hood. Thanks to his civilian commands, he had come to understand what Rebel citizens were capable of and what measures he must take to deal with them. So Slocum felt freer to chance such large expeditions. He also was more interested in using combat troops against Georgia's non-military population.

Slocum's plan resembled Sherman's eventual reality in some of its proposed goals. For instance Sherman would later take Georgia's capital, Milledgeville, and also threaten Macon. Both Sherman and Slocum intended to wreak havoc on Georgia's railroad lines (to the detriment of Lee) and to refit the entire army with fresh horses. Sherman's plans were more audacious. He had more men than Slocum, which meant he could risk more. He intended to, and actually did, make it all the way to the sea. Whether this thought ever occurred to Slocum is not known, but he would have felt obliged to stay close enough to protect Atlanta or to come if Sherman called. Although Slocum does not mention it, he also probably planned to do a good deal of foraging. This can be inferred by the fact that the success of his "bummers" is probably what brought the idea to mind to begin with. Slocum knew that Georgia had plenty of supplies to support such a raid, and that Georgia had no troops to oppose him. Like Sherman he also knew that striking a hard blow there would hurt the Confederacy dearly.

Sherman's plan proved more revolutionary than Slocum's largely because of the philosophy behind it. Sherman intended to strike specifically at the morale of Georgia's civilians, and while Slocum's plan would no doubt have accomplished something similar, Southern morale was an afterthought. Slocum remained focused on tangible goals such as railroads, cities, and horses, displaying no real interest in taking the war to the people in the abstract. Sherman had been interested in the Confederacy's civilian population for years, at least since his infamous letter to Halleck from Tennessee in which he suggested that, in order to truly win the war, the Federal government must focus on civilians. It must exploit the natural divisions within the Confederacy. Now Sherman sought to put his theories into practice. Above all, the men and women of the Confederacy, not to mention any observing foreign powers, had to learn that Sherman could go where he pleased, when he pleased, and do whatever he took a fancy to doing. Although he planned to destroy the rail network and take cities,

Sherman expected all these intangibles to play a larger part in actually ending the war.[12]

Sherman's and Slocum's ideas evolved nearly simultaneously—but relatively independently of each other. Both observed an opportunity, but only Sherman had the position and genius to exploit it to the full. Each man made plans to take advantage of Georgia's weakness, and the results were similar. This does not imply that Slocum gave Sherman the idea for the march, nor did Slocum ever claim it did. Sherman's famous dispatch to Grant, in which he promised to "make Georgia howl" was sent on October 9, 1864, over a week before Slocum made his request to attack Macon.[13] Slocum seemed to think Sherman would settle down for the winter near Hood, and that any fresh campaigning would wait for the new year. He apparently knew nothing of Sherman's intentions before his own suggestion. If indeed he had known anything, he would probably have realized he had little to gain from bringing up the idea of a march of his own. In fact, he had a great deal to lose. It could easily seem to Sherman that Slocum wanted to usurp credit and knew that he must act quickly. A veteran of the political wars of the Army of the Potomac, Slocum probably would not have put himself in such a compromising position.

Slocum's and Sherman's time serving as garrison commanders in occupied territories probably led directly to the independent development of their hard-war philosophies, demonstrated explicitly through their orders and letters. With such a focus already imbedded, it should come as no surprise that both Slocum and Sherman considered Georgia's civilians legitimate targets. With Slocum constantly absorbing more of Sherman's command style, it would also not be surprising to see them both thinking along the same lines.[14]

Sometime between when Slocum sent his dispatch and the arrival of Sherman's reply, Slocum got word of the upcoming march. Sherman curbed Slocum's newfound aggression, telling him to focus on preparing for the "grand march." Sherman wanted everything in readiness by November 1. Defying almost all expectations, Sherman left Hood where he sat and returned to Atlanta. Before leaving, Sherman dispatched Thomas with enough men to deal with the Army of Tennessee. A confused Hood

12. William T. Sherman, *The Memoirs of General William T. Sherman*, 286.
13. Sherman to Grant, *OR*, vol. 39, pt. 2, 162.
14. Those wishing to explore the concept of hard war should read Grimsley, *Hard Hand of War*.

marched north, having grandiose plans of his own to put into action.[15] As Sherman left Hood behind and returned to Atlanta, he sent a flurry of dispatches, all encouraging Slocum to bring in more supplies. Sherman knew for certain that Hood could not reach Atlanta before him, and he emphasized foraging rather than caution. Slocum complied with Sherman's request with gusto, sending out parties in ever-increasing numbers. By the time the armies left on the March to the Sea, the eager Henry Slocum's bummers had accumulated roughly two million pounds of corn and fodder from the Georgia countryside.[16]

Slocum in no way held the monopoly on knowledge about the upcoming march. After the war he made it very clear that Sherman had prepared his other commanders for what they were to do. As he put it:

> There was not an intelligent officer in all of Sherman's command who did not know just what his wagons were to carry, just where the materials and tools for destroying the railroads were to go in the column, just where in the column were to be found the bridges for use in crossing streams, just the right amount and kind of rations to be used each day. Everyone knew beforehand, even before we left Atlanta the exact duty of . . . Sherman's bummers.

Slocum played a very important role in this preparation, if for no other reason than that he had remained in Atlanta.[17]

Although the army would not be ready to leave by Sherman's original deadline of November 1, Slocum set about his duties without delay. He ordered all railroad assets, shops, and so on ready to be put to the torch. All supplies not marked for the march or for destruction he sent back up the rails to Chattanooga. On November 5, Sherman ordered Slocum to have his men ready to move as soon as they received their final orders. After making certain to protect the city, Slocum moved most of his command outside its limits. He generally took care to post provost guards over civilian property whenever the opportunity permitted. On November 7, just over a week before he began marching, Sherman ordered the destruction to begin.[18] That same day, Slocum wrote to Clara about the conditions in Atlanta and the preparations for the march:

15. Sherman to Slocum, *OR*, vol. 39, pt. 2, 370; Bailey, *Chessboard of War*, 48–50; Brian Melton, "March to the Sea," in Tucker, *Encyclopedia*, 2:532.

16. See various dispatches to Slocum, *OR*, vol. 39, pt. 2, 494; Reports of Maj. Gen. Henry Slocum, ibid., 44:157.

17. A. Noel Blakeman, ed., *Personal Recollections of the War of the Rebellion*, 61.

18. Sherman to Slocum, *OR*, vol. 39, pt. 2, 578. See various dispatches to and from Slocum, ibid., 643–44; Sherman to Slocum, ibid., 681.

I have been at the R. R. depot for the past three days several times, and have witnessed many sad and some ludicrous scenes. All citizens (white and black) begin to apprehend that something is about to happen . . . . Hundreds of cars are literally *packed* with them and their dirty bundles, inside and out . . . . Some are gnawing old bones, some squatted by the cars making hoe-cakes, some crying for food . . . . I wish for humanity's sake that this sad war could be brought to a close. While laboring to make it successful, I shall do all in my power to mitigate its horrors.[19]

Apparently, if turned loose on the Georgia countryside on his own, Slocum would not have allowed his men a free hand. During the march itself, he did what he could to limit the unofficial destruction by posting provost guards in various cities (official destruction would be another matter). Even the *Atlanta Journal and Constitution* acknowledged Slocum's relative restraint after the war. Still, Slocum had full intentions of working a somewhat muted brand of hard war, even if it was not as severe as what Sherman wanted. As Slocum put it to Howland, with special reference to South Carolina: "It would have been a sin to have had the war brought to a close without bringing upon its original aggressors some of its pains." Slocum would do his part to deliver the message. As he remarked to Clara in the letter above, "I fear their [the Armies of Tennessee and Georgia] track will be one of desolation." Ironically, under his restrained hard war, the Army of Georgia would contribute a great deal to that devastation, even more than its allegedly more destructive counterpart, the Army of Tennessee.[20]

In the weeks leading up to the march, Sherman took special care to re-tool his army specifically to the task at hand. Sherman himself noted in his memoirs, "most extraordinary efforts had been made to purge this army of non-combatants and of sick men," and historian Joseph T. Glatthaar argues that Sherman's efforts proved much broader. Sherman knew that once he loosed his armies on the Georgia countryside, the conduct of the campaign would depend very much on the abilities of the army officers, down to even the company level. As a result Sherman carefully constructed an army of veterans who could be depended upon to look after themselves and their duties. This obviously included his choice of his two chief subordinates. On the eve of the departure, Sherman issued his fa-

19. Slocum to Clara, November 7, 1864, at Fox, *In Memoriam*, 98.

20. "General Slocum," *Courier*, April 4, 1878; "Gen. Slocum at Atlanta," *Journal*, April 4, 1878 (for the *Atlanta Journal and Constitution*); Slocum to Howland, January 6, 1865, NYHS; Slocum to Clara, November 7, 1864, at Fox, *In Memoriam*, 98. See also John A. Carpenter, *The Sword and Olive Branch: Oliver Otis Howard*, 74–75.

General Slocum and the staff of the Army of Georgia. Library of Congress, Prints & Photographs Division, Civil War Photographs

mous Special Field Orders No. 120. He divided the army into wings, giving Slocum command of the left wing, already known unofficially as the Army of Georgia, composed of the Fourteenth and Twentieth Corps. The armies would carry few supplies aside from a moderate amount of ammunition. Instead Sherman ordered his men to "forage liberally on the country," paying particular attention to the rich planters. He also entrusted corps commanders with the discretion to destroy mills, houses, and cotton gins. Sherman expected them to exercise this power freely, especially with regard to industrial assets.[21]

Sherman left few records addressing specifically why he chose Slocum for this command, but his decision on Slocum and Howard as his chief subordinates is telling. In the general line of command, his choices would seem obvious. Howard kept command of his own army, and with Thomas gone north after Hood, Slocum was the other senior commander in the area. But there is probably more to it than this. Slocum had a long-established

21. Sherman, *Memoirs*, 2:172; Joseph T. Glatthaar, *The March to the Sea and Beyond: Sherman's Troops in the Savannah and Carolinas Campaigns*, 15–38; Special Field Orders No. 120, *OR*, vol. 39, pt. 2, 713–14.

reputation for measured responses and thoughtful handling of Confederate civilians. He could be harsh when necessary but was never overly so. If Sherman's intentions were indeed to cause wanton, pointless damage to the Georgia countryside, he could hardly have chosen more poorly, as he could easily have appointed harsher commanders. Sherman had already shown himself willing to ignore seniority when he passed over Hooker. His choice of Howard, famous as the Christian soldier, and the until recently reserved and cautious Henry Slocum implies that, although Sherman enjoyed destructive language, he did not intend to practice the radical hard war Southern partisans for years afterward accused him of waging. B. H. Liddell Hart alludes to this when he notes that Sherman was of two minds on the subject. Sherman disliked and despised every illegal act but knew that his role must involve punishment and vengeance against the South. He and many of his appointed officers took clear steps to check excesses, although they knew these would still occur despite their best efforts. When such excesses did occur, then they could be justified by the guilt of the South in bringing about disunion.[22]

Sherman's choice also makes sense in light of Slocum's recent ideas about hard war, which he had obviously been discussing with Sherman. He needed to develop his ideas a little further under Sherman's guidance, but he may well have impressed his superior with his understanding of Sherman's aims on a more fundamental level. Slocum obviously had a good understanding of the Georgia situation, especially in the area between Atlanta and Milledgeville and Macon. So, although Slocum clearly did not give Sherman the idea for the March to the Sea, Slocum's plans probably brought him to Sherman's attention and played a role in the decision to name him wing commander.

Sherman, unknowingly, had re-created Burnside's grand divisions. Although in this case called armies, each wing consisted of two corps coordinated by a higher commander who in turn reported directly to Sherman and exercised relatively little initiative. If either man noted this similarity, neither mentioned it. Neither did Slocum complain about this latest incarnation, especially since he now headed one of the wings. A notable difference may help explain why Slocum now voiced no objections. Whereas Burnside's divisions had simply blundered around through mud and eventually into Fredericksburg, Sherman's armies made a real difference. Also, William Marvel noted that Burnside would often skip over layers of the chain of command. In his grand divisions, Burnside often

22. B. H. Liddell Hart, *Sherman: Soldier, Realist, American*, 334.

ignored the overall commander and gave orders directly to his corps, creating an extra level of useless management. Sherman generally used the armies as they were supposed to be used and relied upon his subordinates to make most tactical decisions.

Sherman's plan called for the left wing of the army to advance due east along the Georgia Railroad, heading straight for Augusta. The right wing, under Howard, was to march south initially before turning southeast toward Macon. Both cities were large by Southern standards. Augusta housed a large arsenal while Macon contained some important industrial sites desperately needed by the production-starved Confederacy. Sherman's strategy effectively split any meager force that might be mustered to oppose him. Judson Kilpatrick and a large number of cavalry hovered on the flanks, protecting the army and causing all manner of trouble.[23]

The Twentieth Corps, once again under the command of Brigadier General Alpheus Williams, left Atlanta on the morning of November 15, 1864. Sherman and Brigadier General Jefferson C. Davis with his Fourteenth Corps followed the next day. Sherman and Davis moved almost directly on the Georgia capital, while Slocum and the Twentieth moved east, past the bald frowning face of Stone Mountain. They passed through the towns of Social Circle and Rutledge, destroying every industrial and rail asset that time allowed. Arriving at Madison on November 18, Slocum detached Geary's division to tear up the track as far as the Oconee River to the east. While there Geary destroyed an impressive railroad bridge. The majority of the corps turned south toward Eatonton to meet the rest of the army at Milledgeville. Geary followed as quickly as possible.[24]

Slocum preferred a particular method of railroad destruction, which the Army of Georgia employed throughout the march. First, he detailed a group the night before; the size depended upon the amount of track he hoped to destroy. The next morning he insisted his men get a full breakfast, consisting, preferably, of "roast turkeys, chickens, fresh eggs, and coffee." He noted that in the Georgia countryside these were all readily available and that the men worked better on full stomachs. The officers in charge then divided the men into three smaller details. The first group lined up along a section of track, one man per railroad tie, and turned them over all at once when signaled. Before moving on they loosened the rails from the ties. The second detail would then pile the loose ties into

23. Marvel, *Burnside*, 150; Bailey, *Chessboard of War*, 54–57; McPherson, *Ordeal by Fire*, 465–66; Melton, "March to the Sea," 532.
24. Report of Maj. Gen. Henry Slocum, *OR*, 44:157.

stacks of about thirty each, lay the rails over them, and set them on fire. After the rails had time to heat up, the final group used railroad hooks to bend and twist the soft metal until it had to be processed at a foundry in order to make it useful again. Many miles of track could be destroyed in a single day, depending on how many men Slocum detailed to the task. Although the soldiers could not seize the hot iron barehanded, Slocum thought it was "the only thing looking toward the destruction of property which I ever knew a man in Sherman's army to decline doing."[25]

Meanwhile Howard and the right wing moved south and east toward Macon. On its way the corps passed through the towns of McDonough and Rough and Ready, destroying whatever they could. They came almost to the very edge of Macon before turning northward to meet the rest of the army. Before Howard could leave the area, he was attacked in what became the only large-scale infantry engagement of the march. At Griswoldville a division of untrained old men and boys, remnants of a picked-clean Georgia militia, charged head-on against the entrenched veterans of Howard's army. The dreadful slaughter that followed accomplished nothing.[26]

Slocum, Sherman, and Howard concentrated near Milledgeville, where they discovered the Georgia government had made a hasty departure. They entered town in parade formation, bands playing and flags flying. Slocum made his headquarters at the Milledgeville Hotel on the evening of November 22, 1864. The troops treated the town much as they had others along the march. Some raided the state library, leaving it thoroughly disheveled (Slocum's men had done this also in Madison). Some ransacked stores and shops until the provost guard put an end to the looting. Other, more humorous, incidents also took place. A large group of soldiers convened a mock session of the Georgia legislature in the recently evacuated state house. They elected officers, debated a bit, and when someone asked what issues they had on the table, they placed a protesting soldier on one. After more debates of this nature, they proceeded to repeal the act of secession, bringing Georgia "officially" back into the Union.[27]

While in Milledgeville, Slocum hosted a dinner for Sherman and his large staff. They had the meal in the hotel, making use of its fine china and silverware. Slocum remembered it as a relaxing and entertaining evening, ex-

25. Slocum, "Sherman's March," 4:685–86n.
26. Kennett, *Marching through Georgia*, 254–55; Burke Davis, *Sherman's March*, 53–57.
27. George K. Collins, *Memoirs of the 149th Regiment N.Y. Volunteer Infantry*, 293–94.

cept for one significant moment of embarrassment. At some point during the evening Sherman picked up a spoon and examined it. Of course, it bore the marks of the Milledgeville Hotel. "Slocum, see here!" Sherman exclaimed, "How's this? Have you been taking some other fellow's spoons?" Slocum later admitted to being mortified by the comment, possibly worried that Sherman had taken offense to his disregard for the strict orders on foraging and stealing. After a moment of awkward silence, the conversation started up again, though no one said anything more about the spoons. Not long afterward Sherman returned the favor to Slocum, inviting the general and his considerably smaller staff to dinner at Sherman's headquarters. About halfway through the meal, one of Slocum's officers leaned over and called his attention to the spoons they used, each one clearly marked "Milledgeville Hotel." Slocum made a point of "tax[ing]" Sherman much as Sherman had him before the evening had ended.[28]

Before the army departed Georgia's capital, Sherman entrusted the destruction of all public buildings to Slocum. The fact that Sherman, who still probably thought of Slocum as reserved, left the destruction of both Atlanta and Milledgeville to Slocum may once again be enlightening as to how much damage Sherman really wanted to inflict. Sherman knew Slocum would destroy what he must, but no more. If Sherman had wanted to cause useless collateral damage, he probably would have chosen a man with a temperament more like that of Kilpatrick, who grew famous for his excessive antics.

The Army of Georgia moved swiftly after it left Milledgeville. The two corps reached Saundersville on November 26 and pushed some Confederate cavalry rapidly through town. Burned bridges delayed Sherman shortly at the Ogeechee River and Rocky Comfort Creek. Slocum pushed two divisions of each corps out to the flanks to watch for attacks and to secure the bridges. The armies passed though Habersham, Jacksonborough, and Millen before reaching the enemy's works encircling Savannah on December 10, 1864.[29]

Sherman had reached Savannah with ease, even though Joseph Wheeler's cavalry and others did indeed try to stop him. Governor Joseph Brown called out the militia, but only a few motley and untrained thousands assembled. General P. G. T. Beauregard arrived in the state and tried to rally what troops he could, but his impassioned pleas fell on deaf ears. Calls for a scorched-earth policy, which could have destroyed Sherman's

28. "Notable Talks," *Brooklyn Eagle*, Friday, February 1, 1889, 2.
29. Report of Maj. Gen. Henry Slocum, *OR*, 44:158.

army, went unheeded. Georgia civilians—many of whom had not been for secession to begin with—seemed to prefer the relatively brief presence of the Northern army to the complete and total destruction of their land and belongings. Wheeler's Confederate cavalry did everything they could to slow the Federal march, doing tremendous damage of their own, which Sherman was later blamed for. Grossly outnumbered, Wheeler could do little to slow Sherman's pace, however. Northern engineers had so refined their art over the years that any obstacle Wheeler left in their path they cleared in almost less time than it took to construct it. Wheeler also had his hands full with Kilpatrick's very aggressive cavalry.[30]

When they arrived outside Savannah, Slocum took a position with his left resting on the Savannah River and his right connecting with the Seventeenth Corps. Slocum commanded the water approaches to Savannah from above the city while, on the right, Hazen's division from Howard's army stormed Fort McAlister. There Sherman finally made contact with the outside world again by signaling the Federal blockading fleet. Reconnected to his supplies, he prepared to lay siege to Major General Joseph Hardee, who led the ten-thousand-man garrison in Savannah.

Slocum's position gave him the chance to deal Hardee a killing blow. His left flank had already captured several small steamboats from Augusta trying to break into Savannah. With the Union navy blockading the harbor, Hardee had only one road open for a retreat, and this lay on the South Carolina side of the river. Seeing an opportunity to cut off Hardee, Slocum threw a brigade across and prepared to send more. He entreated Sherman for permission to place an entire corps there. From this position Slocum would have commanded Hardee's only remaining escape route and also been able to fire down into the river approaches to the city with his artillery. Sherman refused to let Slocum act and later explained his hesitation by pointing out two facts. First, he knew that the Confederate Navy had ironclad gunboats in Savannah and feared they might interrupt any large-scale crossings. Also Sherman hoped to contact a Union force under John G. Foster near Hilton Head. He thought that Foster could march south and admirably close the gap. Slocum could then stay united on one side of the river. Sherman went to Hilton Head himself by boat. Fortunately for Savannah, Hardee knew very well the depth of trouble in which he waded. By the time Sherman secured Foster's help and returned, Hardee had safely retreated. Slocum discovered Hardee's

---

30. Bailey, *Chessboard of War,* 57–68.

absence at three in the morning of December 21, 1864, He immediately pushed his troops forward to occupy the city.[31]

Sherman and Slocum had lived out each other's later reputations. Slocum, for so long the picture of a nervous and conservative commander, now wanted to push ahead immediately and crush Hardee. He must have known about the gunboats and Foster but apparently did not care about them. Sherman had Hardee's army in the palm of his hand and Slocum wanted quick action. In the face of possible interference from the gunboats, the reputedly aggressive "War Is Hell" Sherman took no risks, even given the opportunity to achieve decisive results. As a consequence Sherman lost his chance to destroy the only significant opposition between himself and Grant in Virginia.[32]

Slocum's men had met no enemy worth mentioning throughout the entire march, and only a few burned bridges and felled trees had inconvenienced them. For all Slocum's talk of restraint, his men had inflicted extensive damage during the march, particularly to the railroad network. They aimed to remove the possibility that Georgia might ever contribute again to the Confederate war effort, and as Geary put it, they had "almost disemboweled the rebellion." Just in the vicinity of Madison they destroyed all railroad buildings and warehouses and laid waste to virtually every factory, destroying any cotton they came across, over two hundred bales. Slocum's men also spent a good deal of time carrying off as much corn, sweet potatoes, molasses, forage, and so on, and killing as many hogs, chickens, turkeys, and cows as they could find in the countryside. One woman lost over forty-four thousand dollars to Slocum's bummers.[33]

In fact, despite what the *Atlanta Journal and Constitution* would later allege, Slocum's wing far outstripped Howard's in terms of destructiveness. While Howard reported that his men destroyed seventy-two more miles of railroad than Slocum's, Slocum outstripped Howard in most other categories (see table 7.1). While these figures are obviously not precise, it is clear that in terms of livestock taken and cotton destroyed, Slocum's wing manifestly wreaked more havoc than Howard's. Even in the unlikely case that Slocum

31. Ibid., 112–31; Alexander R. Chisolm, "The Failure to Capture Hardee," in *Battles and Leaders of the Civil War*, 4:679; Sherman, *Memoirs*, 204; Glatthaar, *March to the Sea*, 9–10.
32. Glatthaar, *March to the Sea*, 9–10.
33. John W. Geary, *A Politician Goes to War: The Civil War Letters of John White Geary*, 217; Chisolm, "Failure to Capture Hardee," 204; Collins, *Memoirs of the 149th*, 289; David P. Conyngham, *Sherman's March Through the South*, 246; Superior Court of the Ocmulgee Circuit, Execution of Isaac L. Watson's estate, Sherman Folder, Archives of Morgan County, Georgia.

	Army of Georgia	Army of the Tennessee
Horses/Mules	4,090	2,781
Grain	5,000,000	4,500,000a
Fodder taken	6,000,000b	4,500,000
Cotton bales burned	17,000	3,523

Notes: a Howard's figures specifically reference corn, whereas Slocum simply refers to "grain." They are probably the same.

b Slocum notes that this is exclusive of the millions of pounds of fodder eaten by the thousands of cattle they acquired along the way.

Sources: Reports of Maj. Gen. Henry W. Slocum and Maj. Gen. Oliver O. Howard, OR, ser. 1, 44:159, 75–76.

had inflated the number of cotton bales destroyed by half, the real toll of eighty-five hundred would still be double that of Howard's.[34]

Immediately upon entering Savannah, Slocum put Geary temporarily in charge. Later Sherman ordered the army group to camp around Savannah with a mind to convenience rather than to defense. He placed Slocum in command of an area from the Savannah River to the canals. Sherman then set his men to work turning Savannah into the new "grand depot" from which future army operations would spring.[35]

Not long after entering Savannah, a strange thing happened to Slocum that he would not understand for several months. A bottle of excellent wine arrived at his headquarters; the accompanying note claimed it was compliments of General Oliver O. Howard. Knowing that Howard was a teetotaler, Slocum marked this down as odd but said nothing. Later, while preparing for the Carolinas Campaign, he discovered the truth. A British official residing in Savannah maintained a wine cellar of exceptional quality. When Howard's command occupied the area, a number of his officers managed to sneak into the house and replace the man's wine with bottles of water. They sent the wine to other commanding officers in Howard's name as a joke.[36]

Overall, Slocum thought it had been a very pleasant campaign. He called it "the romance of war," with just enough opposition to keep the

34. "General Slocum," Courier, and "Gen. Slocum at Atlanta," Journal, both April 4, 1878.
35. Perkins to Geary, OR, 44:780; Field Orders No. 139, ibid., pt. 3, 793–94.
36. "Notable Talks," Brooklyn Eagle, Friday, February 1, 1889, 2.

soldiers interested but nowhere near enough to put them in any actual danger. Slocum particularly enjoyed the good eating, noting that he had "turkies [sic], chickens, ducks, and sweet potatoes at every meal." The men, he said, looked well and were in better spirits than when they left Atlanta. He thought it amusing to see the "darkies" flocking to the army as they passed through. Slocum said they "danced and howled, laughed cried and prayed all at the same time. They 'had spected Massa Linkum for a long time and now bress de Lord he's come.'" The freed slaves brought with them scores of horses, mules, and provisions, all of which Slocum ordered turned over to the quartermaster.[37] More ominous for the South, even Slocum looked forward to their upcoming advance into South Carolina with relish:

> [Sherman] will soon introduce his mud-sills of the north to the cream of southern aristocracy. The original secessionists, those who boast of having been engaged thirty years in efforts to destroy our country. Now they are to taste the fruit of their labors. The meanest private soldier, knows the history of this contest and the part played by South Carolina. She will pay a fearful penalty.[38]

The most likely reason Slocum got caught up in the anti–South Carolina mania sweeping the army is because the Palmetto State had seceded first, fired the first shots in the war, and aired the most vicious rhetoric. Still, there may also be something more. The time Slocum had spent posted to Fort Moultrie might have left him with personal grudges, if not against individuals then against the state in the abstract. After all, one of the saddest incidents in his life—the death of his first child, Carrie—had occurred in Charleston, and he could not help but associate her sickness and death with the state. Sherman would soon loose an entire army of like-minded men into South Carolina. If Slocum and his men had taken off any kid gloves for Georgia, they would throw them away entirely when they left Savannah.

Slocum presented his men with a new, stricter set of field orders issued on Christmas Day 1864. In general he wanted to streamline the army before the upcoming campaign. First, he took steps to shave off dead weight. He ordered his corps commanders to recommend for dismissal all "officers who, by intemperance, inefficiency, or ignorance of their duties, have shown themselves unqualified for the positions they hold." He curtailed furloughs,

37. Slocum to Howland, January 6, 1865, NYHS. See also Report of Maj. Gen. Henry Slocum, *OR*, 44:159.
38. Slocum to Howland, January 6, 1865, NYHS.

allowing them issued only to men with a surgeon's excuse. Finally, to increase discipline he required that at least one commissioned officer be present with each company and one field officer with each regiment. Those looking forward to their tour ending soon must have been bitterly disappointed when he added that "no officer will be mustered out of service in violation of this rule, until the completion of the ensuing campaign."[39]

Slocum's efforts in Savannah were not nearly as formal or thorough as some of his other disciplinary actions. For instance, when following a similar tack after taking command of the Twelfth, he left most decisions on dismissals to a board of inquiry, which then removed men by court-martial. By comparison his approach after Savannah discarded many of the trappings and red tape he had used while in the Army of the Potomac. Some of these orders no doubt seemed arbitrary to the men dismissed. Those he sent packing probably thought "intemperance and inefficiency" synonymous with being on the bad side of Williams, Davis, or Slocum. In fact one lieutenant went so far as to say that Slocum had been "placed in [a] responsible [position] without the judgment to sustain [himself]. . . . Slocum is about played out. Prosperity has been too much for him." He concluded his statement by saying that the men had liked Slocum a great deal as a division and corps commander but much less so when he was leading the army. Other soldiers such as those of the 149th New York seemed to have no trouble with Slocum's new position. It is safe to say that Slocum probably garnered his share of both defenders and detractors in the army, though which group held a majority is not clear. For his part Sherman still thought highly of Slocum, describing Thomas, Howard, and Slocum all as "men who can be relied upon."[40]

There were two likely reasons for Slocum's change in behavior, neither of which came from his new "prosperity." First, he knew he had only a short time in which to work. Sherman planned on moving through the Carolinas very soon, and all preparations must be cleared up beforehand. If Slocum had taken the time to go through with boards and courts-martial, he could not have completed the process. Second, Slocum had now been six months with Sherman on the campaign; virtually all traces of the cautious McClellan had been wiped away.

Back in Virginia, Grant and the Army of the Potomac stood across the Petersburg trenches from Lee. After Grant had pinned him, Lee responded

39. General Orders No. 3, OR, 44:808.
40. Glatthaar, March to the Sea, 22–23; Brooks D. Simpson and Joan V. Berlin, eds., Sherman's Civil War: Selected Correspondence of William T. Sherman, 1860–1865, 814.

by sending a corps of his army under Jubal Early up the Shenandoah Valley in a lightning-fast assault that actually reached the perimeter of Washington. Grant had Philip Sheridan, Slocum's old roommate from West Point, chase and destroy Early. Sheridan then laid waste to the Shenandoah Valley, hoping to deny the Confederates use of its fertile fields. Meanwhile, Grant continued to hammer Lee against Richmond. Periodically, he tested the Army of Northern Virginia with an assault, knowing that eventually it must break.[41]

Sherman's army marched north in January 1865. He intended to join Grant at Petersburg, where together they could overwhelm Lee. Sherman knew he must cover a great distance in order to get to Grant, and he wanted to make the most of it. Instead of loading Slocum's and Howard's armies on ships at Savannah and depositing them in Virginia, Sherman asked Grant for permission to march straight north through the Carolinas, doing as much damage as he could along the way. As Slocum observed, the army in general looked forward to its trip through South Carolina in particular, and most especially to "smashing things," as Sherman put it, within its bounds.[42]

Sherman's basic plan of operations mirrored the March to the Sea. This time Howard and the right wing advanced as if they intended to attack Charleston. Slocum and the left feinted toward Augusta again, which still fell within striking distance of that side of the army. In the center of the march, between the two wings, lay the state capital of Columbia. Sherman again hoped that by threatening Augusta and Charleston, he would prevent the state's scattered Confederate garrisons from uniting against him. Sherman could then split the horns of the Confederate dilemma and take Columbia before Hardee, who remained in the area, could react.[43]

As it left Savannah, the Army of Georgia found its path obstructed in various ways. First, not long after the march began, a huge storm rolled in, flooding all the rivers and destroying a number of bridges. It was the worst rain to hit the area since 1840, and it turned the normally crossable Savannah River into a lake three miles wide. Most of the Twentieth Corps had crossed beforehand and ended up stranded on the far bank. Slocum, the Fourteenth, and some of the Twentieth could hear no word of their status. Slocum managed to get across the raging torrent on January 29,

41. Matloff, *American Military History,* 266–70; McPherson, *Ordeal by Fire,* 410–71.

42. Matloff, *American Military History,* 266–70; McPherson, *Ordeal by Fire,* 410–71; Sherman to Porter, *OR,* 44:843 (quote); Slocum to Howland, January 6, 1865, NYHS.

43. Glatthaar, *March to the Sea,* 100–118.

Slocum leads his army out of Savannah on the march through the Carolinas.
Library of Congress, Prints & Photographs Division, Civil War Photographs

1865, but still could not find his men. It took him a full day before he could get in touch with Williams, and only then, after resorting to a small row-boat. Man-made difficulties also hampered their initial progress. Hardee's men did their work well, not only burning bridges and felling trees across the path, but also planting a great many torpedoes (a rudimentary sort of landmine) in the road. It took Slocum five days to remove obstructions, a process no doubt slowed by the men's understandable fear.[44]

Slocum later said that the mines played a distinct role in the enormous destruction the army wreaked in South Carolina. The soldiers had little trouble with the idea of using such hidden explosives to defend a clearly marked position, such as the ones that had defended Fort McAlister, but they could not agree to hiding them in a road, where no one had any advance warning of danger. Slocum likened it to poisoning a stream. If the men had looked forward to hurting South Carolina before, they now went

44. Marszalek, *Sherman*, 318; Report of Maj. Gen. Henry Slocum, *OR,* vol. 47, pt. 1, 419–20.

at it with a vengeance and caused a great deal more unofficial destruction in this section than in any before or after. For instance, in his report, Williams noted that although only 2,110 mules and horses had been reported to the quartermaster, he felt certain that a low estimate of the real number of animals stolen by his corps must be in excess of 5,000.[45]

In the beginning of February, Slocum's men finally got under way. Before February 15, both corps concentrated near Lexington, South Carolina. After tearing up some sixty miles of track, they crossed the Saluda River and headed toward the state capital. By the time Slocum reached Columbia, a huge blaze had begun, which his men watched from a distance. Working side by side with the civilians, other Federal soldiers contained the fire but not before it had destroyed much of Columbia. Afterward they followed Hardee across the Great Pee Dee River and into North Carolina. "No sadder scene was presented during the war," Slocum said later, concerning the burning of Columbia. Although not in the immediate vicinity of the town itself, he noted he could see the light of the fire from miles distant. He thought Sherman to be completely innocent of this catastrophe, though he did not completely absolve the Union army, as some might. Slocum blamed the civilians' free distribution of whiskey and other intoxicating drinks to the soldiers. With an interesting turn of phrase, Slocum observed in a postwar essay that a "drunken soldier with a musket in one hand and a match in the other is not a pleasant visitor to have in the house on a dark, windy night, particularly when for a series of years you have urged him to come, so that you might have the opportunity of performing a surgical operation on him." It could be that time had mellowed Slocum, and that he feared to be remembered as a hate-monger, but this seems to be more of an excuse. Whatever the case, Slocum, unlike others, clearly placed the torch in the hand of the Northern soldier, even if he lays the blame elsewhere.[46]

Although more than happy to give South Carolina a good thrashing, Slocum reverted to a relatively restrained approach when the armies entered North Carolina. This may once again point to Sherman's influence. Slocum issued an order noting that the state's "action on the question of secession was undoubtedly brought about by the traitorous acts of other states" and a vocal secession minority. Slocum went so far as to say that

45. Slocum, "Sherman's March," 684. It is notable that there were torpedoes defending Fort McAlister, but few of Sherman's troops, if any, found them legitimate. Report of Bvt. Maj. Gen. Alpheus Williams, *OR*, vol. 47, pt. 2, 589.
46. Slocum, "Sherman's March," 686.

the vast majority of North Carolinians had never approved of it. He therefore wanted his men to be careful with the state's property and be certain not to jump to any conclusions concerning loyalties.[47]

Sherman occupied the town of Fayetteville for several days while planning the next stage of his march, which he hoped would terminate at Goldsboro. Hardee, who up until now had retreated before the much more powerful Union armies, took advantage of this time to rest his men. When Sherman next moved, Slocum's wing performed another feinting maneuver, moving toward Averasboro and Bentonville, while Howard proceeded straight to Goldsboro. Hardee planted himself firmly in Slocum's way by occupying the junction of the Raleigh and Goldsboro roads at Smithville, near Averasboro. Hardee needed to buy time for Johnston to assemble whatever army he could in front of Slocum.[48]

On March 16, 1865, Slocum encountered troops entrenched near Averasboro and started skirmishing with them about daybreak. He found the roads in terrible condition and could not move the bulk of his men forward until late morning. Hardee's first line, commanded by an old friend of Slocum's from Charleston, proved abnormally stubborn, given that the men holding it had no combat experience. It took a flanking movement to dislodge them, but they only fell back to a second line. After a brief stand more in keeping with what could be expected of green troops, that line fell back into a third, more powerful set of entrenchments. Slocum continued to press forward carefully. Finally, vastly outnumbered, Hardee retreated, taking the road through town and leaving the junction uncovered. Slocum followed, heading to his intended rendezvous with the Army of the Tennessee at Goldsboro.[49]

Averasboro has been described as Hardee's finest hour, even better than his retreat from Savannah. He did indeed perform quite well, buying Johnston some desperately needed time. Yet, more important, Hardee's stand gave his inexperienced troops a chance to taste battle before they would make their last real attempt to stop Sherman. Given the shabby state of Johnston's army and its small numbers, experience would be something they could all use. Slocum seems not to have particularly cared

47. General Order No. 8, Army of Georgia, OR, vol. 47, pt. 2, 719; untitled, Journal, March 20, 1865.

48. McPherson, Ordeal by Fire, 471–75; Lawyn C. Edwards, "Bentonville, Battle of," in Tucker, Encyclopedia, 1:96; Mark L. Bradley, "Old Reliable's Finest Hour," 9–10.

49. Report of Maj. Gen. Henry Slocum, OR, vol. 47, pt. 2, 422–23; "Gen. Slocum in the War"; Nathaniel Cheairs Hughes, Jr., Bentonville, 32–35; Herman Hattaway, Shades of Blue and Gray, 235–36.

one way or the other about the battle. He gives it only a cursory mention in his description of the march that appears in *Battles and Leaders*. He performed more along the lines of his old persona but with a flavor of his new: he was careful, yet pushing steadily forward. As far as Slocum was concerned, Hardee stopped, and the Army of Georgia pushed him right back out of the way. There was nothing more to it than that. The battle seems more interesting from Hardee's perspective given the odds he faced, but even there its significance can easily be overstated.[50]

A nasty surprise awaited Slocum just outside Bentonville. On Sunday, March 19, Johnston ambushed Slocum's wing with his newly concentrated army, hoping to destroy it before Howard and the right wing could come to its assistance. On this occasion bad intelligence led to Sherman and Slocum's failure to see the trap. Both believed Johnston's army to be forty miles away, toward Raleigh. When Slocum's men reported firing toward the front of his column, they felt certain it was nothing more than a few cavalry pickets. Sherman ordered Slocum to brush them out of the way and get on with business.[51]

When the Fourteenth Corps moved forward, particularly Morgan and Carlin's divisions, they encountered not cavalry but large numbers of entrenched infantry. Johnston had arranged his men in a sicklelike formation across the road and into the woods on one side. When Slocum's men approached, Johnston attacked the left of the Fourteenth Corps. Although Slocum later maintained that Carlin's division fell back with grace and poise, in reality they just plain scampered for safety. Morgan held out, slowing Johnston's advance substantially. Slocum was still unsure as to exactly what size army faced him until an unwilling Confederate conscript deserted and brought him solid intelligence. Not long before, Slocum had sent a message to Sherman stating that the left wing would need no help, but now he immediately dispatched another messenger to tell Sherman he was actually facing Johnston's entire army. Slocum rapidly moved up the Twentieth Corps and set up a new, more powerful line along a hill a short way behind the wavering front. Johnston's offensive drove through the shattered left and advanced on the second line. Morgan's stubbornness, though, had seen to it that Johnston's forces could not move in unison. Slocum watched in quiet calm as the disorganized, desperate Rebels threw themselves on his second position. Their attack

50. Bradley, "Old Reliable's Finest Hour."

51. Fox, *In Memoriam*, 100; Hughes, *Bentonville*, 68; Edwards, "Bentonville," 96; Hattaway, *Shades of Blue and Gray*, 235–36.

fizzled out under a withering fire of rifle balls and canister. Slocum attacked the next day, regaining all the lost ground. Johnston retreated into his entrenchments. As night fell Slocum ordered his tent pitched on the spot he had originally intended for his headquarters, which the army had taken back during the day.[52] The tattered remnants of what once had been a mighty Southern army remained on the field while Howard's wing joined Slocum. When Sherman ordered Howard to attack, one portion easily broke through Johnston's farce of a defense. Only a last-minute counterattack saved Johnston from total destruction. Finally realizing he could accomplish nothing, Johnston withdrew.[53]

This would be Slocum's last battle and probably the only major engagement in which he had a free hand for more than half the fight, aside from Glendale in 1862. In the first day's fighting, he acquitted himself well. Johnston had indeed caught Slocum off guard, but he had also surprised Sherman. Who could have predicted that Joseph E. Johnston, of all people, would act as he did? Johnston certainly had set no precedent for this kind of daring. When Slocum's predicament became apparent, he maintained his composure and put together a defense that brought Johnston to a halt. The next day Slocum attacked and took back all he had lost. Still, he apparently felt embarrassed by the fact that Johnston had caught him flat-footed. Slocum still reacted defensively over some aspects of the battle even years later, as evidenced in his refusal to admit Carlin's outright flight.[54]

Ironically, only a few days after the Battle of Bentonville, Slocum's army became official. On March 29, 1865, Grant telegraphed Stanton, asking that the Fourteenth and Twentieth officially become the Army of Georgia. The nomenclature actually had come into practical use much sooner. As early as September 8, 1864, the name occurs in reports found in the *Official Records* referring to troops under Sherman's command. Slocum himself used it in his letter to Clara sent on November 7, 1864. By the time the army reached Savannah, Slocum wrote his personal correspondence on official stationary headed with that title. So the official orders naming the two corps simply recognized an already existing state of affairs. According to Grant, the main reason he and Sherman wanted to make it official was that, while Howard could sign discharges and furloughs, Slocum could not.[55]

52. Slocum, "Sherman's March," 695; Report of Maj. Gen. Henry Slocum, *OR*, vol. 47, pt. 2, 424–25; Hughes, *Bentonville*, 89–94; "General Slocum's Victory," and "Gen. Slocum in Battle," *Onondaga Standard*, March 31, 1865.
53. Hughes, *Bentonville*, 150–211; Edwards, "Bentonville," 96.
54. Slocum, "Sherman's March," 695.
55. Grant to Stanton, March 28, 1865, in Grant, *Papers*, 14:240.

	Army of Georgia	Army of the Tennessee
Horses/Mules	4167*a*	4115
Grain	5,456,722	4,867,326
Fodder taken	4,949,461	2,785,721
Cotton bales burned	21,950*b*	Approx. 15,000

Notes: a This figure includes only those animals officially reported to the army's quartermaster.

   b This figure represents only the cotton burned by Williams's Twentieth Corps. Davis did not report figures for the Fourteenth.

Sources: For the Army of Georgia, Report of Bvt. Maj. Gen. Alpheus S. Williams, *OR,* ser. 1, vol. 47, pt. 1, 589; Report of Bvt. Maj. Gen. Jefferson C. Davis, ibid., 436–37; Report of Maj. Gen. Henry W. Slocum, ibid., 418–25. For the Army of the Tennessee, Report of Maj. Gen. Oliver O. Howard, ibid., 209.

After occupying Goldsboro, Sherman prepared his legions for yet another march, this time to Richmond. As it turned out, events at Petersburg made these plans unnecessary. Grant captured Richmond on April 2. Lee managed to pull his army out intact but lost an important rearguard action in the process. Lee tried to get away from Grant and unite with Johnston, but after a brief chase Grant caught him at Appomattox. Lee surrendered on April 9, 1865. Sherman then changed his objective in order to pursue Johnston's army, which he chased through Raleigh. He captured the town on April 13. Next day he and Johnston entered into surrender negotiations, a process that turned out to be both prolonged and controversial, but after two weeks they reached an agreement. For all intents and purposes, the war was finally over.[56]

At the end of his second major campaign as an army commander, Slocum had once again proved to be the more destructive of Sherman's army commanders, this time outstripping Howard in every category sampled (see Table 7.2). Assuming that Davis destroyed roughly the same amount of cotton that Williams did, the Army of Georgia burned roughly twice what the Army of the Tennessee did. Slocum's domination of the amount of fodder taken (2,163,740 pounds more than Howard's men) strongly implies that Williams's off-hand estimates of the real numbers of

56. McPherson, *Ordeal by Fire,* 478–82; Dickson, "Civil War, Land Overview," 197; Hughes, *Bentonville,* 220–21.

horses and mules appropriated from the countryside are by far more accurate than the numbers above. If this is true, then Slocum's men absconded with over seven thousand animals instead of only four thousand. Slocum's friends in the Army of the Potomac must have found this hard to believe.

In the final months of war, Slocum's unconscious tendency to imitate his commanders finally bore good fruit. Sherman's influence obliterated the negative effects of Slocum's time under McClellan and Hooker and brought out the best, most effective aspects of Slocum's character. Slocum saw his best and most useful service in the last months of the war. His experiences in Tennessee and Vicksburg, rather than leading to his disappearance from the national stage, instead fitted him almost perfectly for his new role. By the end of the war he had distinguished himself as an army commander and a friend of Sherman's. He could claim credit for foiling Johnston's last-ditch effort. With his abilities peaking at the end of the war, Slocum seemed poised to turn his military fame into political success.

CHAPTER 8

Trifling with Fair Fame

Political Suicide in 1865

An objective observer at that time would probably have expected Henry Slocum's star to continue its precipitous rise. After having stayed on a plateau for a time between 1862 to 1864, with Hooker's fall Slocum rocketed back into prominence. At the end of the war he had reached the apex of his martial abilities and been identified in the national press as one of Sherman's most trusted subordinates. He could claim to have been (rightly or wrongly) a wing commander at Gettysburg, the first into Atlanta, and the first into Savannah. He had won the last highly publicized battle along the east coast. He had ascended to command of an army, a rank that could be claimed by fewer than a dozen men from over one million in Union blue. Certainly not as famous as Grant or Sherman, Slocum had still garnered enough of a name to translate into considerable political capital. Yet, within the next twelve short months he managed to negate the public value of the past few years and damage his military reputation and political career on the national level in ways from which they would never fully recover.

Slocum remained in command of the Army of Georgia for the short time it would continue to exist. When the armies met at the Bennett place, Slocum and Howard both stood with Sherman as Johnston signed the surrender. During the Grand Review in Washington in late May, Slocum rode at the head of the Army of Georgia. Clara and the rest of his family traveled down to Washington to be with him and rode in a carriage in the parade.[1]

1. Fox, *In Memoriam*, 101; Collins, *Memoirs of the 149th*, 336.

The Army of Georgia in the Grand Review. Library of Congress, Prints & Photographs Division, Civil War Photographs

After the review, the War Department took Slocum's army apart very quickly. He issued his farewell address to the men on June 6, 1865, praising them for all the sacrifices they had made in the service of their country: "I cannot repress a feeling of sadness at parting with you. . . . No generation has ever done more for the establishment of a just and liberal form of government, more for the honor of their nation." He made certain to mention the voting public who "have poured out their wealth in support of these armies with a liberality never before witnessed in any country." The army disbanded on June 17, 1865.[2]

2. The quote is from both "Farewell Address of Gen. Slocum," *Journal*, June 8, 1865, and "Gen. Slocum's Farewell Order," *New York Times*, June 8, 1865, 4. See also Summary of the principal events, *OR*, vol. 47, pt. 1, 1.

Slocum and others busied themselves saying their goodbyes. Within a week of his farewell, Slocum and the officers of the Fourteenth and Twentieth corps sat down to one last dinner in a grove in northwest Washington near Glenwood Cemetery. The area had been decorated with a long pavilion draped in red, white, and blue. The tent covered enough tables and chairs to seat over three hundred persons. The silvery glow of a full moon supplemented the light of hundreds of candles placed on racks affixed to the trees surrounding the tables. Including guests (notably Howard and his staff), the revelers filled the grove completely. Three regimental bands took turns to liven up the night, but the correspondent of the *New York Times* found that of the Thirty-third Massachusetts the most impressive. At nine o'clock that evening, all sat down to dinner, with Slocum presiding over one table and Howard the other. Afterward, Slocum rose to offer the first toast of the evening. He congratulated the men of his army, a hybrid of Eastern and Western commands, for proving their critics wrong. They, like Rosecrans, assumed such men could never work together. He called Lincoln's recent assassination a "sad event" that had "cast a shadow on every meeting of our officers":

> All have felt the absence of one who should have been present to witness these scenes; one to whose great mind and pure heart; to whose perseverance and faith in the right, we are more indebted for our final triumph than to any other cause. I propose a sentiment in which I know you will all unite:—*To the memory of our great leader—Abraham Lincoln.* (Emphasis in the original)

Howard responded to Slocum's toast with one of his own to President Johnson. The group then called on officer after officer, until they had toasted virtually every good thing American they had ever encountered. Any man taking part from the beginning must have ended the night (or early morning) quite drunk. Although he would never command them again, Slocum remained in contact with some of these men for the rest of his life.[3]

Slocum looked forward to the final demise of his army with some cynicism. Williams, trying to find out when he himself might leave for home, called Slocum "an apathetic man in such matters." Having risen to the near top of the Union military hierarchy, Slocum would naturally see the possibility of reverting to nothing more than a small-scale businessman and struggling lawyer as bittersweet. He did not intend to resign immediately,

3. The quote is from both "The Army of Georgia," *New York Times*, June 12, 1865, 8, and "General Slocum," *Journal*, June 13, 1865. Tracey, for instance, attended this dinner and later gave a speech in Slocum's stead after Slocum's death in 1894. "Slocum, Soldier and Man," *New York Times*, May 5, 1894, 9.

but neither did he plan to stay long in the army. He later wrote to Sherman, "I did not like to go out with a crowd of worthless officers who should have been mustered out long ago; but . . . I do not intend to spend the winter [in the army]."[4]

While Slocum and his family visited Washington, President Johnson had already begun to put his reconstruction program together. The atmosphere of the country was no less politically charged than it had been a few months earlier, but over the summer it shifted its focus from war to peace. These changes, especially in the Republican Party, would have drastic effects on Slocum's future. Over the summer, divisions within the Republicans opened into chasms between those who opposed Johnson's lighter-handed approach to reconstruction (the self-labeled Radicals) and those who supported Johnson (the Conservatives). The Radicals wanted to push a harsh legalistic policy that would completely remake the South. They did not want simply to usher a somewhat chastened section back into the Union without punishing it for its sins. They demanded that steps toward complete, total, and immediate black equality be integrated into every aspect of reconstruction. They felt particularly passionate about voting rights. The Conservatives or moderates—who either disliked the idea of black equality or, like Slocum, supported it but thought it impractical to impose so quickly—came out in support of Johnson. The battle to see which side would enforce its will had only just begun.[5]

One of Johnson's first actions was to divide the nation into military districts, including the Military District of Mississippi, once again centered in Vicksburg, and he appointed Slocum to command it. Slocum was a good choice since he already had extensive experience with Vicksburg and its trading villains. On June 13, 1865, Johnson chose William L. Sharkey as provisional governor of Mississippi. He gave Sharkey a mandate to return Mississippi to the rule of civil law as quickly as possible. Johnson ordered the department military commander and all his supporting staff to work with Sharkey, noting that "they are enjoined to abstain from in anyway hindering, impeding or discouraging loyal people from the organization of a State Government, as herein authorized." This arrangement would soon bring Slocum into open conflict with Sharkey.[6]

4. Williams, *Cannon's Mouth*, 390; Slocum to Sherman, August 27, 1865, at Fox, *In Memoriam*, 105.

5. Michael Les Benedict, *A Compromise of Principle: Congressional Republicans and Reconstruction, 1863–1869*, 21–24.

6. "Reconstruction," *New York Times*, June 14, 1865, 1; General Orders No. 118, *OR*, vol. 46, pt. 3, 1299.

Slocum and his family left Washington by June 11, heading back to Syracuse for a leave of absence. Along the way they stopped in New York City, where Slocum visited the Stock Exchange. It suspended operations long enough to applaud him and give him three cheers. By way of response he said he had been encouraged by all the warm expressions of friendship he had received since arriving in New York. He was very glad to see that the war had "left so few marks upon national prosperity." Papers such as the *Albany Knickerbocker* and politicians from both parties began to do their best to lay claim to any part of Slocum's popularity they could.[7]

Slocum tried once again to come into Syracuse with relatively little fanfare. At first he hoped to march in with the 149th New York so he could share the stage with them. When this did not work out, he once again gave the city less than two hours' warning before he arrived. In spite of this, a welcoming committee managed to secure Slocum a flag-draped four-horse carriage and the townspeople raised dozens of flags of varying sizes. As the train carrying Slocum, his family, and several officers from Syracuse neared the station, signal guns announced its arrival. Hundreds of people poured out into the streets and down to the depot to welcome home their most famous hero. The platform filled quickly with onlookers, leaving many more to pack into Washington and Warren streets to catch a glimpse of the general.[8]

Slocum, clad in civilian attire, stepped out onto the platform with members of his staff and family as the crowd gave a loud cheer and Ghem's Brass Band struck up a chorus of "Hail to the Chief." The welcoming committee met them, and they made their way down to the carriage below where L. W. Hall, chairman of the day, gave a speech extolling Slocum's war record. Afterward, the general rose to reply:

> Nearly four years ago I read an article in one of your papers which made a deep impression on me. It contrasted the reception you had given to an officer with one you had given to a private soldier. Both had entered the service from this county—both had been wounded in the same battle and returned under similar circumstances—yet how different their receptions. The officer was met at the depot by a large number of friends and most cordially greeted.

7. *Journal* articles "Gen. Slocum in New York," June 13, 1865 (quote), and "A Story about Slocum" (reprinted from the *Albany Knickerbocker*), June 15, 1865; Fox, *In Memoriam*, 103–4.

8. "Gen. Slocum's Arrival at Home," *Journal*, June 15, 1865; "Gen. Slocum's Arrival at Home" (clipping in OHA), June 18, 1865; "Union Soldiers," *New York Times*, June 18, 1865, 1.

The soldier was met by an only sister, and by her alone accompanied to his home. I presume there are not ten men within reach of my voice who remember the article to which I refer, and I am very confident no one was more impressed than myself. I felt it, for I was the officer to whom the allusion was made, and I could not but acknowledge the justice of the article.

Slocum argued that the bulk of the fighting had been done by the common soldier, and this explained why he had tried so hard to avoid a hero's welcome whenever possible.[9]

It might be easy to interpret this as simple posturing on Slocum's part. Riding a huge wave of popularity, he could be expected to begin channeling his war record and reputation into political gain. If this is so, he could also be expected to don the well-worn mantle of the humble servant of the people who eschewed the fuss made over him by his devoted admirers. Slocum, though he undoubtedly was looking toward a political future, seems to have honestly meant what he said. From the time he read the article until his final return, he had effectively avoided another hero's welcome. This happened long before he had anything tangible or immediate to gain from it. Political ambition may have played a role here, but he consistently exhibited this sentiment long before he could reasonably have imagined himself standing in that carriage.

Slocum also addressed other subjects that would soon lead to a political irregularity, one as remarkable as it was deadly to his career. In particular, he began to offer his opinions of the South and Reconstruction:

[Southerners] are willing to give up slavery, and only ask to be permitted to live in peace with us. I believe it will not be difficult now to establish a new and better Union—a Union of feeling and interest. I would treat the South with kindness, and having extinguished the last hope in the minds of all, for the continuance of slavery, I would adopt such measures as would soonest restore good feeling throughout the land.

This approach conformed much more closely with that of the increasingly unpopular Johnson and would become like a red flag in front of the Radical bull. If anyone noticed the possible conflict between Slocum and a significant portion of his own party, no one remarked on it at the time.[10]

9. "The Address of Welcome and General Slocum's Response" (clipping in OHA), June 19, 1865 (speech); "Union Soldiers," *New York Times*, June 18, 1865, 1; "Gen. Slocum's Arrival at Home," *Journal*, June 15, 1865; "Gen. Slocum's Arrival at Home" (clipping in OHA), June 18, 1865; "Union Soldiers," *New York Times*, June 18, 1865, 1.

10. "The Address of Welcome and General Slocum's Response" (clipping in OHA), June 19, 1865.

Slocum remained in Syracuse a few weeks before departing for his short-lived command in Vicksburg. Traveling in civilian clothes he made several stops along the way, including Lyons, New York, where he searched out a few members of Company B of the Twenty-seventh and visited an uncle. The Republican papers in town gushed over him, calling him a "fine-looking man, of erect bearing, and every inch a soldier." He later arrived without fanfare in Chicago, apparently still out of uniform, and the owners of the boardinghouse where he stayed had no idea that the Henry Slocum on their register was one of Sherman's most famous generals, until some of Slocum's friends found him and declared his presence. Slocum's stop in Chicago made news all the way back into New York. From Illinois he proceeded directly to Mississippi.[11]

Slocum's second tour in Vicksburg would last less than three months, but it would prove eventful. Although he could have been expected just to be marking time, Slocum was not afraid to exercise his authority or to intervene in controversial issues. Like most Northern commanders he had no intention of causing an immediate or total social revolution in his department. Rather, he wanted to maintain Federal authority, forcefully if necessary, and to promote equal rights for everyone concerned. He viewed the state as still at war and worried about threats made against the freedmen, but he also assumed that white Southerners would be inherently reasonable. As a result, though he diligently guarded the rights of former slaves, he also expected that the need for such protections would quickly dissipate. "Our sympathies are due to the white man as well as to the black race," Slocum would remark on his return to Syracuse about two months later, "though we have no constitutional right to control either." The resulting policy exhibited a blind fairness that in the long term proved unsuited for the immediate realities of postwar Mississippi. Slocum really did not fathom the depth of anger and loathing many white Southerners harbored toward blacks, and toward the new system in general. In terms of what he officially handed down, Slocum looked more radical by the day, but in terms of what he thought, he remained somewhat conservative, though in an unstereotypical way.[12]

Slocum's hard-nosed approach and resolute belief in the superiority of military authority soon angered Sharkey and also annoyed Johnson. Some areas of Mississippi still staunchly refused to allow blacks to serve as

---

11. Untitled (clipping in OHA), c. July 1865.
12. "Gen. Slocum's Position," *New York Times,* October 5, 1865, 8 (quote). For a description of the basic Union policy, see James L. Roark, *Masters without Slaves: Southern Planters in the Civil War and Reconstruction,* 114.

courtroom witnesses against whites, and in these counties Slocum insisted on the continued use of military tribunals to try cases involving blacks and whites. This notably irked the white civilian authorities. The situation came to a head with the case of Joseph L. Jackson. On July 4, 1865, Jackson had killed one of the freedmen living on his plantation, he claimed in self-defense. Since his county would not allow testimony from freedmen, military authorities arrested Jackson and sent him to Vicksburg for trial. Jackson's attorney objected, complaining to Warren County Court Judge D. O. Merwin that, as Jackson was not a soldier, authorities had imprisoned him illegally. The attorney called for a writ of habeas corpus. Merwin agreed and issued the writ, arguing that although the military may make any order it felt necessary, a citizen's violation of it did not constitute a violation of military law. He then ordered Slocum himself to appear before his court with Jackson on July 19.[13]

Slocum would not stand for this. He replied that martial law still existed in the state and that as long as the whites denied the freedmen equal standing in the courts he would enforce their rights in military courts. He had Merwin arrested for daring to issue the writ. An angry Governor Sharkey, taking the matter as a personal affront to his dignity, wrote immediately to both Slocum and Seward in protest. Sharkey informed Slocum that Merwin had issued the writ under the governor's express instructions. To Seward Sharkey complained that Slocum's forcible overruling of Merwin (and himself) had violated the provisions of Sharkey's appointment and made the governor subordinate to the military authorities. He also claimed that martial law had ceased with his appointment, which left Slocum no authority over Jackson or Merwin. Seward checked with President Johnson before replying that the government of Mississippi was still "provisional."[14]

Slocum's own response to Sharkey came somewhat later and in a more public fashion. In his General Orders No. 10, issued on August 3, 1865, Slocum further repudiated the governor and strongly supported the freedmen against remaining Confederate sympathizers. Parts of the state, Slocum said, had simply tried to ignore Emancipation and continued to oppress blacks through both pseudo-lawful and outright illegal means. He noted that black men and women had been abused and killed over

13. James Currie, "From Slavery to Freedom in Mississippi's Legal System," *Journal of Negro History* 65.2 (Spring 1980): 120; Currie, *Enclave*, 179–80.
14. Currie, "From Slavery to Freedom," 120–21; James Sefton, *The U.S. Army and Reconstruction*, 36–38; Michael Les Benedict, *A Compromise of Principle*, 128.

trivial matters and that civilian authorities routinely denied them basic rights that were afforded to every white man in the state. In response Slocum reiterated his use of military power to protect the freedmen, though now he also promoted the Freedmen's Bureau in the same role. At the same time Slocum argued that equal treatment under the law for white and black should be the ultimate goal of all their efforts. His new general orders refused to countenance any violence or discrimination against former slaves, but he also insisted that they have no special privileges at the expense of their former masters:

> The class of citizens who are so blinded as to think of still holding these colored men as slaves and who by their unkind treatment are doing all in their power to excite their hatred, are the worst enemies of the State. On the other hand, the professed friend of the negro, who is constantly dwelling on the wrongs inflicted upon him by his former master, constantly representing to him that the Government has not yet granted to him all the privileges to which he is entitled, is the worst enemy of his race. The colored man can be improved not by making him the enemy of the dominant race among whom he must live; not by making him the tool of politicians; but by impressing upon him the importance of education and of forming habits of industry and economy.[15]

Slocum's sense of fairness, belief in truly equal treatment, and practical realism, when mixed with his naive view of white Southerners, spelled potentially disastrous results for the very men and women he meant to protect. He came out against sharper, more decisive government protection of minority rights not because he was opposed to those rights but simply because he thought extra protection unnecessary. Given the chance and faced with the hard reality of slavery's end, he thought, whites and blacks would quickly begin to live and work together in harmony, out of basic humanity and self-interest. As the future would show, however, had this course been adopted the results would have been dire indeed. Fortunately Slocum never had the opportunity to act on this thought.[16]

Slocum's idealism soon left him disgruntled with the freedmen as well. As he began to enforce the tribunals, it quickly became apparent to him that a number of freedmen saw the courts as an opportunity for gain and

15. "Slocum in Mississippi," *Journal*, August 14, 1865.
16. One of Slocum's more developed statements indicating this can be found in *Journal* articles "The Position of General Slocum," October 3, and "Southern Humanity," October 7, 1865.

revenge rather than justice. He believed that some former slaves would accuse any white person who annoyed them, quickly get a conviction from
a friendly military judge, then spread the word around the area as to how
easy and profitable such prosecutions had become. Slocum also took offense at the large numbers of former slaves who simply migrated onto a
plantation, laid claim to the land, and began eating the owner's winter
stores. For Slocum the emphasis of Reconstruction must be to encourage
blacks and whites to live together as equals under the same law and under
the same government: "The object of the Government is not to . . . encourage in [former slaves] the idea that they can be guilty of a crime and
escape its penalties; but simply to secure them the rights of free men, holding them, at the same time, subject to the same laws by which other classes
are governed."[17]

It is notable that Slocum was not alone in his more moderate views.
Other soldiers felt the same way and cautioned the government not to
take too harsh an approach to their former enemies. James McDonough
notes that John Schofield, then commanding in Virginia, felt very much
the same way. Schofield argued for the enforcement of civil law, not military law, and hoped for stern but generous conditions for each state's return to the Union. Unlike Slocum he did not believe that African American
suffrage should be enforced, since he did not think the government was
capable of forcing the South to accept it. Like Slocum he believed that
steps needed to be taken to prepare the freedmen for the responsibilities
of citizenship that lay before them. Both men favored a more relaxed approach, which presumed that equal rights would result from a natural
evolution of sensibilities.[18]

Slocum and Sharkey soon clashed again, this time over the militia.
President Johnson had earlier encouraged the governor of Alabama to
begin the process of rearming and retraining the state's armed forces.
Johnson himself had instituted such a program while governor of
Tennessee and thought it had "worked well." He hoped that rebuilding
the militia would make the states' citizens an active part of Reconstruction
and enlist them in maintaining law and the Union. Besides, Johnson reasoned, since people would form "vigilance" committees in lawless areas

17. "Gen. Slocum's Position," *New York Times*, October 5, 1865, 8; Sefton, *U.S. Army*, 44–
55 (quote). The idea would seem quite foreign to some more recent civil rights activists
who focus more on material wealth than on rights, character, and opportunity.
18. James L. McDonough, *Schofield: Union General in the Civil War and Reconstruction*,
160–61.

anyway, why not try to bring them under the control of the new government? Johnson's Radical Republican opponents attacked him mercilessly on this point, arguing that it was not only dangerous but silly to rearm former Confederates.[19]

On August 19, 1865, Sharkey took matters into his own hands in Mississippi. He issued a proclamation that included a provision for organizing military units from Mississippi to operate under state control. Sharkey, who had not consulted Slocum, specifically called for men who had "distinguished themselves for gallantry" (an obvious reference to former Confederate soldiers) to answer his call. He wanted two companies per county, which could have amounted to a substantial force statewide. The move outraged military authorities in the area. General Carl Schurz, who toured Slocum's command in the midst of the controversy, suggested that Slocum take a stand on the issue and even wrote to President Johnson himself. General Osterhaus, who commanded in northern Mississippi, sent word that most of the outrages the new organizations were supposed to prevent were in fact perpetrated by the very men Sharkey wanted to join up. Slocum needed no prodding. He thought the idea of reforming the militia ridiculous, pointing out that the last thing they needed was to give guns to former Rebels, make them independent of military authority, and place them in the same counties as black troops and freedmen. In a new set of general orders issued on August 24, 1865, Slocum once again overruled Sharkey. He later wrote Sherman, "I did not like to take this step. . . . I hope the United States Military will soon be removed from the State, but until this is done it would certainly be bad policy to arm the militia."[20]

Slocum took seriously the crimes that Sharkey and Johnson wanted to prevent, however, and also took steps to combat them without the need to call upon the militia. In his orders he stipulated that if reports of a crime reached Federal authorities, local commanders were to forcibly disarm everyone in the vicinity. Anyone who resisted would be arrested immediately and held for trial. To make the prospect even more unpleasant, Slocum ordered troops quartered on the perpetrator's premises. James Sefton notes that although Johnson initially thought to side with Slocum,

19. Johnson quoted in Howard K. Beale, *The Critical Year*, 42.
20. Ibid.; Sefton, *U.S. Army*, 26–27; "Gen. Slocum on State Rights," *New York Times*, September 8, 1865, 1 (the order is quoted verbatim); "General Slocum at Vicksburg and Syracuse," *Harper's Weekly*, October 21, 1865; "The Democratic Candidate for Secretary of State," *New York Times*, September 8, 1865, 4; Charles Slocum, *Life and Services*, 326 (quote).

he eventually supported Sharkey. Johnson reprimanded Schurz in particular when he protested the order: "I presume General Slocum will issue no order interfering with Governor Sharkey in restoring the functions of State Government without first consulting the government." By September 4, 1865, Slocum had been forced to rescind his order.[21]

The situation left Slocum in an interesting position. In terms of what he believed, he clearly emerged as a moderate in issues of practical Reconstruction policy. His speeches imply and his letters to Sherman clearly state that he disagreed with the Radical Republican approach, which he thought discriminated against innocent whites as much as it protected blacks. He rightly expected that this would result in a violent reaction, which would undo any civil rights gains for the freedmen as soon as the heavy hand of the Federal army was withdrawn. At the same time his actions spoke louder than his words, especially when the New York papers made sure to publicize them. His escapade with Sharkey actually made the front page of the *New York Times*. In the public eye, and also probably in the opinion of the New York Republican Party, Slocum seemed a Radical's Radical when, in fact, he was moving in the opposite direction.[22]

In New York and elsewhere, a visibly flustered Democratic Party had lost all semblance of a realistic issue. For the past four years the Democrats had generally identified themselves as the antiwar, antiblack party. In 1864 they claimed that the war was a costly failure (this had served them well against Lincoln until Slocum occupied Atlanta under Sherman) and had consistently stood against civil rights, in many cases still following the lead of the intransigent South. Lincoln's reelection devastated their morale. Some Democrats had been willing to reject their proslavery antiwar positions then, but now that the war had been brought to a successful conclusion, they needed to find a way to redefine themselves. The War Democrats broke from their more racist brethren and began to reach out to soldiers they hoped would be receptive, a move resented and opposed by other Democrats.[23]

Slocum received offers from both parties while he was stationed in Vicksburg. The first offer to arrive came from the Republicans, suggesting

21. Sefton, *U.S. Army*, 26–27 (quote); Beale, *Critical Year*, 42–43; Currie, *Enclave*, 186.

22. "Gen. Slocum on State Rights," *New York Times*, September 8, 1865, 1.

23. Guelzo, *Redeemer President*, 401; Lawrence Grossman, *The Democratic Party and the Negro: Northern and National Politics, 1868–1892*, 60–64; "The Democratic Convention: Dissolving Views," *New York Times*, September 8, 1865, 4; *Journal* articles "The Same Old Copperheads," September 12, "Purgation of the Democracy," September 12, and "The New Era," October 6, 1865.

a spot for him on the ticket for secretary of state of New York. Slocum politely refused. He "replied at once that I could not become a candidate for civil office, while in my present position . . . . I do not wish to enter politics at present. I can afford to wait." Whether Slocum really meant this or not, he had manifestly come to believe that the Radical elements controlling the Republican Party were wrong on the most important issue of the day, Reconstruction. Also, though he did not plan to stay long, at this point Slocum apparently thought he would be in Vicksburg at least through the election. "I will not, under any circumstances, be a candidate for civil office this Fall."[24] But even as this response made its way back to New York, Slocum received a letter from none other than John A. Green, Jr., dated August 22, 1865. In it Green offered him the Democratic nomination for the same position: secretary of state. Green rather ridiculously claimed the Democrats would sweep the state that year. He also said that they planned to endorse the reconstruction policy of President Johnson and promised that, if Slocum accepted the offer and was elected, he would get the nomination for governor the following year. Green added, "you will pardon me when I express my belief that everything now indicates the speedy dissolution of the Republican party and the return of the Democracy to power."[25]

Given the chance to support more moderate policies over those of the Radical Republicans, Slocum accepted, but with conditions. He replied that the party's platform must conform to his personal standards, and most important, that it must explicitly support Johnson's policy: "In a few words, I am in favor of returning at the earliest practicable period to a government of civil law . . . . If these views are such as will be endorsed by your convention, and if the convention should nominate me for Secretary of State, I shall accept the nomination . . . . If this convention should not adopt the platform you anticipate, I trust you will not press my name." Slocum's hometown of Syracuse had distinguished itself as a bastion of Republicanism, so it came as no surprise that, on September 16, the *Syracuse Journal* reported Slocum's acceptance with shock and dismay. Slocum turned in his resignation on September 28, 1865.[26]

Slocum's decision to leave Vicksburg so quickly meant that he would have to watch from afar as the fulfillment of his worst fears for Reconstruction

24. Quotes are from *Journal* articles, "Gen. Slocum and the Copperheads," c. September 1, and "New York Politics," September 11, 1865.

25. Green quoted in Fox, *In Memoriam,* 104.

26. *Journal* articles "General Slocum's Letter," September 13 (quote), and "General Slocum Accepts," September 16, 1865; Fox, *In Memoriam,* 106.

came true. Far from their withdrawing from the South in only a few short years, the harsh approach—especially when coupled with blatant instances of carpetbagger opportunism—meant that Federal troops remained in the South until Rutherford B. Hayes and the Compromise of 1877. Predictably, no lasting change had been wrought in the moral fiber of now viciously indignant Southerners, who responded with a counter-reconstruction of their own. The end result—from the perspective of many—was a section of the country that in a number of respects had changed very little from the antebellum period.

For now, though, Slocum had more immediate concerns, and the uncertainty of his decision to change parties must have been foremost among them. What made him defect to the Democrats? From all indications he had always been a Republican. Given the party's prominence in Syracuse it would only be natural for him to link his fortunes with that party. Like so many others, he had joined the party for two overwhelming reasons, the two pillars upon which the party was based in 1858. First, he wanted to deal decisively with the issue of slavery, and second, he wanted to preserve the Union. In the past few years the United States had accomplished both those goals. Why then, Slocum asked, did the Republican Party continue to exist? It had served its purpose and now should relinquish the political stage to groups concerned with more long-term goals. As he himself observed: "Read all their platforms and you will not find in them a single resolution that is pertinent to the issues now before the people." Slocum had seen firsthand the dominance of the Radicals in Congress and in the party as a whole. They had viciously attacked Johnson and the program that Slocum supported. Slocum himself offered this reasoning for his defection:

> I have studied the question carefully, and I believe the policy of the President is the only true one that can be adopted . . . . Upon my return here, I find two parties in the field, one endorsing a policy without a single dissenting voice; the other divided, and in my opinion, the majority of them opposing his policy. I ask, now, as I advocated his measures, what could have been my course except for uniting with the party that united with him?

And so, there it was. Slocum threw in his lot with the Democrats.[27]

The most expedient political option would have been for Slocum simply to accept the Republican nomination and be swept into office on noth-

27. Fox, *In Memoriam*, 106; *Journal* articles "General Slocum's Letter," September 13, "General Slocum Accepts," September 16, "The Position of General Slocum," *Journal*, October 3, 1865 (quote).

ing more than his military record. As secretary of state he would have
been poised to strike for governor and possibly make a presidential bid.
He must have known the switch risked political suicide. If he lost he might
well consider his career over. But Slocum's strict sensibilities doomed him
from the very beginning. The reality was that no amount of military fame
short of that borne by Grant himself could overcome such an obstacle,
whatever he may have hoped. As he would later remark in an 1868 letter
to Sherman: "I cannot curse a man one day and fawn on him the next. I
cannot declare slavery the natural and proper condition of the negro today and to-morrow advocate his right to make constitutions and laws.
Hence, I think I shall never make a politician." What role Sherman may
have played in this political transformation is unclear. It may well be that
the sheer amounts of time the two men spent together in the latter days
of the war affected Slocum, who held Sherman in the highest regard.
Unfortunately for Slocum, the Republicans somehow failed to take his
principles or his friendship for Sherman into consideration when they responded to the news of his decision.[28]

Slocum became part of the vanguard that would eventually sweep the
old-style Democrats entirely from the field. A battle within the party raged
for the next ten years. By 1869–1870, the Democracy of New York had generally abandoned appeals to racism and white supremacy. About the same
time, the Republicans began backing off their commitments to the freedmen, and the Northern Democrats stepped right into the breach hoping
to form a new, more powerful political alliance. With the end of
Reconstruction, the New York Democrats began taking steps beyond rhetoric, and it paid off. In 1882 they recaptured both the state house and the
governorship. Slocum, in this case, proved more forward-thinking than
many of his contemporaries.[29]

The first rumors of Slocum's new political affiliation leaked into the
press before he even left Mississippi. At first they refused to believe he
would ever do such a horrific thing. They stated as much in editorials.
Several papers, particularly the *Syracuse Journal,* trumpeted Slocum's earlier letter of reply to the Republicans where he said he could afford to wait,
as evidence that the Democrats had engaged in some great deception.
Some Republicans refused to accept it even when Green stood up in the
Democratic convention and claimed to have indisputable proof of
Slocum's willingness to accept the nomination and the *Albany Argus* began

28. Slocum to Sherman, March 8, 1868, in Charles Slocum, *Life and Services,* 334.
29. Grossman, *Democratic Party,* 63–65.

reporting it as fact. They called the idea a "'weak invention of the enemy' that could have no solid foundation in fact. . . . Knowing Gen. Slocum, intimately, we should be most grossly and inexplicably deceived in the character of the man, if we should find him turning his back on his friends."[30]

By the middle of September it gradually became clear that Slocum really had left his former party. News of his resignation and arrival, predicted by Green, soon were confirmed. For the Republicans, Slocum had committed the unforgivable sin, and in return they prepared to minimize the political damage by attacking his character. Within the space of just a few short weeks, the same papers that had only recently referred to him as "one of those rare men who has made no mistakes" would describe him as "the zealous and artless Slocum!" One editor slipped up, indirectly pointing to his true motivations in an October 23 article: "But General Slocum has made his choice, as he had a right to do, whatever we may think of the discretion that has guided him in his opinion. If we certainly knew he had had [shady] dealings . . . we should be less at a loss in divining his motives than we confess now to be."[31]

Slocum quickly finished his business in Vicksburg, turned his command over to Osterhaus in late September, and departed for the North. He kept a promise he had made to Sherman to visit him for a few days in St. Louis along the way, but soon he boarded the train for New York and Syracuse where a mixed reaction awaited him. The Republican press offered a somewhat subdued, if hurt, reception upon Slocum's return. At this point they contented themselves with dark references to betrayal and traitors. Slocum once again came home at an odd hour. Expected at two o'clock in the afternoon, he in fact arrived by a midnight train on September 27, thus avoiding both an alleged protest and a Democratic welcoming party. When they found he had slipped past them, a group organized by Green trekked over to his house in the darkness to serenade him. Slocum came out on the front step and gave another speech in response, receiving the cheers of the crowd. The Republicans quickly responded that it must have been a small gathering, since Slocum no longer had any sympathizers in their party, and many notable Democrats reportedly missed it as well.[32]

30. *Journal* articles "The Nomination of Gen. Slocum by the Copperheads," September 8, "New York Politics," September 11, "Gen. Slocum and the Copperheads," c. September 1, 1865 (quote).
31. "General Slocum as a Soldier," *Journal*, August 9, 1865 (much of this the paper excerpted from George Nichols's *Story of the Great March*). *Journal* articles "Political," October 4 ("zealous and artless"), "General Slocum's Implications," October 23, 1865.
32. *Journal* articles "Gen. Slocum's Arrival," September (clipping in OHA), "General Slocum's Return Home," September 25, "The Return of General Slocum," September

A little less than a week later, on October 2, Slocum made his first official speech as a Democratic candidate at the party gathering at Shakespeare Hall in Syracuse. That Monday evening a large number of people turned out to hear him speak. Interrupted by periodic outbreaks of applause, he dwelt on his military experiences and spent some time in discussions of Grant, Sherman, and Sheridan. He reemphasized that he had accepted the nomination because the New York Democrats supported Johnson's lighter-handed version of Reconstruction. Once again it is apparent that his naive views on white Southern acceptance of former slaves led him to this conclusion. "I have never believed that all the humane and kindly impulses implanted by nature in the heart of man were confined to a particular section of country," he said.[33]

Almost before the last of his words had finished echoing through Shakespeare Hall, Republicans launched a nationwide newspaper campaign to destroy Slocum's reputation and career. Papers from Chicago to Albany to New York City opened the assault with exposés and editorials that accused him of everything short of murder. The *Syracuse Journal* called the speech itself "an essay without salient points, and without any close analysis of the political questions it professes to discuss. Much that it said is of no consequence, and will make no impression." The *New York Times* found it "humiliating" and asked rhetorically, "Why will Gen. Slocum thus trifle with his fair fame?" Instead of publishing sickeningly glorious poetry, as it had after Bull Run, the *Journal* offered a new song, called "Slocum Lament," to be sung to the tune of "Carry Me Back":

Oh carry me back to the Union side,
To the faithful and the true;
I feel so queer and homesick here I don't know what to do.[34]

To make matters worse, Slocum himself had inadvertently given his opponents some of their best ammunition with his 1861 donation to the Republican Party and its complimentary letter: "If I were at home, I

27, "Arrival of General Slocum," September 28, "The Committee Heard From," September 28, "General Slocum's Last Order," September 28, "General Slocum's Resignation Accepted," September 30, 1865.

33. "Democratic Meeting at Syracuse," *New York Tribune*, October 3, 1865. Quote is in both "Gen. Slocum's Position," *New York Times*, October 5, 1865, 8, and "The Position of General Slocum," *Journal*, October 3, 1865.

34. "General Slocum's Speech," *Journal*, October 3, 1865; "Gen. Slocum's Speech," *New York Times*, October 5, 1865, 4; William F. Morris, "Slocum's Lament," *Journal*, October 31, 1865.

should join with you most cordially in support of the Republican State and County tickets, for I have yet to learn what good reason any Republican can have for deserting either his party or his principles." Some papers had even titled the short piece "True as Steel." Slocum could not have damned himself more thoroughly if the entire affair had been scripted specifically for that purpose. In one fell swoop, not only had Slocum condemned what he himself would do later on but he seemed to tie his principles explicitly to the party. Republican editors rejoiced to reprint this excerpt, no doubt expecting their readers to agree that, in abandoning his party, he must also have repudiated his principles.[35]

A barrage of other articles appeared, charging him with crime after crime. The indictments nearly universally came from anonymous informants, and these Republican discoveries had a nasty tendency to grow more serious as the election approached. Some papers accused him of smuggling whiskey, others of stealing over one thousand dollars' worth of gold during the March to the Sea. Another blamed his resignations on his dislike of the Lincoln administration. Slocum's old opponent Thomas Alvord (now a Republican) claimed that "so violent was his opposition to the Administration that he openly declared if President Lincoln was re-elected he would resign, convert his effects into money and leave the country." The same papers accused him of trying to prevent soldiers from voting, knowing they favored Lincoln over Slocum's supposedly preferred candidate, McClellan. Slocum's new associates at the *Syracuse Daily Courier* tried to fight back, even threatening a libel suit, but the Republicans would not be put off.[36]

While it is always a difficult task to prove a negative (that is, that Slocum never committed a crime while in the army), there is little evidence to suggest these charges amounted to anything more than quickly

35. "True as Steel," *Onondaga Standard,* November 6, 1861; *Journal* articles "General Slocum's Position," October 29, 1862, "General Slocum in 1861," October 10, 1865, "Condemned by His Own Mouth," October 16, 1865.
36. Alvord quoted from "Political," *Journal,* November 6, 1865. Apparently Alvord had converted to Republicanism, or else he insensibly chose to attack his own party. After having switched parties himself, to attack Slocum for the same sin must have required a great deal of cynicism. *Journal* articles untitled, October 14, "The Impolicy of Coalition Nominations," c. October 15, "General Slocum: Threatened Libel Suit," October 20, "Tears of the Crocodile," October 25, "Political," October 27, "Not of the Bondocracy," November 2, 1865; *Harper's Weekly* articles "Principles and Men," October 14, "General Slocum at Vicksburg and Syracuse," October 21, 1865, OHA; "Gen. Slocum," *New York Tribune,* October 24, 1865; "General Slocum" (clipping in OHA), October 25, 1865 (this is a reprint that probably appeared in the *Journal*); "Gen. Slocum's Political Antecedents," *Onondaga Standard,* October 26, 1865.

manufactured political propaganda. For instance, one persistent correspondent of several papers was A. E. B. (A. E. Bennett), who claimed to be
the former medical inspector for the Twentieth Corps. Bennett provided
many of the anti-Lincoln charges against Slocum. A full text search of the
Official Records reveals that there was indeed a medical inspector for the
Twentieth named W. C. Bennett. Most honest people are not likely to forget their first or middle name and, when creating a pseudonym for fear of
retribution, could be somewhat more creative than to keep their last name.
The charge that Slocum stopped his soldiers from voting can be proved to
be false, as demonstrated by the diary entry for November 8, 1864, by
William Townsend of Company G, Third Wisconsin Volunteers. The accusations were made for political purposes, and in such cases, perception
matters a great deal more than accuracy.[37]

Two effective accusations hit Slocum at both local and national levels.
Locally, he had to contend with his supposed robbery of the Onondaga
County treasurer's office. The *New York Tribune*, the *Syracuse Journal*, and
other papers seized upon the clerical error that had occurred back in 1861
when Slocum departed for Elmira to take command of his regiment.
Although the account had been corrected long ago, the newspapers accused Slocum of stealing over nine thousand dollars from the county.
When the current treasurer—who incidentally opposed Slocum's switch—
wrote to the papers to insist on the general's innocence, the editors heaped
scorn on his explanation. Worried by the fact that he had manifestly cleared
Slocum of any wrongdoing, the staff writers at the paper applied themselves heartily to belittling the vindicating account and attacking Slocum
again on the same points, as if the rejoinder had never even existed.[38]

Republicans also pilloried Slocum in the national papers, not the least
of which were the *Chicago Republican* and the *New York Times*, via the
"Vicksburg Cotton Frauds." Supposedly, during Slocum's initial tenure
in Vicksburg, a man named Joseph Noland had tried to claim over six
hundred bales of cotton in government stores by arguing he was a
Unionist. Part of this lost lot he had burned as the armies approached his
plantation, part of it Grant had taken and used as armor on his "cotton
clads." Slocum refused Noland, but a cotton speculator by the name of
W. S. Grant convinced a panel of officers to honor the claim and thereby
robbed the government of over four hundred thousand dollars. The

37. Special Field Orders No. 11, *OR*, vol. 47, pt. 2, 46; William Townsend Diary.
38. *Journal* articles "The Charges against the Late County Treasurer," October 24,
"General Slocum as County Treasurer," October 23, 1865; "Gen. Slocum's Accounts,"
New York Tribune, October 26, 1865.

Albany Evening Journal (Thurlow Weed's paper) called Slocum out for a response, claiming his honor would be forever tarnished if he refused. The paper also pointed to its political motivations, stating that "no disinterested party or candid person can read this testimony and report, without coming to the conclusion that the Democratic party have drawn an elephant in their candidate for Secretary of State."[39]

Slocum could not refrain from replying, much against the better judgment of his more politically minded friends. He sent a letter that stated he had never decided on any case of private property, and that he had no association whatsoever with this Grant fellow. Slocum included the report of the commission that found Noland's claim valid, which convened sometime after Slocum's initial refusal. He also sent along a letter from his adjutant at the time, Col. F. A. Starring, attesting to his integrity while in Vicksburg. Slocum entertained no illusions about the *Journal*'s purpose: "It has been whispered to me by politicians that you are much more anxious to defeat my election as Secretary of State than you are to protect my honor. However, as reputation is more valuable than office, I shall disregard these suggestions and answer you."[40]

As his friends had feared, the press of course went wild with his response. The *Albany Evening Journal* printed Slocum's letter but only summed up the accompanying material, calling it "utterly worthless, weak, and insufficient." The *Syracuse Journal* reprinted the entire response but did not print the reports with Slocum's letter, placing them elsewhere in the paper, away from the main article on the subject. With his supporting evidence thus divorced from his letter, they tried to dilute the effectiveness of his defense by adding two critical words for each of Slocum's positive ones. The *New York Times* took a more even-handed, but still negative, approach.[41]

In reality it appears Slocum had indeed tried to bring the corruption under control, though in the mess that was wartime Mississippi, it is again impossible to establish his integrity beyond all doubt. O. H. Burbridge, a Treasury agent and brother of a brigadier-general stationed in Kentucky, wrote Lincoln in 1864 of fraud in Vicksburg. He told of his and Starring's

39. The quote is from "The Vicksburg Cotton Frauds," *Albany Evening Journal*, October 1865, OHA. *Journal* articles "Cotton Fraud: General Slocum Implicated," October 5, "The Vicksburg Cotton Frauds," October 14, "The Vicksburg Cotton Fraud," October 24, 1865; *New York Times* articles "A Curious Story," October 5, 8, "More about the Cotton Business: Gen. Slocum's Action," October 6, 1, "The Vicksburgh Cotton Swindle," October 18, 1, all 1865.

40. "The Vicksburg Cotton Frauds," *Albany Evening Journal*, c. October 17, 1865, OHA.

41. Ibid.; "The Vicksburg Cotton Frauds," *Journal*, October 21, 1865; "A Letter from Major-Gen. Slocum," *New York Times*, October 20, 1865, 5.

arrest by General Dana, who confiscated their cotton by military proceedings and refused to turn the bales over to the Treasury Department, exactly the crime of which the papers accused Slocum. He mentions Slocum in the letter, but only in the context of Slocum having sent some corrupt detectives packing. It is certainly notable that both of these charges—the local and the national—disappeared completely after the election.[42]

The best efforts of Slocum's friends only served to embarrass him further. Early in October the *Syracuse Journal* reported with glee that Slocum's supporters had resurrected the "very beautiful and euphonious title of 'The Hunkey Boy.'" It started in the *Elmira Gazette,* and signs began to appear at events in his support using the name. The Democratic papers also began using it frequently. Upon hearing this, the *Syracuse Journal* officially surrendered, arguing, "This is irresistible. We knock under. If Slocum is the 'Hunkey Boy of the Empire State' we do not see what else we can do." The *Journal* later offered this definition to its readers for the title: "a man [in the army] who always claimed a whole loaf of bread, and never divided his rations."[43]

The name, in particular reference to Slocum, meant nothing of the sort. It did originate during the war, but as to exactly what the term meant there can obviously be some leeway. The first definition offered in the *Dictionary of American Slang* for the word "hunky" refers to an immigrant laborer from Central Europe. This does not seem to be the sense in which the word is used here. Slocum's family came from English stock, and he bore no resemblance to the type. Also, his men generally used the term in a complimentary fashion, whereas this is more of an ethnic slur. More probably it just means "satisfactory, fine, or first rate," as in "hunky-dory." The term was used in that manner at the time. For instance, in John Poole's "Song of all Songs," he mentions one titled "A Hunkey Boy Is Yankee Doodle." At any rate the appellation did—and still does—sound childish. To peg Slocum with it at a time when he should have been focusing on his maturity, intelligence, and military accomplishments did him no favors, however good the intent.[44]

42. O. H. Burbridge to Lincoln, November 7, 1864 (Seizure of cotton at Vicksburg), Lincoln Papers.
43. *Journal* articles "Political," October 4 ("irresistible"), untitled, October 6 ("euphonius"), "What It Means," October 18, 1865.
44. John Poole, "The Song of All Songs," at http://lcweb2.loc.gov/cocoon/ihas/loc.natlib.ihas.100005695/pageturner.html. For "hunkie, hunky," and "hunky-dory," see Harold Wentworth and Stuart Berg Flexner, *Dictionary of American Slang* (New York: Thomas Y. Crowell, 1960).

The charges levelled at Slocum produced their intended effect, however. Slocum lost the election, and badly. The Democratic bid to pull in the soldier vote by running him failed, largely because of the Republican choice of Francis C. Barlow, who had been a powerful commander himself and who thus lessened the attraction presented by Slocum to thousands of veterans. Given an atmosphere where soldiers and citizens alike were ordered to "vote the way you shot," any candidate for the formerly Copperhead Democratic Party faced a difficult fight from the outset. Slocum finished several hundred votes behind other Syracuse Democrats. Upon hearing of his defeat, Sherman wrote, "I think I was more disappointed at your non-election than you could have been. . . . But you are young, and can stand it; and I know that, sometime later, your State will recognize and reward, if you need it, military services such as you rendered your country."[45]

Sherman's vote of confidence probably reassured Slocum, who came under steadily increasing pressure in the unfriendly atmosphere around Syracuse. Less than a year before, the city had hailed him as a hero, but now they decried him as a traitor and mocked him. The barrage of insulting articles and accusations hardly lessened with his defeat, as triumphant Republican editors went to drive what they hoped would be the final nails into the coffin of his political career. Other, unconnected events also added to Slocum's woes. He and his family returned home one night during the height of the preelection assaults to find their house had been robbed. Then Slocum's mother died in the last days of October after an illness of several weeks' duration.[46] This would have been enough to try the patience of anyone, and Slocum decided he wanted no more. He began preparations to move his family away from Syracuse.

According to Charles Slocum, for some time the general had in his mind to move to the city of Brooklyn, and the almost tangible hatred in the air around Syracuse would certainly have made the move more tempting. Slocum had originally thought to open a new law practice there, but Brooklyn would also be an excellent chance for "Spec" Slocum to put his business skills to work. In addition, as Brooklyn was a heavily Democratic

45. "Slocum's Votes Compared," *Journal,* November 8, 1865; Sherman to Slocum, December 26, 1865, at Fox, *In Memoriam,* 106–7.

46. *Journal* articles "Poking Sharp Sticks at a Poor Unfortunate!" November 9, "Pelting a Man When Down!" November 10, "A Dismal Fate," November 10, "The Democracy and General Slocum," November 14, "An Appointment for General Slocum," November 20, "General Slocum's House Robbed," October 13, 1865; "Death of Mrs. Mary O. Slocum," *New York Tribune,* November 1, 1865.

town, he would find the atmosphere a good deal friendlier. By January 13, 1866, he had purchased a house there and announced he would soon begin liquidating his assets in Syracuse. In early February, he took a trip west, where he visited with Sherman again for a time. Upon his return on February 13, he began to put his possessions up for auction. His house and salt blocks sold on March 21, for more than six thousand dollars. He placed the family's furniture and kitchenware up for sale on April 27. With nothing left to hold them in Syracuse, Slocum and his family departed for their new home in Brooklyn in the afternoon hours of April 30, 1866.[47]

Only one year and four days after standing with Sherman at the culmination of the Civil War, Slocum's decision and dedication to his own ideals virtually destroyed his local and national reputation. His military fame deserted him; many now called him a turncoat, a Copperhead, and a Rebel sympathizer. He would carry these names at the state level for decades to come. Slocum would have to explore a wide range of different alternatives in order to rebuild his shattered career in Brooklyn, and to create a new life for his family.

47. *Journal* articles "Personal Mention," January 13, "Personal Mention," February 27, "Auction Sale," March 20, "Sales at Auction," March 21, "Auction Sale," April 23, "Auction Sale," April 24, untitled, April 30, 1866.

CHAPTER 9

The Old Soldier Fades Away
Business Booms in Brooklyn

Slocum would spend the rest of his life in his newfound hometown of Brooklyn, New York. He certainly made use of his war record with zeal when it was politically advantageous to do so, especially on the local level, but his decision to switch parties had destroyed much of what that record could once have been worth in non-Democratic areas. Yet he was not a man without aspirations. He would try to link his political future with both a movement and a project, which he hoped would be bigger than the memory of his "betrayal," but unfortunately, neither would prove to be so. His general disinterest in actively and publicly promoting his military legacy led many to forget his role in the war—outside the Battle of Gettysburg and (early on) the March to the Sea. The hatred many had developed for the "traitor" made them happy for the chance to do so. But as a businessman he proved to be an unqualified success.

The Slocums quickly settled into their new home at 465 Clinton Avenue, helped by the friends they still had in Syracuse. The nice new dwelling, described even by Slocum's enemies as "elegant," would also soon boast a new full-length portrait of Slocum in uniform. Several of Slocum's friends, including ex-governor Horatio Seymour and other "prominent citizens," commissioned W. E. McMasters to paint it, and he completed it by the middle of June 1866.[1]

1. *Journal* articles "Portrait of General Slocum," December 12, 1865, untitled, June 19, 1866, "General Slocum," April 14, 1894; "Gen. Slocum Dangerously Ill," *New York Times*, April 10, 1894, 5.

Slocum's new home was the best a former Republican could hope for, and it was in a much friendlier atmosphere than the one they had left behind in Syracuse. New Yorkers at the time continued to look down on Brooklyn from old habit, but by the time Slocum made his home there, their feelings of complete and innate superiority were no longer clearly justified. Just across the East River from New York, Brooklyn had exploded from a village of less than four thousand people in 1800 to a new metropolis of over four hundred thousand by 1869. Although New York still had twice as many people, Brooklyn was rapidly catching up in terms of culture and manufacturing. It was already a larger seaport than New York and had grown to become the third largest city in the nation. It covered more than twenty-five square miles, an area larger than all of Manhattan Island. Business boomed in Brooklyn and would give "Spec" Slocum plenty of opportunity to earn money.[2]

Two other aspects of Brooklyn would have seemed especially attractive to Slocum. First, as David McCullough notes in *The Great Bridge*, Brooklyn was under the firm control of the Kings County Democrats. If Slocum had any hope of bringing about a political resurrection after his demise as a darling of the Republicans, it would have to be in such a place. Second, there were not many Democrats who could hope to match his military record, and fewer still resided in Brooklyn. This meant that Slocum's fame could be regenerated and reused to some extent. Republicans might remember him as a traitor, but he could still be a hero to Brooklyn Democrats, who did not have many other war heroes to their name.[3]

One strategy for making a political comeback would have been for Slocum to attach himself to another cause or issue that was big enough to eclipse the thought of his departure from Republicanism. Slocum found one such cause within a few years of arriving in Brooklyn: the "Eighth Wonder of the World," the Brooklyn Bridge. Slocum was associated with William C. Kingsley, Brooklyn's leading contractor and a powerful impetus in local and state politics in favor of the bridge. Slocum knew about the bridge from the very beginning of the project in 1869. He traveled with the delegation that viewed the other bridges built by the proposed designer, John Roebling, and made sure to purchase stock as soon as the bridge company was formed. He acquired five hundred shares, which netted him a place on the board. It is easy to see what he hoped to gain politically from the project. An undertaking of this magnitude could conceivably erase all memory of his former party switch and transform him back into a political force to

2. David McCullough, *The Great Bridge*, 103–4.
3. Ibid., 83, 104.

be reckoned with. He could also hope to reap rewards in short order; the bridge was originally supposed to be finished by the early 1870s.[4]

Slocum also had a great deal to gain financially from the bridge and its success. It was projected to (and did) greatly increase the prosperity and land values of Brooklyn. Slocum, as an early investor, clearly stood to reap huge returns. The profitability of many of his later business ventures in the Brooklyn railroad system depended upon final completion of the bridge and the increased traffic into Brooklyn that it brought. Slocum may or may not have thought this far ahead in the early years of the Bridge Company, but his own financial future depended almost exclusively on his decision to invest and then on what came of his investment.

McCullough strongly implies that Slocum was in many ways little more than a politically motivated lackey for Kingsley, but Slocum continued to demonstrate a capacity for independent thought and action. If he had indeed been a mere lackey of the Brooklyn Ring Democratic machine, he made a pretty poor one. His tendency to support candidates he thought fit for office, sometimes without regard to party affiliation, continually frustrated his allies and opponents alike. Almost simultaneous to his move to Brooklyn, he wrote a letter to support Republican John W. Geary in his campaign to become governor of Pennsylvania, crediting Geary for the Union victory at Wauhatchie, Tennessee, in October 1863. This may have benefited Geary, but it did Slocum no good. The Republican Party of New York had little interest in favoring Slocum in return; the *Syracuse Journal* called it "the only credible service in the political line that has been done by General Slocum since he resigned his position in the army." Also, given that even years later many Democrats still looked on Slocum's transformation as suspect, open support of a Republican candidate would neither allay fears nor promote his interests. Slocum's independence pleased neither party, leaving him in a vulnerable position, especially in the years before he linked his fortunes with the bridge.[5]

Although he did succeed in gaining some political offices, they were but a shadow of what might have been. In 1866 a coalition of New York and Brooklyn Democrats nominated him for the position of naval officer at New York, but the Senate rejected him in 1867. In 1868 he served on New York's electoral college, where he acted as president. Also in that year he ran successfully for the highest office he would ever achieve, taking New York's Third District seat in the House of Representatives. He held his

4. Ibid., 85, 135.
5. Ibid., 87–88; untitled, *Journal*, March 26, 1866; "Slocum: The General as a Political Quality," *Brooklyn Eagle*, Saturday, May 27, 1876, 4.

Slocum as a congressman. Library of Congress, Prints & Photographs Division

position until 1873. In each case he continued to be dragged down by bad or indifferent press, which usually centered on his ambivalent attitude toward the parties and his betrayal of the Republicans in 1865. As late as 1878, over ten years after his defection, the Republicans still used Slocum as a prime example of "[t]he fate of traitors to the Republican party."[6]

6. *Journal* articles untitled, June 28, 1866, March 28, 1867, "General Slocum's Rejection," March 30, 1867, untitled, December 2, 1868; "Major General Slocum," *Courier* (originally printed in the *Albany Argus,* April 25, 1879); Fox, *In Memoriam,* 108; untitled, *Journal,* November 7, 1878 (quote).

Another charge that sometimes aired involved Slocum's supposed rage at being passed over for command of the Army of the Potomac before Gettysburg or at other times. History has not sustained this charge, but it was an easy accusation to make and seemed to make sense. His opponents would trot it out whenever Slocum engaged in controversy with Republicans (to explain his "hatred" for the party of Lincoln in general) or fellow high-ranking veterans (to explain why he supposedly resented them in particular).[7]

Some rumors went too far even for his most bitter political enemies. One report circulating in New York, Washington, and even Michigan in 1867 alleged that Slocum had somehow insulted a lady in his charge, and that one of her friends had struck him for it. The gossip column does not explain the nature of the offense but called it a serious enough provocation to warrant a duel and then claimed the cowardly Slocum had left town before the fight could take place. Even the *Syracuse Journal* found this preposterous: "We believe General Slocum to be a gentleman, incapable of such an act, and we take pleasure in making this expression on his behalf, more especially as we have had occasion to comment somewhat severely upon his political course."[8]

If Slocum had failed to transcend his past on his own, the Brooklyn Bridge did little to help him. The bridge took far longer to build than anyone had ever expected. Instead of a working bridge by the early to mid 1870s, the project did not span the East River until 1883, fourteen years after Slocum's first involvement with it. Along the way it did nothing but produce bad press for all involved. The allegations of graft and corruption flew so thick that no one connected with the bridge emerged unscathed. Slocum himself attacked the project's chief engineer, Washington Roebling (John Roebling's son), accusing him of conflict of interest when he gave lucrative contracts to his family company. Roebling himself had served with distinction in the war, on the staffs of McDowell, Pope, and later Gouverneur K. Warren. He stayed with Warren from Gettysburg through the end of the war and was brevetted for bravery in the battles around Richmond. An indignant Roebling denied Slocum's accusations. When the committee investigated the matter, the man Slocum claimed had leveled the initial charge against Roebling (which Slocum clearly described as "charges" not "rumors") backed off from his statements. In the end all that resulted from the situa-

7. *Journal* articles "Slocum's Political Pedigree," November 12, 1868, "The Veterans in This Campaign: Slocum to Burnside," October 7, 1872.
8. "Washington Gossip," *Journal*, April 15, 1867.

tion was embarrassment for Slocum, a deep abiding resentment against him on the part of Roebling, and more bad press for everyone.[9]

Slocum's most consistent political success came at the local level where he built himself a reputation as a political reformer. He had quickly integrated into Brooklyn society, joining the Brooklyn Club and spending some of his later years as its president. There, he had the opportunity to meet and court many of the most important figures in Brooklyn politics, associations that paid off at various times, with Slocum serving as president of the board of city works in addition to his work on the bridge. He took on these duties in early 1876. He also continued to demonstrate his cantankerousness. His deep feelings had led him to switch parties in 1865, and before ten years had elapsed some Brooklyn Democrats would have been happy to send him back.[10]

One of Slocum's major efforts at casting himself as a reform candidate came after losing his seat in the House of Representatives for the first time. Slocum, his next-door neighbor William Marshall, and a number of other prominent Democratic mavericks inaugurated a rebellion against Brooklyn's political boss, Hugh McLaughlin. The son of a poor Irish immigrant family, McLaughlin had no education but had managed to get himself a patronage job in the Brooklyn Naval Yard in 1855. By 1862 he had used this position to leverage himself into near total control of the Brooklyn Democratic machine. He did not command absolute, unquestioned power for his entire tenure, but McLaughlin remained more or less in control from then until 1903. In late October 1875, Slocum and his allies held a meeting at the Brooklyn Academy of Music to launch a formal, organized movement against McLaughlin and invited a number of friendly Republicans to attend.[11]

At the meeting Slocum attacked McLaughlin as representative of the evils of one-man government. While Slocum declared himself faithful to

9. McCullough, *Great Bridge*, 466–68; "Washington Augustus Roebling." This resentment seems to be one-sided in at least some ways. Later, when given the chance, Slocum actually voted in favor of keeping Roebling rather than firing him. McCullough, *Great Bridge*, 503–4.

10. *Brooklyn Eagle* articles "Slocum," Thursday, August 27, 1885, 4, "Slocum Elected President of the Brooklyn Club," Saturday, November 15, 1890, 6, "The Testimonial to General Slocum," Monday, April 24, 1893, 10, "A Free Bridge," Wednesday, March 21, 1883, 4; untitled, *Journal*, January 5, 1876.

11. McCullough, *Great Bridge*, 115; "Old-Time Politics" (originally printed in the *New York Advertiser*), c. 1894; "Complete HarpWeek Explanation, Cartoon of the Day," at http://www.harpweek.com/09Cartoon/RelatedCartoon.asp?Year=2003&Month=September&Date=30.

the Democratic Party on the state and national level, he "repudiated the good old Democratic doctrine that to be a Democrat he must vote for all the regular Democratic candidates, no matter how unfitted they were." Slocum particularly objected to McLaughlin's practice of handpicking the officers of Brooklyn's various districts regardless of their qualifications or the desires of district voters. Slocum's group then supported the Republican candidate for mayor. When threatened with being read out of the party for noncompliance, he replied: "Well, gentlemen . . . if this is the pill I am to swallow it will be well to let the reading process begin at once, for I here and now solemnly pledge myself to be governed hereafter in the selection of local agents to do the business of this great city solely by their qualifications for the positions to which they are nominated." Slocum in no way originated this emphasis on civil service reform. In fact a much broader movement swept the country in the post–Civil War era, especially in light of the corruption of the Grant administration just then drawing to a close. Future president Grover Cleveland established his own reputation during this time by fighting party machines in New York. A near simultaneous revolt of Democrats in New York City against Tammany got under way during the time Slocum led his attempt at revolution in Brooklyn. Predating Slocum's offensive by about a year, this may well have been what inspired him to come out for reform.[12]

It should not be surprising, then, that McLaughlin opposed Slocum's nomination to the board of city works in 1876. McLaughlin met with Slocum just before the committee assembled to confirm his appointment and suggested darkly that Slocum have his name removed from consideration. McLaughlin gave Slocum only twenty minutes to make up his mind and get out. Slocum, furious at being talked to in such a manner, refused and left the room immediately. The committee voted in favor of Slocum, and he took up his new position as president of the board, with offices in Brooklyn's city hall.[13]

Slocum began to agitate almost immediately for reform in the Department of City Works, a McLaughlin stronghold. The ink could hardly have dried on his commission when he wrote a letter complaining

12. Quotes are from two *Journal* articles, both untitled and both dated October 25, 1875. See also "The Followers of Slocum," *Brooklyn Eagle*, Wednesday, March 15, 1876, 2; *New York Times* articles "Dissatisfied Democrats," October 15, 1874, 5, "The War against Tammany," October 17, 1874, 12.

13. "Hugh McLaughlin," *Brooklyn Eagle*, Sunday, January 2, 1898, 54; "Old-Time Politics" (clipping in OHA), c. 1894; "Albany," *Brooklyn Eagle*, Saturday, February 10, 1877, 2; Charles Slocum, *Life and Services*, 335.

of waste and graft in the department. By February 8, 1876, Slocum began giving testimony in the ensuing investigation. He described an inefficient operation working nearly exclusively by the spoils system. A year later letters from Slocum on the subject were still appearing in the papers. Finally, in 1877, Slocum and a fellow commissioner began the process of reducing and reorganizing the department's workforce. Slocum himself led the way by lowering his own salary from over $7,000 to $5,010.[14]

Something in the execution of this reorganization still failed to satisfy Slocum. In early January 1878, he used his well-tried tactic of resigning once again. His letter, sent to the mayor and leaked conveniently to the press, charged his fellow commissioners with peddling out the new positions in an attempt to operate the board as yet another political machine. The mayor immediately begged Slocum to take his resignation back and to explain his complaints. Slocum did so, noting his belief that a board of three produced waste and should be consolidated into one position. Whether or not this actually took place, Slocum did choose to resign before the end of his term.[15]

Slocum's political reform movement against McLaughlin grew up alongside his crusade on the board of city works. Out of the initial meeting held in October 1875, he developed a much larger movement that spread through the city. The group next met in March 1876 in the Twentieth Ward. Slocum attended, along with several other prominent Democrats, including a former governor. The total turnout that night ran in excess of 150 persons. At the meeting Slocum and his allies announced the formation of the Kings County General Democratic Committee to promote a sort of democracy that, Slocum said, "appealed to the people and not to a half dozen politicians who hung about the grog shops." The organization already boasted two hundred names on its rolls, which Slocum claimed made it the largest Democratic club in the history of the Twentieth Ward.[16]

Although Slocum apparently intended the committee to be a broad-based coalition (implied by its name), it did not take long for the press to

14. *Brooklyn Eagle* articles "City Works: What General Slocum Knows about Them," Tuesday, February 8, 1876, 2, "Albany," Saturday, February 10, 1877, 2, "Heads Off: Reorganizing the Department of City Works," Monday, July 9, 1877, 4, "Municipal: 'Civil Service' with a Vengeance," Thursday, July 19, 1877, 4; untitled, *Journal,* August 11, 1877.
15. *Brooklyn Eagle* articles "Slocum: The General Disgusted with his Associate Commissioners," Thursday, January 3, 4, "Slocum," Friday, January 4, 4, "Slocum," Saturday, January 12, 4, 1878; Charles Slocum, *Life and Services,* 335.
16. Slocum quoted from "The Followers of Slocum," *Brooklyn Eagle,* Wednesday, March 15, 1876, 2.

dub it the "Slocum Committee," and its following the "Slocum Democrats" or "Slocumites." Whether because of Slocum's name or a broad disgust with Brooklyn politics, the Slocum Committee's influence began to spread across the city. Slocumite groups quickly organized in at least eight wards, with varying degrees of success, and by May 1876, they counted over nine thousand members on their collective rolls. The Seventeenth Ward emerged as a center of strength because of the presence of the depot of the Crosstown Railroad, owned and operated by Slocum. The general criss-crossed the wards speaking at various meetings.[17]

This new political effort pulled Slocum in too many directions at once, however. In addition to his many business ventures, he also found his position as president of the board of city works took up enough of his time that he felt he could not run the Slocum Committee and also maintain his other obligations. By early September, he had decided to resign from the committee, which immediately reorganized itself, and Slocum continued to work with them when he could. In October he led a number of his fellow Independents to the nominating convention in Albany. Once there they tried to protest the recognition of McLaughlin's candidates. The *Syracuse Journal* later reported that the "Slocumites were turned out of the Convention without ceremony."[18]

Like the bridge, Slocum's reform movement did not succeed in actually bringing about a revival great enough to salvage his national reputation. People would spend the next twenty years talking about nominating Slocum for governor or president, but aside from narrowly missing the gubernatorial nomination once, he never realistically came near to either office. As for his campaign against McLaughlin, the old boss proved much too well entrenched to unseat. McLaughlin responded to Slocum's attacks by painting the general as a greedy office seeker concerned only with political gain. McLaughlin went even further, to claim that "he [the Boss] has done a good deal of political dirty work for General Slocum, but found he could not carry it as far as the General wanted to go." At one point McLaughlin even described Slocum's demeanor in one confrontation as

17. *Brooklyn Eagle* articles "Slocum Democrats," Monday, March 27, 2, "Slocumites," Wednesday, March 29, 4, "Slocum Democrats," Thursday, April 6, 4, "Thirteenth Ward Slocum Democrats," Friday, April 7, 4, "Slocum," Friday, April 7, 4, "Slocum Democrats," Tuesday, May 2, 4, "Twelfth Ward Slocum Democrats," Saturday, May 6, 6, "Second Ward Slocum Democrats," Saturday, May 20, 2, "Slocum Democrats," Thursday, May 11, 2, 1876; Morris Werner, *Tammany Hall,* 104–275; Gustavus Myers, *A History of Tammany Hall,* 237–49.

18. Untitled articles, *Journal,* September 7, October 5 (quote), 1877.

"like a monkey's." It is doubtful whether these generic and somewhat childish accusations carried much weight even with Slocum's enemies. The defection of prominent members of the Slocum Committee produced a stronger effect in ending his campaign for reform. Charles S. Higgins, once chairman of the Slocum Committee, resigned and threw in with the McLaughlin ring, claiming Slocum's whole organization had been nothing more than a front for Republicans. Slocum himself accidentally lent credence to this when a private conversation leaked out in which he questioned Samuel Tilden's chances of becoming president. Many Democrats saw this as treason. As one old-line Democrat put it, he found himself "disgusted with Slocum's course."[19]

The apex of Slocum's political hopes came with his near nomination for governor of New York in 1882. The state convention met in Syracuse, where Slocum's "betrayal" still had not been forgotten. That year even impartial observers predicted that Slocum and the King's County Democrats would take the nomination without much trouble. People expected that the only real competition would come from Roswell P. Flower, a Wall Street lawyer. Flower's association with Jay Gould had been hurting him from the beginning of the campaign, and the prospects for Slocum looked excellent. But then, just before the convention began, the *New York World* ran a series of articles recounting all the corruption within the Bridge Company as if it were fresh news, and public opinion began to turn against Slocum. This probably influenced the Brooklyn Democrats to try to gain a little insurance. Kingsley, who led the delegation, negotiated with a party of Tammany Democrats who were fighting to be seated in the convention. He threw his weight behind them, believing they would support Slocum in the balloting. In reality they had made no such promises; Kingsley had presumed too much. Slocum and Flower deadlocked in the first two ballots when the Tammany Democrats split their vote. Grover Cleveland finally won on ballot three, after the full departure of the Tammany delegates to his side. After his failure to achieve the governorship, the party offered Slocum the office of congressman-at-large, which he held for one term before finally retiring from politics.[20]

19. Untitled, *Journal*, October 26, 1875 (quote); *Brooklyn Eagle* articles "Hugh McLaughlin," Sunday, January 2, 1898, 54, "Assembly District Conventions," Saturday, April 22, 1876, 4 (quote), "The Late Chairman of the Slocum Committee on the Inside Workings of That Body," Friday, September 1, 1876, 4, "Slocum: The General as a Political Quality," Saturday, May 27, 1876, 4 (quote), "Slocum: The General Troubled by his Anti-Tilden Interview," Friday, August 18, 1876, 4.
20. McCullough, *Great Bridge*, 506–9; "General Slocum," *Journal*, April 14, 1894.

While holding his various offices Slocum rendered good service, especially regarding the military. Some of his motions in Congress excited little interest, such as his proposal to renovate Willard's Hotel in Washington, D.C., for use by the State Department. By 1884 he definitely had his own opinions of Washington politics. Of Congress he thought: "There's been too much talk . . . . We don't get to work until after 1 o'clock every afternoon . . . . This leaves very little time for debate during the afternoon." He also lamented that so few voters had any real interest in maintaining the economy as few, if any, owned any land. One of his more ambitious moves came when he introduced a bill bearing his name in which he proposed to Congress that they revolutionize the decrepit militia organizations. Sherman, when consulted on the matter by the *New York Tribune,* called it "a great advance in the right direction." The Slocum Bill hoped to improve the National Guard by requiring it to conform in every way possible to the standards of the professional service. To implement this, Slocum called for six hundred thousand dollars to be set aside for distribution to the various congressional districts to pay for uniforms and equipment. He provided for annual inspections and pay for the companies. Slocum also occupied various honorary offices, including serving as Grand Marshal of President Cleveland's first inaugural parade. Cleveland offered Slocum the chance to do so again in 1893, but having openly criticized Cleveland's nomination during the campaign, Slocum refused.[21]

Also in the 1880s Slocum prominently defended Fitz John Porter in his quest for reinstatement. At Second Manassas, Porter had refused a direct order from Pope to attack Jackson's flank. Because of changes on the battlefield that Pope did not comprehend, the order was impossible to follow, but Porter's hatred of Pope left him vulnerable to charges of disloyalty. In 1863 an inquiry found him guilty and expelled him from the army. Porter's appeals for justice began immediately. By the time Slocum took up the issue as a member of the committee of military affairs, it had become a politicized topic. Slocum introduced yet another bill in Porter's favor, following it with a powerful speech. The bill passed both House and Senate, only to be vetoed by President Chester A. Arthur. By the time

---

21. "Slocum," *Journal,* December 15, 1871; "A Talk with Gen. Slocum," *Syracuse Daily Standard,* March 17, 1884 (quote); "General Sherman on the Slocum Bill," *New York Tribune,* December 16, 1884 (quote); *Brooklyn Eagle* articles "Slocum Asked to Be Grand Marshal," Friday, December 16, 1892, 12, "In Democratic Circles," Monday, December 19, 1892, 10.

Cleveland finally exonerated Porter, Slocum had lost his bid for reelection and retired from politics.[22]

The lingering distaste for Slocum's political antecedents may well have also led to the fact that his wartime accomplishments were overlooked and belittled in various accounts of the war, from newspaper reports to memorial exercises to the historians of Slocum's day such as Samuel P. Bates. It may have even affected his subordinate Bartlett and resulted in a drastic change in Bartlett's depiction of Slocum at Crampton's Gap. All that a newspaper clipping from 1865 admitted about his military service was that "[w]e believe his name is somewhat honorably associated with the military operations around Atlanta." An even more blatant instance of willful neglect occurred three years later at a gathering of army officers in Cincinnati at which Sherman and several others gave speeches about the March to the Sea and through the Carolinas. Slocum had chosen not to attend, but what he read of the proceedings shocked him. Even though Slocum had commanded an entire wing of Sherman's army group, his name was not mentioned at all. To make matters worse, the maps used by the event showed George Thomas in command of Slocum's Army of Georgia, and someone gave John A. Logan the credit for the Battle of Bentonville. As Slocum remarked in a letter to Sherman about the incident: "I cannot for the life of me tell what command I had. I begin to doubt whether or not I was with you."[23]

Although Slocum took an active interest in reading postwar history, his general public silence on the war meant that his version of events went largely untold. Although at times he would provide personal responses to authors (he wrote a long, detailed letter to Bates over his Gettysburg history), he wrote no memoirs, gave few public lectures on the war, and generally limited his other war speeches to gatherings of veterans. When he made use of his war reputation, he would often simply let his position as Sherman's top general and army commander speak for itself rather than dwell on the details. Regarding the meeting in Cincinnati, Slocum wrote Sherman: "In order that I may get posted on these matters, I think I shall attend the next meeting; but I assure you I am too lazy or indifferent to

22. Otto Eisenschiml, *The Celebrated Case of Fitz John Porter,* 288, 290, 295, 300; Warner, *Generals in Blue,* 379–80; "Not in the Race," *Brooklyn Eagle,* Thursday, February 20, 1890, 6.

23. "General Slocum's Position," *Journal,* October 27, 1865 (quote); Slocum to Sherman, in Fox, *In Memoriam,* 109 (see also 147, 102 n. 54).

quarrel with my associates for 'the honors' . . . . I never allude to them in conversation with friends, or in letters for the press."[24]

If the press, Republican politicians, and historians disliked Slocum, the veterans generally loved him, however. He remained active in veterans' affairs for the rest of his life. At rare times he spoke to gatherings and meetings about his experiences in the war or his thoughts on its significance. In 1877 veterans elected him president of the Society of the Army of the Potomac at a meeting in Providence, Rhode Island. Although he turned down the position of major general of the New York State Militia, he later accepted the post of president of the board of trustees of the Old Soldiers and Sailors Home at Bath, New York, which he held until 1887. He attended the National Encampment of 1885 but could not be pressed into serving as its commander, pleading the rather ridiculous excuse that he had (rather conveniently) left his uniform back in Brooklyn. When the Gettysburg Monument Commission formed, Slocum became a member, working with them until his death.[25]

At other times the veteran lobby liked him less, however. As the pension controversy heated up in the early 1890s, Slocum took a hard line against what he saw as bounty jumpers repackaged. During the war, Slocum had been one of the strongest supporters of having bounty jumpers shot. At least on one occasion, he had actually circumvented Lincoln in order to enforce execution orders. Slocum thought the increasingly greedy demands for pension money resulted from the same sort of men: "If men would risk disgrace and death during the war to secure the bounty of the government, why should they not seek that bounty in time of peace, when they really risk nothing?" Having never drawn a pension himself, Slocum thought the government support should be gradually reduced beginning in the 1870s. He found himself so irate over the matter that he not only spoke out in the public record about it, but he did so to the veterans themselves at their own meetings.[26]

24. Slocum to Sherman, March 8, 1868, at Fox, *In Memoriam*, 109 (quote); "Address of Horatio C. King," *Brooklyn Eagle*, Monday, May 25, 1896, 4; Slocum, Letter to T. H. Davis and Co.; Slocum, *Military Lessons*.

25. *Journal* articles untitled, July 11, 1868, March 12, 20, 1877, July 5, 1878, April 25, 1879, "The Army of the Potomac," June 28, 1877; Fox, *In Memoriam*, 114–15; *Brooklyn Eagle* articles "Gen. Slocum: His Refusal to Take Charge of the National Encampment," Thursday, July 2, 1885, 4, "Politics," Saturday, August 26, 1876, 4, and "Resignation of General Henry Slocum," Friday, November 11, 1887.

26. *Brooklyn Eagle* articles "Slocum on Pensions," Monday, June 5, 1893, 4 (quote), "Slocum to the Front," Sunday, December 20, 1891, 8, "Slocum Speaks," Wednesday, July 2, 1890, 1.

A scrapbook rendition of Sherman's commanders, displaying a similar layout to the one Sherman mentioned to Slocum in 1889. Library of Congress, Prints & Photographs Division, Civil War Photographs

Slocum kept in contact with his wartime friends and even a few enemies. He and Sherman wrote each other sporadically. Sherman thought of Slocum and Howard as adopted sons and kept track of Slocum's later career not only through Slocum's letters but also through the newspapers. In 1883 he leased his Washington home to Slocum to live in while Slocum served in Congress, and in 1889 Slocum was a prominent guest at Sherman's birthday celebration. Not long afterward Sherman made what he expected would be the final rearrangements to his wall of wartime pictures, placing Slocum's portrait on the right of his own, just below Schofield's. Earlier that year Slocum attended a cordial dinner at the home of Daniel Butterfield, making no mention of his host as being one of Hooker's "gang." Slocum even ran into Hooker himself in May 1875. He wrote Sherman that he had found Hooker to be "very cordial towards me," and Slocum in turn did not denounce Hooker on the spot or call for a court of inquiry. They discussed Sherman's recently published memoirs, and a surprised Slocum did not find Hooker as resentful as he expected him to be. Slocum apparently misread Hooker, however, because less than two weeks later, Hooker declared that, were the two to meet again, he would virtually annihilate Sherman over his depiction of Hooker in his memoirs.[27]

Business opportunities were among the main reasons Slocum moved to Brooklyn, and he made the most of what he found. He experienced far more success in business than he ever did in politics. In 1868 the IRS valued him at $5,029. After ten years had passed, his fortunes had skyrocketed to around $150,000. (It is interesting that neither figure can account for the gigantic sums of money Slocum supposedly absconded with during the war. Either he was innocent or he learned to hide them well.) His newfound wealth came primarily from wise investments in the Brooklyn Railroad system, though like any cautious businessman he also diversified. His own company, the Brooklyn Crosstown Railroad, started service in 1872, probably anticipating the increase in traffic travelling over the new bridge. This made President Slocum, who owned majority stock, an increasingly rich man. The Crosstown line used nearly four hundred horses to pull its seventy-two cars over sixteen miles of track. Slocum's success eventually led to the opening of a similar line, the Brooklyn and Coney Island Railroad Company, in which Slocum's son Henry Jr. (a national ten-

27. Slocum to Sherman, May 20, 1875 (quote), Sherman to Slocum, Dec. 9, 1882, in Fox, *In Memoriam,* 111; Hirshson, *White Tecumseh,* 378, 385; "Notable Talks," *Brooklyn Eagle,* Friday, February 1, 1889, 2; Hebert, *Fighting Joe Hooker,* 294.

nis champion, who authored a book about the sport) played a large role. The completion of the bridge and the rise of Coney Island as a tourist attraction would have made this investment very attractive and probably equally profitable.[28]

Slocum's role in the business life of Brooklyn also led him into public controversy on several occasions, even after his "retirement." At different points in his career he found himself on the receiving end of lawsuits and hence more negative publicity. One of the most prominent cases came from a former Crosstown employee, Demas Strong, who accused him of watering the Crosstown's stock by about one hundred thousand dollars. The term *watering stock* refers to the surreptitious issuance of stock to individuals, without the knowledge of the public or stockholders, which would water down the company's value, thus helping to avoid taxation. Slocum retaliated with two suits alleging illegal issuance of stock by Strong. Courts in Slocum's countersuits either decided for Strong or dismissed the charges, but the case against Slocum dragged on for years. Was Slocum guilty of corruption and wrongdoing? Although he seems to have kept relatively clean of the messes he found at Vicksburg, it seems he might have committed at least some of these business offenses. The reaction of the court to Strong indicates there was clearly a case against Slocum, and Slocum's countersuits, filed for crimes he alleged Strong had committed eight or nine years before, smack of intimidation. Apparently Slocum had come to the conclusion that a successful businessman was also to some extent a businessman who circumvented the law.[29]

The governing authorities also gave Slocum plenty of opportunities to complain. In the late 1880s his Brooklyn–Coney Island line began the process of moving into the modern age by replacing the outmoded horse-drawn cars with new ones powered by single-line electricity. Slocum incorporated the new propulsion method into the line from Coney Island through Flatbush, but the city of Brooklyn refused to let him update inside the city itself. This led to a public row with a city alderman that made headlines all over Brooklyn. Later, in 1891, the *New York Tribune* printed an article entitled "General Slocum's Dubious Methods." The article angered Slocum to the point that he sued the *Tribune* for libel. Slocum, now aged

---

28. *Journal* articles untitled, April 8, 1868, "Slocum," February 19, "Slocum," April 30, 1878; *Brooklyn Eagle* articles "Lawn Tennis," Sunday, August 28, 1887, 9, "Slocum Loses," Wednesday, September 3, 1890, 6; Henry Slocum, Jr., *Lawn Tennis in Our Own Country*.

29. *Brooklyn Eagle* articles "Slocum and Strong," Thursday, November 23, 1876, 4, "Mr. Demas Strong and General H. W. Slocum," Friday, July 8, 1881, 3.

and increasingly infirm, eventually turned the battle over to Henry Jr. and settled down to enjoy a comfortable retirement.[30]

If Slocum worried at all about his health, events would bring his own mortality home to him in a serious way in 1891. In 1888 Sherman had moved his family to New York in the hopes of benefiting his wife's ailing health. Sadly, she died later that year, but Sherman stayed on in New York. So Slocum knew very well when Sherman took a turn for the worse after seeing a play one February night. When doctors notified the family that the final hours had come, someone called both Slocum and Howard, and they waited in another room while the family stood by Sherman in his final moments. At the family's request, Slocum and Howard organized and oversaw the funeral.[31]

By 1893 Slocum was feeling the effects of his own age but overall still seemed in good health. He retired that year as president of the Brooklyn and Coney Island Railroad Company. In February 1894, he and his son-in-law, Capt. H. B. Kingsbury (formerly of Howard's staff), left Brooklyn and traveled about the country. In a month, they visited Colorado, California, and Texas. Slocum returned on March 23, looking and feeling well. About March 31, 1894, he went to Tarrytown with another son, Clarence, to look into purchasing a summer home. While there he complained of pains in his chest and insisted on going inside to rest. He returned to Brooklyn that day and only went out briefly. He fought the illness for the better part of two weeks. By April 10, although confined to bed for the previous week, he showed some signs of improvement, but on April 13, he suffered a serious relapse.[32]

At six o'clock in the evening on April 14, 1894, he began to sink rapidly. His doctors arrived and managed to arrest his descent, but by eight o'clock it was clear he would not recover. The doctors informed the family, who kept vigil while the general slept. Just before midnight, he awoke. He knew he was dying and spoke briefly with his family before passing

30. *Brooklyn Eagle* articles "Slocum Loses: His Road Cannot Use Trolley Wires within the City," Tuesday, May 19, 6, "Trying Again," Thursday, August 27, 4, "A Big Row," Wednesday, December 2, 2, "Slocum Sues," Wednesday, May 6, 6, 1891, and "Squirming under the Tax," Friday, July 14, 1893, 1.

31. Marszalek, *Sherman,* 488–99.

32. "Gen. H. W. Slocum: Death of the Well-Known Veteran of the War" (clipping, probably *Journal,* April 1894); *Brooklyn Eagle* articles, "Gen. Slocum Improving," Tuesday, April 10, 1894, 1, "General Slocum Not as Well," Wednesday, April 11, 1894, 1, "General Slocum has a Relapse," Friday, April 13, 1894, 1; "Gen. Slocum Dangerously Ill," *New York Times,* April 10, 1894, 5.

on in the early hours of the morning. Present with him were his wife, his daughter, and his two sons, Henry Jr. and Clarence. As news of Slocum's death spread, various civil organizations, from his own Brooklyn Club to veterans' groups to the House of Representatives, all voted on official expressions of condolence for the family, nearly burying Clinton Avenue in cards and flower arrangements. His family interred him in Brooklyn's Greenwood Cemetery with military pomp. Sickles, Howard, Butterfield, Porter, and Schofield acted as pallbearers.[33]

Slocum died of pneumonia, a legendary killer of the young, weak, and elderly. Yet there was a possibly ironic aside to his end; doctors ruled a second major cause of death to be cirrhosis of the liver. Although Slocum never acquired a reputation for drunkenness, and although heavy drinking was one of the charges he threw at Hooker, he did drink, and it is tempting to conclude he became an alcoholic at some point. There are a few references scattered here and there throughout his history to show that he enjoyed a good drink. However, the case for alcoholism is far from proved by current evidence. Cirrhosis of the liver is no longer a necessary indication of alcohol abuse. Another cause of the condition is fatty liver associated with obesity and diabetes. Slocum did gain a great deal of weight in his later years, as pictures attest.

His will, filed a week after his death, showed that the general had indeed fared well in business. Although a total value was not specified in the document, the best estimates placed the value of his estate at five hundred thousand dollars. In his will he provided for Clara and made small donations (five thousand dollars each) to two Brooklyn children's charities. He left his now elusive papers and wartime personal effects to Henry Jr. and divided the rest of his estate between his children and their families.[34]

If the newspapers had reviled Slocum while he lived, they forgot all about his alleged sins after his death. Forgiveness had taken time, the various papers growing less antagonistic as the years passed, and his sudden death completed the process in 1894. After the memorial service, a series of articles appeared, praising Slocum as a man of skill and integrity. The

33. *New York Times* articles "Gen. Henry W. Slocum Dead," April 15, 16, "Funeral of Gen. H. W. Slocum," April 18, 9, "Slocum, Soldier and Man," May 5, 9, "In Praise of the Dead Hero," April 17, 9, "Senate's Tribute to Gen. Slocum," April 17, 9, "Voicing the Nation's Grief," April 17, 9; "Gen. Henry W. Slocum Dead," *New York Tribune*, April 17, all 1894.

34. Death Certificate, participant account folder 5, Slocum (Jack Walsh folder, U.S. Military History Institute, GNMP); "Digestive Diseases: Cirrhosis of the Liver"; "Gen. Slocum's Will Filed," *New York Times*, April 21, 1894, 9.

same papers that had earlier referred to him as "the tempter . . . in our fold [who] did not receive the indignant rebuke, 'Get thee behind me, Satan!'" now sought to call attention to his "Career Illustrious." Syracuse quickly reexerted its claim to him, and some people even wanted to mount a campaign to bring his body back to be buried in Oakwood Cemetery.[35]

The state of New York and city of Brooklyn acted quickly to fulfill Sherman's prophecy for honor due Slocum. In 1896 they christened a fortification Fort Slocum, on David's Island, New York. Almost immediately upon his death, talk began of statues to his memory. The city of Brooklyn commissioned the first to be completed, depicting a very uncharacteristic Slocum charging on horseback, waving his saber, and yelling to his troops. This proved a cause for complaint from the surviving veterans, who pointed out that they could not remember the calm and collected Slocum ever striking such a pose.[36]

The Gettysburg Monument Commission, led by Sickles, addressed this in their monument. Sickles himself put forward the unanimously adopted resolution to commission an equestrian statue of Slocum for Culp's Hill on April 17, 1894. He later remarked that "We should not consider our Gettysburg work completed until we have seen a statue erected on Culp's Hill to General Slocum." The commission rejected the first ten models that sculptors brought before it in June 1897, before finally deciding on December 10, 1897, to adopt a design by Edward C. Potter. Potter's statue depicts Slocum seated calmly on his horse, his hat in his hand, staring quietly across the battlefield. Potter first constructed a plaster model from which the cast would be made, while the committee turned its attentions to providing a base for the statue and designing its bronze plaque (which credits him with command of the right wing, no doubt to Meade's post mortem chagrin). By the summer of 1902, everything had been completed at a total cost of $29,941.57. The amount the commission raised for the project totaled $30,000.[37]

35. *Journal* articles "The Nomination of Gen. Slocum by the Copperheads," September 8, 1865 (quote), "General Slocum," April 14, 1894; "Slocum and Onondaga" (clipping in OHA), 1894.

36. "Honors to Slocum," *Brooklyn Eagle*, Friday, July 10, 1896, 6; "Monument to General Slocum," *New York Times*, May 1, 1894, 9; "MacMonnies Latest Work," *Brooklyn Eagle*, Sunday, December 30, 1900, 23.

37. "Sickles to Carr, 11–20-1894," file 17–18, General Henry Slocum Equestrian Statue, GNMP; Fox, *In Memoriam*, 5–24; "Slocum Monument Site Chosen," *Brooklyn Eagle*, Tuesday, May 5, 1896, 1.

The statue's unveiling took place as the highlight of the thirty-third reunion of the Society of the Army of the Potomac. On September 19, 1902, a great crowd of people assembled on Culp's Hill. A parade led the way to the veiled monument. The Seventh New York Regiment served as escort for the procession, which featured General Sickles and his family, several governors, and other persons of import. After speeches they pulled back the cloth as artillery fired a major general's salute in the background. Although history might at times overlook or belittle him, Slocum had finally taken his place among his brethren on the field.[38]

So what are we to make of Henry Slocum, Sherman's forgotten general? If Gettysburg is taken as the totality of the Civil War, then he does not inspire much confidence. It is clear that for Slocum as for other generals Gettysburg became the defining point of the war, though ironically not of his career. Slocum gave much better, more important service under Sherman in the West and indeed reached the height of his powers just before the war ended. Yet it is the Gettysburg Slocum that later generations remember best, because it is here that historians have had the most to say about him. As a result history has absorbed a negative view of him at worst, or a bland mechanical view of him at best.

This affected Slocum's memory more than most. Many other generals and officers had much better political sense than he did. Whereas they often graduated from the field to the canvass with their national reputations intact (or, as in the case of Sherman or Grant, with reputations so gargantuan they stood above all practical political criticism), Slocum managed to exhaust his political capital in less than six months after the war's end. With this, he lost the leverage to secure himself a legacy. Other generals with less military honor to their names were able to outmuscle army commander Slocum in the eyes of historians and the public alike.

Another reason the myopic focus on Slocum at Gettysburg affected him disproportionately is the fact that he served in the army almost from the very first day of the war, in both theaters, and at virtually every level of command from the regiment to just short of Grant himself. Wherever one turns in Civil War history, there is a good chance of encountering Henry Slocum. He was at Bull Run, the Peninsula, South Mountain, Antietam, Chancellorsville, Harpers Ferry, Gettysburg, Tennessee, Vicksburg, Atlanta,

38. "Onondaga Hero Honored in Bronze," *Syracuse Daily Standard*, September 20, 1902; "Slocum Statue Dedication," *Brooklyn Eagle*, Thursday, September 11, 1902.

Savannah, Bentonville, the Bennett Place, and everywhere in between. His life and decisions touch on a vast number of conceptual topics as well: New York politics, raising the army, application of discipline, race relations, wartime civilian administration, hard war, army politics, and press issues are only a few. When historians refer to Slocum in their treatments of these issues, they often view him in light of Gettysburg or treat him like the unknown commodity he was at the time. Many others simply ignore him altogether.

Yet this is not the Slocum a more careful and mature investigation reveals. He was an able and usually competent leader, willing to fight but lacking in killer instinct until almost the last days of the war. He did exactly what his superiors told him to do, in the way they told him to do it, though not always without question. His tendency to emulate his commanders led him to imitate not only their good characteristics but also their bad ones. He would often act on their rhetoric as opposed to their actions. So he was more willing to act like a "Little Napoleon" than McClellan himself, for he would actually attack the enemy when the situation called for it. Although Sherman was supposed to be the ruthless warrior, anxious to destroy his enemy through hard war and maneuver, on the March to the Sea and at Savannah Slocum in reality proved much more destructive and aggressive than Sherman.

Every great commander needs men like Slocum. He must have competent leaders to take the field and see that orders are carried out. These leaders must be intelligent enough to advise their superiors when necessary but also willing to follow orders they disagree with. Although more of a loose cannon in the Army of the Potomac, Slocum provided Sherman with just such a man. Slocum's imitative nature not only served him well, it fitted him perfectly for his role as one of Sherman's chief subordinates. Not only could Sherman count on Slocum carrying out his orders, Slocum might even anticipate them, as he did before the March to the Sea and at Savannah. It would be easy to overemphasize the advantages of Slocum's personal imitative quirk, but it is also difficult to deny that, in Sherman's case, Slocum's adaptability provided Sherman with an ideal army commander. Slocum also distinguished himself as an able administrator and garrison commander, and Sherman trusted him with some of his most hard-earned prizes.

At the same time Slocum had definite failings. He worried himself sick over what he thought his enemies might do and at times greatly overestimated their strength. This could lead to credibility problems with high command. Before 1864 he had not developed the killer instinct of Grant or the restless mind of Sherman. He could hesitate at critical moments when the situation called for energetic actions. He demonstrated this on the first day at Gettysburg. Once a commander truly earned Slocum's enmity, his deeply ingrained sense of honor prevented him from working smoothly with that man again, no matter what greater good lay at stake. Also, he tended to be only as good as the men placed in authority over him. Hence, in the presence of mediocre leaders, his performance suffered greatly. His need for a powerful example left him unsuited to taking over a large-scale independent command, something that luckily never happened during the war.

After the war Slocum proved a terrible judge of politics. Whatever his ultimate reason for defecting to the Democrats, his choice to switch parties was among the worst possible decisions he could have made at the worst possible time. Having tied that albatross around Slocum's neck, public opinion turned so strongly against him in his home of Syracuse that he was compelled to move. Even in Democrat-dominated Brooklyn, he could boast scant few accomplishments when compared with what could have been. His tendency to challenge the powers that controlled the party—whether out of moral obligation or as an attempt at simple maneuvering—hurt his chances in politics. He met with greater success in business, however, and managed to die a wealthy man. But he had devoted so much time to business and local politics that he neglected the postwar debates that could have secured him a more prominent place in history.

Overall, historians owe Slocum a good deal more attention. No study of a campaign or battle he served in can be considered complete without a mention of his presence. Yet in the more than seventy thousand books written on the war since its end, only two others have chosen Slocum as their focus. This biography has been an endeavor primarily to lay out Slocum's life and to provide readers with a more holistic view of his actions and the thinking behind them. Historians and enthusiasts alike need to know more about Slocum as a person, and to meet him in the historical record in a new way. It may be hoped that Sherman's forgotten general will soon be remembered more often.

Appendix

Organization of Slocum's Commands, 1861–1865

Given the regularity, especially in the beginning of the war, with which Slocum changed commands, I have assembled a brief order of battle for his different organizations for ease of reference. Please note that the armies were very much evolving organisms, so it is virtually impossible for a single chart to follow their details concisely over a period of time greater than the time it generally took to fight a battle. Deaths, wounds in battle, leaves of absence, courts martial, changes in political climate, and the significant structural changes that often followed the end of a campaign or the ascension of a new army commander could all throw settled order into chaos with little or no warning. Keeping up with these shifting sands of men—let alone the whys and wherefores connected with them—could easily be a book series in and of itself. It is important always to take with care the specifics of any static presentation of army organizations over a period of more than a few days. The following charts do not even pretend to be an exhaustive treatment of all the comings and goings of Slocum's commands during the Civil War. They are instead snapshots of important and convenient moments, intended to provide a general reference and some perspective. It is also worth noting that I have attempted nothing new here. This appendix is merely, for the convenience of the reader, a compilation of the *Official Records* and other scholars' research.

McDowell's Army, Second Division (Col. Andrew Porter), First Brigade (Col. Andrew Porter), Twenty-seventh Regiment (Infantry) New York Volunteers

Commanded from May 1861 to August 1861

Company	City of Origin	Recruited by	Date Accepted
A	White Plains	Capt. Joseph J. Chambers	April 30, 1861
B	Lyons	Capt. Alex D. Adams	May 2, 1861
C	Binghamton	Capt. Joseph J. Bartlett	May 2, 1861
D	Binghamton	Capt. Hiram C. Rogers	May 2, 1861
E	Rochester	Capt. George G. Wanzer	May 7, 1861
F	Binghamton	Capt. Peter Jay	May 8, 1861
G	Lima	Capt. James Perkins	May 7, 1861
H	Mount Morris	Capt. Charles E. Martin	May 11, 1861
I	Angelica	Capt. Curtis C. Gardner	May 13, 1861
J	No Company J listed.		
K	Albion	Capt. Henry L. Achilles, Jr.	May 16, 1861

Source: Fairchild, History of the 27th, 1.

Fourth Corps (Erasmus Keyes), First Division (William B. Franklin), Second Brigade

Commanded from August 1861 to May 1862

Unit	Commander
16th New York	Col. Joseph Howland
27th New York	Col. Joseph J. Bartlett
5th Maine	Col. N. J. Jackson
96th Pennsylvania	Col. Henry L. Cake

Sources: Sears, *Gates of Richmond,* 361–62; Reports of Col. Joseph J. Bartlett, Col. Jacob G. Frick, Maj. Joel J. Seaver, *OR,* ser. 1, vol. 11, pt. 2, 449–52.

Army of the Potomac (Maj. Gen. George B. McClellan), Sixth Corps (William B. Franklin), First Division

Commanded from May 1862 to October 1862

First Brigade: Brig. Gen. George W. Taylor	
1st New Jersey	3rd New Jersey
2nd New Jersey	4th New Jersey
Second Brigade: Col. Joseph J. Bartlett	
16th New York	5th Maine
27th New York	96th Pennsylvania
Third Brigade: Brig. Gen. John Newton	
18th New York	32nd New York
31st New York	95th Pennsylvania
Artillery: Capt. Edward R. Platt	
Massachusetts Light, Battery A	Second United States, Battery D
New Jersey Light, Battery A	

Source: Sears, *Gates of Richmond,* 373.

Army of the Potomac (variously Ambrose Burnside, Joseph Hooker, George Meade), Twelfth Corps, later under Hooker in Western Theater, Army of the Cumberland (William Rosecrans, George Thomas)

Commanded from October 1862 to April 1864

At the time of Antietam (September 1862), just before Slocum assumes command

First Division: Brig. Gen. Alpheus S. Williams	
First Brigade: Brig. Gen. Samuel Crawford (wounded) Col. Joseph F. Knipe	
5th Connecticut	10th Maine
28th New York	46th Pennsylvania
124th Pennsylvania	125th Pennsylvania
128th Pennsylvania	
Third Brigade: Brig. Gen. George H. Gordon (wounded) Col. Thomas H. Ruger	
27th Indiana	2nd Massachusetts
13th New Jersey	107th New York
3rd Wisconsin	
Second Division: Brig. Gen. George S. Greene	
First Brigade: Lieut. Col. Hector Tyndale (wounded) Maj. Orrin J. Crane	
5th Ohio	7th Ohio
66th Ohio	28th Pennsylvania
29th Ohio	

Second Brigade: Col. Henry Stainrook	
3rd Maryland	102nd New York
111th Pennsylvania	

Third Brigade: Col. William B. Goodrich (killed) Lieut. Col. Jonathan Austin	
3rd Delaware	Purnell Legion (Maryland)
60th New York	78th New York

Artillery: Capt. Clermont L. Best	
Maine Light, Batteries Four and Six	First New York Light, Battery M
New York Light, Tenth Battery	Pennsylvania Light, Batteries E and F
Fourth United States, Battery F	

At the time of the Chancellorsville Campaign (May 1863)

Provost Guard: Three Companies of the Tenth Maine Chief of Artillery: Clermont L. Best	
First Division: Brig. Gen. Alpheus S. Williams	

First Brigade: Brig. Gen. Joseph F. Knipe	
5th Connecticut	128th Pennsylvania
28th New York	46th Pennsylvania

Second Brigade: Col. Samuel Ross (wounded) Brig. Gen. Joseph F. Knipe	
20th Connecticut	3rd Maryland
123rd New York	145th New York

Third Brigade: Brig. Gen. Thomas H. Ruger	
27th Indiana	2nd Massachusetts
13th New Jersey	107th New York
3rd Wisconsin	
Second Division: Brig. Gen. John W. Geary	
First Brigade: Col. Charles Candy	
5th Ohio	7th Ohio
66th Ohio	28th Pennsylvania
29th Ohio	147th Pennsylvania
Second Brigade: Brig. Gen. Thomas L. Kane	
29th Pennsylvania	109th Pennsylvania
111th Pennsylvania	124th Pennsylvania
125th Pennsylvania	
Third Brigade: Brig. Gen. George S. Greene	
60th New York	78th New York
102nd New York	137th New York
149th New York	
Artillery: Capt. Joseph M. Knap	
Pennsylvania Light, Battery E	Pennsylvania Light, Battery F

At the time of Gettysburg (July 1863)

Provost Guard: Four Companies of the Tenth Maine	
First Division: Brig. Gen. Alpheus S. Williams	
First Brigade: Col. Archibald L. McDougall	
5th Connecticut	20th Connecticut
3rd Maryland	123rd New York
145th New York	46th Pennsylvania
Second Brigade (not officially assigned until after the battle): Brig. Gen. Henry Lockwood	
1st Maryland, Potomac Home	1st Maryland, Eastern Shore
150th New York	
Third Brigade: Brig. Gen. Thomas H. Ruger	
27th Indiana	2nd Massachusetts
13th New Jersey	107th New York
3rd Wisconsin	
Second Division: Brig. Gen. John W. Geary	
First Brigade: Col. Charles Candy	
5th Ohio	7th Ohio
66th Ohio	28th Pennsylvania
29th Ohio	147th Pennsylvania

Second Brigade: Brig. Gen. Thomas L. Kane	
29th Pennsylvania	109th Pennsylvania
111th Pennsylvania	
Third Brigade: Brig. Gen. George S. Greene	
60th New York	78th New York
102nd New York	137th New York
149th New York	
Artillery Brigade: Lieut. Edward D. Muhlenberg	
Pennsylvania Light, Battery E	1st New York Light, Battery M
4th United States, Battery F	5th United States, Battery K

Sources: For Antietam, James V. Murfin, *The Gleam of Bayonets: The Battle of Antietam and the Maryland Campaign of 1862,* 357–58, and Sears, *Landscape Turned Red,* 365–66; for Chancellorsville, Sears, *Chancellorsville,* 464–65; for Gettysburg, Pfanz, *Gettysburg,* 394–95, and Coddington, *Gettysburg Campaign,* 584–85.

The District of Vicksburg

Commanded from April 1864 to August 1864

First Division, Seventeenth Army Corps (Not present in Vicksburg, reported present with Seventeenth Corps)	
Maltby's Brigade Brig. Gen. Jasper Maltby	
124th Illinois	58th Ohio
1st Regiment, Mississippi Marines	72nd Illinois
8th Ohio Battery	26th Ohio Battery

Unattached Forces	
5th U.S. Colored Heavy Artillery	64th U.S. Colored Troops
Cavalry Forces Col. Emory Osband	
5th Illinois	11th Illinois
3rd U. S. Colored	2nd Wisconsin
Artillery at Vicksburg Maj. Charles Mann	
2nd Illinois Light, Battery L	Ohio Light, 7th Battery
Post and Defenses of Natchez	
8th New Hampshire	48th Ohio
4th Illinois Cavalry	2nd Illinois Light Artillery
58th U.S. Colored Troops	63rd U.S. Colored Troops
70th U.S. Colored Troops	71st U. S. Colored Troops
6th U.S. Colored Heavy Artillery	

Note: These figures represent a compilation of the more general returns made while Slocum was in command and the more specific ones made by his successor, not long after taking command. While it is likely they represent the forces Slocum commanded, there may be some inaccuracies in certain details.

Sources: Abstract from returns of the Department of the Tennessee, *OR,* ser. 1, vol. 32, pt. 3, 561, vol. 38, pt. 5, 318, 744; District of Vicksburg, ibid., vol. 39, pt. 3, 568.

Army of the Cumberland (George H. Thomas), Twentieth Corps
Commanded August 1864 to November 1864

Escort: 15th Illinois Cavalry, Company K	
First Division: Brig. Gen. Alpheus S. Williams	
First Brigade: Brig. Gen. Joseph F. Knipe	
5th Connecticut	123rd New York
141st New York	46th Pennsylvania
3rd Maryland (detachment)	3rd Maryland
20th Connecticut	145th New York
Second Brigade: Brig. Gen. Thomas H. Ruger	
27th Indiana	2nd Massachusetts
13th New Jersey	107th New York
150th New York	3rd Wisconsin
Third Brigade: Col. James S. Robinson Col. Horace Boughton	
82nd Illinois	101st Illinois
45th New York	143rd New York
61st Ohio	82nd Ohio
31st Wisconsin	
Artillery: John D. Woodbury	
1st New York Light, Battery I	1st New York Light, Battery M

Second Division: Brig. Gen. John W. Geary	
First Brigade: Col. Charles Candy Col. Ario Pardee, Jr.	
5th Ohio	7th Ohio
66th Ohio	28th Pennsylvania
29th Ohio	147th Pennsylvania
Second Brigade: Col. Adolphus Bushbeck Col. John T. Lockman Col. Patrick H. Jones Col. George Mindil	
33rd New Jersey	119th New York
134th New York	154th New York
27th Pennsylvania	73rd Pennsylvania
109th Pennsylvania	
Third Brigade: Col. David Ireland Col. William Rickards, Jr. Col. George Cobham, Jr. Col. David Ireland	
60th New York	78th New York
102nd New York	137th New York
149th New York	29th Pennsylvania
111th Pennsylvania	
Artillery: Capt. William Wheeler	
Pennsylvania Light, Battery E	New York Light, 18th Battery

Third Division: Maj. Gen. Daniel Butterfield Brig. Gen. William T. Ward	
First Brigade: Brig. Gen. William T. Ward Col. Benjamin Harrison	
102nd Illinois	105th Illinois
129th Illinois	70th Indiana
79th Ohio	
Second Brigade: Col. Samuel Ross Col. John Coburn	
20th Connecticut	33rd Indiana
85th Indiana	19th Michigan
22nd Wisconsin	
Third Brigade: Col. James Wood, Jr.	
20th Connecticut	33rd Massachusetts
136th New York	55th Ohio
73rd Ohio	26th Wisconsin
Artillery: Capt. Marco B. Gary	
1st Michigan Light, Battery I	1st Ohio Light, Battery C
Artillery Brigade: Maj. John A. Reynolds	
1st Michigan Light, Battery I	1st New York Light, Battery I
1st New York Light, Battery M	New York Light, 13th Battery
1st Ohio Light, Battery C	Pennsylvania Light, Battery E
5th United States, Battery K	

Source: These statistics represent the Twentieth during the Atlanta Campaign. Returns of the Military Division of the Mississippi, *OR,* ser. 1, vol. 38, pt. 1, 97–100.

William T. Sherman's Army Group, Army of Georgia (Left Wing)

Commanded November 1864 to March 1865

Before Savannah

Pontoniers: 58th Indiana	
Engineers: 1st Michigan (detachment)	
Fourteenth Corps: Maj. Gen. Jefferson C. Davis	
First Division: William P. Carlin	
First Brigade: Col. Harrison C. Hobart	
104th Illinois	42nd Indiana
88th Indiana	33rd Ohio
94th Ohio	21st Wisconsin
Second Brigade: Lieut. Col. Joseph H. Brigham	
13th Michigan	21st Michigan
69th Ohio	
Third Brigade: Col. Henry Hambright (sick) Lieut. Col. David Miles	
38th Indiana	21st Ohio
74th Ohio	79th Pennsylvania

Second Division: Brig. Gen. James D. Morgan	
First Brigade: Col. Robert F. Smith	
16th Illinois	60th Illinois
10th Michigan	14th Michigan
17th New York	
Second Brigade: Lieut. Col. John S. Pearce	
34th Illinois	78th Illinois
98th Ohio	108th Ohio
113th Ohio	121st Ohio
Third Brigade: Lieut. Col. James Langley	
85th Illinois	86th Illinois
110th Illinois	125th Illinois
22nd Indiana	52nd Ohio
Third Division: Brig. Gen. Absalom Baird	
First Brigade: Col. Morton C. Hunter	
82nd Indiana	23rd Missouri
17th Ohio	31st Ohio
89th Ohio	92nd Ohio
Second Brigade: Col. Newell Gleason	
75th Indiana	87th Indiana
101st Indiana	2nd Minnesota
105th Ohio	

Third Brigade: Col. George P. Este	
74th Indiana	18th Kentucky
14th Ohio	38th Ohio
Artillery: *Maj. Charles Houghtaling*	
1st Illinois Light, Battery C	2nd Illinois Light, Battery I
Indiana Light, 19th Battery	Wisconsin Light, 5th Battery
Twentieth Corps: Brig. Gen. Alpheus S. Williams	
First Division: Brig. Gen. Nathaniel J. Jackson	
First Brigade: Col. James L. Selfridge	
5th Connecticut	123rd New York
141st New York	46th Pennsylvania
Second Brigade: Col. Ezra A. Carman	
2nd Massachusetts	13th New Jersey
107th New York	150th New York
3rd Wisconsin	
Third Brigade: Col. James S. Robinson	
82nd Illinois	101st Illinois
143rd New York	61st Ohio
82nd Ohio	31st Wisconsin

Second Division: Brig. Gen. John W. Geary	
First Brigade: Col. Ario Pardee, Jr.	
5th Ohio	66th Ohio
28th Pennsylvania	29th Ohio
147th Pennsylvania	
Second Brigade: Col. Patrick H. Jones	
33rd New Jersey	119th New York
134th New York	154th New York
73rd Pennsylvania	109th Pennsylvania
Third Brigade: Col. Henry A. Barnum	
60th New York	102nd New York
137th New York	149th New York
29th Pennsylvania	111th Pennsylvania
Third Division: Brig. Gen. William T. Ward	
First Brigade: Col. Franklin C. Smith	
102nd Illinois	105th Illinois
129th Illinois	70th Indiana
79th Ohio	

Second Brigade: Col. Daniel Dustin	
33rd Indiana	85th Indiana
22nd Wisconsin	19th Michigan
Third Brigade: Col. Samuel Ross	
20th Connecticut	33rd Massachusetts
136th New York	55th Ohio
73rd Ohio	26th Wisconsin
Artillery Brigade: Maj. John A. Reynolds	
1st New York Light, Battery I	New York Light, 13th Battery
1st New York Light, Battery M	Pennsylvania Light, Battery E
1st Ohio Light, Battery C	

Source: Organization of Union Forces, *OR,* ser. 1, 44:22–25.

The Army of Georgia at Bentonville

Pontoniers: 58th Indiana	
Fourteenth Corps: Maj. Gen. Jefferson C. Davis	
First Division: William P. Carlin	
First Brigade: Bvt. Brig. Gen. Harrison C. Hobart	
104th Illinois	42nd Indiana
88th Indiana	33rd Ohio
94th Ohio	21st Wisconsin

Second Brigade: Bvt. Brig. Gen. George P. Buell	
13th Michigan	21st Michigan
69th Ohio	

Third Brigade: Lieut. Col. David Miles	
38th Indiana	21st Ohio
74th Ohio	79th Pennsylvania

Second Division: Brig. Gen. James D. Morgan

First Brigade: Brig. Gen. William Vandever	
16th Illinois	60th Illinois
10th Michigan	14th Michigan
17th New York	

Second Brigade: Brig. John G. Mitchell	
34th Illinois	78th Illinois
98th Ohio	108th Ohio
113th Ohio	121st Ohio

Third Brigade: Bvt. Brig. Gen. Benjamin D. Fearing (wounded) Lieut. Col. James Langley	
86th Illinois	110th Illinois
125th Illinois	22nd Indiana
37th Indiana (one company)	52nd Ohio

Third Division: *Bvt. Maj. Gen. Absalom Baird*	
First Brigade: Col. Morton C. Hunter	
82nd Indiana	23rd Missouri
11th Ohio (4 companies)	17th Ohio
31st Ohio	70th Ohio
89th Ohio	92nd Ohio
Second Brigade: Lt. Col. Thomas Doan	
75th Indiana	87th Indiana
101st Indiana	2nd Minnesota
105th Ohio	
Third Brigade: Col. George P. Este	
74th Indiana	18th Kentucky
14th Ohio	38th Ohio
Artillery: *Maj. Charles Houghtaling*	
1st Illinois Light, Battery C	2nd Illinois Light, Battery I
Indiana Light, 19th Battery	Wisconsin Light, 5th Battery

Twentieth Corps: Bvt. Maj. Gen. Alpheus S. Williams	
First Division: Brig. Gen. Nathaniel J. Jackson	
First Brigade: Col. James L. Selfridge	
5th Connecticut	123rd New York
141st New York	46th Pennsylvania
Second Brigade: Col. William Hawley	
2nd Massachusetts	13th New Jersey
107th New York	150th New York
3rd Wisconsin	
Third Brigade: Brig. Gen. James S. Robinson	
82nd Illinois	101st Illinois
143rd New York	61st Ohio
82nd Ohio	31st Wisconsin
Second Division: Bvt. Maj. Gen. John W. Geary	
First Brigade: Bvt. Brig. Gen. Ario Pardee, Jr.	
5th Ohio	66th Ohio
28th Pennsylvania	29th Ohio
147th Pennsylvania	

Second Brigade: Col. George W. Mindil	
33rd New Jersey	119th New York
134th New York	154th New York
73rd Pennsylvania	109th Pennsylvania
Third Brigade: Bvt. Brig. Gen. Henry A. Barnum	
60th New York	102nd New York
137th New York	149th New York
29th Pennsylvania	111th Pennsylvania
Third Division: *Bvt. Maj. Gen. William T. Ward*	
First Brigade: Col. Henry Case	
102nd Illinois	105th Illinois
129th Illinois	70th Indiana
79th Ohio	
Second Brigade: Col. Daniel Dustin	
33rd Indiana	85th Indiana
22nd Wisconsin	19th Michigan

Third Brigade: Bvt. Brig. Gen. William Cogswell	
20th Connecticut	33rd Massachusetts
136th New York	55th Ohio
73rd Ohio	26th Wisconsin
Artillery Brigade: Maj. John A. Reynolds	
1st New York Light, Battery I	1st Ohio Light, Battery C
1st New York Light, Battery M	Pennsylvania Light, Battery E

Sources: Organization of the Union Forces Commanded by Maj. Gen. William T. Sherman, Jan.–April 1865, *OR,* ser. 1. vol. 47, pt. 1, 55–55.

Selected Bibliography

Newspapers

Albany Evening Journal. 1865–1866. In the Slocum Biographic Clippings File, OHA.

Brooklyn Eagle. 1875–1905. Online at http://www.brooklynpubliclibrary.org/eagle.

Harper's Weekly. 1864–1902. Online at http://app.harpweek.com.

New York Times. 1865–1894. On microfilm at the Texas Christian Library.

New York Tribune. 1865–1866. In the Slocum Biographic Clippings File, OHA.

Onondaga Standard. (After 1880, *Syracuse Daily Standard.*) 1856–1902. In the Slocum Biographic Clippings File, OHA.

Syracuse Daily Courier. 1858–1902. Most are in the Slocum Biographic Clippings File, OHA. Some (cited with volume number and sometimes issue number) are on microform from the OHA.

Syracuse Daily Standard. See *Onondaga Standard.*

Syracuse Herald. In the Slocum Biographic Clippings File, OHA.

Syracuse Journal. 1858–1961. In the Slocum Biographic Clippings File, OHA.

Collections and Manuscript Repositories

Brooklyn Historical Society, Brooklyn, New York.

Gettysburg National Military Park (GNMP) Archives, Gettysburg, Pennsylvania.

Huntington Library Collection, San Marino, California.

Abraham Lincoln Papers, Library of Congress (Lincoln Papers). Transcribed and annotated by the Lincoln Studies Center, Knox College. Galesburg, Illinois. Online at http://memory.loc.gov/ammem/alhtml/malhome.html.

Morgan County Archives, Madison, Georgia.

National Archives (NA), Washington, D.C.

New-York Historical Society Collections, New York (NYHS).

New York State Archives and Library, Albany, New York.

William T. Sherman Papers, University of Notre Dame. Online at http://www.archives.nd.edu/findaids/ead/index/SHR001.htm.

Slocum Biographic Clippings File. Onondaga Historical Association (OHA), Syracuse, New York.

Slocum Letters to Howland. At Slocum, [General] H. W. Miscellaneous Manuscripts, H (NYHS).

John Ostrander Slocum Papers, OHA.

Town of Pompey Historical Society, Pompey Town, New York.

U.S. Military History Institute, Carlisle, Pa. Civil War Miscellaneous Collection, Brake Collection.

F. F. Wead Papers. New York State Library.

Primary Sources

Bartlett, J. J. Report of Col. Joseph J. Bartlett. *OR*, vol. 11, pt. 2, 449.

———. Report of Col. Joseph J. Bartlett. *OR*, vol. 19, pt. 1, 388–90.

———. Report of Maj. J. J. Bartlett. *OR*, 2:388–89.

Battles and Leaders of the Civil War. Edited by Robert Underwood Johnson and Clarence Clough Buel. Vols. 2, 4. New York: Thomas Yoseloff, 1956.

Blakeman, A. Noel, ed. *Personal Recollections of the War of the Rebellion.* 2d ser. Reprint. Wilmington, N.C.: Broadfoot, 1992.

Boatner, Mark M, III. *The Civil War Dictionary.* New York: David McKay, 1959.

Boyd's City Directory, 1859–1860. Syracuse, N.Y.: Thacher and Lawrence, 1859.

Canby, Courtland, ed. *Lincoln and the Civil War.* New York: George Braziller, 1960.

Chisolm, Alexander R. "The Failure to Capture Hardee." In *Battles and Leaders of the Civil War,* 4:679.

City Directory for 1862–1863. Published by the *Syracuse Daily Journal.* Syracuse, N.Y.: Truair, Smith and Miles, Daily Journal Office, 1862.

Collins, George K. *Memoirs of the 149th Regiment N.Y. Volunteer Infantry.* Rpt. Hamilton, N.Y.: Edmonston, 1995.

Conyngham, David P. *Sherman's March Through the South.* New York: Sheldon and Co., 1865.

"Diary of William Townsend." Transcribed by Jeanne Rinesmith. Online at http://www.3rdwisconsin.org/letters/townsend/townsend_10.html.

"Diploma: Medical School at Castleton." Transcribed by Rebekah Ambrose. Papers of John Ostrander Slocum, OHA.

Doubleday, Abner. *Chancellorsville and Gettysburg.* Wilmington, N.C.: Broadfoot, 1989.

Fairchild, Charles B. *History of the 27th Regiment New York Volunteers.* Binghamton, N.Y.: Slocum and Wells, 1888. Available at the U.S. Army Military History Research Collection, Carlisle, Pa.

"First Fifty Years of Cazenovia Seminary, 1825–1875." Cazenovia, N.Y.: Nelson and Phillips, 1877.

Geary, John W. *A Politician Goes to War: The Civil War Letters of John White Geary.* Edited by William A. Blair. University Park: Pennsylvania State University, 1995.

"Gen. Slocum in the War." *Brooklyn Eagle,* Sunday, February 5, 1888, 15.

Gould, John M., with Leonard G. Jordan. *History of the First-Tenth-Twenty-ninth Maine Regiment.* Portland: Stephen Berry, 1871.

Grant, Ulysses. *The Papers of Ulysses S. Grant.* Edited by John Y. Simon. Carbondale: Southern Illinois University Press, 1985.

Howard, Oliver O. "To the Memory of Henry Slocum: A Eulogy by Oliver O. Howard." In *Civil War Times Illustrated,* ed. Thomas E. Hilton, 21 March 1982, 38–41.

Judd, David W. *The Story of the Thirty Third New York Volunteers.* Rochester, N.Y.: Benton and Andrews, 1864.

"Letter concerning Slocum's status after Bull Run." Veterans Records for Henry Warner Slocum. National Archives.

Lincoln, Abraham. *Abraham Lincoln: Complete Works Comprising His Speeches, State Papers, and Miscellaneous Writings.* Edited by John G. Nicolay and John Hay. New York: Century, 1894, 1902. Two vols.

———. *The Collected Works of Abraham Lincoln.* Edited by Roy P. Balser. New Brunswick, N.J.: Rutgers University Press, 1953. Nine vols.

"The Loyal Legion." *Syracuse Daily Journal,* May 11, 1894, 1–2.

Meade, George Gordon. *The Life and Letters of George Gordon Meade.* Vols. 1, 2. Edited by George Meade. New York: Charles Scribner's Sons, 1913.

"Monument to the New York Brigade at Lookout Mountain." Available in the Slocum Biographic Clippings File (OHA).

Morse, Charles F. "History of the Second Massachusetts Regiment of Infantry." Boston: George H. Ellis, 1882.

Nichols, George Ward. *The Story of the Great March: From the Diary of a Staff Officer.* New York: Harper & Brothers, 1865.

Osborn, Thomas Ward. *The Fiery Trail: A Union Officer's Account of Sherman's Last Campaigns.* Edited by Richard Harwell and Philip N. Racine. Knoxville: University of Tennessee Press, 1986.

Priest, John. *Before Antietam: The Battle for South Mountain.* Shippensburg, Pa.: Whitemane, 1992.

Sears, Stephen W., ed. *The Civil War Papers of George B. McClellan.* New York: Ticknor and Fields, 1989.

Seventh and Eighth Annual Reunion Proceedings of the Survivors Association of the 27th Regiment, New York Volunteers, 1st New York Veteran Cavalry, 33rd Regiment New York Volunteers. 1891.

Sheridan, Philip. *Personal Memoirs of P. H. Sheridan.* Vols. 1, 2. New York: C. L. Webster & Company, 1888.

Sherman, William T. *The Memoirs of General William T. Sherman.* Edited by Charles Royster. New York: New York Library of America, 1990.

Simpson, Brooks D., and Joan V. Berlin, eds. *Sherman's Civil War: Selected Correspondence of William T. Sherman, 1860–1865.* Chapel Hill: University of North Carolina Press, 1999.

Slocum, Henry W. Correspondence with Clara Slocum. Reprinted in Fox, *In Memoriam,* and Charles Slocum, *Life and Services.*

———. Correspondence with Joseph Howland. In Slocum, [General] H. W., Miscellaneous Manuscripts, H (NYHS).

———. "Gettysburg, Thirty Years After." *North American Review,* ed. Lloyd Bruce. Vol. 152. New York, 1891. Accessed via the Cornell University Web site.

———. Letter to T. H. Davis and Co. (publishers of Bates, *Battle of Gettysburg*). September 8, 1875. Slocum Folder, Robert L. Brake Collection, U.S. Army Military History Institute, Carlisle Barracks, Carlisle, Pa.

———. *Military Lessons Taught by the War: An Address before the Long Island Historical Society.* New York: George F. Nesbitt, Printers, 1869; Huntington Library, Alpha Numeric HIS-199.

———. "Sherman's March From Savannah to Bentonville." In *Battles and Leaders of the Civil War,* 4:681–95.

Stockton, Joseph. *War Diary.* Chicago: John T. Stockton, 1910.

Townsend, William. Diary. Transcribed by Jeanne Rinesmith. Online at http://www.3rdwisconsin.org/letters/townsend/townsend;10.html.

U.S. War Department. *The War of the Rebellion: A Compilation of the Official Records of the Union and Confederate Armies.* 128 vols. Washington, D.C.: GPO, 1881–1901. Series 1.

Wheeler, Richard. *Lee's Terrible Swift Sword: From Antietam to Chancellorsville: An Eyewitness History.* New York: HarperCollins, 1992.

Wilcox, Orlando B. *Forgotten Valor: The Memoirs and Civil War Letters of Orlando B. Wilcox.* Edited by Robert Garth Scott. Kent, Ohio: Kent State University, 1999.

Williams, Alpheus. *From the Cannon's Mouth.* Detroit: Wayne State University Press, 1959.

Winsor's Syracuse City Directory. Syracuse, N.Y.: H. P. Winsor, 1857.

Secondary Sources

Adams, Michael C. C. *Our Masters the Rebels: A Speculation on Union Military Failure in the East, 1861–1865.* Cambridge, Mass.: Harvard University Press, 1978.

"Albion Winegar Tourgee." In *Dictionary of American Biography* Base Set. American Council of Learned Societies, 1928–1936. Reproduced in *Biography Resource Center.* Farmington Hills, Mich.: Thomson Gale. 2006. Online at http://galenet.galegroup.com/servlet/BioRC.

"Albion Winegar Tourgée." In *Encyclopedia of World Biography.* 2nd ed. 17 vols. Gale Research, 1998. Reproduced in *Biography Resource Center.* Farmington Hills, Mich.: Thomson Gale. 2006. Online at http://galenet.galegroup.com/servlet/BioRC.

"The Atlanta Campaign, Order of Battle." Online at http://www.civilwarhome.com/atlantaorderofbattle(union).htm. Accessed April 22, 2006.

Bailey, Anne J. *The Chessboard of War: Sherman and Hood in the Autumn Campaigns of 1864.* Lincoln: University of Nebraska Press, 2000.

Bailey, Thomas A. *Democrats vs. Republicans: The Continuing Clash.* New York: Meredith, 1968.

Barrett, John Gilchrist. *Sherman's March through the Carolinas.* Chapel Hill: University of North Carolina Press, 1956.

Bates, Samuel P. *The History of the Battle of Gettysburg.* Philadelphia: T. H. Davis and Company, 1875.

Beale, Howard K. *The Critical Year.* New York: Harcourt Brace, 1930.

Beatie, Russel H. *Road to Manassas: The Growth of Union Command in the Eastern Theatre from the Fall of Fort Sumter to the First Battle of Bull Run.* New York: Cooper Square, 1961.

Bell, Valerie Jackson. "The Onondaga New York Salt Works, 1654–1926." *Science Tribune,* October 1998. Online at http://www.tribunes.com/tribune/sel/bell.htm.

Benedict, Michael Les. *A Compromise of Principle: Congressional Republicans and Reconstruction, 1863–1869.* New York: W. W. Norton, 1964.

"Billy Bowlegs (Holatta Micco)." The National Portrait Gallery: Native Americans. Online at http://www.npg.si.edu/col/native/bowlegs.htm.

Bradley, Mark L. "Old Reliable's Finest Hour." *Blue and Gray* (October 1998): 9–10.

———. *This Astounding Close: The Road to Bennett Place.* Chapel Hill: University of North Carolina Press, 2000.

Broadwater, Robert Paul. *Battle of Despair.* Macon, Ga.: Mercer University Press, 2004.

Cannan, John. *The Atlanta Campaign, May–November 1864.* Conshohocken, Pa.: Combined Books, 1991.

Caraway, Roger. "Hooker, Joseph," in Tucker, *Encyclopedia,* 2:400–402.

Carpenter, John A. *The Sword and Olive Branch: Oliver Otis Howard.* New York: Fordham University, 1999.

Castel, Albert E. *Decision in the West: The Atlanta Campaign of 1864.* Lawrence: University Press of Kansas, 1992.

Catton, Bruce. *Gettysburg: The Final Fury.* Garden City, N.Y.: Doubleday, 1974.

———. *Glory Road: The Bloody Route from Fredericksburg to Gettysburg.* New York: Doubleday, 1952.

———. *Grant Moves South.* Boston: Little Brown, 1960.

———. *A Stillness at Appomattox: The Army of the Potomac.* New York: Doubleday, 1953.

———. *This Hallowed Ground: The Story of the Union Side of the War.* Garden City, N.Y.: Doubleday, 1956.

"Civil War Generals from West Point." Online at http://sunsite.utk.edu/civil-war/wpclasses.html. Accessed April 20, 2006.

Cleeves, Freeman. *Meade of Gettysburg.* Norman: University of Oklahoma, 1960.

Coddington, Edwin B. *The Gettysburg Campaign: A Study in Command.* New York: Scribner, 1968.

Connelly, Thomas L. *Autumn of Glory: The Army of Tennessee, 1862–1865.* Baton Rouge: Louisiana State University Press, 1971.

Cox, Jacob D. *Atlanta.* New York: C. Scribner's Sons, 1882.

———. *The March to the Sea: Franklin and Nashville.* New York: C. Scribner, 1913.

Currie, James. *Enclave: Vicksburg and Her Plantations.* Jackson: University of Mississippi Press, 1980.

———. "From Slavery to Freedom in Mississippi's Legal System." *Journal of Negro History* 65.2 (Spring 1980): 112–25.

Davis, Burke. *Sherman's March.* New York: Random House, 1980.

Davis, Stephen. *Atlanta Will Fall.* Wilmington, Del.: SR Books, 2001.

Davis, William C. *Battle at Bull Run.* Garden City, N.Y.: Doubleday, 1977.

Dickson, Keith. "Civil War, Land Overview." In Tucker, *Encyclopedia*, 1:194–97.

"Digestive Diseases: Cirrhosis of the Liver." *Web MD.* Online at http://my.webmd.com/content/article/90/100596.htm.

Dodge, Grenville M. *The Battle of Atlanta, and Other Campaigns, Addresses, etc.* Denver: Sage Books, 1965.

Dodge, Theodore Ayrault. *The Campaign of Chancellorsville.* New York: Da Capo Press, 1999.

Donald, David. *Lincoln.* London: Jonathan Cape, 1995.

Dowdey, Clifford. *The Seven Days: The Emergence of Robert E. Lee.* New York: Fairfax Press, 1978.

Eisenschiml, Otto. *The Celebrated Case of Fitz John Porter.* Indianapolis: Bobs-Merrill, 1950.

Engle, Stephen. *Yankee Dutchmen: The Life of Franz Sigel.* Fayetteville: University of Arkansas Press, 1993.

Evans, David. *Sherman's Horsemen: Union Cavalry Operations in the Atlanta Campaign.* Bloomington: Indiana University Press, 1996.

Fishel, Edwin. *The Secret War for the Union.* Boston: Houghton Mifflin Trade and Reference, 1996.

Fleming, Thomas J. *West Point: The Men and Times of the United States Military Academy.* New York: William Morrow, 1969.

Foner, Eric. *Free Soil, Free Labor, Free Men: The Ideology of the Republican Party before the Civil War.* New York: Oxford University, 1970.

———. *Politics and Ideology in the Age of the Civil War.* New York: Oxford University, 1980.

Forman, Sidney. *West Point: A History of the United States Military Academy.* New York: Columbia University, 1950.

Fox, William F. *In Memoriam: Henry Warner Slocum.* Albany, N.Y.: J. B. Lyon, 1904. Also known as *Slocum and His Men: The Twelfth Corps.*

———. *New York at Gettysburg.* Albany, NY: J. B. Lyon, 1900.

Gallagher, Gary W. *The First Day at Gettysburg: Essays on Confederate and Union Leadership.* Kent, Ohio: Kent State University Press, 1992.

———. *The Richmond Campaign of 1862: The Peninsula and the Seven Days.* Chapel Hill: University of North Carolina Press, 2000.

Gallagher, Gary W., ed. *Chancellorsville: The Battle and Its Aftermath.* Chapel Hill: University of North Carolina Press, 1996.

———. *The Second Day at Gettysburg: Essays on Confederate and Union Leadership.* Kent, Ohio: Kent State University Press, 1993.

Gibson, John M. *Those 163 Days: A Southern Account of Sherman's March from Atlanta to Raleigh.* New York: Bramhall House, 1961.

Gienapp, William E. "'Politics Seem to Enter into Everything': Political Culture in the North, 1840–1860." In Gienapp, *Essays on Antebellum Politics.*

Gienapp, William E., et al. *Essays on Antebellum Politics, 1840–1860.* College Station: University of Texas at Arlington, 1982.

Glatthaar, Joseph T. *The March to the Sea and Beyond: Sherman's Troops in the Savannah and Carolinas Campaigns.* New York: New York University Press, 1985.

Goss, Thomas J. *The War within the Union High Command: Politics and Generalship during the Civil War.* Lawrence: University Press of Kansas, 2003.

Greene, A. Wilson. "A Step All-Important and Essential to Victory." In Gallagher, *Second Day at Gettysburg,* 87–135.

Grimsley, Mark. *The Hard Hand of War.* New York: Cambridge University Press, 1995.

Groom, Winston. *Shrouds of Glory: From Atlanta to Nashville.* New York: Atlantic Monthly Press, 1995.

Grossman, Lawrence. *The Democratic Party and the Negro: Northern and National Politics, 1868–1892.* Urbana: University of Illinois, 1976.

Guelzo, Allen C. *Abraham Lincoln: Redeemer President.* Grand Rapids, Mich.: William B. Eerdmans, 1999.

Hall, H. Seymour. "A Volunteer at First Bull Run." In *War Talks in Kansas.* A series of Papers Read Before the Kansas Commandery at Military Order of the Loyal Legion of the United States, Commandery of the State of Kansas. Kansas City: Franklin Hudson, 1906. Reprint, Wilmington, N.C.: Broadfoot, 1992. 144–84.

Harper, Robert S. *Irvin McDowell and the Battle of Bull Run.* Columbus, Ohio: Civil War Centennial Commission, 1961.

Hassler, Warren W. *Commanders of the Army of the Potomac.* Baton Rouge: Louisiana State University Press, 1962.

Hattaway, Herman. *Shades of Blue and Gray.* Columbia: University of Missouri Press, 1997.

Hearn, Chester G. *Six Years of Hell: Harpers Ferry during the Civil War.* Baton Rouge: Louisiana State University Press, 1996.

Hebert, Walter H. *Fighting Joe Hooker.* Lincoln: University of Nebraska, 1999.

Hennessy, John J. *Return to Bull Run: The Campaign and Battle of Second Manassas.* New York: Simon and Schuster, 1993.

———. "We Shall Make Richmond Howl." In Gallagher, *Chancellorsville,* 1–13.

Herndon, William, and Jesse W. Weik. *Herndon's Life of Lincoln.* Albert and Charles Boni, 1930. Reprint, Cleveland: World Publishing Company, 1942.

Hettle, Wallace. *The Peculiar Democracy: Southern Democrats in Peace and Civil War.* Athens: University of Georgia, 2001.

Hirshson, Stanley P. *The White Tecumseh: A Biography of General William T. Sherman.* New York: John Wiley and Sons, 1997.

Hoke, Jacob. *The Great Invasion.* New York, London: Thomas Yoseloff, 1959.

Holt, Michael F. *The Political Crisis of the 1850s.* New York: W. W. Norton, 1978.

Hughes, Nathaniel C., Jr. *Bentonville.* Chapel Hill: University of North Carolina, 1996.

Hyman, Harold M., ed. *The Radical Republicans and Reconstruction: 1861–1870.* Indianapolis: Bobbs-Merrill, 1967.

Jamieson, Perry D. *Death in September.* Fort Worth: Ryan Place, 1995.

Kennett, Lee. *Marching through Georgia: The Story of Soldiers and Civilians during Sherman's Campaign.* New York: HarperCollins, 1995.

Key, William. *The Battle of Atlanta and the Georgia Campaign.* New York: Twayne, 1958.

Kise, Tom. "Salt in Upstate New York." The Salt Institute. Online at http://www.saltinstitute.org/nyhist.html.

Lash, Jeffrey. *A Politician Turned General: The Civil War Career of Stephen Augustus Hurlbut.* Kent, Ohio: Kent State University Press, 2003.

Liddell Hart, B. H. *Sherman: Soldier, Realist, American*. New York: Dodd, Mead, 1929.

"The Life of Henry Warner Slocum: Program for General Slocum Day." Delphi Falls, N.Y.: Town of Pompey Historical Society, 1996.

Luvaas, Jay, and Harold W. Nelson, eds. *The U.S. Army War College Guide to the Battles of Chancellorsville and Fredericksburg*. Carlisle, Pa.: South Mountain Press, 1988.

Marszalek, John F. *Sherman: A Soldier's Passion for Order*. New York: Free Press, 1993.

Martin, David G. *Gettysburg, July 1*. Conshohocken, Pa.: Combined Books, 1995.

——. *Jackson's Valley Campaign: November 1861–June 1862*. Conshohocken, Pa.: Combined Books, 1994.

——. *The Peninsula Campaign, March–July 1862*. Conshohocken, Pa.: Combined Books, 1992.

——. *The Second Bull Run Campaign, July–August 1862*. Conshohocken, Pa.: Combined Books, 1997.

Marvel, William. *Burnside*. Chapel Hill: University of North Carolina Press, 1991.

Matloff, Maurice, ed. *American Military History*. Washington, D.C.: Center of Military History, 1988.

McCullough, David. *The Great Bridge*. New York: Simon and Schuster, 1972.

McDonough, James L. *Schofield: Union General in the Civil War and Reconstruction*. Tallahassee: Florida State University Press, 1972.

McDonough, James L., and James Pickett Jones. *"War So Terrible": Sherman and Atlanta*. New York: Norton, 1987.

McPherson, James. *Battle Cry of Freedom: The Civil War Era*. New York and Oxford: Oxford University Press, 1988.

——. *Ordeal by Fire*. New York: Knopf, 1982.

Melton, Brian. "Gettysburg, Battle of." In Tucker, *Encyclopedia*, 2:347–48.

Morrison, James L., Jr. *"The Best School in the World": West Point, the Pre–Civil War Years, 1833–1866*. Kent, Ohio: Kent State University Press, 1986.

Murfin, James V. *The Gleam of Bayonets: The Battle of Antietam and the Maryland Campaign of 1862*. New York: T. Yoseloff, 1965.

Murphy, Justin D. "Bull Run/Manassas, Second Battle of." In Tucker, *Encyclopedia*, 1:132–34.

Myers, Gustavus. *A History of Tammany Hall*. New York: Boni and Liveright, 1917.

Nevins, Allan. *The War for the Union: The Organized War to Victory, 1864–1865*. 4 vols. New York: Scribner and Sons, 1959–1971.

"Opposing Forces at the Battle of Bentonville, North Carolina." Official Web site of the Battle of Bentonville. Online at http://www.ah.dcr.state.nc.us/sections/hs/bentonvi/battle.htm. Accessed on June 6, 2006.

Palfrey, Francis W. *The Antietam and Fredericksburg*. New York. Scribner's Sons, 1882.

Parish, Peter J. *The American Civil War*. New York: Holmes and Meier, 1975.

Patterson, Gerard. *Rebels from West Point*. New York: Doubleday, 1987.

Pfanz, Harry W. *Gettysburg—Culp's Hill and Cemetery Hill*. Chapel Hill: University of North Carolina Press, 1993.

———. *Gettysburg, the Second Day*. Chapel Hill: University of North Carolina Press, 1987.

Potter, David M. *The Impending Crisis, 1848–1861*. Edited by Don Fehrenbacher. New York: Harper Torch Books, 1976.

Pratt, Fletcher. *A Short History of the Civil War*. New York: Pocket Books, 1961.

Priest, John. *Before Antietam: The Battle for South Mountain*. Shippensburg, Pa.: Whitemane, 1992.

Rable, George. *Fredericksburg! Fredericksburg!* Chapel Hill: University of North Carolina, 2002.

Rafuse, Ethan. *A Single Grand Victory*. Wilmington, Del.: Scholarly Resources, 2002.

Randall, J. G., and David Donald. *The Civil War and Reconstruction*. Boston: Heath, 1961.

Rawley, James A. *The Politics of Union: Northern Politics during the Civil War*. Lincoln: University of Nebraska, 1974.

Reardon, Carol. *Pickett's Charge in History and Memory*. Chapel Hill: University of North Carolina Press, 1997.

Roark, James L. *Masters without Slaves: Southern Planters in the Civil War and Reconstruction*. New York: W. W. Norton, 1977.

Sandburg, Carl. *Abraham Lincoln: The War Years*. Vols. 1–4. New York: Harcourt Brace, 1939.

Sears, Stephen W. *Chancellorsville*. Boston: Houghton Mifflin, 1996.

———. *Controversies and Commanders: Dispatches from the Army of the Potomac*. Boston: Houghton-Mifflin, 1999.

———. *Gettysburg*. Boston: Houghton Mifflin, 2003.

———. *Landscape Turned Red: The Battle of Antietam*. New York: Ticknor and Fields, 1983.

————. *To the Gates of Richmond: The Peninsula Campaign.* New York: Ticknor and Fields, 1992.

Sefton, James E. *The United States Army and Reconstruction.* Baton Rouge: Louisiana State University, 1967.

Silbey, Joel H. *A Respectable Minority: The Democratic Party in the Civil War Era, 1860–1868.* New York: Norton, 1977.

Simpson, Brooks. *America's Civil War.* Wheeling, Ill.: Harlan Davidson, 1996.

————. *Ulysses S. Grant: Triumph over Adversity, 1822–1865.* Boston: Houghton Mifflin, 2000.

Slocum, Charles E. *The Life and Services of Major-General Henry Warner Slocum.* Toledo: Slocum Publishing, 1913.

Slocum, Henry Jr. *Lawn Tennis in Our Own Country.* New York, Philadelphia, Chicago: A. G. Spalding & Bros. 1890.

Smith, Michael. "Chancellorsville, Battle of." In Tucker, *Encyclopedia,* 1:162–64.

Stackpole, Edward J. *Chancellorsville: Lee's Greatest Battle.* Harrisburg, Pa.: Stackpole, 1958.

————. *From Cedar Mountain to Antietam.* Harrisburg, Pa.: Stackpole Books, 1993.

Sutherland, Daniel E. *Fredericksburg and Chancellorsville: The Dare Mark Campaign.* Lincoln: University of Nebraska Press, 1998.

Tanner, Robert G. *Stonewall in the Valley: Thomas J. "Stonewall" Jackson's Shenandoah Valley Campaign, Spring 1862.* Garden City, N.Y.: Doubleday, 1976.

Tap, Bruce. "Antietam/Sharpsburg, Battle of." In Tucker, *Encyclopedia,* 1:49–52.

————. "Fredericksburg, Battle of." In Tucker, *Encyclopedia,* 1:329–32.

"Third Seminole War." Online at http://www.u-s-history.com/pages/h1156.html.

"Thomas Lincoln Casey." *Dictionary of American Biography, Supplements 1–2 to 1940.* American Council of Learned Societies, 1944–1958. Reproduced in *Biography Resource Center.* Farmington Hills, Mich.: Thomson Gale. 2006. Online at http://galenet.galegroup.com/servlet/BioRC.

"Thomas Lincoln Casey." *Virtual American Biographies.* Online at http://www.famousamericans.net/thomaslincolncasey. Accessed April 20, 2006.

Tucker, Spencer, ed. *The Encyclopedia of American Military History.* 3 vols. New York: Facts on File, 2003.

Walker, Peter. *Vicksburg: A People at War, 1860–1865.* Chapel Hill: University of North Carolina, 1960.

Warner, Ezra J. *Generals in Blue.* Baton Rouge: Louisiana State University, 1964.

———. *Generals in Gray.* Baton Rouge: Louisiana State University Press, 1959.

Waskey, A. J. L. "Seminole War, First," "Seminole War, Second," "Seminole War, Third." In *Encyclopedia of American Military History,* ed. Spencer Tucker. Vol. 3.

Werner, Morris. *Tammany Hall.* Garden City, N.Y.: Doubleday, Dorian, 1928.

Williams, Kenneth P. *Lincoln Finds a General: A Military Study of the Civil War.* Vols. 3–5. New York: Macmillan, 1956–1959.

Woodworth, Steven E. *Beneath a Northern Sky: A Short History of the Gettysburg Campaign.* Wilmington: Scholarly Resources, 2003.

———. *Davis and Lee at War.* Lawrence: University Press of Kansas, 1995.

———. *Six Armies in Tennessee.* Lincoln, Neb.: Bison Books, 1998.

Index

Acoustic shadow, 121, 125, 128

African Americans, 16, 17, 73, 162, 163, 165, 166, 184, 209, 210, 211, 212

Agan, P. H., 32

Alabama, 176, 178, 212

Albany, New York, 9, 12, 28, 29, 30, 31, 34, 54, 97, 219, 234

Albany Argus, 217

Alexander's Bridge, 72

Alvord, Thomas, 24, 25, 26, 27, 28, 29, 220

Antietam (Sharpsburg), Battle of, 6, 15, 60, 83, 85, 87, 88, 94, 117, 124, 134, 139, 245

Army of Georgia, 6, 184, 185, 187, 189, 192, 195, 199, 200, 201, 203, 237

Army of Northern Virginia, 71, 79, 98, 103, 114, 115, 117, 118, 139, 167, 195

Army of the Potomac 66–68, 75, 78, 80, 84, 88, 91, 94, 95, 96, 98, 109, 114, 117, 118, 119, 120, 121, 125, 126, 142, 143, 149, 153, 154, 155, 159, 167, 182, 194, 202, 230, 238, 245, 246; Eleventh Corps, 88, 96, 100, 101, 103, 105–6, 118, 122, 126–27, 135, 146, 157, 160–61, 172; Fifth Corps, 71, 76, 96, 101, 117, 119, 123, 159; First division, 91, 101, 104, 129, 131, 133, 139, 143, 156, 158, 159; Fourth Corps, 60, 172, 251; Ninth Corps, 88, 99; receives corps insignia, 95; Second Corps, 84, 96; Second division, 92, 129, 130, 131; Sixth Corps, 68, 73, 80, 84, 96, 99, 158–59; Third Corps, 106, 127, 130, 131; Twelfth Corps, 3, 84, 85, 86, 87, 88, 89, 90, 91, 92, 95, 100, 101, 102, 106, 108, 109, 111, 112, 115, 119, 120, 121, 124, 128, 129, 130, 131, 132, 134, 135, 137, 139, 140, 143, 145, 146, 147, 148, 149, 153, 154, 155, 157, 159, 160, 161, 162, 172, 194

Army of Virginia, 78

Arthur, Chester A., 236

Atlanta, Georgia, 17, 142, 167, 168, 170, 173, 175, 177, 179, 180, 181, 182, 183, 186, 189, 193, 237; Battle of, 1, 3, 170, 172, 187, 203, 245; occupation of, 176, 214; Slocum's management of, 177, 178, 180

Augusta, Georgia, 187, 190, 195

Averasboro, Battle of, 198

Baltimore, Maryland, 42

Barlow, Francis C., 224

Bartlett, Joseph J., 5, 34, 49, 50, 51, 52, 54, 72, 76, 81, 82, 96, 237

Bates, Samuel P., 5, 123, 124, 127, 132, 237

Battle above the Clouds, 157

Beauregard, Pierre G. T., 44, 47, 85, 189

Belden, James, 53, 57

Bennett, A. E. B. *See* W. C. Bennett

Bennett, W. C., 221

Bentonville, Battle of, 6, 198, 199, 200, 237, 246

Bobb, John, 165

Bounty jumping. *See* Deserters

Bragg, Braxton, 145, 157, 167

285